D0076492

Democracy Incorporated

Democracy Incorporated

Managed Democracy and
the Specter of Inverted Totalitarianism

NEW EDITION

SHELDON S. WOLIN

WITH A NEW INTRODUCTION
BY CHRIS HEDGES

Princeton University Press
Princeton and Oxford

Copyright ©2008 by Princeton University Press
Introduction copyright © 2017 by Princeton University Press
Published by Princeton University Press, 41 William Street,
Princeton, New Jersey 08540
In the United Kingdom: Princeton University Press, 6 Oxford Street,
Woodstock, Oxfordshire OX20 1TW
All Rights Reserved

First edition 2008
First paperback edition, with a new preface by the author, 2010
New edition, with an introduction by Chris Hedges, 2017
New paperback ISBN: 978-0-691-17848-6

The Library of Congress has cataloged the cloth edition of this book as follows

Wolin, Sheldon S.
Democracy incorporated : managed democracy and the specter of
inverted totalitarianism / Sheldon S. Wolin.
p.   cm.
Includes bibliographical references and index.
ISBN 978-0-691-13566-3 (hardcover : alk. paper)
1. Democracy—United States. 2. Corporate state—United States.
3. United States—Politics and government. 4. Political science—History.
5. Political science—Philosophy—History. 6. Totalitarianism. 7. Fascism. I. Title.
JK1726.W66 2008
320.973—dc22   2007039176

British Library Cataloging-in-Publication Data is available

This book is composed in Electra

Printed on acid-free paper. ∞

press.princeton.edu

Printed in the United States

1 3 5 7 9 10 8 6 4 2

To Carl and Elizabeth Schorske

Contents

Preface to the First Paperback Edition

SPARE CHANGE

Democracy Incorporated describes certain *tendencies* in American politics and argues that they are serving to consolidate a unique political system of "inverted totalitarianism." Rather than attempting a summary of the volume, I want to examine a contemporary political development that, it could be argued, invalidates or undermines my thesis. I am referring both to the unprecedented election in 2008 of an African American as president and to the widely held expectation that the Obama administration would proceed promptly to undo the excesses of the Bush regime, many of which I had used as evidence in support of the thesis of *Democracy Incorporated*.

In adopting "change" as the signature theme of his presidential campaign, Obama chose an idea as American as the proverbial apple pie. Ever since the nation's beginnings, Americans have seen themselves as futurists, notable for their receptiveness, even their addiction, to change and to its counterfeit, novelty. Typically, change was considered to be virtually synonymous with progress, with the promise of steady material improvement in the lives of most citizens as well as a better future for their children. Change thus tended to be identified with expanded opportunity rather than with a fundamental shift such as that represented by Jacksonian democracy, when power relationships among groups and classes were significantly altered. Another example of fundamental change was the abolition of slavery, although arguably the political promise of the Fourteenth and Fifteenth amendments was not realized until the presidential election of 2008.

Throughout much of American history, government has been an active promoter of fundamental change. The Civil War amendments were aimed at undoing past wrongs associated with the institution of slavery. New Deal programs significantly improved the lives of ordinary people, especially the poor, and marked a change in direction, away from free-market capitalism and toward a mixed economy notable for significant governmental initiatives and "interference" in the economy.

Thus we have two distinct conceptions of change, each involving active governmental intervention. One we can call mitigative or tactical change. It seeks to redress a situation or condition without significantly modifying power relationships (e.g., a "tax break for the middle class"). The other, paradigmatic or strategic change, institutes not only a new program but recasts basic power relationships: it reforms, empowers, sets a new direction (e.g., a single-payer health care system). *Democracy Incorporated* describes the paradigmatic change represented by the amalgamation of state and corporate power.

Sometimes a paradigmatic change takes the form of an attack on an entrenched or longstanding status quo—for example, reducing the power of the antebellum plantation owners. Sometimes a mitigative change might seek to undo a previous paradigmatic change in order to restore, to a limited extent, the status quo ante. For example, the repressive paradigm shift initiated after September 11, 2001, that included governmental wire tapping, surveillance, and denial of due process, might be undone by restoring prior practices more respectful of due process and First Amendment rights.

Paradoxically, Obama's victory might turn out to be a reaction, a yearning for a certain status quo ante that would rescind some of the changes introduced by the Bush-Cheney administration, such as torture of detainees. If so, then the change promised by the 2008 election may be more mitigative than paradigmatic, aiming to restore or modify rather than opting for a sharply different direction.

In the mid-twentieth century, starting with the Cold War and its anti-communist crusade at home and abroad, and attaining its consolidation in the Reagan counterrevolution, the national fixation on change, while it retained a strong economic and technological driving force, was joined to a new and self-conscious conservatism. The result was a unique dynamic: change that professed to look backward to some distant "city on a hill." It was not regressive in the sense of actually restoring the past. Rather the "new conservatism" appealed to an idealized, mythical past as a strategy in its "culture war" against "liberalism." It combined political, religious, and cultural elements into an ideology that appealed to Founding Fathers, the "original" constitution, biblical texts, "family values," the sanctity of "traditional marriage," and a militant patriotism. ("America, Love It or Leave It.") Its economic ideology also looked to an imagined past, to a "free economy" where harmony and prosperity had resulted from enlightened selfishness and "small government."

Conservative politics, however, was far from being merely nostalgic. In deliberately promoting inegalitarianism it qualified as paradigmatic. The celebration of the unchanging provided ideological cover for the basic aim of reversing or modifying as much as possible the changes previously introduced by egalitarian social programs. By reducing or eliminating programs that had helped to empower the Many, inegalitarianism reinforced a structure which combined state and corporate power. Although the administration of George W. Bush would continue and even intensify the attacks on liberal social programs and the "liberal culture of permissiveness," it substituted a new paradigm that would refocus the dynamics which anticommunism had first generated. It would push outward in an aggressive quest for imperial hegemony, an emphasis different from the somewhat more provincially minded Reagan conservatives. The new paradigm would display a unique feature, one virtually unknown to previous versions of national identity. It would define the scope of its dominion by postulating an enemy—terrorism—that had no obvious limits, neither temporal nor spatial, nor a single fixed form. Thus the new paradigm introduced a monumental change that redefined national identity, overshadowing "republic" and "democracy." The "United States," hitherto a name that denoted the lower half of a continent, now signified a global empire.

Empire constituted a paradigmatic change, yet, like that love that dare not speak its name, it was repressed during the 2008 campaign even as the role of the presidency was evolving from a national to an imperial office. Attention was directed instead to the unprecedented spectacle of an African American candidate competing for and winning the highest office in the land. Before gauging the extent and type of change represented by that election, we need to ask: against what background has that change taken place? One might argue that throughout much of the twentieth-century white Americans have accepted and adulated African American public performers—musicians, actors and actresses, and writers—even as most white Americans tolerated segregation, discrimination, and racial slurs. Following the 2008 election all manner of established groups began to press their agendas on the incoming administration: environmentalists, health care advocates, state governors, antiwar groups, and, inevitably, corporate lobbyists. Strikingly less prominent were those advocacy groups representing African Americans. Had the election of "one of their own" had the ironic result of inhibiting instead of empowering?

Before August 2008, when the public first began to become (or be made) aware of the brewing economic crisis, "change" had been primarily associated with ending the American military operations in Iraq and Afghanistan and with a promise both of sweeping socioeconomic changes (e.g., health care reform, environmental safeguards) and of political reforms (e.g., restoring constitutional protections, outlawing the practice of torture, disavowing an expansive notion of executive power). Yet there was no talk of halting construction of the huge permanent American embassy in Baghdad, only Obama's promise to honor the Bush timetable for withdrawing most troops from Iraq during the summer of 2009 while redoubling the military commitment to Afghanistan and pursuing the Taliban into Pakistan: in short, no talk of disentangling from our imperial commitments.

In the immediate aftermath of the election it became increasingly apparent that Obama's notion of change was a highly pragmatic one. The specific kinds of change and their scope and depth would be contingent on circumstance and political calculations, rather than determined by the intensity of the public reaction against Bush-Cheney policies—that is, mitigative rather than paradigmatic.

At the outset there was the opportunity of choosing the actual agents of change, those who would head the departments and preside over the courts. The controlling premise appeared to be that there was a relatively small political class, an elite, from which crucial appointments should be made. The operatives who were selected to be in charge of finance, economic policy, foreign affairs, regulatory policy, and health care proved to be seasoned deciders. Before the debacle of compromised cabinet nominees (Daschle, et al.), Obama's original cabinet selections consisted primarily of Clintonistas, suggesting that they had been chosen before the gravity of the economic situation became widely acknowledged. They represented, in other words, a decision which assumed that the economy would remain more or less on course and that the situation in Iraq was being stabilized. This is borne out by the fact that, even before Obama took the oath of office, he and the leaders of the Democratic Party largely followed the initiatives proposed by the Bush administration during its final weeks. The major one was the $600 billion bailout of the major banks and credit institutions whose arcane and largely unregulated practices were mainly responsible for the crisis. At the same time, the Obama administration hastened to staff its councils with seasoned veterans from the financial world. Save for the huge sums involved and the brazenness of the giveaway, what could be more unchanging than the perpetuation of the cozy and longstanding relationship between Washington and Wall Street?

One might conjecture that paradigmatic change is less likely during periods of prosperity when members of society are presumably contented, but that when things are going very wrong society is apt to be more receptive to major, even paradigmatic changes. However, as the interval between November 4, 2008, and January 20, 2009, began to shrink, grandiose promises of change gave way to proposals for rescuing the economy rather than altering its fundamentals. Once the economy began to slide ever more downward, it was widely reported as inevitable that notions of change would have to be scaled down and subordinated to new priorities of confronting a worsening economic climate. Thus as change yielded to the priorities and requirements of policy and administrative decision making, the scope of change "contracted" and got lost in translation. Supporters, too, began to change, consoling themselves that Obama would at least be better than Bush: if not change, then a respite.

Politically sobered by the encounter with complexity, Obama adopted nuance and exchanged the rhetorical flourishes of the political campaign for the measured, insider discourse of "policy" and "decision making." Policy is commonly defined as the attempt to formulate a set of rules and guiding principles of action for achieving a specified purpose or outcome. It might also be described as the revelatory moment when the commitment to substantive change is tested. Judging from some of the early decisions of the Obama administration, the two paradigmatic opportunities presented by the apparent stabilization of Iraq and the economic recession were squandered in favor of "rescuing" or restoring as quickly as possible the economic status quo ante and of increasing the imperial military presence in the Afghanistan-Pakistan region. Crisis called for continuity, not departures.

It was not the banks alone that failed; so too did the political and economic imagination. In desperation liberal pundits and think-tank employees decided to go "historical," hoping to find inspiration in FDR's New Deal and its response to the Depression. Besides overlooking that FDR had no more embittered opponent than the great bankers of his day (he called them "economic royalists"), it seems not to have occurred to establishment theoreticians that the main point of FDR's action was that he did not try to imitate his predecessors or seek an earlier precedent for his programs. He chose, instead, to innovate, or, more accurately, to experiment with paradigmatic changes. It is revealing of the deep conservatism of our times that references to the New Deal have largely avoided associating it with the notion of "experimentation" even though during the 1930s the phrase familiarly used was "the New Deal experiment," which was suggestive of a departure from business as usual and of a commitment to trying new and untested ideas. It was also overlooked that FDR was pressured from below by popular movements demanding programmatic action: Huey Long's "Share the Wealth," the Townsend Plan for guaranteed incomes for all citizens.

If FDR and the New Deal exploited an opportunity for change, Obama and his administration assumed automatically the limits of change. Which raises the question of whether the truly profound change of the twentieth century, the dominance of corporate power— politically, economically, and culturally—has not produced an equally profound change: the effective management of the citizenry. Clearly, these two developments—corporate dominance and a managed electorate—point to a certain political rigidity that is reflected in perhaps the most striking aspect of the present predicament: the absence of alternatives other than variations on the theme of economic orthodoxy. When the idea of nationalizing the banks was being suggested it provoked an immediate storm: it was alleged as tantamount to "socialism." The Obama administration panicked and immediately declared it had no such plans, thereby denying itself a range of more imaginative remedies.

That reaction points to another great regressive change: the paucity of intellectual proposals that deviate from the current orthodoxies. This reflects a quiet but paradigmatic change: a shift in intellectual and ideological influence from academia to think tanks, the vast majority of which were conservative and dependent upon corporate sponsorship. Whereas the former had on occasion housed and nurtured deviants, "impractical dreamers" of new paradigms and challengers of orthodoxy, the think-tank inmates are committed to influencing policy makers and hence their horizons are restricted by the demands of practicality and constricted by the interests of their corporate sponsors to proposing mitigative changes.

Shortly before his inauguration President-elect Obama tried to explain why it would be necessary to scale down some of his promises for wide-sweeping social and economic reforms by saying that "we must look forward rather than back." In effect, that was then, this is now. Yet Obama's remark was misleading on both accounts. First, the new administration was being less than candid about the systemic significance of the solutions it was introducing. In using the financial institutions as the means of recovery it was reinforcing the state-corporate alliance. The significance of the placement of governmental representatives on the boards of various banks and financial institutions was in effect the legitimation of that alliance and of the paradigm shift which it represented. The fundamental nature of that shift was underscored in the bailout of General Motors Corporation. The terms of the settlement involved the co-optation and neutralization of a powerful trade union, the United Automobile Workers. Under the terms of the bailout, the government—or as it was said "the taxpayers"—lent GM $50 billion. The union, which had also been forced to buy a 55 percent share in

Chrysler, now had to draw upon its pension fund to purchase 17.5 percent of the shares in GM. The union further agreed to a wage freeze and pledged not to strike. In return it received representation on the corporation's governing board but with the proviso that its shares would not bring voting rights. The workers' union also agreed to accept the loss of several thousand jobs of its members. Thus, under the terms of the "agreement," the union was, in effect, incorporated and rendered a party to its own humiliation and, given the highly doubtful future of GM itself, facing a possible chance of losing everything.

Obama's reluctance to look backward had a more profound significance than the abandonment of a policy promised during the presidential campaign. From the beginning of his presidency he made it clear that he would strive to "reach out" to congressional Republicans and to make change a bipartisan affair. The crucial consequence of that strategy was to suppress any serious attempt to educate the public concerning certain potentially impeachable actions of Bush administration officials, most notably the extreme expansion of presidential powers (including "signing statements"), the practice of torture, the denials of due process, and, above all, the lies that were employed to justify the war waged against Iraq. Rarely has Santayana's famous dictum— roughly, "those who forget the past are doomed to repeat it"—been more relevant. When the actions of the Bush administration are compared to the one that led to the attempted impeachment of President Clinton, we have the clearest indication of the limited vision of the Obama administration. While "the audacity of hope" which Obama wrote about in his autobiography certainly has been fulfilled by the fact of his own election, that audacity does not appear to challenge the system of power which has brought the nation an endless war, bankruptcy, recession, and high unemployment. Change aplenty and all feeding the drift toward the system described in the pages that follow.

July 2009

Preface

As a preliminary I want to emphasize certain aspects of the approach taken in this volume in order to avoid possible misunderstandings. Although the concept of totalitarianism is central to what follows, my thesis is *not* that the current American political system is an inspired replica of Nazi Germany's or George W. Bush of Hitler.[1] References to Hitler's Germany are introduced to remind the reader of the benchmarks in a system of power that was invasive abroad, justified preemptive war as a matter of official doctrine, and repressed all opposition at home—a system that was cruel and racist in principle and practice, deeply ideological, and openly bent on world domination. Those benchmarks are introduced to illuminate tendencies in our own system of power that are opposed to the fundamental principles of constitutional democracy. Those tendencies are, I believe, totalizing in the sense that they are obsessed with control, expansion, superiority, and supremacy.

The regimes of Mussolini and Stalin demonstrate that it is possible for totalitarianism to assume different forms. Italian fascism, for example, did not officially adopt anti-Semitism until late in the regime's history and even then primarily in response to pressure from Germany. Stalin introduced some "progressive" policies: promoting mass literacy and health care; encouraging women to undertake professional and technical careers; and (for a brief spell) promoting minority cultures. The point is not that these "accomplishments" compensate for crimes whose horrors have yet to be fully comprehended. Rather, totalitarianism is capable of local variations; plausibly, far from being exhausted by its twentieth-century versions would-be totalitarians now have available technologies of control, intimidation and mass manipulation far surpassing those of that earlier time.

The Nazi and Fascist regimes were powered by revolutionary movements whose aim was not only to capture, reconstitute, and monopolize state power but also to gain control over the economy. By controlling the state and the economy, the revolutionaries gained the leverage necessary to reconstruct, then mobilize society. In contrast, inverted totalitarianism is only in part a state-centered phenomenon. Primarily it represents the *political* coming of age of corporate power and the *political* demobilization of the citizenry.

Unlike the classic forms of totalitarianism, which openly boasted of their intentions to force their societies into a preconceived totality, inverted totalitarianism is not expressly conceptualized as an ideology or objectified in public policy. Typically it is furthered by power-holders and citizens who often seem unaware of the deeper consequences of their actions or inactions. There is a certain heedlessness, an inability to take seriously the extent to which a pattern of consequences may take shape without having been preconceived.[2]

The fundamental reason for this deep-seated carelessness is related to the well-known American zest for change and, equally remarkable, the good fortune of Americans in having at their disposal a vast continent rich in natural resources, inviting exploitation. Although it is a cliché that the history of American society has been one of unceasing change, the consequences of today's increased tempos are, less obvious. Change works to displace existing beliefs, practices, and expectations. Although societies throughout history have experienced change, it is only over the past four centuries that promoting innovation became a major focus of public policy. Today, thanks to the highly organized pursuit of technological innovation and the culture it encourages, change is more rapid, more encompassing, more welcomed than ever before—which means that institutions, values, and expectations share with technology a limited shelf life. We are experiencing the triumph of contemporaneity and of its accomplice, forgetting or collective amnesia. Stated somewhat differently, in early modern times change displaced traditions; today change succeeds change.

The effect of unending change is to undercut consolidation. Consider, for example, that more than a century after the Civil War the consequences of slavery still linger; that close to a century after women won the vote, their equality remains contested; or that after nearly two centuries during which public schools became a reality, education is now being increasingly privatized. In order to gain a handle on the problem of change we might recall that among political and intellectual circles, beginning in the last half of the seventeenth century and especially during the eighteenth-century Enlightenment, there was a growing conviction that, for the first time in recorded history, it was possible for human beings to deliberately shape their future. Thanks to advances in science and invention it was possible to conceive change as "progress," an advancement benefiting all members of society. Progress stood for change that was constructive, that would bring something new into the world and to the advantage of all. The champions of progress believed that while change might result in the disappearance or destruction of established beliefs, customs, and interests, the vast majority of these deserved to go because they mostly served the Few while keeping the Many in ignorance, poverty, and sickness.

An important element in this early modern conception of progress was that change was crucially a matter for political determination by those who could be held accountable for their decisions. That understanding of change was pretty much overwhelmed by the emergence of concentrations of economic power that took place during the latter half the nineteenth century. Change became a private enterprise inseparable from exploitation and opportunism, thereby constituting a major, if not the major, element in the dynamic of capitalism. Opportunism involved an unceasing search for what might be exploitable, and soon that meant virtually anything, from religion, to politics, to human wellbeing. Very little, if anything, was taboo, as before long change became the object of premeditated strategies for maximizing profits.

It is often noted that today change is more rapid, more encompassing than ever before. In later pages I shall suggest that American democracy has never been truly consolidated. Some of its key elements remain unrealized or vulnerable; others have been exploited for antidemocratic ends. Political institutions have typically been described as the means by which a society tries to order change. The assumption was that political institutions would themselves remain stable, as exemplified in the ideal of a constitution as a relatively unchanging structure for defining the uses and limits of public power and the accountability of officeholders.

Today, however, some of the political changes are revolutionary; others are counterrevolutionary. Some chart new directions for the nation and introduce new techniques for extending American power, both internally (surveillance of citizens) and externally (seven hundred bases abroad), beyond any point even imagined by previous administrations. Other changes are counterrevolutionary in the sense of reversing social policies originally aimed at improving the lot of the middle and poorer classes.

How to persuade the reader that the actual direction of contemporary politics is toward a political system the very opposite of what the political leadership, the mass media, and think tank oracles claim that it is, the world's foremost exemplar of democracy? Although critics may dismiss this volume as fantasy, there are grounds for believing that the broad citizenry is becoming increasingly uneasy about "the direction the nation is heading," about the role of big money in politics, the credibility of the popular news media, and the reliability of voting returns. The midterm elections of 2006 indicated clearly that much of the nation was demanding a quick resolution to a misguided war. Increasingly one hears ordinary citizens complaining that they "no longer recognize their country," that preemptive war, widespread use of torture, domestic spying, endless reports of corruption in high places, corporate as well as governmental, mean that something is deeply wrong in the nation's politics.

In the chapters that follow I shall try to develop a focus for understanding the changes taking place and their direction. But first—assuming that we have had, if not a fully realized democracy, at least an impressive number of its manifestations, and assuming further that some fundamental changes are occurring, we might raise the broad question: what causes a democracy to change into some non- or anti-democratic system, and what kind of system is democracy likely to change into?

For centuries political writers claimed that if—or rather when—a full-fledged democracy was overturned, it would be succeeded by a tyranny. The argument was that democracy, because of the great freedom it allowed, was inherently prone to disorder and likely to cause the propertied classes to support a dictator or tyrant, someone who could impose order, ruthlessly if necessary. But—and this is the issue addressed by our inquiry—what if in its popular culture a democracy were prone to license ("anything goes") yet in its politics were to become fearful, ready to give the benefit of the doubt to leaders who, while promising to "root out terrorists," insist that endeavor is a "war" with no end in sight? Might democracy then tend to become submissive, privatized rather than unruly, and would that alter the power relationships between citizens and their political deciders?

A word about terminology. "Superpower" stands for the projection of power outwards. It is indeterminate, impatient with restraints, and careless of boundaries as it strives to develop the capability of imposing its will at a time and place of its own choosing. It represents the antithesis of constitutional power. "Inverted totalitarianism" projects power inwards. It is not derivative from "classic totalitarianism" of the types represented by Nazi Germany, Fascist Italy, or Stalinist Russia. Those regimes were powered by revolutionary movements whose aim was to capture, reconstitute, and monopolize the power of the state. The state was conceived as the main center of power, providing the leverage necessary for the mobilization and reconstruction of society. Churches, universities, business organizations, news and opinion media, and cultural institutions were taken over by the government or neutralized or suppressed.

Inverted totalitarianism, in contrast, while exploiting the authority and resources of the state, gains its dynamic by combining with other forms of power, such as evangelical religions, and most notably by encouraging a symbiotic relationship between traditional government and the system of "private" governance represented by the modern business corporation. The result is not a system of codetermination by equal partners who retain their distinctive identities but rather a system that represents the political coming-of-age of corporate power.

When capitalism was first represented in an intellectual construct, primarily in the latter half of the eighteenth century, it was hailed as the perfection of decentralized power, a system that, unlike an absolute monarchy, no single person or governmental agency could or should attempt to direct. It was pictured as a system but of decentralized powers working best when left alone (laissez-faire, laissez passer) so that "the market" operated freely. The market furnished the structure by which spontaneous economic activities would be coordinated, exchange values set, and demand and supply adjusted. It operated, as Adam Smith famously wrote, by an unseen hand that connected participants and directed their endeavors toward the common benefit of all, even though the actors were motivated primarily by their own selfish ends.

One of Smith's fundamental contentions was that while individuals were capable of making rational decisions on a small scale, no one possessed the powers required for rationally comprehending a whole society and directing its activities. A century later, however, the whole scale of economic enterprise was revolutionized by the emergence and rapid rise of the business corporation. An economy where power was dispersed among countless actors, and where markets supposedly were dominated by no one, rapidly gave way to forms of concentrated power—trusts, monopolies, holding companies, and cartels—able to set (or strongly influence) prices, wages, supplies of materials, and entry into the market itself. Adam Smith was now joined to Charles Darwin, the free market to the survival of the fittest. The emergence of the corporation marked the presence of private power on a scale and in numbers thitherto unknown, the concentration of private power unconnected to a citizen body.

Despite the power of corporations over political processes and the economy, a determined political and economic opposition arose demanding curbs on corporate power and influence. Big Business, it was argued, demanded Big Government. It was assumed, but often forgotten, that unless Big Government, or even small government, possessed some measure of disinterestedness, the result might be the worst of both worlds, corporate power and government both fashioned from the same cloth of self-interest. However, Populists and Progressives of the late nineteenth and early twentieth centuries, as well as trade unionists and small farmers, went a step further to argue that a democratic government should be both disinterested and "interested." It should serve both the common good and the interests of ordinary people whose main source of power was their numbers. They argued, perhaps naively, that in a democracy the people were sovereign and government was, by definition, on their side. The sovereign people were fully entitled to use governmental power and resources to redress the inequalities created by the economy of capitalism.

That conviction supported and was solidifed by the New Deal. A wide range of regulatory agencies was created, the Social Security program and a minimum wage law were established, unions were legitimated along with the rights to bargain collectively, and various attempts were made to reduce mass unemployment by means of government programs for public works and conservation. With the outbreak of World War II, the New Deal was superseded by the forced mobilization and governmental control of the entire economy and the conscription of much of the adult male population. For all practical purposes the war marked the end of the first large-scale effort at establishing the tentative beginnings of social democracy in this country, a union of social programs benefiting the Many combined with a vigorous electoral democracy and lively politicking by individuals and organizations representative of the politically powerless.

At the same time that the war halted the momentum of political and social democracy, it enlarged the scale of an increasingly open cohabitation between the corporation and the state. That partnership became ever closer during the era of the Cold War (1947–93). Corporate economic power became the basis of power on which the state relied, as its own ambitions, like those of giant corporations, became more expansive, more global, and, at intervals, more bellicose. Together the state and corporation became the main sponsors and coordinators of the powers represented by science and technology. The result is an unprecedented combination of powers distinguished by their totalizing tendencies, powers that not only challenge established boundaries—political, moral, intellectual, and economic—but whose very nature it is to challenge those boundaries continually, even to challenge the limits of the earth itself. Those powers are also the means of inventing and disseminating a culture that taught consumers to welcome change and private pleasures while accepting political passivity. A major consequence is the construction of a new "collective identity," imperial rather than republican (in the eighteenth-century sense), less democratic. That new identity involves questions of who we are as a people, what we stand for as well as what we are willing to stand, the extent to which we are committed to becoming involved in common affairs, and what democratic principles justify expending the energies and wealth of our citizens and asking some of them to kill and sacrifice their lives while the destiny of their country is fast slipping from popular control.

I want to emphasize that I view my main construction, "inverted totalitarianims," as tentative, hypothetical, although I am convinced that certain tendencies in our society point in a direction away from self-government, the rule of law, egalitarianism, and thoughtful public discussion, and toward what I have called "managed democracy," the smiley face of inverted totalitarianism.

For the moment Superpower is in retreat and inverted totalitarianism exists as a set of strong tendencies rather than as a fully realized actuality. The direction of these tendencies urges that we ask ourselves—and only democracy justifies using "we"—what inverted totalitarianism exacts from democracy and whether we want to exchange our birthrights for its mess of pottage.

Acknowledgments

Ian Malcolm has guided the manuscript throughout the long process from gestation to completion. I am deeply indebted for his comments and criticisms. Thanks also to Lauren Lepow for her skillful editing and encouragement. Anne Norton contributed several pointed and helpful suggestions. Arno Mayer took time off from his own writing to offer encouragement, invaluable criticisms, and intellectual companionship despite our continental divide. All of the above are absolved from responsibility for any errors or missteps in the pages that follow.

Finally, special thanks beyond words to Emily Purvis Wolin for companionship extending over more than sixty years.

Introduction to the 2017 Edition

Sheldon Wolin was our most important contemporary political theorist. He gave us a modern vocabulary to describe our decayed democracy and the poisonous effects of empire. He was a scholar who detested orthodoxies, rooted his understanding of democracy in the ancient concept of the Athenian demos and believed, like Max Weber, that politics was a vocation.

Ralph Nader gave me *Democracy Incorporated: Managed Democracy and the Specter of Inverted Totalitarianism* when it first came out in 2008. Nader, who has been fighting the abuse of corporate power longer and with perhaps more success than any other American, called it a "masterpiece." Wolin captured the political mutations caused by neoliberalism and coined the term "inverted totalitarianism" for the novel political and economic system it had spawned. He foresaw that this system of inverted totalitarianism would, as it has, eventually crush or hollow out our democratic institutions and give rise to an authoritarian or even totalitarian regime.

Inverted totalitarianism is different from classical forms of totalitarianism. It does not find its expression in a demagogue or charismatic leader but in the faceless anonymity of the corporate state. Inverted totalitarianism pays outward fealty to the facade of electoral politics, the Constitution, civil liberties, freedom of the press, the independence of the judiciary, and the iconography, traditions and language of American patriotism, but it has effectively seized all of the mechanisms of power to render the citizen impotent.

"Unlike the Nazis, who made life uncertain for the wealthy and privileged while providing social programs for the working class and poor, inverted totalitarianism exploits the poor, reducing or weakening health programs and social services, regimenting mass education for an insecure workforce threatened by the importation of low-wage workers," Wolin wrote. "Employment in a high-tech, volatile, and globalized economy is normally as precarious as during an old-fashioned depression. The result is that citizenship, or what remains of it, is practiced amidst a continuing state of worry. Hobbes had it right: when citizens are insecure and at the same time driven by competitive aspirations, they yearn for political stability rather than civic engagement, protection rather than political involvement."

Great writers and intellectuals give us a vocabulary that allows us to make sense of reality. They excavate depths that we, without their help, are unable to fathom. We are captive to systems of power until we can name the dominant myths and the intricate systems of coercion and control that extinguish our freedom.

We are a society awash in skillfully manufactured lies. Reality is whatever hallucination flickers on a screen. Solitude that makes thought possible—a removal from the electronic cacophony that besieges us—is harder and harder to find. We have severed ourselves from a print-based culture. We are unable to grapple with the nuances and complexity of ideas. We have traded ideas for fabricated clichés. We speak in the hollow language we are given by our corporate masters. Reality, presented to us as image, is unexamined and therefore false. We are culturally illiterate. And because of our cultural illiteracy we are easily manipulated and controlled.

The great writers—Marcel Proust, Anton Chekhov, Hannah Arendt, Simone Weil, Max Weber, Samuel Beckett, George Orwell, W.E.B. Du Bois, James Baldwin, and others—knew that thought is subversive. They challenged and critiqued the dominant narrative, assumptions, and structures that buttress power. They freed us. They did not cater to the latest fashion of the academy or popular culture. They did not seek adulation. They did not build pathetic monuments to themselves. They elucidated difficult and hard truths. They served humanity. They lifted up voices the power elites seek to discredit, marginalize, or crush. Wolin was a writer of this stature. He gave us the words and the ideas to understand our corporate despotism—what he called "inverted totalitarianism." He did so by battling the dominant trend within university political science departments that, as he lamented, has seen them become de facto social science departments "addicted" to quantitative projects, chasing after an unachievable scientific clarity and refusing to take a stand or examine the major issues facing the wider society.

This quantitative gathering of "value-free" facts may get you tenure. It may get you invited as a courtier into the machinery of power—indeed, academic writing too often serves the ends of power. But these pursuits, as Wolin reminded us, are intellectual treason. Wolin was not afraid to ask the huge, esoteric, uncomfortable, and often unanswerable questions that make the life of the mind and political thought vital and important. He called out corporate power for its destruction of our capitalist democracy. He railed against the commodification of the individual and the ecosystem. He unmasked the mechanisms of manipulation. He denounced our corporate coup d'état. He upheld the integrity of the scholar. And he was often alone.

I met Wolin at his home in Salem, Oregon, in 2014 to film a nearly-three hour interview. It was the last major interview he would give. He said then that "inverted totalitarianism" constantly "projects power upwards." It is "the antithesis of constitutional power." It is designed to create instability to keep a citizenry off balance and passive.

"Downsizing, reorganization, bubbles bursting, unions busted, quickly outdated skills, and transfer of jobs abroad create not just fear but an economy of fear, a system of control whose power feeds on uncertainty, yet a system that, according to its analysts, is eminently rational," he wrote.

Inverted totalitarianism also "perpetuates politics all the time," Wolin said when we spoke, "but a politics that is not political." The endless and extravagant election cycles, he said, are an example of politics without politics.

"Instead of participating in power," he wrote, "the virtual citizen is invited to have 'opinions': measurable responses to questions predesigned to elicit them."

Political campaigns rarely discuss substantive issues. They center on manufactured political personalities, empty rhetoric, sophisticated public relations, slick advertising, propaganda, and the constant use of focus groups and opinion polls to loop back to voters what they want to hear. Money has effectively replaced the vote. Every presidential candidate—including Bernie Sanders—understands, to use Wolin's words, that "the subject of empire is taboo in electoral debates." The citizen is irrelevant. He or she is nothing more than a spectator, allowed to vote and then forgotten once the carnival of elections ends and corporations and their lobbyists get back to the business of ruling.

"If the main purpose of elections is to serve up pliant legislators for lobbyists to shape, such a system deserves to be called 'misrepresentative or clientry government,'" Wolin wrote. "It is, at one and the same time, a powerful contributing factor to the depoliticization of the citizenry, as well as reason for characterizing the system as one of antidemocracy."

The result is that the public is "denied the use of state power." Wolin deplored the trivialization of political discourse, a tactic used to leave the public fragmented, antagonistic, and emotionally charged while leaving corporate power and empire unchallenged.

"Cultural wars might seem an indication of strong political involvements," he wrote. "Actually they are a substitute. The notoriety they receive from the media and from politicians eager to take firm stands on nonsubstantive issues serves to distract attention and contribute to a cant politics of the inconsequential."

"One cannot point to any national institution[s] that can accurately be described as democratic," he wrote, "surely not in the highly managed, money-saturated elections, the lobby-infested Congress, the imperial presidency, the class-biased judicial and penal system, or, least of all, the media."

"The ruling groups can now operate on the assumption that they don't need the traditional notion of something called a public in the broad sense of a coherent whole," he said in our interview. "They now have the tools to deal with the very disparities and differences that they have themselves helped to create. It's a game in which you manage to undermine the cohesiveness that the public requires if they [the public] are to be politically effective. And at the same time, you create these different, distinct groups that inevitably find themselves in tension or at odds or in competition with other groups, so that it becomes more of a melee than it does become a way of fashioning majorities."

In classical totalitarian regimes, such as those of Nazi fascism or Soviet communism, economics was subordinate to politics. But "under inverted totalitarianism the reverse is true," Wolin argued. "Economics dominates politics—and with that domination comes different forms of ruthlessness."

He continued: "The United States has become the showcase of how democracy can be managed without appearing to be suppressed."

The corporate state, Wolin told me, is "legitimated by elections it controls." To extinguish democracy, it rewrites and distorts laws and legislation that once protected democracy. Basic rights are, in essence, revoked by judicial and legislative fiat. Courts and legislative bodies, in the service of corporate power, reinterpret laws to strip them of their original meaning in order to strengthen corporate control and abolish corporate oversight.

He wrote: "Why negate a constitution, as the Nazis did, if it is possible simultaneously to exploit porosity and legitimate power by means of judicial interpretations that declare huge campaign contributions to be protected speech under the First Amendment, or that treat heavily financed and organized lobbying by large corporations as a simple application of the people's right to petition their government?"

Our system of inverted totalitarianism will avoid harsh and violent measures of control "as long as . . . dissent remains ineffectual," he told me. "The government does not need to stamp out dissent. The uniformity of imposed public opinion through the corporate media does a very effective job."

The elites, especially the intellectual class, have been bought off. "Through a combination of governmental contracts, corporate and foundation funds, joint projects involving university and corporate researchers, and wealthy individual donors, universities (especially so-called research universities), intellectuals, scholars, and researchers have been seamlessly integrated into the system," Wolin wrote. "No books burned, no refugee Einsteins."

But, he warned, should the population—steadily stripped of its most basic rights, including the right to privacy, and increasingly impoverished and bereft of hope—become restive, inverted totalitarianism will become as brutal and violent as past totalitarian states. "The war on terrorism, with its accompanying emphasis upon 'homeland security,' presumes that state power, now inflated by doctrines of preemptive war and released from treaty obligations and the potential constraints of international judicial bodies, can turn inwards," he wrote, "confident that in its domestic pursuit of terrorists the powers it claimed, like the powers projected abroad, would be measured, not by ordinary constitutional standards, but by the shadowy and ubiquitous character of terrorism as officially defined."

The indiscriminate police violence in poor communities of color is an example of the ability of the corporate state to "legally" harass and kill citizens with impunity. The cruder forms of control—from militarized police to whole-sale surveillance, as well as police serving as judge, jury, and executioner, now a reality for the underclass—will become a reality for all of us should we begin to resist the continued funneling of power and wealth upward. We are tolerated as citizens, Wolin warned, only as long as we participate in the illusion of a participatory democracy. The moment we rebel and refuse to take part in the illusion, the face of inverted totalitarianism will look like the face of past systems of totalitarianism.

"The significance of the African-American prison population is political," he wrote. "What is notable about the African-American population generally is that it is highly sophisticated politically and by far the one group that throughout the twentieth century kept alive a spirit of resistance and rebelliousness. In that context, criminal justice is as much a strategy of political neutralization as it is a channel of instinctive racism."

Wolin expressed consternation for a population severed from print and the nuanced world of ideas. He saw cinema, like television, as "tyrannical" because of its ability to "block out, eliminate whatever might introduce qualification, ambiguity, or dialogue." He railed against what he calls a "monochromatic media" with corporate-approved pundits used to identify "the problem and its parameters, creating a box that dissenters struggle vainly to elude. The critic who insists on changing the context is dismissed as irrelevant, extremist, 'the Left'—or ignored altogether."

The constant dissemination of illusions permits myth rather than reality to dominate the decisions of the power elites. And when myth dominates, disaster descends upon the empire, as sixteen years of futile war in the Middle East and our failure to react to climate change illustrate. Wolin wrote:

> When myth begins to govern decision-makers in a world where ambiguity and stubborn facts abound, the result is a disconnect between the actors and the reality. They convince themselves that the forces of darkness possess weapons of mass destruction and nuclear capabilities: that their own nation is privileged by a god who inspired the Founding Fathers and the writing of the nation's constitution; and that a class structure of great and stubborn inequalities does not exist. A grim but joyous few see portents of a world that is living out "the last days."

Wolin was a bombardier and a navigator on a B-24 Liberator heavy bomber in the South Pacific in the Second World War. He flew fifty-one combat missions. The planes had crews of up to ten. From Guadalcanal, he advanced with American forces as they captured islands in the Pacific. During the campaign the military high command decided to direct the B-24 bombers—which were huge and difficult to fly in addition to having little maneuverability—against Japanese ships, a tactic that saw tremendous losses of planes and American lives. The use of the B-24, nicknamed "the flying boxcar" and "the flying coffin," to attack warships bristling with antiaircraft guns exposed for Wolin the callousness of military commanders who blithely sacrificed their air crews and war machines in schemes that offered little chance of success.

"It was terrible," he said of the orders to bomb ships. "We received awful losses from that, because of these big, lumbering aircraft, particularly flying low trying to hit the Japanese navy—and we lost countless people in it, countless."

"We had quite a few psychological casualties . . . men, boys, who just couldn't take it anymore," he said, "just couldn't stand the strain of getting up at five in the morning and proceeding to get into these aircraft and get shot at for a while and coming back to rest for another day."

Wolin saw the militarists and the corporatists, who formed an unholy coalition to orchestrate the rise of a global American empire after the war, as the forces that extinguished American democracy. He called inverted totalitarianism "the true face of Superpower." These war profiteers and militarists, advocating the doctrine of total war during the Cold War, bled the country of resources. They also worked in tandem to dismantle popular institutions and organizations such as labor unions to politically disempower and impoverish workers. They "normalized" war. And Wolin warned that, as in all empires, they eventually will be "eviscerated by their own expansionism." There will never be a return to democracy, he cautioned, until the unchecked power of the militarists and corporatists is dramatically curtailed. A war state cannot be a democratic state.

Wolin wrote:

> National defense was declared inseparable from a strong economy. The fixation upon mobilization and rearmament inspired the gradual disappearance from the national political agenda of the regulation and control of corporations. The defender of the free world needed the power of the globalizing, expanding corporation, not an economy hampered by "trust busting." Moreover, since the enemy was rabidly anticapitalist, every measure that strengthened capitalism was a blow against the enemy. Once the battle lines between communism and the "free society" were drawn, the economy became untouchable for purposes other than "strengthening" capitalism. The ultimate merger would be between capitalism and democracy. Once the identity and security of democracy were successfully identified with the Cold War and with the methods for waging it, the stage was set for the intimidation of most politics left or right.

The result is a nation dedicated almost exclusively to waging war.

"When a constitutionally limited government utilizes weapons of horrendous destructive power, subsidizes their development, and becomes the world's largest arms dealer," Wolin wrote, "the Constitution is conscripted to serve as power's apprentice rather than its conscience."

He went on:

That the patriotic citizen unswervingly supports the military and its huge budget means that conservatives have succeeded in persuading the public that the military is distinct from government. Thus the most substantial element of state power is removed from public debate. Similarly in his/her new status as imperial citizen the believer remains contemptuous of bureaucracy yet does not hesitate to obey the directives issued by the Department of Homeland Security, the largest and most intrusive governmental department in the history of the nation. Identification with militarism and patriotism, along with the images of American might projected by the media, serves to make the individual citizen feel stronger, thereby compensating for the feelings of weakness visited by the economy upon an overworked, exhausted, and insecure labor force. For its antipolitics inverted totalitarianism requires believers, patriots, and nonunion "guest workers."

Sheldon Wolin was often considered an outcast among contemporary political theorists whose concentration on quantitative analysis and behavioralism led them to eschew the examination of broad political theory and ideas. Wolin insisted that philosophy, even that written by the ancient Greeks, was not a dead relic but a vital tool to examine and challenge the assumptions and ideologies of contemporary systems of power and political thought. Political theory, he argued, was "primarily a civic and secondarily an academic activity." It had a role "not just as an historical discipline that dealt with the critical examination of idea systems," he told me, but as a force "in helping to fashion public policies and governmental directions, and above all civic education, in a way that would further . . . the goals of a more democratic, more egalitarian, more educated society." His 1969 essay "Political Theory as a Vocation" argued for this imperative and chastised fellow academics when they focused their work on data collection and academic minutiae. He wrote, with his usual lucidity and literary flourishes, in that essay:

In a fundamental sense, our world has become as perhaps no previous world has, the product of design, the product of theories about human structures deliberately created rather than historically articulated. But in another sense, the embodiment of theory in the world has resulted in a world impervious to theory. The giant, routinized structures defy fundamental alteration and, at the same time, display an unchallengeable legitimacy, for the rational, scientific, and technological principles on which they are based seem in perfect accord with an age committed to science, rationalism and technology. Above all, it is a world which appears to have rendered epic theory superfluous. Theory, as Hegel had foreseen, must take the form of "explanation." Truly, it seems to be the age when Minerva's owl has taken flight.

Wolin's magnificence as a scholar was matched by his magnificence as a human being. He stood with students at UC Berkeley, where he taught, to support the Free Speech Movement and wrote passionately in its defense. Many of these essays were published in "The Berkeley Rebellion and Beyond: Essays on Politics and Education in the Technological Society." Later, as a professor at Princeton University, he was one of a handful of faculty members who joined students to call for divestment of investments in apartheid South Africa. He once accompanied students to present the case to Princeton alumni. "I've never been jeered quite so roundly," he said. "Some of them called me [a] 50-year-old . . . sophomore and that kind of thing."

From 1981 to 1983, Wolin published *Democracy: A Journal of Political Renewal and Radical Change*. In its pages he and other writers called out the con game of neoliberalism, the danger of empire, the rise of unchecked corporate power and the erosion of democratic institutions and ideals. The journal swiftly made him a pariah within the politics department at Princeton.

"I remember once when I was up editing that journal, I left a copy of it on the table in the faculty room hoping that somebody would read it and comment," he said. "I never heard a word. And during all the time I was there and doing *Democracy*, I never had one colleague come up to me and either say something positive or even negative about it. Just absolute silence."

Max Weber, whom Wolin called "the greatest of all sociologists," argued in his essay "Politics as a Vocation" that those who dedicate their lives to striving for justice in the modern political arena are like the classical heroes who can never overcome what the ancient Greeks called *fortuna*. These heroes, Wolin wrote in "Politics and Vision," rise up nevertheless "to heights of moral passion and grandeur, harried by a deep sense of responsibility." Yet, Wolin goes on, "at bottom, [the contemporary hero] is a figure as futile and pathetic as his classical counterpart. The fate of the classical hero was that he could never overcome contingency or *fortuna*; the special irony of the modern hero is that he struggles in a world where contingency has been routed by bureaucratized procedures and nothing remains for the hero to contend against. Weber's political leader is rendered superfluous by the very bureaucratic world that Weber discovered: even charisma has been bureaucratized. We are left with the ambiguity of the political man fired by deep passion — 'to be passionate, *ira et studium*, is . . . the element of the political leader' — but facing the impersonal world of bureaucracy which lives by the passionless principle that Weber frequently cited, *sine ira et studio*, 'without scorn or bias.'"

Wolin wrote that even when faced with certain defeat, all of us are called to the "awful responsibility" of the fight for justice, equality and liberty.

"You don't win," Wolin said at the end of our talk. "Or you win rarely. And if you win, it's often for a very short time. That's why politics is a vocation for Weber. It's not an occasional undertaking that we assume every two years or every four years when there's an election. It's a constant occupation and preoccupation. And the problem, as Weber saw it, was to understand it not as a partisan kind of education in the politicians or political party sense, but as in the broad understanding of what political life should be and what is required to make it sustainable. He's calling for a certain kind of understanding that's very different from what we think about when we associate political understanding with how do you vote or what party do you support or what cause do you support. Weber's asking us to step back and say what kind of political order, and the values associated with it that it promotes, are we willing to really give a lot for, including sacrifice."

Wolin embodied the qualities Weber ascribes to the hero. He struggled against forces he knew he could not vanquish. He never wavered in the fight as an intellectual and as a citizen. He was one of the first to explain to us the transformation of our capitalist democracy into a new species of totalitarianism. He warned us of the consequences of unbridled empire or superpower. He foresaw the moral and political decay that would see a culture entranced by celebrity and reality television elect Donald Trump to the presidency. He called on us, always, to resist.

Democracy Incorporated was ignored by every major newspaper and journal in the country. This did not surprise him. He knew his power. So did his enemies. All his fears for the nation have come to pass. A corporate monstrosity rules us. A demagogue is in the White House. Our rights as citizens have been abolished. Our democracy is a fiction. If we held up a scorecard we would have to say Wolin lost, but we would also have to acknowledge the integrity, brilliance, courage, and nobility of his life.

Chris Hedges
Princeton, New Jersey, 2017

Democracy Incorporated

Preview

... the eminence and richness of a Reich which
has become a superpower.

—*German commentator at the opening of a
new Reich Chancellery in 1939*[1]

i

The Triumph of the Will, Leni Riefenstahl's famous (or infamous) propaganda tribute to Hitler, memorialized the 1934 rally of the Nazi Party
at Nuremberg. It begins with a dramatic, revelatory moment. The camera is trained on a densely clouded sky. Magically, the clouds suddenly
part and a tiny plane glides through. It swoops down, lands, and The
Leader, in uniform, emerges and strides triumphantly past the salutes
of admiring throngs and the party faithful. As the film draws to a close,
the camera becomes riveted on a seemingly endless parade, row on
row, of uniformed Nazis, shoulder to shoulder, goose-stepping in the
flickering torchlight. Even today it leaves an impression of iron determination, of power poised for conquest, of power resolute, mindless, its
might wrapped in myth.

On May 1, 2003, in another tightly orchestrated "documentary," television viewers were given an American version of stern resolve and its
embodiment in a leader. A military plane swoops from the sky and
lands on an aircraft carrier. The camera creates the illusion of a warship
far at sea, symbolizing power unconfined to its native land and able to
project itself anywhere in the world. The leader emerges, not as a plain
and democratic officeholder, but as one whose symbolic authority is
antidemocratic. He strides resolutely, flight helmet tucked under his
arm, outfitted in the gear of a military pilot. Above, the banner "Mission
Accomplished." He salutes a prearranged crowd of uniformed military
personnel. Shortly thereafter, swaggering, he reemerges in civilian garb

1

but without discarding the aura of anticivilian authority. He speaks magisterially from the flight deck of the carrier *Abraham Lincoln*, now cleared with the military carefully ringed about him. He stands alone in the ritual circle expressive of a sacrament of leadership and obedience. They cheer and clap on cue. He invokes the blessing of a higher power. He, too, has promised a triumph of the will:

The United States will:

- champion aspirations for human dignity;
- strengthen alliances to defeat global terrorism;
- . . . defuse regional conflicts;
- prevent our enemies from threatening us [and] our allies . . . with weapons of mass destruction;
- ignite a new era of global economic growth
- expand the circle of development by opening societies and building the infrastructure of democracy;
- transform America's national security institutions.[2]

Myth wrapped in might? Will to power?

ii

Both spectacles are examples of the distinctively modern mode of myth creation. They are the self-conscious constructions of visual media. Cinema and television share a common quality of being tyrannical in a specific sense. They are able to block out, eliminate whatever might introduce qualification, ambiguity, or dialogue, anything that might weaken or complicate the holistic *force* of their creation, of its *total* impression.

In a curious but important way these media effects mesh with religious practice. In many Christian religions the believer participates in ceremonies much as the movie or TV watcher takes part in the spectacle presented. In neither case do they participate as the democratic citizen is supposed to do, as actively engaged in decisions and sharing in the exercise of power. They participate as communicants in a ceremony prescribed by the masters of the ceremony. Those assembled at Nuremberg or on the USS *Abraham Lincoln* did not share power with their leaders. Their relationship was thaumaturgical: they were being favored by a wondrous power in a form and at a time of its choosing.

The underlying metaphysic to these dreams of glory, of an "American century," of Superpower, was revealed in the musings of a high-level administration official when he or she attributed a view of "reality" to reporters and then contrasted it with that held by the administration: reporters and commentators were "in what we [i.e., the administration] call the reality-based community [which] believe[s] that solutions emerge from your judicious study of discernible reality. That's not the way the world works anymore. We're an empire now, we create our own reality. And while you're studying that reality—judiciously as you will—we'll act again, creating other new realities, which you can study, too, and that's how things will sort out. We're history's actors . . . and you, all of you, will be left to just study what we do."[3]

It would be difficult to find a more faithful representative of the totalitarian credo that true politics is essentially a matter of "will," of a determination to master the uses of power and to deploy them to reconstitute reality. The statement is a fitting epigraph to Riefenstahl's *Triumph of the Will*—is it a possible epitaph for democracy in America?

CHAPTER ONE

Myth in the Making

i

> Robert S. Mueller III [director of the FBI] and Secretary of
> State Powell read from the Bible. Mr. Mueller's theme
> was good versus evil. "We do not wrestle against flesh and
> blood, but against the rulers, against the authorities,
> against the cosmic powers over the present darkness, against
> the spiritual forces of evil in the heavenly places," he said,
> reading from Ephesians 6:12–18.
>
> Mr. Powell, who followed, touched on trust in God.
> "Therefore do not be anxious about tomorrow, for tomorrow
> will be anxious about itself," Mr. Powell said, reading from
> Matthew 6:25–34.[1]
>
> In choosing [the World Trade Center] as their target the
> terrorists perversely dramatized the supremacy of the free
> market and of the political system intimately associated
> with it in the United States and elsewhere, democracy, as
> defining features of the world of the twenty-first century.
> —*Michael Mandelbaum*[2]

If the burning of the German Parliament (Reichstag) in 1933 produced
the symbolic event portending the destruction of parliamentary government by dictatorship, the destruction of the World Trade Center and
the attack upon the Pentagon on September 11, 2001, were a revelatory
moment in the history of American political life.

What did the selected targets symbolize? Unlike the Reichstag fire
the attacks were not aimed at what could be characterized as the archi-
tecture of constitutional democracy and the system of power that it represented. Neither the congressional buildings nor the White House was

attacked;[3] nor were the symbols of democracy, not the Statue of Liberty, the Lincoln Memorial, or Independence Hall. Instead the buildings symbolic of financial and military power were struck practically simultaneously. Once the United States declared war on terrorism, attention naturally focused on the projection abroad of the actual forms of globalizing power symbolized by the targets of 9/11. Yet the impact of 9/11 may prove equally significant in accelerating the threat to the domestic system of power whose architectural symbols were ignored.

ii

On cue to 9/11 the media—television, radio, and newspapers—acted in unison, fell into line, even knew instinctively what the line and their role should be.[4] What followed may have been the modern media's greatest production, its contribution to what was promptly—and darkly—described as a "new world." Their vivid representations of the destruction of the Twin Towers, accompanied by interpretations that were unwavering and unquestioning, served a didactic end of fixing the images of American vulnerability while at the same time testing the potential for cultural control.

The media produced not only an iconography of terror but a fearful public receptive to being led, first by hailing a leader, the mayor of New York, Rudolf Giuliani, and then by following one, the president of the United States, George W. Bush.[5] As one pundit wrote approvingly, "the fear that is so prevalent in the country [worked as] a cleanser, washing away a lot of the self-indulgence of the past decade." Washed in the blood of the lambs . . . Actually, those who could afford self-indulgence would continue to do so while those who could not would send their sons and daughters to Afghanistan and Iraq.

September 11 was quickly consecrated as the equivalent of a national holy day, and the nation was summoned to mourn the victims. Soon thereafter, when memory receded, the date itself was perpetuated and made synonymous with terrorism.[6] On the second anniversary of the event "a senior White House official" explained the two different rituals of grieving adopted by the president: "Last year you had an open wound, physically and metaphorically. This year it is about healing—you don't ever want to forget, and the war goes on, but the spiritual need is different."[7]

September 11 was thus fashioned into a primal event, the principal reference point by which the nation's body politic was to be governed and the lives of its members ordered. From the crucified to the redeemer-nation.

But was it "holy politics" or wholly politics?[8] How was it possible for a notably gimlet-eyed administration, flaunting its prowess for unchristian hardball politics, to overlay its unabashed corporate culture with the cloak of piety without tripping itself up? To be sure, its devotional mien would occasionally be joked about. The jokes, however, would trail off, as though the jokesters themselves were uneasy about mocking some higher powers. That the overwhelming majority of Americans declare they "believe in God" is likely to give pause to expressions of irreverence.

In attempting to characterize an emerging symbolic system reported as "a spontaneous outpouring," one must bear in mind that, although pressures from the administration were undoubtedly at work, television largely conscripted itself. Unprompted, stations replayed endlessly the spectacle of the collapsing Twin Towers while newspapers, in a macabre version of Andy Warhol's prediction of fifteen minutes of fame for everyone, published continuing stories of heroism and self-sacrifice by firemen and police and thumbnail biographies of individual victims.[9] The media then announced, disingenuously, that "9/11 had forever been printed on the national consciousness." Which is to say, the date was enshrined and readied, not merely to justify but to sanctify the power of those pledged to be its avengers.[10]

In a society where freedom of speech, media, and religion are guaranteed, where quirkiness is celebrated, why was the result unison? How is it that a society that makes a fetish of freedom of choice can produce a unanimity eerily comparable to that of a more openly coercive system? Is it a process like the "hidden hand" of Adam Smith's free market where, unprompted by any central directorate, the uncoordinated actions of individuals, each concerned to advance his self-interest, nonetheless produce an overall effect that is good for all?

Smith's model assumes that all of the actors are similarly motivated by rational self-interest, but the aftermath of 9/11, its production and reproduction, is remarkable for the incongruity of the actors, for the diversity of motivations that nonetheless were combined to perpetuate a spectacular moment that permitted only one response. September 11 became that rare phenomenon in contemporary life, an unambiguous truth, one that dissolved contradictions, the ambiguities of politics, the claims and counterclaims of political ideologies and pundits. Critics transformed themselves into penitents defending a preventive war as just and celebrating a constitution sufficiently flexible to be suspended at the pleasure of the chief executive. The truth of 9/11 did more than set free the nation's citizens; it rendered them innocent, able to repress their involvement in the vast expanse of power of empire and globalization, and to ask plaintively, "Why does the rest of the world hate us?"

What explains and promotes such unanimity? In an earlier time it was common to liken the free circulation of ideas to competition in a free marketplace: the best ideas, like the superior product, would prevail over inferior competitors. In the highly structured marketplace of ideas managed by media conglomerates, however, sellers rule and buyers adapt to what the same media has pronounced to be "mainstream." Free circulation of ideas has been replaced by their managed circularity. The self-anointed keepers of the First Amendment flame encourage exegesis and reasonable criticism. Critics who do not wish to be considered as "off-the-wall" attract buyers by internalizing co-optation. Accepting the conventions of criticism entails accepting the context created and enforced by the "house" voices. The result is an essentially monochromatic media. In-house commentators identify the problem and its parameters, creating a box that dissenters struggle vainly to elude. The critic who insists on changing the context is dismissed as irrelevant, extremist, "the Left"—or ignored altogether. A more sophisticated structure embraces the op-ed page and letters to the editor. In theory everyone is free to submit articles or letters, but the newspaper chooses what suits its purpose with meager explanation of standards for acceptance—although it is obvious that the selected opinions represent limits set by the editors. From the paper's viewpoint the best of all worlds is attained when the authors of op-ed pieces or letters criticize not the paper but its pundits, who are carefully selected according to a Dorothy Parker principle of representing all opinions in the range between A and B.[11] The point is the appearance of freedom: critics are encouraged to "score points." to trade insults, although these jabs do not add up to anything beyond venting.

The responsibility of the responsible media includes maintaining an ideological "balance" that treats the "Left" and the "Right" as polar opposites as well as moral and political equivalents. Over the years the *New York Times* has faithfully discharged that responsibility. In 1992 it featured a story about South Africa, still struggling with the effects of apartheid. The reporter interviewed some young black people who favored a war to "end the colonial settler regime." That sentiment gave the *Times* reporter the sense that he was caught in "some cold war time warp." It inspired him to balance off the anticolonial rebels by inserting a description of an Afrikaner neo-Nazi gang who wanted "a people's army." His conclusion: "the two groups have much in common." One of their commonalities, he discovered, was the small numbers in each group. After "a two-hour conversation" with the blacks he was ready with his conclusion: the conversation was "a refresher course in the ideological lexicon that has been discredited from Moscow to Mogadishu."[12]

iii

By the most recent count, more than three thousand innocent persons were murdered on September 11 without apparent provocation or justification. The damage to property and the impact upon the city of New York and upon the general economy were enormous. These facts, at once familiar yet impossible to fully comprehend, had a stark and brutal immediacy. Quantitatively they were as crudely "real" as reality is ever likely to be. Since then the reality of that day has been reproduced in a variety of guises and practical applications that are, in their own way, as amazing as the event invoked to justify them.

The nation was immediately declared to be at war against an enemy whose nature, number, and location were largely unknown. Nonetheless, "enemy aliens" were rounded up and held under constitutionally dubious conditions. The nation's population was periodically placed on a state of alert. The powers of government were expanded and made more intrusive, while simultaneously its social welfare functions were radically scaled back. Amidst a faltering economy, widening disparities between social classes, and escalating national debt, the administration responded by promoting its own version of "class actions." It became more aggressively biased in favor of the wealthier, while, equally signifi-cant, the less wealthy and poor remained politically apathetic, unable to find a vehicle for expressing their helplessness. A provocative foreign policy was adopted with the aim of releasing American power from the restraints of treaties and of cooperation with allies. "At some point," a senior administration official warned, "the Europeans with butterflies in their stomachs—many of whom didn't want us to go into Afghani-stan—will see that they have a bipolar choice: they can get with the plan [to invade Iraq] or get off."[13] New enemy states were identified, not as hostile or enemy but as "evil," and threatened. The notion of preemptive war was embraced and put into practice against Iraq.

The general effect of this expansion of powers created a new world where everything became larger-than-life, strange, filled with huge powers locked in a contest that would determine the fate of the world: "Axis of Evil," "weapons of mass destruction," "civilization against bar-barism." The reality of September 11 became clothed in a myth that dramatized an encounter between two world-contending powers and prophesied that after severe trials and marvelous events the power blessed by the Creator would triumph over the evil power.

The mythology created around September 11 was predominantly Christian in its themes. The day was converted into the political equiva-lent of a holy day of crucifixion, of martyrdom, that fulfilled multiple functions: as the basis of a political theology, as a communion around a mystical body of a bellicose republic, as a warning against political apostasy, as a sanctification of the nation's leader, transforming him from a powerful officeholder of questionable legitimacy into an instru-ment of redemption, and at the same time exhorting the congregants to a wartime militancy, demanding of them uncritical loyalty and support, summoning them as participants in a sacrament of unity and in a crusade to "rid the world of evil."[14] Holy American Empire?

iv

Myth, in its original form [in ancient Greece], provided
answers without ever explicitly formulating the problems.
When [Greek] tragedy takes over the mythical traditions, it
uses them to pose problems to which there are no solutions.
—*Jean-Pierre Vernant*[15]

Let us weigh the gain and the loss in wagering that God is.
Let us estimate these two chances. If you gain, you gain
all; if you lose, you lose nothing. Wager, then, without
hesitation that He is.
—*Blaise Pascal*[16]

May God continue to bless America.
—*President George W. Bush*

In the aftermath of September 11 the American citizen was propelled into the realm of mythology, a new and different dimension of being, unworldly, where occult forces were bent on destroying a world that had been created for the children of light. Myth recounts a story, in this case of how the armies of light will arise from the ruins to battle and overcome the forces of darkness. Myth presents a narrative of exploits, not an argument or a demonstration. It does not make the world intelligible, only dramatic. In the course of its account the actions of the myth's heroes, no matter how bloody or destructive, acquire justification. They become privileged, entitled to take actions that are morally denied to others. No need to tally the Iraqi civilian casualties.

Myths come in many sizes and shapes. Our concern is with a particular species, the cosmic myth, and with a unique permutation that occurs when the cosmic myth is combined with secular myth. A cosmic myth might be defined as a dramatic form with epical aspirations. Its subject is not a simple contest but an inevitable, even necessary showdown between irreconcilable forces, each claiming that ultimately its power draws upon supernatural resources. Their capabilities far exceed the scales of ordinary politics. Typically, one force portrays itself as defending the world, and it depicts the other as seeking to dominate it by a perverse strategy that thrives on chaos. Although each possesses a different form of power from its rival, each claims that its power alone is drawn from a sacred source, that therefore it alone is blessed while its foe is diabolical. Not only are the claims of each party mutually exclusive of the other and impossible to disprove; each is intolerant of opposition (= doubt) and distrustful of a free and genuinely democratic politics.

In his State of the Union address of January 2007 President Bush, having suffered a clear defeat in the midterm elections of 2006 and a popular repudiation of his Iraq policies, responded by, in his turn, repudiating that most down-to-earth democratic process and called for increasing the troop levels in Iraq by more than twenty thousand troops. Defiantly the decider decided to transcend mere elections, ignoring their legitimizing role, and to substitute a mythical representation of the stakes. If American forces were to "step back before Baghdad is secure," he warned, then chaos would threaten the world.

> [T]he Iraqi government would be overrun by extremists on all sides. We could expect an epic battle between Shia extremists backed by Iran and Sunni extremists aided by Al Qaeda and supporters of the old regime. A contagion of violence could spill out across the country, and in time the entire region could be drawn into the conflict.
>
> For America this is a nightmare scenario. For the enemy, this is the objective. Chaos is their greatest ally in this struggle. And out of chaos in Iraq, would emerge an emboldened enemy with new safe havens, new recruits, new resources and an even greater determination to harm America.

The president then presented his contribution to the structure of inverted totalitarianism and in the process demonstrated that even when all of the main elements of a "free society" are in place—free elections, free media, functioning Congress, and the Bill of Rights—they can be ignored by an aggrandizing executive. First he emphasized

that the battle against chaos had no discernible end. "The war on terror," he declaimed, "is a generational struggle that will continue long
after you [i.e., Congress] and I have turned our duties over to others."
He then threw down the gauntlet to the vast majority of Americans and
Congress by declaring that he would seek authorization from Congress
to increase the army and Marine Corps by ninety-two thousand over
five years, and, equally significant, he pressed Congress to assist in devising "a volunteer Civilian Reserve Corps." That corps would, in effect, function as a private army. He envisaged a corps of "civilians with
critical skills to serve on missions abroad when America needs them."[17]
A praetorian guard for the new empire?

v

In the early part of the twentieth century the great social and political
theorist Max Weber wrote feelingly of the "disenchantment of the
world" brought about by the triumph of scientific rationalism and skepticism. There was, he contended, no room any longer for occult forces,
supernatural deities, or divinely revealed truth. In a world dominated
by scientifically established facts and with no privileged or sacrosanct
areas, myth would seemingly have a difficult time retaining a foothold.[18]
Not only did Weber underestimate the staying power of credulity; he
could not foresee that the great triumphs of modern science would
themselves provide the basis for technological achievements which, far
from banishing the mythical, would unwittingly inspire it.

The mythical is also nourished from another source, one seemingly
more incongruous than the scientific-technological culture. Consider
the imaginary world continuously being created and re-created by contemporary advertising and rendered virtually escape-proof by the enveloping culture of the modern media. Equally important, the culture
produced by modern advertising, which seems at first glance to be resolutely secular and materialistic, the antithesis of religious and especially
of evangelical teachings, actually reinforces that dynamic. Almost every
product promises to change your life: it will make you more beautiful,
cleaner, more sexually alluring, and more successful. Born again, as

it were. The messages contain promises about the future, unfailingly optimistic, exaggerating, miracle-promising—the same ideology that invites corporate executives to exaggerate profits and conceal losses, but always with a sunny face. The virtual reality of the advertiser and the "good news" of the evangelist complement each other, a match made in heaven. Their zeal to transcend the ordinary and their bottomless optimism both feed the hubris of Superpower. Each colludes with the other. The evangelist looks forward to the "last days," while the corporate executive systematically exhausts the world's scarce resources.

Virtual reality has about it the character of unreality, of transcending the ordinary world and its common smells and sights, its limiting rhythms of birth, growth, decline, death, and renewal. For Americans, the chosen people of advertising, technology, capitalist orthodoxy, and religious faith, the greatest triumph of virtual reality is war, the great unexperienced reality. Ever since the Civil War Americans have fought wars at a distance: in Cuba, the Philippines, France, on almost every other continent in World War II, then in Korea, Vietnam, the Middle East. War is an action game, played in the living room, or a spectacle on a screen, but, in either case, not actually experienced. Ordinary life goes on uninterruptedly: work, recreation, professional sports, family vacations. After 9/11 terrorism becomes another virtual reality, experienced only through its re-created images, its destructiveness (= wonders) absorbed through the spectacle of the occasional and hapless terrorist or captive journalist put on public display. In contrast, official policy decrees that the coffins of dead soldiers are not to be seen by the public.

vi

In an age poised between the scientific rationalism of modernity and a deeply skeptical postmodernity for which truth or fact is simply "another story" and irony a badge of courage, myth is no straightforward matter, no "easy sell" to a generation for whom cynicism is second nature. For reality to be transmuted into popular mythology certain conditions had to obtain, or be created; only then could the mythic become a defining element in both the popular understanding of the post–September 11 world and the self-justifying rhetoric of the governing elite. That susceptible public is one whose secularism is continually overestimated and its credulousness underestimated, especially by liberals. There were many who believed in a virtual reality and marvels long before they were simulated. Additionally, when myth emerges, not in a prescientific or pretechnological world, but in a power-jaded world accustomed to scientific revolutions and technological marvels (cloning, man on the moon), and, at the same time, credulous—for such an audience myth has to portray prodigies of power that are both familiar and uncanny. Not space aliens armed with the weaponry of a more advanced civilization, an "above world," but their opposite: primitive, satanic, invisible denizens of an "underworld" who (through devious money-laundering schemes) are able to purchase and operate contemporary technology. The power-jaded world, so jaded it names its own mythical champion "Superpower" after a comic strip character, will engage terrorism for control of the world. Before that contest can be cleanly represented, before power can be mythified, it needs a new world, a fresh context at once mythical and believable, though not necessarily credible.

When myth begins to govern decision-makers in a world where ambiguity and stubborn facts abound, the result is a disconnect between the actors and reality. They convince themselves that the forces of darkness possess weapons of mass destruction and nuclear capabilities; that their own nation is privileged by a god who inspired the Founding Fathers and the writing of the nation's constitution; and that a class structure of great and stubborn inequalities does not exist. A grim but joyous few see portents of a world that is living out "the last days."

That disconnect raises the question of what kind of politics could best restore reality, could press decision-makers to take account of it. Is it a politics dominated by a combination of the elite and the elect? or a politics more closely connected, not with "the" reality nor with those who are convinced of their power to remake reality on their own terms—a politics, rather, involving and representing those for whom reality is more stubborn, more a fact of life that has to be engaged daily?

Totalitarianism's Inversion: Beginnings of the Imaginary of a Permanent Global War

i

> The fact of the matter is that there is a little bit of the
> totalitarian buried somewhere, way down deep, in each
> and every one of us. It is only the cheerful light of confidence
> and security which keeps this evil genius down. . . . If
> confidence and security were to disappear, don't think that he
> would not be waiting to take their place.
> —*George Kennan (1947)*[1]

Is an American version of totalitarianism plausible, even conceivable? Or is inverted totalitarianism merely a contemporary libel imposed on an innocent past; or, perhaps, like profane love, an identity which cannot be acknowledged by a public discourse that assumes totalitarianism is the foreign enemy?

Underlying those questions is an important preliminary consideration: how would we go about detecting the signs of totalitarianism? how would we know what we are becoming? how, as a citizenry, would we set about separating what we are from the illusions we may have about who we are?

One could start by scrutinizing certain actions of the current administration (denial of due process, torture, sweeping assertions of executive power) and then decide whether they add up to, or are indicative of, a system that, while unique, could fairly be labeled totalitarian. One might go further and ponder the behavior of friends, neighbors, associates, and public figures, including politicians, celebrities, officials, and the police, and decide whether their actions contribute to or have a place in a totalitarian scheme. Proceeding in this way would, however, not quite resolve the problem.

It is not alone what we observe but what we are becoming. What formative experiences of recent years could have made us, as a citizenry, contributors to the tendencies toward a totalitarianism? That question suggests a direction. That possibility, in turn, implies a past, a history of what we may have collectively experienced, sublimated, and perpetuated. In thus lending contemporary events historical depth we reset the limits of the plausible regarding what we are becoming as a people that could dispose us twice to approve an administration which has expanded presidential power beyond that claimed by any previous president, and to support a war founded on lies to the Congress and the public, a war that bears responsibility for the deaths of thousand of innocents, reduced to rubble a nation which had done us no harm, and burdened coming generations with a shameful and costly legacy— without generating massive revulsion and resistance.

Antecedents and *precedents*: both notions perpetuate past experiences. They raise the query, "What went before" that might have continuing effects? Plausibly one could ask, were there antecedents of inverted totalitarianism that could become precedents, and could some antecedents derive from opposed doctrines and political alignments, liberal as well as conservative, Democratic as well as Republican?

ii

More than a half century ago, and in sobriety, totalitarianism was imagined in a form that seemed plausible despite a political setting where there was virtual unanimity that totalitarianism was the exact antithesis of the nation's understanding of itself. More than a half century ago, in the immediate aftermath of the Second World War, a war in which our main enemies were understood to be totalitarian regimes, Edward Corwin, a distinguished constitutional scholar of his day and no sci-fi enthusiast or radical, published a short book titled *Total War and the Constitution* (1947). Like many of his contemporaries Corwin was responding to the novel possibility of nuclear war. He tried to imagine the kind of national transformation likely to occur in the event of a nuclear threat. There would be, he speculated, a streamlining of the system of constitutional government into a "functional totality":

> the politically ordered participation in the war effort of all personal and social forces, the scientific, the mechanical, the commercial, the economic, the moral, the literary and artistic, and the psychological.[2]

Corwin depicted total mobilization of all "forces" as an instinctive reaction to a threat of annihilation emanating from "outside." In short, not a totalitarianism taking shape gradually but one mobilized as an immediate reaction setting off a radical transformation of the old structure of governance and the imposition of a new and, one would hope, temporary political identity. Corwin had depicted a totalitarian system resulting from a series of deliberate, self-conscious actions, a deviation provoked by an emergency of uncertain duration rather than an inversion evolving from a succession of seemingly unrelated, heedless decisions.

iii

Why should a sober and highly respected constitutional authority indulge in this particular flight of fancy? In depicting a state of war in the nuclear age, Corwin ventured beyond the actual mobilization of American society during the Second World War, beyond what Americans had experienced but not beyond what was known. Corwin's formulation could be described as an act of political imagination, a self-conscious projection of a state of affairs that did not in fact exist, involving an unidentified enemy at a time when no other nation possessed nuclear weapons. Yet he also extrapolated some elements (e.g., nuclear bombs) that did exist. Above all, looking backwards, he assumed that the recent wartime mobilization constituted the meaning of "total."

I want to pause over the idea of "political imagination" and its product, the "political imaginary." My concern is not so much with an individual thinker's formulation as with the consequences when a particular political imaginary gains a hold on ruling groups and becomes a staple of the general culture; and when the political actors and even the citizens become habituated to that imaginary, identified with it.

Bearing in mind that totalitarianism is first and foremost about power, we can see that the ideas of imagination and of the imaginary, while pointing toward the fanciful, are power-laden terms, striking because they seem to join power, fantasy, and unreality. Consider the following standard dictionary definitions:

> imagination: The power which the mind has of forming concepts beyond those derived from external objects . . . a scheme, plot; a fanciful project.
> imaginary: existing only in imagination . . . not really existing.[3]

The idea of an imaginary has special relevance to a society where continuous technological advances encourage elaborate fantasies of individual prowess, eternal youthfulness, beauty through surgery, action measured in nanoseconds: a dream-laden culture of ever-expanding control and possibility, whose denizens are prone to fantasies because the vast majority have imagination but little scientific knowledge.

A political imaginary involves going beyond and challenging current capabilities, inhibitions, and constraints regarding power and its proper limits and improper uses. It envisions an organization of resources, ideal as well as material, in which a potential attributed to them becomes a challenge to realize it. What is conceived by the imagination is not a mere improvement but a quantum leap that nonetheless preserves elements of the familiar. For example, in his imaginary, *The Secret of Future Victories* (1992), a four-star general imagined an attack by the Soviet bloc which would be met by an American force that "draws adroitly on advanced technology, concentrates forces from unprecedented distances with overwhelming suddenness and violence, and blinds and bewilders the foe."[4]

As the quotation suggests, while a strong element of fantasy may figure the imaginary, there is likely to be a significant "real," verifiable element as well. Postmodern weaponry has in fact demonstrated its "Star Wars" potential, and suicide bombers do blow up schoolchildren.

iv

I want to sketch two contrasting types of imaginary. One I shall call the "power imaginary," the other the "constitutional imaginary." On the face of it, the two seem mutually exclusive; I shall treat them as cohabiting uneasily. The constitutional imaginary prescribes the means by which power is legitimated, accountable, and constrained (e.g., popular elections, legal authorization). It emphasizes stability and limits. A constitution partakes of the imaginary because it is wholly dependent on what public officials, politicians in power, and, lastly, citizens conceive it to be, such that there is a reasonable continuity between the original formulations and the present interpretations. The power imaginary seeks constantly to expand present capabilities. Hobbes, the theorist par excellence of the power imaginary and a favorite among neocons, had envisioned a dynamic rooted in human nature and driven by a "restless" quest for "power after power" that "ceaseth only in death." But, according to Hobbes, unlike the individual whose power drives cease with death, a society can avoid collective mortality by rationalizing the quest for power and giving it a political form. Hobbes proposed to combine a constitutional with a power imaginary. It took the form of a permanent contract, a constitutional imaginary, which provided the basis for the power imaginary. The individual members of society, driven by fear and insecurity, agree to be ruled by an absolute sovereign or chief executive in exchange for assurances of protection and domestic peace.[5] He becomes the custodian of the power imaginary, "the great Leviathan," as well as the final interpreter of the constitutional imaginary.

The main problem is that pursuit of the power imaginary may undermine or override the boundaries mandated in the constitutional imaginary. A power imaginary is usually accompanied by a justifying mission ("to defeat communism" or "to hunt out terrorists wherever they may hide") that requires capabilities measured against an enemy whose powers are dynamic but whose exact location is indeterminate. The enemy's aims and powers may have some verifiable basis, but they are typically exaggerated, thereby justifying a greater claim on society's resources, sacrifices by society's members, and challenges to the safeguards prescribed in the constitutional imaginary.[6]

One consequence of the pursuit of an expansive power imaginary is the blurring of the lines separating reality from fancy and truth telling from self-deception and lying. In its imaginary, power is not so much justified as sanctified, excused by the lofty ends it proclaims, ends that commonly are antithetical to the power legitimated by the constitutional imaginary. At present, according to one apologist, "empire has become a precondition for democracy." The United States, he continues, should "use imperial power to strengthen respect for self-determination [and] give states back to abused, oppressed people who deserve to rule them for themselves."[7] Thus, instead of imperial domination as the antithesis of democracy or of imposed government as the opposite of self-government, we have a fantasy of benevolence, of opposites harmonized through the largesse of a superpower.

I want to suggest that an American imaginary, centered on the nation's projection of unprecedented power, began to emerge during World War II (1941–45). However, that shift was as significant for the imaginary it displaced as for the one it established. Before the war, during the first two terms of FDR's presidency (1933–41), a substantial attempt was made to establish a liberal version of social democracy. Looking back upon that experience, one has difficulty recognizing an America in which, unapologetically, public debate and discussion centered on matters such as planning; focusing resources on the poor and unemployed; bringing radical changes to agriculture by limiting production; regulating business and banking practices while not fearing to castigate the rich and powerful; raising the standard of living of whole regions of the country; introducing public works projects that created employment for millions and left valuable public improvements (libraries, schools, conservation practices, subsidies to the arts); and promoting all manner of participatory schemes for including the citizenry in economic decision-making processes.

However, the combination of expanded state power and genuine mass enthusiasm for the new president gave pause to some observers.[8] At FDR's inaugural address in 1933 Eleanor Roosevelt found the enthusiasm of the crowd "a little terrifying because when Franklin got to that part of the speech when he said it might become necessary for him to assume powers ordinarily granted to a president in war time, he received his biggest demonstration."[9]

At the time the country's economy was in desperate straits. Millions were unemployed and hungry; agricultural prices had fallen so low that products were not marketed and countless farms were being foreclosed, sparking violent protests; manufacturing had come to a virtual halt and the fortunate few who were employed received meager wages. In the background, Hitler had assumed office, while Mussolini was firmly ensconced in power. A distinctive power vocabulary began to take hold suggesting that the world was witnessing the emergence of a novel, more expansive power imaginary. Usages such as "dictatorship," "totalitarianism," and "mobilization" were not uncommon. Although the carnage of the First World War remained a fresh memory, there arose a spontaneous belief, shared among politicians, pundits, business leaders, and the public, that the nation's economic crisis qualified as the equivalent of a state of war which justified an unprecedented expansion of state power in peacetime.

Early in the New Deal in what some Americans saw as "economic nihilism" threatening the nation, there was a clamor for a different imaginary that was clearly at odds with the constitutional imaginary. Congressman Hamilton Fish referred approvingly to FDR's administration as "an American dictatorship." Al Smith, a former Democratic presidential candidate, seemed to be appealing to experience when he demanded hyperbolically, "What does a democracy do in a war? It becomes a tyrant, a despot, a real monarch. In the [First] World War we took our Constitution, wrapped it up and laid it on the shelf and left it there until it was over." The Republican presidential nominee in 1936, Governor Alf Landon, declared: "Even the hand of a national dictator is in preference to a paralytic stroke. . . . If there is any way . . . a Republican governor in a mid-western state can aid [the president] in the fight, I now enlist for the duration of the war."[10]

What was unusual or perhaps naive about such reactions was that the United States had not experienced the actuality of war at home since 1865. For the vast majority of Americans modern warfare was, in large measure, imagined rather than actually felt or observed firsthand. Similarly, dictatorship had never been established. In 1933 there was not yet a common awareness of the brutality of Mussolini's regime or of the deadly effects of the liquidation of the kulaks and forced collectivization in the Soviet Union.[11]

Although the Roosevelt administration was granted exceptional powers to deal with the crisis, and although it attempted to raise wages and to control manufacturing, retailing, and agricultural output, many of its programs were voluntary or required the cooperation of trade associations and agricultural groups. There was certainly far more chaos, improvisation, and haphazard enforcement than regimentation, yet it was also clear that a new power imaginary had come into existence. The everyday vocabulary of government officials, politicians, publicists, and academics bandied expansive power terms and envisioned new scales of operation: national planning, mobilization of labor, controls over agricultural production, consumer protection.[12] In some official circles there was even talk of "socialism." The vision of power was, however, strictly domestic and mostly involved economic relations; the influential economists favored economic nationalism rather than globalism.[13] There was no attempt to control education, culture, newspapers, or radio broadcasting. There was no foreign enemy. Although capitalist greed was often attacked,[14] FDR and most of his closest advisers believed that the aim of the New Deal was to save the capitalist system from unreconstructed capitalists. Government regulation, instead of being the enemy of capitalism, was conceived as the means of saving it by promoting employment, decent wages, education, and a cushion against the cyclical swings endemic to capitalism.

v

But while the New Deal imaginary stimulated hopes of fundamental social and economic reforms within the framework of capitalism, it also aroused panic among business and financial leaders and provoked a counterimaginary. Once the economy appeared to be recovering, a powerful public relations campaign was mounted. The New Deal was depicted as the creature of leftist forces bent on transforming the country's economy.

The alarums sounded by business and financial leaders were not without foundation. The 1930s were years of extraordinary political ferment, most of it directed against the economic status quo. There were substantial numbers of communists as well as socialist followers of Norman Thomas, but perhaps more important were the popular political movements that openly challenged the political and economic power of capital.

The most important of these was the Share-the-Wealth movement of Huey Long, the Townsend movement for old-age pensions, and the National Union for Social Justice, galvanized by the Catholic priest Father Coughlin, that called for a guaranteed annual wage, the nationalization of public utilities, and the protection of labor unions. The striking feature of the three movements was their success in mobilizing the support of the poor, the unemployed, the workers, small-business owners, and members of the middle class, *and* accomplishing much of this mobilization through the new medium of national radio.[15] The fact that millions of citizens were stirred to support leaders and become emotionally and practically involved in movements outside the main political parties lent a different, potentially more populist meaning to "mobilization." An American version of a demos, demagogic warts and all, had emerged. Huey Long's movement centered its protests on the maldistribution of wealth. He called for taxation that would eliminate all income over a million dollars and inheritances over five million. There were to be homestead allowances of five thousand dollars to every family and a guaranteed annual income of at least two thousand, old-age pensions, limitations on the hours of labor, and college education for the qualified. In a few short years he succeeded in actually changing and improving the lives of poor people, but primarily by means of corruption, intimidation, and personal charisma.[16] A plausible case could be, and has been, made that he had created, if briefly, a thin form of fascism. But it might also be argued that all three movements were versions of a "fugitive" democracy which, while destined to be short-lived because of its reliance on the limited resources of ordinary people, succeeded nonetheless in challenging the democratic credentials of a system that legitimates the economic oppression and culturally stunted lives of millions of citizens while, for all practical purposes, excluding them from political power.[17]

Each movement was received coolly by the New Deal leadership and kept at arm's length, despite agreement with many of the proposals put forward by the dissidents. The lesson for the political establishments of the major parties was that "mobilization" should be carefully controlled so as to preclude its becoming a challenge to the far narrower notions of popular participation represented by the two major party organizations.

By the late 1930s the question beginning to emerge was whether liberalism with a primarily domestic focus would survive and flourish once the New Deal was suspended by World War II; and whether its counterimaginary of a state-regulated capitalism would survive after the shooting war ended or, instead, give way to a radically altered power imaginary for a new kind of war that followed, and for the kind of demos needed for its support.[18]

vi

A clue to the modest influence of foreign affairs in the political imaginary before World War II was suggested in some remarks of 1941 by Senator Robert Taft, a major Republican spokesman for isolationism and a constrictive view of American power:

> Frankly, the American people don't want to rule the world, and we are not equipped to do it. Such imperialism is wholly foreign to our ideals of democracy and freedom. It is not our manifest destiny or our national destiny.[19]

Before the end of the twentieth century Taft's insular vision would be abandoned by conservative elites. President Reagan assured the nation that it had the "power to begin the world over again."[20] The old imaginary, confined to a continent, was defeated by World War II when the global reach of American power was first explored, and the New Deal dream of a planned and more equitable economy was temporarily, if unintentionally, realized by wartime austerity. American military power was engaged on every continent, save for Latin America. Its economic resources were expanded to support not only American forces but those of its allies.

On the "home front" of World War II the entire society was, for the first time, mobilized for a lengthy period. The government sought to organize all of society's resources under central control and direct them toward the single purpose of defeating the enemy. It represented the break as a change from peacetime "normalcy" to wartime "emergency," although what was passed off as "normal" had been the New Deal regulatory state of the 1930s. Censorship and a military draft were introduced. Resources were allocated and assigned priorities, not by the market but by the government. Class distinctions seemed suspended as a wartime egalitarianism was imposed. Wages, profits, and prices were controlled, and all citizens were subjected to food rationing. Nonetheless, domestically the formal constitution of the system remained largely untransformed.

While an impressive systematization of governmental regulatory power had been introduced and executive authority expanded, the enlarged scope of government's legal powers was understood as temporary, confined to the duration of the "wartime emergency." With the possible exception of a somewhat deferential judiciary, the constitutional order functioned more or less normally. Congress met uninterruptedly and did not refrain from criticizing the conduct of the war; the two political parties continued their contests for office; and elections remained free. Except for the shameful "relocation" of Americans of Japanese ancestry, very few governmental actions could be described as dictatorial. Although an enlarged power imaginary had clearly taken hold, it lacked mythological status. Perhaps this was due to the fact that at the time the nature of the enemy was not truly comprehended.[21] The Nazi concentration camps and the murder of millions of Jews, Gypsies, homosexuals, and Jehovah's Witnesses were not major themes of wartime propaganda.

Or perhaps the imaginary was restrained by an inhibition that could be relaxed only after the war was over. The wartime American imaginary had been incomplete, not only because it was assembled hastily in response to a war that the United States had not instigated, and which, before December 7, 1941, was strongly opposed, but also because wartime expediency dictated the suppression of hostility toward a major ally whom many politicians and pundits considered to be at least as evil as the Nazis.

vii

For the imaginary spawned by World War II contained one embarrassment: the alliance with the communist dictatorship of the Soviet Union, without whose contributions and horrific sacrifices the Allied victory would have been highly problematic. Distrust of this ally had its beginnings as far back as the Bolshevik Revolution of 1917 and the "red scare" of the 1920s.[22] The motive at that time was not solely geopolitical worries about the Bolshevik regime but that regime's candidacy as an alternative to capitalism.[23]

The wartime imaginary was not abandoned after 1945 but reconceived as a "Cold War" between the United States and the Soviet Union, a showdown between capitalism and anticapitalism. The undeclared stake concerned domestic policy. Would the egalitarian tendencies encouraged by the New Deal and its accompanying faith in governmental regulation of the economy be resumed after World War II? The policy-makers of the Cold War would decide that issue by assigning a huge proportion of the nation's resources to defense rather than welfare.

The Cold War consolidated the power of capital and began the reaction against the welfare state *but* without abandoning the strong state. What was abandoned was all talk of participatory democracy. "Mobilization" was participation's sublimation. The propaganda of business interests depicted the combination of social democracy and political regulation of the economy as simple socialism and therefore the blood relative of communism.[24] The new state would continue to promote business but without requiring it to be socially responsible. Rearmament would be financed to an important extent by cuts in social spending, while the costs of national security would be largely borne by the less well-off.[25] The lasting effects of the Cold War encounter included not only the elimination of the USSR but also the containment and rollback of the social and political ideals of the New Deal. The unifying ideology for the masses was a "dematerialized" one, a combination of patriotism, anticommunism, and — in the new nuclear era — fear.

The Democrats, the party most closely identified with New Deal social and economic reforms, were the original, most enthusiastic cold warriors. A new species of liberalism came into being: the "Cold War liberal" who was resolutely anticommunist and convinced that "national security" constituted the nation's highest priority.[26] The Cold War liberal even discovered the political utility of a civil religion. He was prepared to put aside the secularism and rationalism that, historically, had been among liberalism's defining elements and to seek validation for liberal anticommunism abroad and at home by appealing to theology, most notably that of Reinhold Niebuhr's Christian realism. Niebuhr was notoriously pessimistic, subscribing to a view that stressed the dark side of human nature. Sobered by Niebuhr's pessimism, the Cold War liberals set about to scale down liberalism by relocating it in what an admirer of Niebuhr christened "the vital center." "The old liberal," according to one of the leading neoliberals, viewed "man as perfectible, as endowed with sufficient wisdom and selflessness to endure power and to use it infallibly for the general good," while the new liberal has been "reminded" by totalitarian regimes "that man was, indeed, imperfect and that the corruptions of power could unleash great evil in the world. We discovered a new dimension of experience in the dimension of anxiety, guilt, and corruption." The new liberal was fired less by hopes for socioeconomic reform than by the wish to distance himself from "the Left" and populist democracy and to celebrate a new, more clear-eyed elite, one committed to the Cold War, lukewarm or indifferent toward social democracy, and increasingly unreceptive to egalitarian ideals. "I am persuaded, too," wrote the theorist of the "vital center," "that liberals have values in common with most members of the business community — in particular a belief in a free society."[27] The bonds between liberalism and democracy began to unravel.

The Cold War (1947–91) provided the framework for a radically new imaginary of a war that was "cold" in the sense of being calibrated to stop short of actual battle. To champion that oxymoron required hyperbole. Its proponents proclaimed it a "total war" of global dimensions and of uncertain but prolonged duration.[28] Rearmament was institutionalized as a huge, albeit controversial, and permanent part of the nation's economy and annual budget. A "defense establishment," comprising the economy, the military, and the state, came into being. It would alter the political identity of the society for decades to come. For the first time, too, "war," for the most part, would be fought without actual battles and against an enemy who operated secretively, "undercover." Although few Americans encountered the enemy, they were assured by politicians, publicists, preachers, and the FBI that he was "hidden" and had to be confronted abroad and rooted out at home. New categories of "loyalty," "internal security," and "subversion" were introduced and given the status of legal standards.

The constitutional imaginary underwent profound changes as it adapted to the new power imaginary and its totalizing categories. For almost a half century the new war was defined in starkly Manichaean terms, as an epical struggle for the fate of the world between totalitarian dictatorship promoting atheism and communism, and the freedom-loving, God-fearing capitalist democracy of the United States and its Western European allies.[29] Public officials insisted that the Cold War was "in fact a real war" against an enemy bent on "world domination." One high-ranking official declared that the United States was "in a war worse than any we have experienced . . . not a cold war but a hot war." Henceforth the nation must disavow the "sharp line between democratic principles and immoral actions" and be ready to fight "with no holds barred."[30]

viii

The prime example of a power imaginary and the best indicator of the turning point from a politics of social reform to the pursuit of a global politics is an official report to President Truman by the National Security Council in April 1950. A leading scholar has described *NSC-68: United States Objectives and Programs for National Security* as "the bible of American national security and the fullest statement of the new ideology that guided American leaders" during the Cold War.[31] It was also prophetic of how "mobilization" would provide the form by which totalizing power would become normalized.

The highly charged language of NSC-68 seems out of character for a classified "top secret" policy paper composed by and for policy-making elites. One expects a document for the sober. While there are plenty of economic statistics and military strategies, the report contains myth making of epical proportions and high melodrama as well. "The issues that face us," the document announced sweepingly, "are momentous, involving the fulfillment or destruction not only of this Republic but of civilization itself."

NSC-68 begins with the favorite ploy of many myths, a dualism where innocence and virtue are confronted by unnuanced evil.[32] The postwar world is, unqualifiedly, polarized: "power [has] increasingly gravitated to . . . two centers."

> [While] the fundamental purpose of the U.S. is to assure the integrity and vitality of our free society, which is founded upon the dignity and worth of the individual . . . the Soviet Union, unlike previous aspirants to hegemony, is animated by a new fanatic faith, antithetical to our own, and seeks to impose its absolute authority over the rest of the world. Conflict has, therefore, become endemic and is waged, on the part of the Soviet Union, by violent or non-violent methods in accordance with the dictates of expediency. With the development of increasingly terrifying weapons of mass destruction, every individual faces the ever-present possibility of annihilation should the conflict enter the phase of total war.[33]

The shape of the power imaginary is dictated not only by the threat posed by the USSR but by the nature of its power dynamic, which is described as "inescapably militant because it possesses and is possessed by a world-wide revolutionary movement." It rules by enslaving: "The system becomes God and submission to the will of God becomes submission to the will of the system."[34] Its tactics display "extraordinary flexibility," which "derives from the utterly amoral and opportunistic conduct of Soviet policy" and from the "secrecy" of its operations.[35] At present, its power outstrips that of the United States. Even our advantage in nuclear weapons is temporary. The conclusion is that if a freedom-loving democracy is to survive, it must organize its resources and accept "the responsibility of world leadership."[36] This means mustering "clearly superior overall power in its most inclusive sense."[37] How totalizing a Cold War becomes is suggested in a summary of American strategy:

> Intensification of affirmative and timely measures and operations by covert means in the fields of economic warfare and political and psychological warfare with a view to fomenting and supporting unrest and revolt in selected strategic satellite countries.[38]

On occasion the NSC report avowed that the aim of mobilization was limited to "containment" of Soviet power so as to avoid a shooting war. Given the report's repeated emphasis on the "dynamic" character of *both* Soviet and American power, "containment" served to cloud the main consequence of seeking American global dominance. The United States had adopted the same goals as the Soviets: global supremacy and a regime change by means of subversion. "We should take dynamic steps to reduce the power and influence of the Kremlin inside the Soviet Union and other areas under its control. . . . In other words, it would be the current Soviet cold war technique used against the Soviet Union."[39] Thus a fanatical, repressive, totalitarian regime sets the standard of power a free society must surpass if civilization is to be preserved.

At the same time that the report calls for establishing nuclear superiority and for subverting the Soviet regime, it reasserts American innocence, even anticipating April 2003 in Iraq, by repeatedly insisting that our efforts will not hurt the Soviet people, although the document expresses hope that the Soviet people will take the initiative against their government.[40]

Not least, the new imaginary of global power accompanies an estimate of America's power—its industrial capacity, its nuclear advantage—with a scrutiny of our weaknesses. Some measure of regime change at home will be required to overcome our "lack of will" and difficulty in pursuing a set purpose.[41] "A large measure of sacrifice and discipline will be demanded of the American people. They will be asked to give up some of the benefits which they have come to associate with their freedoms."[42] The demands of "internal security" include increased taxes, reduced federal spending except for defense, and acceptance of a lower standard of living.[43] "The democratic way" requires a changed civic culture so that citizens are less naive, more discriminating:

> [In] the search for truth [the individual] knows when he should commit an act of faith; that he distinguish between the necessity for tolerance and the necessity for just suppression. A free society is vulnerable in that it is easy for people to lapse into excesses — the excesses of a permanently open mind wishfully waiting for evidence that evil design may become noble purpose, the excess of faith becoming prejudice, the excess of tolerance degenerating into indulgence of conspiracy and the excess of suppression when moderate measures are not only more appropriate but more effective.[44]

The report cautions that a public relations strategy at home must counter "any adverse psychological effects" of the "dynamic steps" needed: "in any announcement of policy and in the character of the measures adopted, emphasis should be given to the essentially defensive character and care should be taken to minimize, so far as possible, unfavorable domestic and foreign reactions."[45]

ix

Unquestionably the Soviet Union was a brutal murderous dictatorship that sought to expand its influence and power globally by encouraging communist parties in Greece, Western Europe, and Asia, supporting "satellite regimes" in central Europe, liquidating all opposition at home, and engaging in espionage. There was, then, a significant element of reality to what became the Cold War imaginary.

But why the insistence by American political, economic, and opinion-making elites on declaring a "war" instead of invoking the notion of, say, "a Great Power rivalry"? Was it that in combating an evil enemy, "rivalry" smacked of appeasement or, worse, of moral equivalence? Although doubtless there are other possible answers to that question, I would suggest that what attracted decision-makers to choosing "war" is that Americans of the twentieth century had no direct experience of it and hence were receptive to having warfare imagined for them—and Hollywood happily obliged with "war movies." Save for actual combatants sent overseas and economic shortages at home, World War II was unexperienced. After 1945 "war" was akin to a tabula rasa on which opinion-makers and governmental decision-makers were free to constitute its meaning in terms that pretty much suited their purposes, allowing them to set the character of public debate and to acquire a vastly enlarged range of governmental powers—powers that, when they did not violate the Constitution, deformed it. For almost a half century, from the late 1940s to the early 1990s, war served as the omnipresent background in the imaginary constructed by news- and movie-makers, television producers, and the rhetoric of politicians. The meaning of war was given a plasticity that allowed the new image-makers to set its parameters as they pleased.

"War" also had its effects upon politics, causing a shift in emphasis from socioeconomic issues to ideological ones where partisanship had far fewer material consequences. During the 1950s the ideological battles were centered on "loyalty," "subversion," "communism," and civil rights. While politics of the decade seemed intense, it was also narrower: socioeconomic problems were subordinated to ideological battles in which anticommunist ideologues did their best to link liberalism, the main force behind socioeconomic reform, with communism.[46]

Nowhere was this more apparent than when the authors of NSC-68—after first declaring "that the integrity and vitality of our system is in greater jeopardy than ever before in our history"—then remark: "Even if there were no Soviet Union we would face the great problem of the free society of reconciling order, security, the need for participation, with the requirement of freedom. We would face the fact that in a shrinking world the absence of order among nations is becoming less and less tolerable." We have "an uneasy equilibrium without order" causing men to doubt "whether the world will long tolerate this tension without moving toward some kind of order, on somebody's terms."[47]

Elsewhere the report acknowledges that at present the Soviets are not planning to actually attack the United States and its allies, although, the authors hasten to add, "the possibility of such deliberate resort to war cannot be ruled out."[48] In the last analysis the "fact" of "the absence of order . . . imposes on us the responsibility of world leadership." Even were we to win a "military victory" over the Soviets, that "would only partially and perhaps only temporarily affect the fundamental conflict." There would be "the resurgence of totalitarian forces and the re-establishment of the Soviet system, or its equivalent. . . . We have no choice but to demonstrate the superiority of the idea of freedom."[49]

It was not alone the designation "war" that mattered but equally its "cold," enveloping character. As Hubert Humphrey, Democratic senator and presidential nominee, noted approvingly, "it is hard to tell . . . where war begins and where it ends."[50] Secretary of State Dulles noted that while "in the present state of world opinion we could not use an A-bomb, we should make every effort now to dissipate this feeling."[51] Just as terrorism would later become useful to American policymakers for its "fear factor," so during the Cold War the stockpiling of atomic weapons served that same end of normalizing an atmosphere of fear. As then Vice President Nixon explained, "tactical atomic explosives are now conventional."[52] When the Cold War threatened to become too normal and abstract, déjà vu all over again, there would be "war scares," including air raid drills during which children practiced protecting themselves from nuclear attacks by huddling under their schoolroom desks.[53]

Perhaps the most unnerving example of the mentality at work constructing a Cold War power imaginary was the doctrine of "Mutual Assured Destruction" formulated in the aftermath of the Cuban Missile Crisis of 1962. Instead of targeting an enemy's military facilities "each side should target the other's cities" in order to cause the most casualties possible. "The assumption behind it," according to one historian, "was that if no one could be sure of surviving a nuclear war, there would not be one."[54] If there had been one, incinerated parents could die comforted with the knowledge that, thanks to school desks, their children would have been spared.

x

The development of an extended relationship between the military and the corporate economy began in earnest. National defense was declared inseparable from a strong economy. The fixation upon mobilization and rearmament inspired the gradual disappearance from the national political agenda of the regulation and control of corporations. The defender of the free world needed the power of the globalizing, expanding corporation, not an economy hampered by "trust-busting." Moreover, since the enemy was rabidly anticapitalist, every measure that strengthened capitalism was a blow against the enemy. Once the battle lines between communism and the "free society" were drawn, the economy became untouchable for purposes other than "strengthening" capitalism. The ultimate merger would be between capitalism and democracy. Once the identity and security of democracy were successfully identified with the Cold War and with the methods for waging it, the stage was set for the intimidation of most politics left of right.

Throughout the 1950s there was a steady erosion in the power of various nongovernmental groups and institutions. Universities and government initiated what would prove to be an intimate relationship.[55] While the political influence of trade unions was strong during the Truman years, a long and seemingly irreversible decline set in even before the Republican victory of 1952. The Taft-Hartley Act (1947) outlawed the closed or union shop. An independent trade union movement, with its disruptive "weapons" of strike and boycott, was portrayed as a potential threat to the mobilization of America's economic power, especially if, as was frequency alleged, communists had "penetrated" unions involved in war production.

There was much talk about molding a new type, "the citizen soldier" who would be a model of discipline, physical fitness, patriotism, and work habits that would carry over and create a more reliable workforce.[56] Even before World War II ended, there were repeated efforts to preserve the draft and several attempts to create a system of "universal military training" (UMT) aimed at requiring all young men, after high school or having reached their eighteenth birthday, to undergo a brief period of military training followed by longer service in the organized reserves or National Guard. The concern was to create a prepared nation, one that would be forever ready and never again caught by surprise. For the first time a totalitarian imaginary emerged, but because traces of the World War II sensibility persisted, critics, especially those in the academy, preferred the euphemism "garrison state."[57]

xi

A crucial element in the imaginary inspired by the Cold War had been absent from the imaginary accompanying World War II. Practically speaking, no significant ideological opposition had developed to a war that began with the Japanese attack on Pearl Harbor and with the Germans immediately joining in by declaring war against the United States. There was no internal enemy to fight, no suspected disloyal elements to expose, as there had allegedly been with German Americans during World War I. The glaring exception was the internment of several thousand Americans of Japanese descent, most of whom were "relocated" in Western deserts far from public view. Nationalism and patriotism, rather than ideology, sufficed to control the population and gain its support. Patriotism required no collective self-examination, only the spontaneous response to the simple fact that we had been attacked.[58]

This changed dramatically with the advent of the Cold War when the power imaginary turned inwards. Communism was depicted as a domestic contagion to be eradicated as well as a foreign threat to be combated. The appearance of a new set of political actors—the FBI, the House Un-American Activities Committee, loyalty and security boards to eliminate the "disloyal" from government service—marked a new form of governmental power: thought policing to enforce ideological conformity. Disloyalty became a broad-brush category that included communists, alleged communist sympathizers, and those who refused to expose colleagues or acquaintances who were communists. *Rouge et noir*: "blacklists" were drawn up by authorities to identify and root out suspected "reds" and their sympathizers in the entertainment industries, in the media, and among intellectuals. Opposition required unusual courage. For the first time in the nation's history universities became the object of a widespread purge. "Loyalty oaths" were introduced as a precondition of employment in many state institutions of higher learning, while some intellectuals and academics were recruited as government agents to report on the political activities of colleagues.[59] The Internal Security Act (1950) established six concentration camps. Police and federal law enforcement authorities undertook the systematic surveillance of suspect political activity. Not surprisingly, homosexuals were singled out and were said to be entrenched in the State Department. A 1950 Senate report bore the title *Employment of Homosexuals and Other Sex Perverts in Government.*[60]

The domestic version of anticommunism was aimed at even larger targets alleged to be connected: social democracy, trade union power, anticapitalist beliefs associated with the New Deal, and the political liberalism identified with academia and the media. The targets were (in the language of the times) "smeared" as being either communist or sympathetic to communism, disloyal, or, at the least, "soft" on communism. There was much discussion of how educational reform might serve to "strengthen national security" by instructing the citizenry in the meaning of democracy and the importance of patriotism.[61]

Certain elements in the domestic side of the Cold War imaginary displayed an uncomfortable similarity to elements of the Soviet regime: purges; loyalty tests; violations of due process; criminalization of a political party for its beliefs rather than its actions; development of an elaborate, largely secretive agency with a global network of spies and assassins (CIA), dedicated to subverting regimes deemed unfriendly or uncooperative and installing sympathetic ones. A study group reporting to President Eisenhower urged explicitly that the United States not only follow the Soviet example but seek to surpass it:

> We are facing an implacable enemy whose avowed object is world domination by whatever means and at whatever cost. . . . [T]here are no rules in such a game. Hitherto acceptable norms of human conduct do not apply. We must develop effective espionage and counterespionage services and must learn to subvert, sabotage, and destroy our enemies by more clever, more sophisticated, and more effective means than those used against us.[62]

Thus anticommunism as mimesis: the character of the enemy supplied the norm for the power demands that the democratic defender of the free world chose to impose on itself.

xii

The phenomenon that best captured the transformation of the nation was the pandemic of the 1950s known as McCarthyism. In a short-lived career that began and ended in obscurity, Senator Joseph McCarthy turned anticommunism into a spectacle: thanks to television, a nation watched the drama of disloyalty and betrayal unfolding.

McCarthy was remarkable for a simple but matchless talent: he lied endlessly and spectacularly. No matter how often the lies were brought to light, he plunged on, exposing one after another alleged spy, traitor, red, or pinko, and in the process recklessly damaging or ending careers. His sheer destructiveness did not stop with the charges thrown at obscure officials or hapless academics or Senate colleagues. His accusations of communist or Soviet sympathies extended to cabinet officers and some of the country's most revered icons, including General (later Secretary of State) George Marshall, President Dwight Eisenhower, and the U.S. Army itself. With very few exceptions the media caved in or kowtowed.

The fact that the Soviet regime was dogmatically atheist made it easy for the anticommunist crusade to gain the blessing of the hierarchy of the Catholic Church and its unwavering support. A cardinal and an archbishop attained celebrity status through their fiery sermons and broadcasts in support of McCarthy and denunciation of communism. The pope blessed McCarthy's marriage; even after the senator had died in disgrace, a "McCarthy Mass" was celebrated annually at St. Patrick's Cathedral.[63]

A new messianism and the reaffirmation of a civil religion began to figure in the power imaginary, and it would later register in a wondrous afterglow with which a reputable historian could look back upon the Cold War. He wrote that the triumph of the American vision of "a society in which universal morality, state morality, and individual morality might all be the same thing" pointed to a superhuman agency at work: "At which point God, or at least His agents, intervened to to make that vision an unexpected—and to the Kremlin a profoundly alarming—reality."[64]

xiii

That a political figure as bizarre, crude, and unscrupulous as McCarthy could generate the tidal wave of McCarthyism was no doubt due in part to the support he received from reputable politicians, such as Senator Taft, and from influential intellectuals, such as William Buckley, but it was the Cold War itself that lent resonance to his antics and an inward turn to what seemed primarily a matter of foreign and defense policy. Many of the public officials, trade union leaders, intellectuals, and academics who were villified or purged actually adhered to the social democratic ideals and programs of the New Deal; this suggested that a domestic power struggle was in the making that would redefine American politics for the next half century or more. Put simply: New Deal values of social democracy were effectively purged from the national power imaginary. Notable casualties of that drama were Lyndon Johnson and Hubert Humphrey, both Democrats who believed deeply in social programs but found themselves forced to shoulder a Cold War that had turned hot in Vietnam and left little or no public resources for social spending. The populist surge of the 1930s that had carried over into support for the democratized effort of World War II was reconfigured.

The Cold War effected a radical change in the American political identity to accompany the new power imaginary. One of the major themes of Cold War propaganda was that although the American economy far oustripped that of any other nation or combination of nations, Americans would be required to forgo the prospect of substantial and steady improvement in their social, economic, cultural, and political prospects. In confidential discussions public officials pondered how to get "our people" to recognize "that the cold war is in fact a real war in which the survival of the free world is at stake." The effort would require "sacrifice," "unity," and "tenacity of purpose." The meaning of "sacrifice" was cast in the bureaucratic euphemism of "significant domestic financial and economic adjustments."[65] Less opaque, one official estimate was that if a nuclear war broke out, it was possible that ten million Americans might die.[66]

All of the elements aimed at the "mobilization" of society—from proposals for universal military training to the institutionalization of a huge defense economy that represented a business version of a New Deal; from loyalty purges and red scares to government-sponsored propaganda to promote political orthodoxy ("Freedom Trains" displaying the artifacts illustrative of the saga of freedom in America)—spelled the transformation of popular participation, from New Deal experiments in participatory democracy to a populism exchanging socioeconomic power for loyal conformism, hope for fear.[67]

Two crucial consequences of the Cold War upon domestic politics contributed major elements to the power imaginary evolving from the conflict. One was the shrinking place occupied by politics and the enlargement of state power. The growing dominance of foreign policy and military strategy altered the scope and status of public participation. Public officials, experts, and pundits were quick to declare these to be privileged subjects where partisan politics should defer to national unity and experts should decide among themselves. The second development was intimately connected with the priority of foreign policy and military preparedness: the emergence and legitimation of elitism, of a political class, "the best and the brightest." The social science literature of the period was heavy with discussions of elitism, and few questioned its legitimacy.[68] That direction was bolstered by the invention of "voting studies" touted as the social scientific investigation into the behavior of the voter. The electorate was not infrequently portrayed as inattentive to politics, ill-informed, and indifferent—qualities that some academics considered functionally useful.[69] The clear implication was that elitism was the antidote to mass ignorance and essential to victory in the struggle for freedom. Elitism signified a privileged claim to power on the part of those who not only manifested proven intelligence, experience, and sterling character but also, unlike the fantasy-prone masses, were "realists."[70] A whole ideology emerged to legitimate elitism: the "realists" and "neoliberals" such as Niebuhr, George Kennan, and Arthur Schlesinger, Jr.

That war was "cold" only in the sense that the two antagonists did not engage each other in a shooting war. During that era, which lasted until the fall of the Berlin Wall in 1989, the United States fought two very hot wars, first in Korea, then in Vietnam. It suffered a stalemate in one and defeat in the other, both by Soviet proxies. If we add the defeat in Iraq, we might be tempted to redefine superpower as an imaginary of power that emerges from defeat unchastened, more imperious than ever. Nonetheless, with the "defeat" or collapse of the USSR and the emergence of the United States as the sole standing Superpower, the imaginary constructed after 9/11 perpetuated elements designed during the Cold War. The new imaginary, too, depicted a foe global, without contours or boundaries, shrouded in secrecy. And like the Cold War imaginary, not only would the new form seek imperial dominion; it would turn inwards, applying totalitarian practices, such as sanctioning torture, holding individuals for years without charging them or allowing access to due process, transporting suspects to unknown locations, and conducting warrantless searches into private communications. The system of inverted totalitarianism being formed is not the result of a premeditated plot. It has no *Mein Kampf* as an inspiration. It is, instead, a set of effects produced by actions or practices undertaken in ignorance of their lasting consequences. This is the achievement of a nation that gave pragmatism, the philosophy of consequences, to the world.

CHAPTER THREE

Totalitarianism's Inversion, Democracy's Perversion

i

By God, we've killed the Vietnam syndrome once and for all.
    —*George H. W. Bush (1991).*[1]

Our nation stands alone right now in terms of power.
And that is why we have got to be humble.
    —*Presidential candidate George W. Bush*[2]

Totally united.
    —*Bumper sticker*

In some respects, Nazi expansionist policy accelerated the
process of internal dissolution, because the methods of rule in
the occupied territories were subsequently transferred to
the Reich itself and contributed to the progressive destruction
of public administration, which became more and more
controlled by party functionaries.
    —*Hans Mommsen*[3]

We are not just any hegemon. We run a uniquely benign
imperialism . . . it is a fact manifest in the way that
others welcome our power.
    —*Charles Krauthammer*[4]

Save for the shameful "relocation" of American citizens of Japanese
ancestry, very few governmental actions during World War II could be
described accurately as repressive. Perhaps that was why Corwin's *Total
War and the Constitution* had not entertained the possibility that, in-

41

stead of a sweeping regulation of economy and society, a rapid increase in the size of the federal bureaucracy, and a unified front to a singular outside threat, totality might take the form of a convergence: between an external threat, part real, part imaginary, part concocted, and the indirect totalizing "forces" already at work "inside." Under that scenario a significant portion of the resources of society might be focused upon a single great objective, say a war on terrorism, with no *apparent* drastic reconstitution of the current system or ruffling of everyday life. Because significant change would then appear as a modest accentuation of previous tendencies, it could gain the protective cover of "continuity" or "precedent." If most lives were lived normally—if, in other words, radical change, by gradually meshing with normalcy so that, for example, "yellow alerts" seemed familiar and reassuring rather than exceptional—normalcy would then have ceased to serve as a restraint and measure of sanity.

The acceptance of restraints on personal freedom and being resigned to political impotence: such possibilities are not wildly implausible for a society that is accustomed to exchanging new habits for old, to adapting to rapid change, uncertainty, and social dislocation, to having one's fate determined by distant powers over which one has no control (globalization, market "forces"). Especially plausible for a society addicted to a virtual reality where cosmic mayhem rules: where planets are routinely destroyed every evening, environmental catastrophes are created by (what else?) "blockbusters," and whole civilizations wiped out—a virtual reality readily available on several channels, a daily "experience."[5] If we have already had the preview, what's unusual about the projection of overwhelming power even if it exceeds anything classic totalitarians might have achieved or even imagined? After all, it may be simply a question of virtuality: of genre, not genus.

ii

Notwithstanding these possibilities, to liken American democracy to a dictatorship, our constitutional system to a totalitarian one, is to invite outrage tempered by disbelief. Only a visceral Bush-hater would discern similarities between an American president and the Nazi *Führer* or argue that American democracy displays totalitarian tendencies. Because so much rides on the plausibility of what follows, my hope is that skeptical readers will resist the impulse to dismiss it and persevere instead. And this for a particular reason beyond the foreign and domestic record of the present administration.

The stakes in this volume are two: the first is prompted by President Bush's remark that the United States is "the greatest power in the world." Not only must we ask how this "greatest power" is constituted; we must also question the process by which it is legitimated. Does, or can, our Constitution, which typically has been understood as intending to limit power, actually authorize power of the magnitude being claimed by the president, or is an extraconstitutional justification being claimed? In light of the lofty, even sacred place that the "original Constitution" occupies in the ideology of the administration's most fervent supporters, that question should be of some interest, particularly to those who consider themselves conservatives.

The president frequently declares that our system is a democracy. The traditional understanding of democracy is that it is a system by which the citizenry delegates power to the government, and hence the latter has only such powers as are delegated to it. How, and when, did the people delegate "the greatest power in the world" to their government? If the people did not have that power in the first place, where does it come from? or has there been an acquisition of powers unanticipated in the founding document or in the theory of democracy, and are such powers inherently antagonistic to the spirit and logic of both constitutionalism and democracy?

Our second concern relates to an equally fundamental and jeopardized institution: can the citizen relearn the demands that democracy places on its highest, most difficult office — not, as commonly supposed, on the office of the president, but on that of the citizen? And that question has a practical corollary: the reinvigoration of citizenship requires more than a civics lesson. It would necessitate a reordering of basic power arrangements and a different understanding of civic commitments from that of spectator.

My main point will not be that the Bush administration was a facsimile of the Nazi dictatorship, or that the unremarkable George W. Bush resembled the charismatic *Führer*, or that his supporters were Naziphiles who dreamed of a racist nation of goose-steppers. Rather, in coining the term "inverted totalitarianism" I tried to find a name for a new type of political system, seemingly one driven by abstract totalizing powers, not by personal rule, one that succeeds by encouraging political disengagement rather than mass mobilization, that relies more on "private" media than on public agencies to disseminate propaganda reinforcing the official version of events.

In classic totalitarianism the conquest of total power did not result from a coalescence of unintended consequences; it was the conscious aim of those who led a political movement. The most powerful twentieth-century dictatorships were highly personal, not only in the sense that each had a dominant, larger-than-life leader, but each system was peculiarly the creation of a leader who was a self-made man. Mussolini, Stalin, and Hitler did not just invent their personae; they literally built the organizations of their respective dictatorships. Each system was inseparable from its *Führer*, or *Duce*. Inverted totalitarianism follows an entirely different course: the leader is not the architect of the system but its product. George W. Bush no more created inverted totalitarianism than he piloted a plane onto the USS *Abraham Lincoln*. He is the pliant favored child of privilege, of corporate connections, a construct of public relations wizards and of party propagandists.

The classic totalitarian regimes, Stalin's Russia, Mussolini's Italy, and Hitler's Germany, were, importantly, the creation of a charismatic leader and unimaginable without his imprint. Inverted totalitarianism, on the other hand, is largely independent of any particular leader and requires no personal charisma to survive: its model is the corporate "head," the corporation's public representative. Among the classical dictatorships only Stalin died while still in power, although his dictatorship did not survive the century. In the inverted system the leader is a product of the system, not its architect; it will survive him. While Hitler, Mussolini, and Stalin were the principal authors of schemes that eventually led to disastrous overreaching, those who counsel the titular head of Superpower, the equivalents of the CEO, supply the hubris that confuses opportunity with capability and grossly underestimates the resources needed to accomplish the grandiose end of world hegemony.

One prominent Washington insider, notable for his influence and close ties with the Bush inner circle, declared that he looked forward to the day when the national government will have been ruthlessly shrunken so that its pathetic remains can be washed down a bathtub or (the versions vary) flushed down a toilet.[6] Whatever its sound-bite value, that fantasy imagines either that the military will go the way of other major political institutions, or, while the latter are flushed, the armed forces remain. In either case, since nothing is intimated about the structure of corporate power, presumably it survives, flushed by success, as it were, protected by a now privatized military. Such fantasies ignore the facts of huge defense spending accompanied by an aggressive foreign policy, a fervent nationalism, and a military that, unlike the German *Wehrmacht* in its contempt for business values, cohabits comfortably with corporate America.[7] Be careful what you flush.

What we are in fact witnessing is something new, a conservative form of *étatisme* that, while it is hostile toward social spending, is eager to intervene in the most personal of affairs: sexual relations, marriage, reproduction, and family decisions about life and death. The case of Terri Schiavo was the perfect illustration of a conservative version of *étatisme*. The Republican-dominated Congress was hurriedly called in to special session; Dr. Frist, the Senate majority leader, offered his professional judgment from a distance; the president flew back to Washington; evangelicals and Catholic groups besieged the media, Congress, and the Florida legislature—and all for the cause of a person whom medical opinion had pronounced to be hopelessly brain-dead. What was significant was not the particular case but the tacit threat of quickly mobilized power, public and private, and orchestrated zeal. Intelligent design?

iii

An inversion is conventionally defined as an instance of something's being turned upside down. Unlike the classic totalitarian regimes which lost no opportunity for dramatizing and insisting upon a radical transformation that virtually eradicated all traces of the previous system, inverted totalitarianism has emerged imperceptibly, unpremeditatedly, and in seeming unbroken continuity with the nation's political traditions. For our purposes an inversion occurs when seemingly unrelated, even disparate starting points converge and reinforce each other. A giant corporation includes prayer sessions for its executives, while evangelicals meet in "franchised" congregations and millionaire preachers extol the virtues of capitalism.[8] Each is a reliable component in a system of which the administration is the public face. An inversion is present when a system, such as a democracy, produces a number of significant actions ordinarily associated with its antithesis: for example, when the elected chief executive may imprison an accused without due process and sanction the use of torture while instructing the nation about the sanctity of the rule of law. The new system, inverted totalitarianism, is one that professes to be the opposite of what, in fact, it is. It disclaims its real identity, trusting that its deviations will become normalized as "change." Again exactly the opposite of the classic totalitarians, who, far from disguising their break with the constitutional system of the past, celebrated it.

What is typically meant by "totalitarianism"? First and foremost, it is the attempt to realize an ideological, idealized conception of a society as a systematically ordered whole, where the "parts" (family, churches, education, intellectual and cultural life, economy, recreation, politics, state bureaucracy) are premeditatedly, even forcibly if necessary, coordinated to support and further the purposes of the regime. The formulation of those purposes is monopolized by the leadership. In classical totalitarian regimes it was assumed that total power demanded that the entirety of society's institutions, practices, and beliefs had to be dictated from above and coordinated (*gleichgeschaltet*), that total power was achievable only through the control of everything from the top. In actual fact, no totalitarian regime succeeded in perfectly realizing that vision. Although each of the classic forms of totalitarianism was rife with corruption, plagued by incompetence, and corroded by cynicism, they did not fail for lack of trying.

Inverted totalitarianism works differently. It reflects the belief that the world can be changed to accord with a limited range of objectives, such as ensuring that its own energy needs will be met, that "free markets" will be established, that military supremacy will be maintained, and that "friendly regimes" will be in place in those parts of the world considered vital to its own security and economic needs. Inverted totalitarianism also trumpets the cause of democracy worldwide. As we shall point out in later chapters, "democracy" is understood as "managed democracy," a political form in which governments are legitimated by elections that they have learned to control, the most recent example being the presidential election in Egypt in September 2005. President Mubarak, who had served for more than two decades, easily triumphed over a dozen rivals. Intimidation, corruption, unequal access to the media, and similar tactics reportedly were widespread.

Managed democracy is centered on containing electoral politics; it is cool, even hostile toward social democracy beyond promoting literacy, job training, and other essentials for a society struggling to survive in the global economy. Managed democracy is democracy systematized.

The United States has become the showcase of how democracy can be managed without appearing to be suppressed. This has come about, not through a Leader's imposing his will or the state's forcibly eliminating opposition, but through certain developments, notably in the economy, that promoted integration, rationalization, concentrated wealth, and a faith that virtually any problem—from health care to political crises, even faith itself—could be managed, that is, subjected to control, predictability, and cost-effectiveness in the delivery of the product. Voters are made as predictable as consumers; a university is nearly as rationalized in its structure as a corporation;[9] a corporate structure is as hierarchical in its chain of command as the military. The regime ideology is capitalism, which is virtually as undisputed as Nazi doctrine was in 1930s Germany. The political challenge has been to harness these various dynamics: a military that wants ever more futuristic technology and more deadly weaponry; a corporate economy that is continually searching for new markets and outlets; churches that are on the prowl for converts; news and entertainment media as eager to expand their market share as they are to pay court to the political establishment; and an intelligentsia avid to secure a measure of status by cozying with executives, politicos, and generals, and, no doubt, "speaking truth to power."

The genius of the Republican Party is to perceive the possibilities present in these systematizing and dynamic institutions and to combine them into something entirely new in U.S. politics, a dynamic reactionary movement professing to be a party of conservatism dedicated to small government, fiscal austerity, and a return to our Ur-myth, the "original Constitution of the Founders." Not least a party that has developed an impressive system for recruiting future apparatchiks.

Although I shall indicate some similarities between the American political system and Nazi Germany, my main argument is that while both systems belong to the same genus of totalitarianism, they represent different versions with some parallels and occasionally striking similarities. For example, the Nazi ideology of *Lebensraum* was the official justification for conquering peaceful neighboring countries and extending German hegemony. According to the doctrine, Germany needed "living space" to accommodate the dynamics of a superior master race that, if it was to avoid lapsing into decadence, had to provoke the challenges of war. That doctrine bears a striking similarity to the Bush doctrine of preemptive war.

Preemptive war entails the projection of power abroad, usually against a far weaker country, comparable, say, to the Nazi invasion of Belgium and Holland in 1940. It declares that the United States is justified in striking at another country because of a perceived threat that U.S. power will be weakened, severely damaged, unless it reacts to eliminate the danger before it materializes. Preemptive war is *Lebensraum* for the age of terrorism. The global character of terrorism offers endless opportunities for the preemptor to invade other countries on the grounds that they "harbor" terrorists. The neoconservative ideologists had, however, selected Iraq for invasion shortly after the end of the first Gulf War; indeed, they had been arguing that the only means by which America could expiate the shame of Vietnam and prove its mettle was in battle against other states.[10]

It can be objected, nonetheless, that unlike the Polish army in 1939, which the Nazis claimed was about to strike, terrorists are capable of terrible harm. However, Bush's declaration of a "war" on terrorism was fraught with serious constitutional implications; and whether or not it is legally justified, there is no guarantee that such a war could be won in any conventional sense. It was not Poland that brought about the defeat of the Nazi war machine but hubris, overreaching, the decision to launch two unwinnable wars virtually simultaneously, first against the Soviet Union, then against the United States. The doctrine of pre-emptive war seems irrelevant if the foe is not another state, and when, typically, collection of evidence that proves a conventional state is "harboring" terrorists takes time.

In the case of Iraq the script for applying the preemptive doctrine produced a disaster. Following the invasion of April 2003 and the rapid defeat of an army that mostly disappeared, the United States and its allies found their forces, as well as the Iraqi population, under continuous attack by an enemy whose exact identity seemed elusive. While failing to link Saddam and terrorists, the United States succeeded in provoking the very terrorism that it had failed to find. The misadventure in Iraq suggests that the difference between an expansive doctrine of *Lebensraum* and Superpower's expansive doctrine of globalization is that the one was genocidal in intention and results, while the other had the more modest goals of reorganizing the Middle East, ensuring oil supplies, and securing Israel. Instead of laying waste to a whole continent and killing millions, Superpower's toll—thousands of innocent lives, widespread economic devastation and social dislocation, and years of military occupation—was unintended rather than deliberate.

Over time, perhaps, and with good fortune, the contrasts between classic and inverted totalitarianism will emerge more sharply. Under the one the lives of ordinary people were relentlessly drab, unpromising, and harsh, save for the few able to collaborate successfully.[11] Under the inverted form there is a good chance that eventually ordinary lives will be materially tolerable and safer; whether the regime will be democratic is problematic. The main reason for believing that the future might bring material improvement and social stability is that these objectives suit the needs of a conqueror concerned to avoid actually governing conquered land. A globalizing power wants military bases abroad, trading partners, markets, and consumers: suzerainty, not an old-fashioned empire.

The benignity of inverted totalitarianism as contrasted with the harshness of classic totalitarian regimes is revealed in the ecumenical character of the one and the xenophobia of the other. The three classic totalitarianisms, while extending their domination over other societies, never sought to incorporate them in the sense that, say, the Romans did when they extended Roman citizenship to conquered peoples. Instead Hitler and the other dictators strove to keep *die Heimat* clean of foreigners while glorifying its own native-born, and making citizenship seem precious by reserving virtually all positions of power and wealth for its own subjects. In contrast, globalizing superpower blurs the distinction between homeland and *Ausland*: it enthusiastically exports culture and jobs—while missing no opportunity to weaken trade union power at home and abroad—and just as enthusiastically welcomes skilled and unskilled foreign workers, especially if the unskilled understand that they are "guests," with few legal or political entitlements, rather than future citizens.

Nazism and Italian fascism both barely concealed their intention of dismantling the existing parliamentary governments of their countries; both recognized that their goal of total power depended upon the elimination of freely competing parties and fair elections. The Bush administration, having failed to make the case that its invasion of Iraq was a response to an imminent threat of "weapons of mass destruction," shifted its rationale to one of bringing "democracy" to a nation despoiled by tyranny. What ensued was a curious variation on Corwin's scenario that threat of nuclear war would produce domestic totalizing powers and suspension of constitutional democracy at home in order to obliterate an enemy abroad; instead, the nuclear threat allegedly posed by Saddam Hussein's regime was invoked to justify an invasion for the purpose of imposing democracy *ab nihilo* upon a society that, while it most likely wanted to be rid of Saddam Hussein, had expressed no clear wish to be democratized, especially if that meant secularization. Meanwhile, at home, the war against Iraq is declared by the Bush administration to be simultaneously part of the ongoing war against terrorism, although the evidence of links between Saddam and al Qaeda appears to be as slender as the evidence that Saddam possessed weapons of mass destruction. And, it might be added, almost as dubious as the evidence supporting Hitler's claim of 1939 that the Poles were poised to invade Germany.

Thus far the promoters of American superpower have evinced no interest in abolishing a system that enables them to maximize power: a free politics, under the right conditions and controls, interposes no barriers to their kind of totalizing powers and may even serve as their auxiliary. The "right conditions" refers to the porousness of institutions that enables a different form of power—one ostensibly nonpolitical in its origins, unbound to constitutional limits or to democratic processes (call it "corporate power")—to turn access or simple influence over legislators and policy-makers into copartnership: not as in a corporate state of Mussolini's fantasies but as in the incorporated state. Why negate a constitution, as the Nazis did, if it is possible simultaneously to exploit porosity and legitimate power by means of judicial interpretations that declare huge campaign contributions to be protected speech under the First Amendment, or that treat heavily financed and organized lobbying by large corporations as a simple application of the people's right to petition their government?

To invert Marx: the first time, totalitarianism as tragic farce; the second, as farcical tragedy.

iv

> [If] political preferences are simply plugged into the
> system by leaders (business or other) in order to extract
> what they want from the system, then the model of
> plebiscitary democracy is substantially equivalent to
> the model of totalitarian rule.
> —Robert Dahl[12]

Within minutes of the strikes [of 9/11], U.S. law-enforcement and intelligence-gathering authorities mobilized to find the culprits and prevent another attack. They ramped up the tapping of Americans' phone calls and voice-mails. They watched Internet traffic and e-mails as never before. They tailed greater numbers of people and into places deemed off-limits, such as mosques.

> They clandestinely accessed bank accounts and credit
> card transactions and school records. They monitored travel.
> And they broke into homes without notice, looking for
> signs of terrorist activity and copying entire file cabinets
> and computer hard drives.
>
> Authorities even tried to get inside peoples' heads, using
> supercomputers and "predictive" software to analyze
> enormous amounts of personal data about them and
> their friends and associates in an effort to foretell who
> might become a terrorist, and when.
> —Josh Meyer, *Los Angeles Times*[13]

Unlike classical totalitarian regimes, which boasted of their totalitarian character, inverted totalitarianism disclaims its identity. Doubtless most Americans would indignantly protest that their political institutions and Constitution are the antithesis of a totalitarian regime. The contrast—at one extreme my claim that a species of totalitarianism is coming into being and, at the other, a claim by the putative totalitarians and the citizenry that theirs is an exemplary democracy; or, stated differently, the polarity between my denial that ours is a democracy and their denial that that system is totalitarian—may be too stark. Perhaps the actuality is a combination of both elements, which suggests that they are not mutually exclusive.

While robust democratic practices would be in contradiction to imperial power and its basic principle of domination and exploitation, democratic myths that have become detached from democratic practice may prove useful to inverted totalitarians. Plausibly, democratic mythology might linger on after democratic practices have lost substance, thereby enabling mythology, passivity, and empty forms to serve a type of totalitarian regime.

Whether democracy and totalitarian rule are necessarily incompatible might depend upon what kind of democracy and what kind of totalitarianism are combined. Recent studies have argued that democracy contributed importantly to the rise of the Nazis and the Fascists, and even served as a preparation. "[F]ascism," according to one prominent scholar of the subject, "is the product of democracies gone wrong, that had working constitutional systems which they gave up voluntarily."[14] To expand that interpretation: Hitler and Mussolini did not instantly "overthrow" parliamentary systems but, while cultivating a mass following, exploited popular elections to gain office and, once in power, proceeded to eviscerate the system of parliamentary governance, party competition, and the rule of law.[15] Democracy, according to this line of analysis, signified not an active citizenry but a politically disenchanted and alienated "mass" whose support was useful for conferring legitimacy on dictatorship and extending its control over the population. An artful combination of propaganda flattered the mass, exploited its antipolitical sentiments, warned it of dangerous enemies foreign and domestic, and applied forms of intimidation to create a climate of fear and an insecure populace, one receptive to being led. The same citizenry, which democracy had created, proceeded to vote into power and then support movements openly pledged to destroy democracy and constitutionalism. Thus a democracy may fail and give way to antidemocracy that, in turn, supplies a populace—and a "democratic" postulate—congenial to a totalitarian regime.

Eventually the dictatorships of Mussolini and Hitler were toppled, not by popular revulsion but by military defeats. Was it democracy that failed, or, instead, was it a failure of certain parliamentary systems to effectively translate democracy into actual practice? One line of argument, aimed at exonerating democracy's complicity in totalitarian regimes, contends that prior to the totalitarian seizure of power there was a thin democracy that included little beyond voting rights and formal legal guarantees. Democracy failed because of the superficial democratic civic culture in both societies. At the turn into the twentieth century monarchs were still important political actors in both societies. Germany's Weimar constitution had been in existence for a mere dozen years; Italy's parliamentary monarchy, while a creation of the nineteenth century, was notoriously corrupt and lacking in public support. Neither country could draw on a fund of democratic political experience or a tradition of participatory politics; its citizenry was prepolitical. The shallowness of democracy's hold in those countries was underscored by the astonishing rapidity with which Hitler and Mussolini consolidated their dictatorships and opposition collapsed.[16]

The "democracy" that failed in Italy and Germany was primarily an electoral democracy, the most easily managed and transformed into plebiscitary democracy. Mass participation was simulated through appeals to patriotism and nationalism, and satisfied by mass rallies and membership in various auxiliaries (e.g., *Hitler-Jugend*) created by the regime. Fascist and Nazi totalitarianism was made possible by the methodical transformation of passive citizens into ardent followers, uncomplaining patriots, willing executioners, and, finally, cannon fodder.

v

Paradoxically, while totalitarian regimes had a strong popular element, their principal institutions were self-consciously antidemocratic. They were notorious for trumpeting the "leadership principle" (*Führerprinzip*), legitimizing the predominance of elites, and elevating the status of the "loyal follower." Power was monopolized, not shared. In addition to unflinching loyalty a strict orthodoxy was required of those who aspired to powerful positions in the hierarchy; as we would say today, they had "to stay on message." Further, in both Italy and Germany the most powerful social and economic classes, as well as many of the members of the political elites, were hostile to democracy and, at best, lukewarm toward liberalism. Especially potent was the combination of a prepolitical demos and highly self-conscious, resentful elites convinced of their natural right to rule. Unlike the political elites of the late eighteenth and early nineteenth centuries, the elites who gravitated toward totalitarianism were less fearful of the mass than contemptuous of its gullibility.

The denial that democracy could have spawned a totalitarian regime assumes that a "healthy" democracy would abhor a Nazi-style dictatorship and resist being its accomplice. In one sense, a definitional or conceptual one, a true democracy and a dictatorship are mutually exclusive. Our thesis, however, is this: it is possible for a form of totalitarianism, different from the classical one, to evolve from a putatively "strong democracy" instead of a "failed" one. A weak democracy that fails, such as that of Weimar, might end in classical totalitarianism, while a failed strong democracy might lead to inverted totalitarianism. The latter possibility becomes greater if the strong democracy is shallower than advertised—and greater still if, historically, that democracy was acknowledged rather than embraced by elites.

vi

America must be able to fight Iraq and North Korea, and *also* be able to fight genocide in the Balkans and elsewhere without compromising its ability to fight two major regional conflicts. And it must be able to contemplate war with China or Russia some considerable (but not infinite) time from now.
—Frederick W. Kagan[17]

Twentieth-century totalitarian systems aspired to total control over every aspect of society and to the elimination or neutralization of all possible forms of opposition. In the German version this served the all-consuming purpose of waging war and expanding beyond established boundaries. In practice control was extended over family life and reproduction, education, economy, all forms of cultural expression, the courts, bureaucracy, and military. By imposing a single ideology the Nazis created a self-justifying regime. The complete rearrangement of German society was the preliminary to their rearranging the world by taking over and administering other countries, using their populations as slave laborers, resettling some peoples and liquidating others. For our purposes the crucial question is, how did both Nazism and fascism, as well as Soviet communism, invent systems of power that, by the standards of the last century, were awesome and incomparable, and, by any standard, lethal?

The answer is this: by forced organization, coordination of power centers, and imposed mobilization and disciplining of the general population, not least by introducing a measure of economic improvement and an atmosphere of fear. In Germany these techniques were accompanied by an official ideology that promised Germans a superior place in a New Order; in Soviet Russia citizens were told to expect a future society of abundance and equality. From today's perspective, colored as it is by postmodern sensibilities, these older ideologies both demanded, and exacted, severe sacrifices from present generations, raising the question of how such ideologies of postponed and nebulous rewards were able to generate a dynamic instead of provoking widespread active or passive resistance. A short answer might invoke the potency of calibrated doses of fear, combined with excitement at being a part of a great undertaking and expectations about opportunities in the present—a present that, despite its dangers and shortcomings, offered greater hope of advancement than did the dreary existence in the depressed economy of Weimar or the premodern, rigid class society of tsarist Russia.

Unlike the Bolsheviks, Nazis, and Italian Fascists, inverted totalitarianism does not require as the condition of its success the overthrow of the established system. It has no overt plan to suppress all opposition, impose ideological uniformity or racial purity, or seek the traditional form of empire. It allows free speech, venerates the Constitution, and operates within a two-party system that, theoretically, secures a role for an opposition party. Rather than revolting against an existing system, it claims to be defending it. This suggests that a different kind of dynamic is at work, one that for the most part does not depend upon resentments against the prevailing form of government or social system.

Inverted totalitarianism has learned how to exploit what appear to be formidable political and legal constraints, using them in ways that defeat their original purpose but without dismantling or overtly attacking them. One strategy is to exploit institutions to facilitate certain favored forms of power while checking rival ones. Thus it will accept reform of campaign financing that prohibits contributions from trade unions and corporations, knowing that in practice it is relatively easy for corporations to evade such prohibitions. Besides, the same interests that have invested in the political campaigns of senators who sit on the Judiciary Committee receive "returns" on their investment when the politicized courts decide that campaign reforms violate the rights of free speech guaranteed to corporations. Which is one more application of the doctrine that for legal purposes corporations are to be considered persons—

except in those cases where the "persons" agree to a "settlement" whereby the wrongdoers avoid prison terms by paying a large sum to the government while, according to the formula, not "admitting any wrongdoing." As numerous corporate and political scandals have revealed, corruption is systemic to inverted totalitarianism as it had been with classical totalitarianism.

Our totalizing system, nonetheless, has evolved its own methods and strategies. Its genius lies in wielding total power without appearing to, without establishing concentration camps, or enforcing ideological uniformity, or forcibly suppressing dissident elements so long as they remain ineffectual.[18] However, the parallel lines of classic totalitarianism and inverted totalitarianism occasionally intersect. It is true that aliens, and even some citizens, who are suspected of having "links" to terrorists have been hauled away, kept incommunicado, and even transported abroad to countries with more cost-effective, less tender methods of interrogation, yet such practices are meant more as object lessons than as standard procedures. In the same vein the United States has established only a few extrajudicial courts (e.g., so-called military tribunals) and does not have concentration camps, only some "detention centers" and "brigs" where, under harsh conditions, prisoners may be held without being charged with a specific crime. The point is to preserve an economy of fear and not to saturate the "market." For what is most revealing of totalitarian tendencies in our inverted regime are not the publicized denials of due process to enemy nationals or to misguided "freedom fighters." The more important consideration is ensuring domestic tranquillity. But, specifically, against whom?

The United States has the highest rate of incarceration of any country in the world, a prison system with brutalizing conditions, and one that has been significantly privatized.[19] Equally striking, a disproportionately high percentage of the imprisoned are African Americans. Assuming that most of the imprisoned African Americans have committed some crime, their incarceration would appear to contrast with the Nazi policies that herded millions of Jews, Gypsies, homosexuals, political opponents, and Slavs into slave labor camps for no other reason than to satisfy irrational ideological beliefs ("racial purity") and obtain "free" labor. Or do the high incarceration rates among blacks reflect not only old-fashioned racism but inverted totalitarianism's fear of political dissidence?

The significance of the African American prison population is political. What is notable about the African American population generally is that it is highly sophisticated politically and by far the one group that throughout the twentieth century kept alive a spirit of resistance and rebelliousness. In that context, criminal justice is as much a strategy of political neutralization as it is a channel of instinctive racism.

Our government need not pursue a policy of stamping out dissidence—the uniformity imposed on opinion by the "private" media conglomerates performs that job efficiently. This apparent "restraint" points to a crucial difference between classical and inverted totalitarianism: in the former economics was subordinate to politics. Under inverted totalitarianism the reverse is true: economics dominates politics—and with that domination come different forms of ruthlessness. It is possible for the government to punish by withholding appropriated funds, failing to honor entitlements, or purposely allowing regulations (e.g., environmental safeguards, minimum wage standards) to remain unenforced or waived. What seem like reductions in state power are actually increases. Withholding appropriated money is an expression of power that is not lost on those adversely affected; waiving minimum wage standards is an act of power not lost on those who benefit and those who suffer.[20] Such strategies play a major role in the incorporation of state and corporate power. Incorporation need not always require, for example, that corporate representatives sit on review committees that judge new drugs or gather in the office of the vice president to consult on energy policies. Power is typically exercised in a context where the participants know their cues. Recently a major television network withdrew a program dealing with Ronald Reagan after the Republican National Committee protested a scene where the former president was portrayed as less than inclusive about homosexuals.[21] This surrender occurred at the precise moment when the Republican-dominated Federal Communications Commission was promoting greater concentration of media ownership and, in the process, ignoring an unprecedented outcry from thousands of citizens.

vii

The fact that politically organized interest groups with vast resources operate continuously, that they are coordinated with congressional procedures and calendars, that they occupy strategic points in the political processes, is indicative of how the meaning of "representative" government has radically changed. The citizenry is being displaced, severed from a direct connection with the legislative institutions that are supposed to "stand in" for the people. If the main purpose of elections is to serve up pliant legislators for lobbyists to shape, such a system deserves to be called "misrepresentative or clientry government." It is, at one and the same time, a powerful contributing factor to the depoliticization of the citizenry, as well as reason for characterizing the system as one of antidemocracy.

How is the role of the citizen being redefined and to whose advantage? Almost from the beginning of the Cold War the citizenry, supposedly the source of governmental power and authority as well as a participant, has been replaced by the "electorate," that is, by voters who acquire a political life at election time. During the intervals between elections the political existence of the citizenry is relegated to a shadow-citizenship of virtual participation. Instead of participating in power, the virtual citizen is invited to have "opinions": measurable responses to questions predesigned to elicit them.

There is an especially revealing contrast between the Nazi use of public opinion surveys and the methods of contemporary pollsters. The Nazis were interested primarily in constructing a "mass" opinion, a monolithic expression of the citizens without qualification or nuance. Hence the plebiscite and its stark choice of "yes" or "no." In contrast, the American method is to prepare for elections by first splintering the citizenry into distinct categories, such as "between 20 and 35 years old," or "white male over 40," or "female college graduate." The potential electorate is thus divided into small subgroups that candidates can then "target" with messages tailored to the "values," prejudices, or habits of the particular category. The effect is to accentuate what separates citizens, to plant suspicions and thereby further promote demobilization by making it more difficult to form coherent majorities around common beliefs. At the same time, the dicing of the public into ever more refined categories renders their constituent members more easily manipulable: cheaply reproduced in "focus groups," their conclusions are represented as political reality. The respondents, for their part, are not obligated to act on their opinions: giving an opinion entails no political responsibility.

The advanced stage of the art of opinion construction and its manipulation is indicative of the forces molding the political system. It combines advanced technology, academic social science, government contracts, and corporate subsidies. We shall encounter this same combination of powers in later pages; it plays a vital role in coordinating the powers on which Superpower depends.

In a genuinely democratic system, as opposed to a pseudodemocratic one in which a "representative sample" of the population is asked whether it "approves" or "disapproves," citizens would be viewed as *agents* actively involved in the exercise of power and in contributing to the direction of policy. Instead citizens are more like "patients" who, in the dictionary definition, are "bearing or enduring (evil of any kind) with composure; long suffering or forbearing."[22]

A demotion in the status and stature of the "sovereign people" to patient subjects is symptomatic of systemic change, from democracy as a method of "popularizing" power to democracy as a brand name for a product manageable at home and marketable abroad.[23]

viii

"Superpower" signifies the emergence of a new system. Its guiding purposes are not democratic ones of promoting the well-being of its citizens or involving them in political processes. The new identity and how it is to be measured were stated by the administration: "the United States possesses unprecedented—and unequalled—strength and influence in the world."[24] Implicit in that declaration is a reformulation of the nation's identity: it stands for sheer power, economic and military, that is measured by a global standard rather than the nation's constitution; freed not only from constitutional democracy but from any truly political character.

Inverted totalitarianism, the true face of Superpower, represents a blend of powers that includes modern as well as archaic ones. It comprises the business corporation—once hailed as "the city of God on earth" and even formally theologized[25]—the organization of science for continuous advance, and the systematic conversion of new scientific knowledge into new technological applications, especially military ones. A common characteristic of each of these powers is a presumption of virtually limitless development. That dynamic governs economic behavior, the pursuit of knowledge, the production of culture, and military weaponry. The paradox is that the inevitable changes accompanying the development of these powers, indeed, changes that are often consciously sought, are promoted by an administration and a political party advertising themselves as "conservative."

Democracy proposes a radically different conception of power. Democracy is first and foremost about equality: equality of power and equality of sharing in the benefits and values made possible by social cooperation. Democracy is no more compatible with world domination than is "the political," which is first and foremost about preserving commonality while legitimating and reconciling differences. Both democracy and the political become distorted when the scales are continually expanded. In the United States, from the beginning, there has been a persistent tension between the drive for expansion (the Louisiana Purchase, "Westward, Ho!") and the struggle to devise new institutions for adapting the practices of democracy and its ethos of political commonality. An enlarged spatial scale both requires and promotes a technology of power that can make occupation and rule effective. America's westward migration was facilitated by new technology, from the covered wagon, the Pony Express, the railroad, and the telegraph to the Winchester rifle. To the technology of expansion there should be added the ideology of "Manifest Destiny," which served to legitimate and fuel the "drive" westward. Ideology can be as vital a part of the technology of power as any mechanical invention, provided it is dynamic—that is, if it possesses a "thrust" forward in time (e.g., the "Last Days") to accompany the occupation of new space. Such an ideology reassures those who are applying mundane forms of technology that the act of "taking over" what was not previously theirs is "just" by some higher principle. Manifest Destiny, religious conversion, the counterparts to *Lebensraum*, the Redskin to the Jew.

The preconditions for Superpower are the availability of a totalizing technology of power and an accompanying ideology that encourages the regime's aspirations to global domination. These preconditions were satisfied during the Bush administration. It succeeded in systematizing and exploiting a dynamic complex of powers already existing. Its principal elements include the state, corporate economic power, the powers represented in the integration of modern science and postmodern technologies, a military addicted to technological innovation, and a religious fundamentalism that is no stranger to politics and markets. By "dynamic" I mean to emphasize that they are powers which constantly supersede their own previous limits and are totalizing in the sense that infinity, or the persistent challenging of the constraints of existing practices, beliefs, and taboos, rather than simple superiority, is the driving force. This is accompanied by a systematic effort to establish the conditions that facilitate power and eliminate those which interfere—from government regulations that frustrate entrepreneurial energies to the "wall separating church and state" that constrains religious zealots from purifying schools, placing the Ten Commandments in courthouses, preaching redemption to a captive audience of welfare recipients, sometimes using terrorist violence against medical clinics, and setting the limits of scientific research in the name of protecting "life" before birth but less zealous about promoting health care for the postnatal poor. Such religiosity fits comfortably with a regime promising a "compassionate conservatism" that "will leave no child behind" although, in practice, it frequently fails to provide adequate funds for social and educational programs designed to assist poor families. It does not emulate the rhetoric of Nazis and Stalinists by extolling the values of "hardness" and "steel." Instead, it coexists easily with a culture of softness, indulgence, and fantasy, of comfortable viewers watching superb athletes perform physical prodigies of grace and violence.

ix

Hitler was a parvenu in relation to the existing political system. He and his intimate circle began as "outsiders" who were not a part of the conventional system of political parties and elites in pre-Hitler Germany. In keeping with that character they adopted unconventional, often illegal, means to gain power. The court circle of George II, in contrast, was composed of highly seasoned political operatives, such as Dick Cheney, Donald Rumsfeld, and Karl Rove, insiders rather than outsiders. Not only were they experienced in government, but most of them were intimately familiar with the inner workings of the corporate world. Their talents lay in managing the dual system of state and corporation. In Hitler's regime the subjectivity of arrivistes reigned; in Bush's governing circle the "objectivity" of professional politicians, the aggrandizing of corporate managers on loan, and the stratagems of consultants prevailed. The revolving door of the dual system suggests a certain parity between corporate and state power; the actuality is asymmetrical. While the corporate ethos has overwhelmed the ideal of government as the servant of the people, the old governmental ideals—such as the view that power is to be used for the public good, not for private profit—supply no model for corporate behavior.

One truly fundamental difference between classical and inverted totalitarian regimes is that in the years before assuming power, the Nazis had attracted only limited support from the representatives of "big business." And during their years of rule it was abundantly clear that capitalism was subordinate to the power of the state and the party. In contrast the Bush administration openly flaunts its connections with corporate powers by appointing their representatives to high positions in government and in the hierarchy of the Republican Party. Another revealing difference: alongside their highly selective celebration of *Kultur* (e.g., Wagner) the Nazis celebrated a certain barbarism that was contemptuous of "civilization," seeing in high culture an effete decadence that sapped the will to power. The Bush administration's spokespersons, as well as supporters of the attack on Iraq and the war against terrorism, portray the United States as the defender of "civilization" against "barbarians" and "apocalyptic nihilists."[26]

In one instance the distinction between "real" and "inverted" totalitarianism nearly—or, perhaps, ironically—appears to break down. The Nazis came to power by an election in which they won more votes than any rival party, although not a majority. The election, while formally free, was marred by episodes of violence enacted by party thugs. George II was also elected or, better, anointed without a popular majority. Thanks to the manipulation of a dubious electoral process in the state of Florida, an aggressive, experienced, and highly paid "hit team" of lawyers and political consultants, a timid opposition party, and a highly partisan Supreme Court, the high-handed violations of elementary principles of legitimacy were treated as just another bit of dirty politics, easily forgotten in the rush to "get on with the nation's business."[27]

Behind the benevolent rhetoric of the Bush administration lies perhaps the most crucial inversion. One of the striking features of the three principal twentieth-century totalitarian regimes was a focus on maintaining their societies in a state of continuous political mobilization. Hitler's Germany, Mussolini's Italy, and Stalin's Soviet Union all held periodic plebiscites in which, unfailingly, more than 95 percent of a mobilized citizenry went to the polls and voted yes. There were endless political rallies, public spectacles, rousing oratorical performances by the leadership, tireless propaganda extolling the leaders, the party, and the ideology, and warnings that heavy sacrifices lay ahead.

In contrast, inverted totalitarianism thrives on a politically demobilized society, that is, a society in which the citizens, far from being whipped into a continuous frenzy by the regime's operatives, are politically lethargic, reminiscent of Tocqueville's privatized citizenry. Roughly between one-half and two-thirds of America's qualified voters fail to vote, thus making the management of the "active" electorate far easier. Every apathetic citizen is a silent enlistee in the cause of inverted totalitarianism. Yet apathy is not simply the result of a TV culture. It is, in its own way, a political response. Ordinary citizens have been the victims of a counterrevolution that has brought "rollbacks" of numerous social services which were established only after hard-fought political struggles, and which the earlier Republican administrations of Eisenhower and Nixon had accepted as major elements in a national consensus. Rollbacks don't simply reverse previous social gains; they also teach political futility to the Many. And along the way they mock the ideal and practice of consensus.

Where classic totalitarianism—whether of the German, Italian, or Soviet type—aimed at fashioning followers rather than citizens, inverted totalitarianism can achieve the same end by furnishing substitutes such as "consumer sovereignty" and "shareholder democracy" that give a "sense of participation" without demands or responsibilities. An inverted regime prefers a citizenry that is uncritically complicit rather than involved. President Bush's first words to the citizenry after 9/11 were not an appeal for sacrifice in a common cause but "unite, consume, fly."

Yet elements of inverted totalitarianism could not crystallize in the absence of a stimulus that would rouse the apathetic just enough to gain their support and obedience. The threat of terrorism supplied that element. It could evoke fear and obedience on demand ("according to unverified reports . . .") without causing paralysis or skepticism.

What is the temptation of a democracy without citizens?

A clue was suggested in the recent remarks of a member of the president's inner circle: "Even the president is not omnipotent. Would that he were. He often says that life would be a lot easier if it were a dictatorship. But it's not, and he is glad it's a democracy."[28] Presumably, the nation exhaled.

x

The Nazis developed an extreme form of politicalization. The leadership continuously drummed into its population the necessity of personal sacrifice, of subordinating one's personal concerns to the good of the whole. It was, however, a "politicalization without politics." It actively suppressed free public discussion, discouraged the airing of policy alternatives, and clamped down upon the expression of group conflicts. Instead of a politics of open contestation and public involvement, the Nazis pursued a vicious politics of cronyism, intrigue, ruthless ambitions, and periodic purges within the party and its various auxiliaries (SA, SS, etc.). There, hidden from view, individuals and cliques fought over the spoils and prerogatives of office.

Inverted totalitarianism reverses things. It is all politics all of the time but a politics largely untempered by the political. Party squabbles are occasionally on public display, and there is a frantic and continuous politics among factions of the party, interest groups, competing corporate powers, and rival media concerns. And there is, of course, the culminating moment of national elections when the attention of the nation is required to make a choice of personalities rather than a choice between alternatives. What is absent is the political, the commitment to finding where the common good lies amidst the welter of well-financed, highly organized, single-minded interests rabidly seeking governmental favors and overwhelming the practices of representative government and public administration by a sea of cash.

xi

The twentieth-century totalitarian systems in Italy and Germany were made possible by the weakness and eventual collapse of parliamentary government and the failure of the conventional political parties to mount and sustain an effective opposition. The latter proved incapable of countering the tactics and appeals of both extreme Right and Left that had made no secret of their ultimate purpose of dismantling elected governments and outlawing the system of free politics. Classic totalitarianism first gained power by capturing the existing system and, once in power, proceeded to destroy it. The break was abrupt and complete.

Inverted totalitarianism has a different background, undramatic, no mass movement driving it, no putsches or Marches on Rome, no abrupt discontinuity. Instead a scarcely noticeable evolution, an undramatic convergence of tendencies and unintended consequences. In historical terms, corporate power itself is at least as old as the "trusts" of the nineteenth century; similarly, the role of big money in corrupting politics was well established by the end of the nineteenth century and had aroused a whole generation of "muckrakers" in the early years of the twentieth. In the 1920s political scientists were already describing interest groups and lobbies as "the fourth branch of government." What is unprecedented in the union of corporate and state power is its systematization and the shared culture of the partners.

Inverted totalitarianism begins to crystallize amidst the affluence of the world's most dynamic economy. In contrast, the Nazis' ascendancy was aided in no small measure by the severe economic depression, high inflation, and acute unemployment afflicting Germany during much of the 1920s and early 1930s. Once in power they began to mobilize the society for total war. The resulting full employment reduced the regime's need to exploit economic fears. Where Hitler's party, the National Socialists, had—for a brief period—made gestures in the direction of socialism and the working classes but remained cool toward capitalism, inverted totalitarianism is just the opposite. It is resolutely capitalist, no friend of the working classes, and, of course, viscerally antisocialist. In contrast to the Nazis, the ever-changing economy of Superpower, despite its affluence, makes fear the constant companion of most workers. Downsizing, reorganization, bubbles bursting, unions busted, quickly outdated skills, and transfer of jobs abroad create not just fear but an economy of fear, a system of control whose power feeds on uncertainty, yet a system that, according to its analysts, is eminently rational.

xii

One of the most revealing contrasts between classic and inverted totalitarianism is in their treatment of what an inspired university president designated "the knowledge industry." Under classic totalitarianism, schools, universities, and research were conscripted into the service of the regime. Scientific establishments and independent critics were either silenced, purged, or eliminated. Those who survived were expected to faithfully echo the party or government line. The primary task of all educational institutions was the indoctrination of the population in the ideology of the regime.

Inverted totalitarianism, although at times capable of harassing or discrediting critics,[29] has instead cultivated a loyal intelligentsia of its own. Through a combination of governmental contracts, corporate and foundation funds, joint projects involving university and corporate researchers, and wealthy individual donors, universities (especially so-called research universities), intellectuals, scholars, and researchers have been seamlessly integrated into the system. No books burned, no refugee Einsteins. For the first time in the history of American higher education top professors are made wealthy by the system, commanding salaries and perks that a budding CEO might envy. During the months leading up to and following the invasion of Iraq, university and college campuses, which had been such notorious centers of opposition to the Vietnam War that politicians and publicists spoke seriously of the need to "pacify the campuses," hardly stirred. The Academy had become self-pacifying.

CHAPTER FOUR

The New World of Terror

i

> The victor will not be asked later whether he
> had spoken the truth or not.
> —*Adolf Hitler*[1]

> Extremism in the defense of liberty is no vice. . . .
> Moderation in the pursuit of justice is no virtue.
> —*Barry Goldwater*[2]

> Weakness is provocative.
> —*Donald Rumsfeld, "Rules of Life"*[3]

In Western thought the idea of a New World was typically used to support a myth of a fresh beginning, a place of promise, a new birth. As the "first new nation," the United States was widely regarded as fulfilling that promise, even though there were several old nations already occupying the land. But today the myth of a "new world" is not superimposed on an uncharted land, a tabula rasa, or blank tablet, awaiting inscription. Rather the idea is necessarily superimposed on an existing world. To the extent that it envisions a radically changed system, a new world represents a willful act of power, a determination to supersede not an old order—for in postmodernity maturity and old age are unacceptable—but a current one.

The most recent example of this mode of thinking—although it seems long ago—was the celebration of the arrival of a new millennium in 2000. At the time it was widely prophesied that advanced societies were poised at the threshold of a new age of dazzling technological marvels.[4] A year later, following September 11, 2001, many public officials and commentators were quick to declare that a different kind of "new world" had come into being, a world of fears where "barbarians" were turning sophisticated technologies against the advanced civilization that had invented them. Citizens were told that the destruction of the Twin Towers and part of the Pentagon meant as well the destruction of the comforting assumption of invulnerability that had implicitly underlain American foreign policies and military strategies as well as their own daily lives.[5] The most complete statement of the ideology of will-to-power was *The National Security Strategy of the United States* issued in 2002. In that document the administration declared its intention to reshape the current world and define the new one. "In the new world we have entered," it declared grandly, "the only path to safety is the path of action."[6]

Clearly neither politicians nor the news media could truly *know* that a new world had been born that instant *and* that an old world had been superseded. Declaring a new world is a positive act canceling an old one and discarding along with it the old restraints and inhibitions upon power. "If they [Iraq and North Korea] do acquire WMD [weapons of mass destruction] their weapons will be unusable," Condoleezza Rice warned, "because any attempt to use them will bring national obliteration"[7]—the wrath, if not of an angry god, then of a divinely appointed agent. The United States, the president announced, is the "greatest force for good on the earth," and in fighting terrorism the nation is responding to "a calling from beyond the stars."[8] Terrorism is both a response to empire and the provocation that allows for empire to cease to be ashamed of its identity. Under empire the claims of power can be relocated in a context different from the one defined by the traditions and constraints of constitutional government and of democratic politics. Among the first actions of the administration, with the acquiescence of Congress and strong public support, were the creation of a Homeland Security Department, Superpower's super-agency, and passage of the Patriot Act, introducing super-citizens to their diminished bill of rights.

These and other actions were responses to 9/11. But they were simultaneously attempts to reshape the existing political system, most notably by enlarging the powers of the executive branch of government, including the military and police functions, while reducing the legal protections of citizens. In the shaping of a fearful new world much would depend on the administration's definition of the enemy, the evidence supporting that definition, and the definition's problematic nature. Definition, evidence, and consequences, however, were to be preceded by the invention of a context consistent with the new world. Following 9/11 and virtually every day thereafter, government announcements and news bulletins sounded a drumbeat, cautioning citizens that a furtive network of fanatical enemies was tirelessly plotting death and destruction—especially for occasions when citizens congregated—and only awaited the opportunity when a free society relaxed its guard.

Accompanying the invention of a new world was the concerted effort to fix in the public mind a certain shapeless character and identity to terrorism. The *National Security Strategy*—more of its doctrine later—declared that terrorism was "[a] shadowy network of individuals [that] can bring great chaos and suffering to our shores for less than it costs to purchase a single tank. Terrorists are organized to penetrate open societies and to turn the power of modern technology against us."[9] Thus the diffuse character attributed to terrorism is reproduced in an enveloping atmosphere whose effect is to arouse a primal fear about the precariousness of every moment in daily life, to surround the most taken-for-granted routines with uncertainty. As many commentators have been quick to point out, terrorists do not present the single, determinate threat of an enemy nation-state. Potentially they are everywhere—and nowhere. The amorphous character assigned to the new world of terrorism then justifies enlarging the power of the avenging state both at home and overseas. "The best way to protect America," the president claimed, "is to go on the offensive, and stay on the offensive."[10] Power becomes not only spatially but also temporally limitless.

At the same time, the character of absolute evil assigned to terrorism—of a murderous act without reasonable or just provocation—works toward the same end by allowing the state to cloak its power in innocence.[11] In the immediate aftermath of 9/11 Americans asked, "What have we done to deserve this?" The official silence that met the question made plain the obvious answer: Nothing. When a few voices suggested that acts of terrorism had been committed in retaliation for U.S. government actions abroad, the media quickly dismissed the notion as implausible and vaguely unpatriotic. (It was an object lesson in how the system can enforce censorship and stifle opposition without appearing to do so.) Terrorism was made to appear as irrational violence, without apparent cause or reasonable justification. It became stylized as "threatening," its intentions unknown until too late. Action in response to it could thereby appear as "pure," without ulterior or mixed motives, provoked. An innocence that under normal circumstances might raise suspicions about motives served to justify extensions of power at home and abroad. In the ponderous summary of one commentator, "The most carefree and confident empire in history now grimly confronts the question of whether it can escape Rome's ultimate fate."[12]

The moment that marked the turning point from the old to the new was not the immediate, horrified response of the citizenry but the astonishing speed with which the entire nation was to be defined in a single, all-encompassing purpose. By declaring a war on terrorism, America had, in the pastoral language of its president, found "its mission and its moment." In his message urging the expansion of the government's powers under the intrusive Patriot Act, the president turned from his New Testament friendly god to assume the role of the Old Testament god of vengeance and wrath, vowing, "We will never forget the servants of evil who plotted the attacks and we will never forget those who rejoiced at our grief."[13]

"The struggle against global terrorism," according to the administration's *National Security Strategy* (NSS), "is different from any other war in our history. It will be fought on many fronts against a particularly elusive enemy over an extended period of time." The characteristics of the hastily constructed new world were like terrorism, vague and indeterminate. "The war against terrorists of global reach," according to NSS, "is a global enterprise of uncertain duration."[14]

A world where warfare has no boundaries, spatial or temporal, and hence no limits was not the simple product of terrorism but that of its exploitation. "Progress," according to NSS, " will come through the persistent accumulation of successes—some seen, some unseen."[15] The dark vision of a radically new condition produced a wish, an opportunity, and a justification for converting an event into a permanent crisis. Terrorism, power without boundaries, becomes the template for Superpower; the measureless, the illegitimate, becomes the measure of its counterpart.

To be sure, before September 11 government had, on more than one occasion, manufactured and manipulated fear. This time, however, because of the indefinite spatial and temporal character of terrorism, fear became pervasive and invasive, the rule and no longer the exception, the mockery of FDR's counsel, "We have nothing to fear except fear itself." The focus on terrorism elevated fear into a public presence, creating a new atmospherics that could be appealed to and exploited.[16] Miraculously, out of the rubble and phoenixlike emerged a stronger state, a "superpower" or "empire."[17] Superpower was commonly defined as the capability of a state to project force anywhere in the world and at a time of its own choosing. It might also be described as power that is continually challenging the forbidden as its predestined other. The terrorism being combated by Superpower, while real enough, is one whose image Superpower's representatives have constructed. Superpower's understanding of the requirements of its own powers has been guided by the character it has chosen to bestow upon terrorism. Terrorism repays the mimicry by embracing advanced military technology and countering "shock and awe" with displays of beheadings on television. Two irreconcilable forms of power, terrorism and Superpower, locked together, each dependent on the other.

No previous administration in American history had demanded such extraordinary powers in order to muster the resources of the nation in pursuit of an enterprise as vaguely defined as "the war against terrorism" or demanded such an enormous outlay of public funds for a mission whose end seemed far distant and difficult to recognize if and when it might be achieved. World Wars I and II ended conclusively when armistices were negotiated by representatives from both sides. Terrorists, however, are reported as operating a highly decentralized organization—even assuming that they could properly be described as having "an" organization—making it unlikely that any individual or group could plausibly claim to negotiate on behalf of all terrorists.

Since that September day it is not only the ordinary routines and liberties of citizens that have been changed. The constitutional institutions designed to check power—Congress, courts, an opposition political party—swore allegiance to the same ideology of vengeance and enlisted themselves as auxiliaries. Despite some solitary dissident voices, none of these institutions attempted consistently to block or resist as the president proceeded to mount an unprovoked invasion of one country and threaten others, nor to question as he and members of his cabinet bullied allies, demanding uncritical support from all nations while proclaiming the right of the United States to walk away from solemn treaty obligations whenever convenient and to undercut the efforts of other nations seeking to develop international institutions for curbing wars, genocide, and environmental damage.[18]

ii

> The end of worship amongst men, is power.
> —Thomas Hobbes[19]

> [I]n every Christian commonwealth, the civil sovereign
> is the supreme pastor.
> —Thomas Hobbes[20]

The new prominence of terror and fear brings to mind Thomas Hobbes, perhaps the first Western political theorist to correlate fear and power and explain how those two elements could be exploited to promote an awesome concentration of state power and authority, and, crucially, how that outcome could be represented as the product of popular consent. It is appropriate that apologists for the Bush administration's imperialistic foreign policy should have suddenly discovered Hobbes's relevance for "an anarchic world." According to neoconservative intellectuals, "The alternative to American leadership is a chaotic Hobbesian world" where "there is no authority to thwart aggression, ensure peace and security or enforce international norms."[21] It is striking that, without exception, the neo-Hobbesians have suppressed that half of Hobbes's story which dealt with the domestic implications of his defense of the principle of absolute authority and of the sovereign's role as "supreme pastor."

Hobbes asks us to imagine what life would be like in the absence of a strong authority armed with the power to enforce law, administer justice, and keep the peace. He likened that condition to a "state of nature" in which human beings lived in constant fear of violent death, an unending war of each against all.[22] Hobbes's solution to the problem of fear and terror required individuals to agree to establish, and then to obey unconditionally, an absolute power. He named that state "Leviathan" to emphasize that the price of peace was the investiture of a power freed from the restraints of other institutions such as courts or parliaments. "There is nothing on earth," Hobbes wrote, "to be compared with him."

Leviathan was the first image of superpower and the first intimation of the kind of privatized citizen congenial with its requirements, the citizen who finds politics a distraction to be avoided, who if denied "a hand in public business," remains convinced that taking an active part means "to hate and be hated," "without any benefit," and "to neglect the affairs of [his] own family."[23] Hobbes had not only foreseen the power possibilities in the oxymoron of the private citizen, but exploited them to prevent sovereign power from being shared among its subjects. Hobbes reasoned that if individuals were protected in their interests and positively encouraged by the state to pursue them wholeheartedly, subject only to laws designed to safeguard them from the unlawful acts of others, then they would soon recognize that political participation was superfluous, expendable, not a rational choice. Hobbes's crucial assumption was that absolute power absolutely depended not just on fear, but on passivity. Civic indifference was thus elevated to a form of rational virtue, the sovereign having established and maintained the conditions of peace that enable individuals to pursue their own interests in the sure knowledge that the law of the sovereign would protect, even encourage them. Virtually unlimited power, on the one hand, and, on the other, an apolitical citizenry now assured of its security so that it can single-mindedly pursue private concerns: a perfect complementarity between apolitical absolutism and economic self-interest.

Hobbes insisted that the power of "that mortal god to which we owe under the immortal God, our peace and defence" could be instituted and endure only if legitimated—if, in other words, those it defended became willing collaborators, conscious accomplices. According to his argument extraordinary, concentrated power had to originate in the freely given consent of individuals: the sovereign could therefore claim that his act was that of their "Sovereign Representative," hence the act of the whole body of citizens.[24] His power was their power, the power they were to transfer to him who would protect them from what they most feared, not death itself but "violent death"—the kind of death visited upon Americans on September 11.[25] He was to have an absolute right to their bodies and their fortunes. In that "covenant" each would swear obedience and surrender to the sovereign his own power of self-defense and natural freedom. The consequence of the exchange was that the citizen reverted to the status of subject.[26] As subject he would receive protection as compensation for complicity in every future action of the sovereign.

Once the original covenant was adopted, the obligation to obey its authority was perpetual. There was no requirement for it to be periodically reaffirmed. The one exception to absolute obedience was that if the sovereign failed to protect the citizens, they were freed from their obligations toward him. That stipulation, far from tempering power, was an incitement for the sovereign to take advantage of any opportunity to extend his authority as far as circumstances allowed and all in the name of the security of his subjects.

The most striking aspect of Hobbes's argument was the increased potential of "fear" and "terror" for justifying unlimited power and authority. The "fear" and "terror" caused by external enemies did double duty, as it were. Not only did they serve to justify giving the sovereign all the power necessary to combat threats from abroad, but fear and terror could be made reflexive. Instead of being fearful only of foreign enemies, the citizenry, having observed the effects of extraordinary power used against foreigners, would become conditioned to fear its own sovereign, to hesitate before voicing criticism. By periodically reminding subjects of the example of his own unchecked actions and triumphs, the sovereign authority could convert fear and terror from a threat posed by foreigners into one more veiled and redirected against its own citizenry: "By this authority given him by every particular man in the commonwealth, he hath the use of so much power and strength conferred on him, that by terror thereof he is enabled to form the wills of them all, to peace at home and mutual aid against their enemies abroad."[27]

In anticipation of the 2004 presidential campaign a Bush aide described the strategy to be followed by the president as "a healthy mix of optimism and the fear factor."[28]

iii

It is tempting to dismiss Hobbes's account by arguing that in times of crisis American citizens should be willing to concede extraordinary powers to the state, secure in the knowledge that they retain safeguards against the danger of absolute authority and the abuse of power. According to this argument our Constitution places limits on authority, prescribing what it can and cannot do. The limits, in turn, are enforced by a system of checks and balances whereby each of our major institutions of Congress, the executive, and the judiciary is given authority to check the actions of the other branches. In addition, unlike Hobbes's stipulation that individual consent would be given once and for all time, our democratic system of periodic elections and of free political parties makes it possible to remove officeholders. Moreover, the Constitution guarantees to every citizen the right to criticize and organize opposition, and grants to the press and other media of communication the right to expose and criticize the actions of public officials.

Thus constitutional guarantees, a two-party system, institutionalized opposition, democratic elections, and a free press would seem formidable safeguards against the emergence of a Hobbesian sovereign. Unfortunately, in the aftermath of September 11 those guarantees have proved ineffectual.

A classic example was the charade that was played out shortly before the midterm elections of 2006. With the prospect of severe losses at the polls the Republican administration and its congressional supporters proposed a sweeping bill curtailing the rights of detainees, including those who were American citizens. The charade began when three prominent Republican senators, two of whom harbored presidential ambitions, assumed the lofty pose of protesting the provisions covering the interrogation techniques applied to detainees. They threatened to block the bill unless it respected the articles of the Geneva Conventions proscribing certain forms of torture. After much huffing, puffing, and public posturing they claimed that the White House had given in to their demands. When the bill was passed and its details made public, it was clear that the senators had participated in a shell game. The illusion was promoted that presidential power had been checked when in fact presidential authority was expanded. What they and sixty-two other senators had accepted was the most radical invasion of the rights of defendants since the Alien and Sedition laws of 1798. The act reduced the power of the courts to hear appeals from detainees and relied instead on military commissions to handle the cases—and this an obvious attempt to reverse the setback that the administration had received in the Hamdan case a few months earlier when the Supreme Court had struck down the military tribunals the administration had established following 9/11. The Court had held that the tribunals were in violation of the Constitution and of international law. The most striking provision of the new law denied detainees the right to habeas corpus and to challenge the legality of their detention. As for the Geneva Conventions and their prohibitions against torture, the law gave the president the authority to decide the meaning of the human rights treaties while relieving courts of jurisdiction over any appeals to his interpretation. Moreover, the provision also allowed the president to delegate that authority to (of all people) the secretary of defense. Yet during the political campaigns of fall 2006 neither party called attention to the law.

The sole form of protest against the preemptive war and the repressive policies of the administration took place not in the Congress, the courts, or an opposition party, but outside "official channels," in the streets where hundreds of thousands of ordinary citizens organized themselves to protest the actions of the administration. Equally striking, the administration consistently ignored the protesters. The major media, attentive to official cues, followed suit with belated, condescending, and minimal coverage.

iv

Two centuries after Hobbes had conceived of a superpower based upon democratic consent, and about a half century after the ratification of the U.S. Constitution, Alexis de Tocqueville published the final volume of *Democracy in America*. That work was the first comprehensive inquiry into the phenomenon of American democracy and, while not uncritical, was largely sympathetic and, on occasion, even admiring.[29] Toward the close of that work Tocqueville posed the question of how democracy might go wrong and what form a perverted democracy might take. Unlike Hobbes, whose theory of the absolute sovereign was inspired by the historical reality of an England whose political order had been shattered by revolution and civil war, Tocqueville imagines "the new features" of a despotism evolving naturally and peacefully out of a democracy.

> I see an innumerable crowd of like and equal men who revolve on themselves without repose, procuring the small and vulgar pleasures with which they fill their souls. Each of them, withdrawn and apart, is like a stranger to the destiny of all the others: his children and his particular friends form the whole human species for him; as for dwelling with his fellow citizens, he is beside them but he does not see them. . . .
>
> Above these an immense tutelary power is elevated, which alone takes charge of assuring their enjoyments and watching over their fate. It is absolute, detailed, regular, far-seeing, and mild. . . . It seeks only to keep [men] fixed irrevocably in childhood. . . . It provides for [the citizens'] security, foresees and secures their needs, facilitates their pleasures, conducts their principal affairs, directs their industry, regulates their estates, divides their inheritances; can it not take away from them entirely the trouble of thinking and the pain of living?
>
> Thus after taking each individual by turns in its powerful hands and kneading him as it likes, the sovereign extends its arms over society as a whole; it covers its surface with a network of small, complicated, painstaking uniform rules through which the most

original minds and the most vigorous souls cannot clear a way to surpass the crowd; it does not break wills, but it softens them, bends them, and directs them. . . . it does not destroy, it prevents things from being born; it does not tyrannize, it hinders, compromises, enervates, extinguishes, dazes, and finally reduces each nation to nothing more than a herd of timid and industrious animals of which the government is the shepherd.[30]

Tocqueville's democratic despotism might seem as far-fetched from contemporary America as Hobbes's Leviathan. Instead of embracing Big Brother and submitting to government regulations most Americans want government "off their backs." Far from meekly living in a drab condition of equality, the United States is a land where success is richly rewarded, so much so that it is at least as notable for its striking inequalities as for its professions of equal rights and equality before the law. Far from being passive Americans are renowned for their drive and inventiveness. In their high energy Americans more closely resemble Hobbes's chilling portrait of a man who cannot remain content "with moderate power" because "he cannot assure the power and means to live well, which he hath present, without the acquisition of more." If, as Hobbes claimed, there "is a general inclination of all mankind, a perpetual and restless desire of power after power that ceaseth only in death," how might that translate into the culture of state power?[31]

Tocqueville's democrat comfortable with despotism and Hobbes's free rationalist who opts for absolutism share an elective affinity. Tocqueville imagines a despotism made possible because citizens have chosen to relinquish participatory politics, which he had singled out as the most remarkable, widespread, and essential element of American political life. By abandoning their intense involvement with the common affairs of their communities in favor of personal ends they, like the signatories to Hobbes's contract, have chosen to be apolitical subjects rather than citizens.

v

The contemporary moral to be drawn from our detour through Hobbes and Tocqueville is this: while it may prove possible to mobilize voters around the slogan "Anything to beat Bush!" it takes more persistence,

more thoughtfulness to dismantle Superpower and to nurture a democratic citizenry. The lesson of Hobbes and Tocqueville can be boiled
down to a brief but chilling dictum: concentrated power, whether of a
Leviathan, a benevolent despotism, or a superpower, is impossible without the support of a complicitous citizenry that willingly signs on to the
covenant, or acquiesces, or clicks the "mute button."

CHAPTER FIVE

The Utopian Theory of Superpower: The Official Version

i

to show . . . the very age and body of
the time his form and pressure.
—*Shakespeare, Hamlet, 3.2.27*

We have to make it clear that we didn't just come [to Iraq]
to get rid of Saddam. We came to get rid of the status quo.
—*An official in the Bush administration*[1]

[W]e don't need anyone's permission.
—*President George W. Bush*[2]

Superpower is not just a system of aggrandizing power but an attempt at reconstituting the nation's identity. A compact statement of the ideology of Superpower was set out in *The National Security Strategy of the United States* of September 9, 2002 (hereafter NSS).[3] It represented the clearest formulation of the administration's understanding of the mission of Superpower and of its totalizing reach. The document is also the best evidence of the ideology promoting inverted totalitarianism. In the course of its claims one can clearly see the components on which a grandiose conception of power relies and the global ambitions that a Superpower alone could contemplate. In the end it provides a unique example of how hard-nosed realism can combine with utopianism at the expense of reality—among other casualties.

Utopia is usually associated with a soft-headed idealism that dreams of a time when the ills afflicting humankind—poverty, disease, strife—will have been eliminated. That understanding seriously underestimates the extent to which utopians have been fascinated by and dependent upon power for the realization of their hopes and dreams.

There have been three recurrent elements or prerequisites in many visions of utopia. One is that the founders of utopia possess some form of knowledge, some unquestionable truth, concerning what the right order of society should be, what should be the proper arrangement of its major institutions. The second element is that utopians must imagine it possible to possess the powers capable of establishing and realizing the utopian order. The third element is the opportunity of bringing utopia into existence and the skill in seizing and exploiting that moment. The NSS document embodies the first element, the blueprint, and suggests the second, the powers that seem to put utopia within reach. The third element, opportunity, was concocted in the preemptive war against Iraq.

ii

Depending on one's taste, the NSS document can be described as either forthright or crude; either way, there is no mistaking its single-minded concern and myth mentality. It begins by positing a conception of an expansive power that goes beyond previous understandings, and justifies it, not by an appeal to legal authority or political principle, but by a Manichaean myth that depicts two formations locked in a death struggle. One is the representative of absolute justice, the other of absolute injustice. On the one side, unprecedented but just power: "Today, the United States enjoys a position of unparalleled military strength and great economic and political influence"; on the other, "terrorists of global reach" who employ methods of violence devoid of justification: "premeditated, politically motivated violence perpetrated against innocents."[4] All of the might of one side is mustered to defend and avenge the innocents; all of the cunning of the other is dedicated to slashing, again and again, at the world's greatest power by attacking the innocent. Utopia versus Dystopia.

Does innocence mean not being implicated in wrongdoing such as torture of prisoners or the "collateral damage" to hapless civilians? And is it that the citizens are innocent but not their leaders? If that is the case, isn't the system closer to the dictatorships whose horrendous crimes were attributed solely, or overwhelmingly, to the leadership and not to the followers? Perhaps the answer is somewhere in between the categories of innocence and complicity. A clue is the frequency with which *NSS* invokes "we" to indicate that Superpower is a collaborative project. As citizens are we collaborationists? To collaborate is to cooperate; to be complicit is to be an accomplice.

iii

War is the state of affairs which deals in earnest with the
vanity of temporal goods and concerns.
—*G.W.F. Hegel*[5]

Because "the struggle against global terrorism" is declared to be "different from any other war in our history," it crowds out all other distinctions, reducing politics to one focal point, a politics fixated upon a single foe, mobilized to combat an enemy unlike any encountered previously, "a new condition of life." Exhilarated by the prospect of a contest between good and evil, as confident of its own rectitude as it is of the unalloyed evil of its foe, *NSS* offers assurance that our society will emerge invigorated from the contest with terrorists: "We will adjust to it and thrive—in spite of it."[6]

While declaring terrorism a unique phenomenon, the author(s) of *NSS* hasten to fill the vacuum left by earlier contests with evil powers.

For most of the twentieth century, the world was divided by a great struggle over ideas: destructive totalitarian visions versus freedom and equality.

The great struggle is over. The militant visions of class, nation, and race which promised utopia and delivered misery have been defeated and discredited.[7]

In fact, the totalitarian systems of Hitler and Mussolini, far from promising utopia, had demanded endless heroic sacrifices from their populaces. Utopianism, far from being discredited, reemerges in those who wield America's power. Its manifesto is in the opening sentence of the NSS document: "The great struggles of the twentieth century between liberty and totalitarianism ended with a decisive victory for the forces of freedom—and a single sustainable model for national success: freedom, democracy, and free enterprise."[8] That "single sustainable model" embodies the new utopianism and has its own breathless version of totalizing power: "the United States will use this moment of opportunity to extend the benefits of freedom across the globe. We will actively work to bring the hope of democracy, development, free markets, and free trade to every corner of the world."[9]

As the vision unfolds, it reveals, if unwittingly, how "democracy, development, free markets, and free trade" will converge to further their opposites and the ambitions of Superpower.

The Nazis and Fascists exalted strength and domination and were contemptuous of weakness; the new utopians are proud of their unparalleled strength but, paradoxically, feel threatened by weakness in others: "The events of September 11, 2001, taught us that weak states, like Afghanistan, can pose as great a danger to our national interests as strong states. . . . [P]overty, weak institutions, and corruption can make weak states vulnerable to terrorist networks and drug cartels within their borders." The power that will come to the aid of weak states is identified with the particular "freedoms" which the new utopians are eager to promote: "Free trade and free markets have proven their ability to lift whole societies out of poverty."

The freedoms being dangled before the unfree are, in reality, disguised power. Free trade and free markets in the hands of the already powerful are not symmetrical with free trade and markets in the hands of "weak" societies. Instead, the effect upon the poor nations of opting for them invariably turns simple weakness into dependence on those nations whose economies have made them dominant powers and who, accordingly, have the right to declare a state weak and call its performance to account. "For freedom to thrive, accountability must be expected and required."[10] Thus when the NSS document presents the "free market" as one of the three constituent elements of the ideal political system, the market is a surrogate, a stand-in for globalization/empire.

Thus freedom is granted conditionally and performance is account-able to the power that makes freedom possible. What began as the challenge posed by terrorism becomes conflated into "a great mission" that comprehends virtually all of the world's ills and, in the process, inflates national power into global power:

> Throughout history, freedom has been threatened by war and ter-ror; it has been challenged by the clashing wills of powerful states and the evil designs of tyrants and it has been tested by widespread poverty and disease. Today, humanity holds in its hands the oppor-tunity to further freedom's triumph over all these foes. The United States welcomes our responsibility to lead in this great mission.[11]

The new utopians, while proclaiming that the United States must exercise power commensurate with the demands of its campaign against terrorism and the global mission of reconstituting the world's economies, insist that Superpower will be devoted to reducing the power of the state universally. "The lessons of history are clear: market economies, not command-and-control economies with the heavy hand of government, are the best way to promote prosperity and reduce pov-erty. Policies that further strengthen market incentives and market insti-tutions are relevant for all economies—industrialized countries, emerg-ing markets, and the developing world."[12]

Taken at face value, the pronouncement devaluing the state seems at cross-purposes with the utopian aim of reconstructing societies in "every corner of the world." What kind of power is it that, in effect, can reconstruct the world without employing "the heavy hand of govern-ment," and what kind of power is being contemplated that is both ef-fective and nongovernmental? The questions become unsettling in light of the original goal of combating, without necessarily eradicat-ing, global terrorism. "Modern life," we are warned, is particularly "vulnerable," and that "vulnerability" "will persist long after we bring to justice those responsible for the September eleventh attacks."[13] Terrorism, then, is the kind of problem which can be viewed in two ways that are not mutually exclusive: where there is not even a promise of light at the end of the tunnel or where there is endless opportunity for investment.

Light-handed government in regard to economic policy—a conception that might be termed "antipolitical economy"—and heavy-handed state power to fight terrorism: the two represent a unique power combination. In the economies of contemporary capitalist societies relationships reek of unequal power, but dominant powers differ from those of the government or state. Great corporations attribute their immense resources to the fact that they are able to operate free from state interference. One might, of course, cite endless examples of government favors and subsidies ("corporate welfare"); moreover, the global power that, for a domestic audience, decries state intervention into the economy has not hesitated countless times to lift its heavy hand abroad and to intervene, even to covertly subvert, when some free society's elected representatives have opted for elements of socialism, such as government ownership and operation of a nation's extensive petroleum resources: vide Guatemala (1964), Chile (1971), Nicaragua (1980s), or Venezuela, Brazil, and Bolivia (2003). Perhaps, then, free trade and free markets, while meant to restrain government intervention in foreign countries, actually extend the global power of the United States, although not the power of the U.S. government as such. "Free trade" and "free markets" expose weaker, less economically developed societies to the highly advanced forms of economic power wielded by corporations and tacitly backed by American political and military power. Against superior economic might native governments are largely defenseless.

Nor, in the NSS formulation, is U.S. power abroad to be restricted to military or economic matters. Unilaterally, the United States declares it is justified in reconstructing the infrastructure of other societies. "As humanitarian relief requirements are better understood, we must also be able to help build police forces, court systems and legal codes, local and provincial governmental institutions, and electoral systems."[14]

Iraq proved this to be no idle boast. That country was fated to be selected as a testing ground for the ambitious forces assembled under Superpower. The test took the form of a catch-22. First the display of the awesome destructive power, the "shock and awe" and "bunker busters" made possible by science and technology. Then, having employed weapons of mass destruction to smash and disrupt the economy and society of Iraq in order to prevent Saddam from using his nonexistent weapons of mass destruction, Superpower attempted to close the circle by applying the power of the free market to the reconstruction of the infrastructure it had shattered. The most redoubtable corporate powers—Bechtel, Halliburton, the Carlyle Group—entered the newly established "free" market from which Russian, French, and Canadian business firms were initially excluded because of their opposition to the preemptive war.[15] Presumably Micronesia, which had joined "the coalition of the willing," was free to compete.

In order to fulfill the role envisaged by NSS the political power of the United States has to be conceived in imperial rather than constitutional terms. Accordingly, "It is essential to reaffirm the essential role of American military strength." This requires "defenses beyond challenge" and "dissuad[ing] future military competition"—"competition" signifying the integration of the military as a permanent part of the market economy and the expansion of the market to accommodate "corporate warriors" and a thriving private security industry.[16] Security for securities . . .

An unchallengeable military power, not a merely preeminent one, means that "the United States will require bases and stations within and beyond Western Europe and Northeast Asia, as well as temporary access for the long-distance deployment of U.S. forces." The power needed must defend not only "critical U.S. infrastructure" but also "assets in outer space."[17] Like Tocqueville's benevolent despot, the United States reassures the world that it will act "with a spirit of humility."[18]

iv

There is one master theme whose frequent recurrence supplies the overall context for the several concerns and proposals in the NSS document. The "dangerous technologies" acquired by terrorists demand that "America . . . act against such emerging threats before they are fully formed."

While the United States will constantly strive to enlist the support
of the international community, we will not hesitate to act alone,
if necessary, to exercise our right of self-defense by acting preemptively against such terrorists, to prevent them from doing harm
against our people and our country. . . . The greater the threat, the
greater is the risk of inaction—and the more compelling the case
for taking anticipatory action to defend ourselves, even if uncertainty remains as to the time and place of the enemy's attack. . . .
We will be prepared to act apart (from friends and partners) when
our interests and unique responsibilities require.[19]

In order to act preemptively and to call attention to its might, Superpower exempts itself from the constraints of treaties, such as the Anti-
Ballistic Missile Treaty. Although the United States often turns over war
criminals of other nations to international tribunals, its own officials or
agents "are not [to be] impaired by the potential for investigations, inquiry, or prosecution by the International Criminal Court whose jurisdiction does not extend to Americans and which we do not accept."[20]
Since state and corporate power have become increasingly intertwined,
that composite identity requires that the renunciation of restraints is also
extended to treaties, such as the Kyoto Accords intended to control
global warming, the rationale being that they impose an unacceptable
burden on American economic enterprises.[21] The unspoken assumption
is that a burden on American enterprise detracts from American power.

　The totalizing impulses underlying the drive to be rid of restraints
are not limited to the projection of power abroad. For, while terrorists
have their networks based outside the borders of the United States, their
targets are inside the country. Accordingly, state power must pursue
them by projecting power internally, the power that, in keeping with
Hobbesian logic, casts off external restraints whenever and wherever
the necessity arises. The justification for increased domestic powers is
that "the distinction between domestic and foreign affairs is diminish-
ing." "In a globalized world" we are affected by events outside our borders; more important, because "our society must be open to people,
ideas, and goods from across the globe," we are inherently vulnerable
to terrorist attacks.[22]

The vanishing line between foreign and domestic is crucial because of the contention that constraints on power in domestic matters ought not to carry over to foreign affairs, especially when military action is involved.[23] This claim might seem to be an appeal to the old doctrine of "reason of state," which asserted that when issues of war and diplomacy were at stake, those who were responsible for the safety of the nation should be allowed a freer hand, greater discretionary power, to meet external threats without being hampered by the uncertainty attending the cumbersome and time-consuming legitimating processes of legislatures or courts.

In fact, the NSS doctrine goes beyond the old reason of state. It places reason of state in the context of terrorism, that is, in a context which, by the administration's definition of terrorism, knows no boundaries, spatial or temporal. The reason-of-state argument for discretionary power had assumed a demarcation between matters of war and diplomacy, where state actors would have a comparatively freer hand, and matters of internal governance, where they would be subject to ordinary constraints.[24] The war on terrorism, with its accompanying emphasis upon "homeland security," presumes that state power, now inflated by doctrines of preemptive war and released from treaty obligations and the potential constraints of international judicial bodies, can turn inwards, confident that in its domestic pursuit of terrorists the powers it claimed, like the powers it had projected abroad, would be measured, not by ordinary constitutional standards, but by the shadowy and ubiquitous character of terrorism as officially defined. The Hobbesian line between the state of nature and civil society begins to waver.

v

It is not only the line between foreign and domestic matters that is being blurred but the distinction between economic and political power. Once upon a time it was believed that in a democracy the power of the government was derived from a citizenry who, by the political duty of participating in politics and exercising their political rights, transmitted a distinctively political character to governmental authority that served to justify its exercise of power. Now, however, the power of government is not an emanation of the *political* power of the citizens. Rather government appears as autonomous, distanced from the citizens because the power of the citizenry is given a sharply different focus: not as political power expressive of the will of engaged citizens but as "political and economic freedom" which ensures that the *nation* "will be able to unleash the potential of their people and assure their future prosperity." Political involvement is reduced to minimal, anodyne terms: "People everywhere want to say what they think; choose who will govern them; worship as they please; educate their children—male and female; own property; and enjoy the benefits of their labor."[25] Quietly, economic mobilization is accompanied by a de-emphasis on politics, by a political demobilization. That unthreatening ideal inspires the peroration to NSS, where economy supersedes the political and is designated the real basis of national security:

> Ultimately, the foundation of American strength is at home. It is in the skills of our people, the dynamism of our economy, and the resilience of our institutions. A diverse, modern society has inherent, ambitious, entrepreneurial energy. Our strength comes from what we do with that energy. That is where our national security begins.[26]

This statement represents the clear admission that the American economy is acknowledged to be more than a system of providing goods and services. It is, in its own right, a system of power that deserves to be considered as much a part of the "foundation" of political society as the institutions prescribed by the Constitution. The consecration of economy means that in the trinity of "freedom, democracy, and free enterprise" the three elements are not of equal standing. Freedom and democracy are clearly subservient to free enterprise, a relationship that, by providing "cover" for the political incorporation of the corporation, assumes great significance in light of the fact that the economic structures defining free enterprise are inherently autocratic, hierarchical, and primed for expansion. When the claims and needs of the economy trump the political, and bring in their wake strikingly unequal rewards and huge disparities in wealth and power, inequality trumps demo-cratic egalitarianism.

The later transformation of the market, from one of small-scale pro-ducers into one dominated by large corporations and monopolies and near monopolies, lent a new meaning to market "forces." The market was now the site of great powers: powers that determined prices, wages, patterns of consumption, the well-being or poverty of individuals, the fate of entire neighborhoods, cities, states, and nations. Several of the larger corporations possess wealth rivaling or exceeding that of many of the smaller nations of the world. The power of great corporations underwent further change toward the end of the twentieth century when corporate power conjoined with state power. The "market" ceased to be an entity distinct from, and contrasting with, state power, becoming its extension—and vice versa, becoming the "hidden hand" in "public" policies.

Once the hybrid or dual nature of contemporary state action is un-derstood, it is possible to put in their true light the coupling in NSS of "freedom" and "democracy" with "free enterprise." The porous charac-ter that freedom and democracy create in society—"our society must be open," as NSS noted, "to people, ideas, and goods from across the globe"—provides the conditions that enable the economic power gen-erated in the market to easily penetrate and control politics. Freedom and democracy, far from posing a threat to "free enterprise," become its instrument and its justification. And rather than serving as the means for furthering the political project of democratization, the state helps to inter it.

vi

It is one of the consequences of aggression that it hardens
the conscience, as the only means of quieting it.
—*James Fenimore Cooper*, The Deerslayer[27]

The test case of the NSS doctrine is Iraq, its utopian opportunity. There all the might of Superpower was mobilized in defiance of world opinion; there the great corporate giants of the American economy were poised to reconstruct the Iraqi economy according to the principles of the free market; and there the corporate warriors, well-paid and armed with the latest weaponry, were gearing up to join forces with the American military largely composed of young men and women from working-class and recent immigrant backgrounds who had enlisted, not to fight a war, but to improve their economic status or finance a college education otherwise unattainable.

And, despite the blueprint for a new democratic Middle East, the power of modern technology and corporate resources straining to exploit Iraq, and the pretext that was supposed to provide the opportunity, Superpower failed. Instead of achieving conquest, it provoked an insurgency that left Iraq virtually ungovernable and close to being uninhabitable; instead of dealing terrorism a damaging blow, it exacerbated the problem and multiplied the ranks of the enemy; instead of seeing the world cowering before its might, Superpower faced a world where many governments and their peoples found common ground in opposing the United States.

In Iraq Superpower succeeded only in providing the answer to the plaintive question of 9/11, "Why do they hate us?"

vii

In attempting to explain the debacle of Iraq several commentators have pointed to the highly ideological group of "neoconservatives" who, it is alleged, had long been dreaming of a new order in the Middle East and were only waiting for an opportune moment. Although the neocon factor matters, there is a far more significant and ominous source encouraging the hubris of Superpower. The Superpower revealed in Iraq was quintessentially power without legitimacy, as was demonstrated by every claim that Saddam was linked to al Qaeda and that he possessed weapons of mass destruction. The shabby and unverifiable arguments, especially those before the UN, were unconvincing precisely because everyone was aware that Superpower had long since made up its mind. Superpower made no secret that its preparations for invasion were under way and that no amount of argument would persuade the American leaders to abandon or significantly postpone their plans. Superpower's operatives no more needed the consent of the UN than they needed an accurate counting of ballots in the presidential election of 2000. The moment when the breaking of limits and the subsequent assertion of expansive powers suddenly became possible was that moment when political and constitutional legitimacy was cynically discarded and George II was crowned. Much became possible that previously was unthinkable or, if thinkable, then done surreptitiously: class-based tax cuts,[28] the undermining of decades of environmental safeguards, the crude collusion with corporate power, the decimation of social programs benefiting the poor, the steady dismantling of the "wall" separating church and state, the nomination of highly ideological candidates for judicial appointment. In short, Iraq had its origins in Florida: there power without legitimacy was first envisioned. That was when power brokers found that, if sufficiently determined, they could overcome the inhibitions of democratic constitutionalism.

CHAPTER SIX

The Dynamics of Transformation

i

A decent society will not go to war except for a just cause.
But what it will do during a war will depend to a certain
extent on what the enemy—possibly an absolutely
unscrupulous and savage one—forces it to do. There are
no limits which can be defined in advance, there are no
assignable limits to what might become just reprisals. . . .
But societies are not only threatened from without.
Considerations which might apply to foreign enemies
may well apply to subversive elements within society.
—*Leo Strauss*[1]

One of the oldest political platitudes teaches that political systems can experience changes of such magnitude and velocity that their identity is altered, literally trans-formed. The city-states of ancient Greece underwent frequent and often dizzying transformations, from cities governed by aristocracies to ones run by those characterized as democrats; Athenian democracy transformed itself into an empire and the Roman republic did the same; eventually both Athenian democracy and the Roman republic disappeared, eviscerated by their own expansionism. Seventeenth-century England went full cycle in little more than two decades, from monarchy to rule by Parliament to the dictatorship of Cromwell to the restoration of the monarchy. For France, beginning in the last quarter of the eighteenth century, it is difficult to count the number of different political identities following the Revolution of 1789 and continuing throughout the nineteenth century into the twentieth. There were periods of dictatorship, a first empire under Napoleon, restoration of a monarchy combined with a parliament, a second empire and dictatorship under Louis Napoleon, then a series of republics interrupted in the twentieth century by the Vichy dictatorship (1940–44) sponsored by and beholden to the Nazis.

Nor is American experience an exception. The thirteen colonies were originally part of the British Empire; the colonial system was overthrown by a confederation of the former colonies; it was succeeded by a new federal system and national government that would be challenged in the next century by a secessionist movement that culminated in a civil war and two systems of government. Throughout the nineteenth century the structure, even the form, of the American system, including its politics, was continually changing as new states from the Midwest, Southwest, and West, some with cultures strikingly different from that of the eastern states, were admitted—and all this against the background of Indian "wars," the first chapter in the national commitment to eradicating terrorists while extending the reach of its government.

Perhaps Americans tend to accept, even welcome, change while resisting the idea of transformation. Change suggests a modification that retains a prior "deeper" identity. Transformation implies supersession, or submergence, of an old identity and the acquisition of a new one. Between the two poles of change and transformation there is a third possibility in which transformation occurs yet the older form is preserved. Thus throughout most of its history England (and later the United Kingdom) preserved the trappings of monarchy after having long since hollowed out its substance.

Change is the rule rather than the exception: that platitude is easy for Americans to acknowledge when applied, say, to the economy or to "lifestyles." Americans, accustomed to, even insistent upon, continuous progress in scientific knowledge and innovative technology, assume that their main political institutions, the Constitution, and the protections of citizenship are firmly established and admirably difficult to amend. They believe, perhaps with a trace of desperation, that their fundamentalist view of the Constitution is vindicated because the United States is "the world's oldest continuous democracy." Although Americans recognize that their politics is changing, as the presence and influence of television continually reminds them, they shy away from transformation when "basic" political forms are involved for fear of rendering identities problematic, the nation's as well as their own. And, equally important, they have become blindly accepting of the notion that whatever is pronounced "outdated" or relegated to the "past" is no longer recoverable. There is no going back: an identity, such as "democracy," once lost is gone forever.

When terms like "American superpower," "American empire," or "the greatest power in history" acquire a certain notoriety, as they did during the controversy over the invasion of Iraq, the sheer dissonance produced by the effort to comprehend oxymorons such as "superpower democracy" or "imperial constitution" raises the possibility that a different type of political system is evolving within the familiar framework. Instead of a system in which governmental powers are measured by a constitution of enumerated powers, there appears to be an expansive conception of power and a triumphalist ideology alien to the Constitution. Despite its "exceptionalism," or perhaps because of it, the United States may be undergoing a political transformation that includes not only significantly different political and civic identities but also a different kind of politics. The distance between Superpower's claims of global hegemony and democracy's ideal of self-government has been bridged by the concept of "managed democracy," which acquired some currency in connection with the reconstruction of Iraq. Superpower and managed democracy might comfortably coexist. It is, as a pastorly president might put it, a match made in heaven.

Before we consider the changes that promote Superpower's managed democracy, it is worth bearing in mind that, from ancient times to the end of the eighteenth century, when political theorists referred to constitutional transformations they were not primarily concerned with alterations in the "basic" laws except as these registered shifts in the distribution of power. That focus led to attempts at identifying the sources of political reconfigurations, some of which might have originated within the system of power (e.g., the legislature reduces kingship to a ceremonial figurehead), but, more often, transformations were attributed to developments originating "outside" the formal system (e.g., the rise of a merchant or industrial class that challenged the ruling landed aristocracy and demanded representation in the councils of governance; or conquest by a foreign power and the imposition of a new system, as in Japan after World War II). In general, while a constitution may "constitute" power by creating institutional authorities virtually de novo—as in the invention of the presidency and the Supreme Court—more often it demonstrates flexibility by recognizing and investing de facto power with authority—as when, in 1933, the Weimar Reichstag declared Hitler to be chancellor (or prime minister) but only after changing the law that had declared Austrians ineligible for the office.

A constitution, or rather its authoritative interpretation, may be made to legitimate powers originating elsewhere: in the changing character of class relations, economic structures, social mores, ideological and theological doctrines, or the emergence of powerful social movements (e.g., opposition to abortion rights). A constitution may also serve as the means of deflecting external powers: for example, a supreme court may zealously turn back "attacks" on property rights and business interests from the regulatory powers of state legislatures, as happened from roughly 1871 to 1914 in the United States. To cite another example: challenges to racial segregation were resisted by all branches of government and the two major political parties until the mid-twentieth century. Here transformation was resisted in favor of tactical acquiescence in change that, while acknowledging the emergence of new forces, signals adaptation to, not necessarily reconstitution of, the dominant powers.

In theory a constitution prescribes a distinctive organization of power (e.g., a constitutional monarchy or a republic) and identifies the purposes for which power can be used legitimately. A constitutional form lends power shape, definition, and a genealogy ("We, the People . . . do ordain and establish this Constitution"). The portent of transformation is a lack of fit between power and authority. Authority sanctions, authorizes, the use of power ("The Congress shall have power to lay and collect taxes") and sets limits ("but all duties, imposts and excises shall be uniform throughout the United States" (art. I, sec. 8, cl. 1). Yet, while Congress alone has the authority to declare war (art. I, sec. 8, cl. 11), that power was, in effect, preempted by the president in the war on Iraq, and Congress meekly capitulated.

The technology of power, however, evolves more or less independently of constitutional conceptions of authority. In a society that strongly encourages technological innovation, definitions of constitutional authority tend to lag well behind the actual means of power and their capabilities. For example, the so-called war powers authorized by the American Constitution are invoked to justify the use of "weapons of mass destruction" capable of inflicting death and misery upon thousands of noncombatants, among them the populations of Dresden and Hiroshima. A war power may be authorized by a constitution drawn up more than two centuries ago, but "advances in weaponry" have altered dramatically the meaning of warfare without formally rewriting the authorization to use them.

What does it mean to be "victorious" in the age of "shock and awe," nuclear weapons, and global terrorism, or to "defend the nation" when it has become an empire? It is possible that the powers available to twenty-first-century rulers and to their terrorist foes are such as to outstrip the ability of fallible mortals to control their effects—and that may be what the jargon of "collateral damage" serves to obscure. When a constitutionally limited government utilizes weapons of horrendous destructive power, subsidizes their development, and becomes the world's largest arms dealer, the Constitution is conscripted to serve as power's apprentice rather than its conscience.

Such considerations expose an underlying assumption of our Constitution. At the time of its formulation, the authors, as well as those who ratified the final document, naturally assumed that in the future the weapons of destruction would not be radically different from existing ones. But while it is in Superpower's interest that the Constitution should appear unchanging, the technology of war has been revolutionized. The likely consequence of that imbalance is suggested in the summary remarks by the authors of a mainstream textbook in constitutional law:

> The circumstances of nuclear warfare would, not improbably, bring about the total supplantation for an indefinite period of the forms of constitutional government by the drastic procedures of military government.[2]

Accordingly, we need to broaden our definition of Superpower: power unanticipated by a constitutional mandate *and* exceeding the political abilities and moral sensibilities of those who employ it. Superpower does not automatically guarantee super(wo)men, only outsized temptations and ambitions.

The formlessness of "Superpower" and "empire" that accompanies concentrated power of indefinite limits is subversive of the idea of constitutional democracy. Although, strictly speaking, traditional accounts of political forms do not anticipate superpower, some writers, notably Niccolò Machiavelli (1469–1527) and James Harrington (1611–77), proposed a distinction between a political system content to preserve itself rather than expand and a political system, such as that of ancient Rome, eager to "increase" its power and domain.[3] Applying that distinction, we might say that the United States combines both. In the view of those who venerate the "original Constitution," the Founders had established a government of limited powers and modest ambitions. The constitution of Superpower, in contrast, is meant for "increase."[4] It is based not on the intentions of the framers but on the unlimited dynamic embodied in the system whereby capital, technology, and science furnish the sources of power. Accordingly, when certain reformers, such as environmental activists and anticloning advocates, seek to use constitutional authority to control the powers associated with the "constitution for increase" (e.g., regulating nuclear power plants or cloning labs) they find their efforts blocked by those who invoke the conception of a constitution as one of limited authority. But typically when representatives of the "constitution for increase" press for favors from those who man the "constitution for preservation," they get their way. While Superpower's constitution is shaped toward ever-increasing power, but has no inherent political authority, the constitution for preservation has limited authority while its actual power is dependent upon those who operate the constitution for increase. The two constitutions—one for expansion, the other for containment—form the two sides of inverted totalitarianism.

ii

Only who has the bigger pot, who controls more money than the other. There are no values in this election. There are no principles. It's only who gets power. Nothing more. It's a shame.
—*A Nigerian pro-democracy activist commenting on Nigerian elections of 2003*[5]

If Superpower signifies form-free power, sophisticated and "advanced," at the disposal of those who govern in the name of constitutional democracy, it cannot mean, practically or theoretically, "government by the people." Not practically because the global "responsibilities" of Superpower are incompatible with participatory governance; not theoretically, because the powers that make Superpower formidable do not derive either from constitutional authority or from "the people." Stated more strongly, the condition for the ascendance of Superpower is the weakening or irrelevance of democracy and constitutionalism—except as mystifications enabling Superpower to fake a lineage that gives it legitimacy.

The crucial event exposing how deeply political deterioration had penetrated the system was the Florida recount in the presidential election of 2000. That event also provided a glimpse into the inverted totalitarian character of Superpower. Unlike the crude plebiscites of the Nazis with their yes-or-no choice and atmosphere of latent violence, the recount, while it was accompanied by some intimidation of voters, relied mainly on tactics that made it difficult for the poor and African Americans to deal with the ballot or even to find their proper polling place. Once the polls closed, the slanted process began: actual counting and decisions about which ballots qualified were supervised by a loyal Republican official whose politico-mathematical correctness was later rewarded by elevation to a safe seat in the U.S. Congress. Then the high-powered legal talents and public relations experts took over, fought the case through the Florida Supreme Court, and appealed to the U.S. Supreme Court. There a pliant judiciary hurriedly produced a contorted justification for a manipulated result. What was striking was not so much the highly coordinated attack on the system of democratic elections by the Bush loyalists as the feebleness of opposition.[6]

A healthy democracy would have ignited the opposition party in Congress to denounce the coup and contest its legitimacy for as long as necessary. Throughout the nation there should have been massive protests, even a general strike and acts of civil disobedience, at the cynical subversion of elections, the one nonnegotiable supposition of a democracy. Instead, an illegitimate president took office amidst scarcely a ripple of discontent.[7] The masters of the ceremony and the media ensured that the inauguration was made to seem like all previous ones: authority was transferred, continuity preserved, as the former president, whom for all practical political purposes the Republicans had earlier destroyed, looked on: constitutional democracy is dead; long live the president.

The Florida events reveal concisely how inverted totalitarianism operates and, without ceasing to be totalitarian, differs from classic totalitarianism. The uniquely inverted character of the totalitarian coup was that, while tacit racism and class discrimination informed the proceedings, at no point was there a latent threat of violence; nor did the media respond with a chorus of support for the result. Instead they made a circus of the events—one act after another—and once the Supreme Court had spoken, they dropped the series, leaving the public with an impression that a hiccup had occurred, and with the unintentionally sardonic reassurance that "continuity" remained unbroken. In contrast to the postmortem on the Watergate scandal, assurance that "the system had worked," such a verdict after Florida would be an expression of black (*sic*) humor.

In the saga of the Florida recount was a clear demonstration of managed democracy. Earlier I referred to Superpower as "formless." That requires amending: Florida demonstrated that Superpower indeed has a form, and, moreover, revealed its lineaments. Unlike all traditional conceptions of a constitutional form, where the *political* character was primary and defining, Superpower represents a substantive transformation. A corporate or economic model of governance has been superimposed upon a political form whose constitution consisted partly of republican, antipopulist elements and partly of democratic elements. The Florida recount was as much an example of a corporate takeover as of a coup d'état. In the new model the presidency bears little resemblance to the original conception of a national leader and chief executive; it owes even less to the later ideal of the president as "the tribune of the people." Instead the office is modeled after the corporate CEO. The president is neither above politics nor is he a popular tribune, although if circumstance requires, he may momentarily assume those stances. Rather his role is, in part, to protect and advance the economic and ideological interests that form the dynamic of Superpower. (These will be discussed in chapter 7.) But the president is also what might be called a cinemythological figure, the embodiment of a popular myth constructed of Hollywood movies: the genial patriarch (Reagan) or the straight-shooting defender of order (George II).[8] Underneath the myths the president, like the CEO, is the dominant power in the organization. In contrast, Congress, which was once thought to be the predominant branch of government because it supposedly stood "closer to the people," has been demoted to a position of power comparable to that of a corporate board. The latter tend to be creatures of the CEO rather than the independent supervisory power to which the CEO is theoretically responsible. Like a board, Congress may occasionally display independence, especially when it and the president represent opposing parties. But the main point is that Congress has lost its close connection with the citizenry. Poll after poll has shown that, of all national political institutions, it ranks lowest in terms of public confidence. Finally, in the image of shareholders, who wield small power over their CEOs or boards and are stirred to protest only when dividends disappoint, so the citizenry has embraced a diminished role. Like shareholders they can vote out their own CEO, the president, or their board of directors, Congress, but mostly they want to be assured that the CEO-president is "heading the country in the right direction."

iii

The virtual unanimity of Congress and the initial broad public support for the second Gulf War are a measure of how recent is the decay of our representative institutions and of the political consciousness of the citizenry. We have forgotten the great divisions over the first Gulf War (1991) when a conservative such as Senator Sam Nunn of Georgia, long a supporter of the armed forces, opposed it. A poll of June 1991 found that 46 percent of Americans would approve of war if Iraq did not withdraw from Kuwait by January 15, while 47 percent thought that the United States should wait longer for sanctions and other forms of pressure to work.[9]

Even more striking was the contrast between, on the one hand, the passivity of Congress and of the Democratic "opposition" party in the weeks preceding the buildup and directly following the invasion of Iraq

(April 2003) and, on the other, the determined opposition during the 1960s and 1970s to the Vietnam War and the invasion of Cambodia. In that earlier crisis Congress made strenuous efforts to regain some of the ground it had lost by supinely condoning an undeclared war. It proceeded to condemn the invasion of Cambodia by cutting off funds for the bombing. Although Nixon's subsequent veto of the bill was sustained, Congress continued to press the matter until the president agreed to end the bombing by a specific date and to consult with Congress should further action be necessary. Throughout 1973 members of Congress continued to petition the courts in an effort to halt the bombing. Finally, late in 1973 Congress overrode a presidential veto and enacted the War Powers Resolution, which reasserted the role of Congress in the decision to go to war.[10]

While Congress was pressing its case for regaining its lost constitutional authority over war making, its efforts were supported by continuing demonstrations across the nation, especially on college campuses, and by a passionate national debate over the war. Not only did democracy come to life in the decade of the sixties and early seventies, but the parallel resistance by Congress underscored the true meaning of "constitutional democracy." Concurrent with popular debate all across the nation, much of it improvised, there was the formal institutional opposition by Congress. The union of two powers, one populist and uninstitutionalized, the other representative and institutional: *constitutional democracy*.

Small wonder that ever since those days conservatives and hawks have waged their own relentless "culture war" against the sixties. The effort to overcome "the Vietnam syndrome" involved more than a wish to exorcise the shame of a military defeat; it aimed to discredit the democratic and constitutional impulses of that era as well, an aim consistent with totalitarianism, inverted or not.[11] As the legatee of that campaign George II remarked, "Sometimes I listen to the American people and sometimes I don't." A democracy evoked at the whim of its highest elected official cannot count for much.

That the Congress and administration ignored the massive protests throughout the nation did not invalidate the fact that a rump democracy persisted, even flourished, "outside" the Washington system—in "the streets" and the more than one hundred city councils throughout the nation that passed resolutions opposing the invasion of Iraq.

The Iraq war of 2003 is symptomatic rather than paradigmatic. The seriousness of the situation goes beyond the slowly growing opposition to the war. One cannot point to any national institution(s) that can accurately be described as democratic: surely not in the highly managed, money-saturated elections, the lobby-infested Congress, the imperial presidency, the class-biased judicial and penal system, or, least of all, the media.

iv

To identify the antecedents of inverted totalitarianism, we must bear in mind that throughout much of the past century the American political system was repeatedly subjected to the strains and pressures of war. During the twentieth century war became normalized.

To reiterate, the century saw major conventional wars: the two world wars, Korea, and Vietnam. And other conflicts abounded: the small war against Filipinos fighting for their independence (1911); the war against Mexican revolutionaries (1913–14); the armed occupation of Siberia (1918–21), which tacitly was a war against the Bolshevik Revolution; invasions of the Dominican Republic, Grenada, and Panama; the Gulf War of 1991; the war against terrorism declared in 2001; and the war against Iraq (2003). And, of course, the invention of a "cold war."

Wars, especially undeclared ones, invariably boost the powers and status of the president as commander-in-chief. Just as surely war presses Congress and the courts to "defer" to the wishes and judgments of the chief executive. A president, however feckless or unimposing, is transformed, rendered larger than life. He becomes the supreme commander, the unchallengeable leader and the nation incarnate.

The Second World War marked a particularly notable moment in the evolution of expanding American power. The Roosevelt administration measured its wartime powers against the challenge posed by a totalitarian system that made no secret of its aim to control as much of the globe as possible.[12] The defeat of totalitarianism demanded the creation of a "home front" and "total mobilization." It was necessary, so the justification ran, "to fight fire with fire." "Universal" (i.e., male) military conscription was instituted; the economy was controlled by government "planning" directed toward prescribed production goals, prohibited from producing most consumer goods, and subjected to central allocation of vital materials. The labor force, for all practical purposes, was conscripted: its mobility was restricted, wages and prices were fixed, while collective bargaining was put on hold. Food and fuel were rationed, censorship was introduced, and the government undertook to wage a propaganda war, enlisting radio, newspapers, and the movie industry in the single purpose of winning the war. There was an all-enveloping atmosphere of apprehension: uniformed soldiers everywhere, warnings about spies, news censorship, propaganda films, heroic war movies, patriotic music, casualty figures. As a leading constitutional scholar warned shortly after the end of World War II, "The effects of the impact of total war on the Constitution will . . . become embedded in the peacetime Constitution."[13]

Strikingly, in the post-1945 wars, whether hot or cold, warfare became normal, incorporated into ordinary life without transforming it. No attempt was made to reintroduce the kinds of controls and mobilization that had temporarily brought the system closer to a total system. Costly long wars as in Korea (1951–54), Vietnam (1961–73), the shorter first Gulf War (1991), and now Iraq have been prosecuted without imposing economic hardships, only some inconveniences, never U.S. civilian casualties.[14] Korea and Vietnam were not even "declared wars" as the Constitution required. After 1945 wars acquired a certain abstract quality. They were, in a popular phrase, "distant wars" that no longer needed to enlist a "home front." Hostilities lasting more than four decades and, though more than once edging toward nuclear catastrophe, were nonetheless characterized as a "Cold War."

The contrast with Nazi Germany could not be sharper. Where the Nazis kept the German population in an agitated state of continuous mobilization and made no secret of their preparation for war, U.S. leaders promoted a paradox in which the government was fighting a war while the citizenry remained demobilized: no conscription, no economic controls, no rationing. It might seem at first that the horrific events of 9/11 would revive the idea of a "home front," but instead of actively engaging the citizenry, the administration set about to manage it. Unlike the Nazis, who may accurately be described as "control freaks" obsessed by the need to rule everything, American rulers prefer to manage the population as would a corporate CEO, manipulatively, alternately soothing and dismissive, relying on the powerful resources of mass communication and the techniques of the advertising and public opinion industries. In the process the arts of "coercion" are refined. Physical threat remains but the main technique of control is to encourage a collective sense of dependence. The citizenry is kept at a distance, disengaged spectators watching events in the formats determined by an increasingly "embedded" media whose function is to render warfare "virtual," sanitized, yet fascinating.[15] To satisfy viewers with an urge for vicarious retaliation, for blood and gore, a parallel universe of action movies, computer war games, and television, saturated with images of violence and triumphalism, are but a click away.

The growth of Superpower and the corresponding decline of democracy can be measured by the concentration of media ownership and its accompanying discipline over content. The relationship between democratic decline and the media ownership is illustrated in the contrast between the attention paid by Washington and the national media to the sixties' protest movements against the Vietnam War and, four decades later, the virtual blackout of the protests against the invasion of Iraq.[16] In the sixties, thanks to the antiwar movements and the publicity given to them by national and local television and radio, the nation truly agonized over that preemptive war and tried to work through it. The true significance of the continuing conservative resentment against the sixties, the real "Vietnam syndrome," appears in the growing intolerance toward opposition and especially toward the disorderliness that has always been the hallmark of a vibrant democracy.

In the fall of 2003 Congress passed an $87 billion appropriation for Iraqi reconstruction that also contained $9 million for the Miami police force to enable it to suppress the expected popular opposition to a meeting in Miami on trade relations with Latin America. The media dutifully reported the $87 billion and almost universally ignored the funding of the Miami police, just as they ignored the force's brutal treatment of dissent. The current censorship of popular protest against Superpower and empire serves to isolate democratic resistance, to insulate society from hearing dissonant voices, and to hurry the process of depoliticization.

v

Thus the Hobbesian fear factor is kept alive and well. Hobbesian fear, unlike Nazi terror, afflicts a society in which the preeminence of safety and security ("law and order") has been drummed into the popular consciousness over the course of many political campaigns and television and movie seasons. Nowhere is the manipulation of fear better illustrated than by the numerous invasions of privacy authorized under the Patriot Act and encroachments upon constitutional guarantees, particularly those pertaining to right to counsel, confidentiality of communications between lawyers and their clients, and the resort to secret tribunals.[17] Since the vast majority of the cases involve males of Middle Eastern origins, the broader public is reassured and simultaneously given an object lesson. Equally important is the reinforcement of the fear factor by the economic recession that began in 2001 and left more than a million workers unemployed while rendering many more insecure, a condition exacerbated by the more than one million jobs lost to the movement of American manufacturing abroad.

Doubtless the second Bush administration did not intentionally cause the economic downturn, but what was most striking was its response. The deep economic depression of the late 1920s had been a principal cause in attracting German voters to the Nazi Party then in opposition.[18] By mobilizing the German economy for war the Nazis succeeded in easing unemployment. Unlike the Nazis the administration has done little to allay the recession's effects and much that exploits the accompanying insecurities. Far from calling for "equal sacrifice" from the citizenry, as would be the case in a genuinely democratic society involved in a war, it has openly practiced a politics of inequality that feeds on the fears of the most insecure members of society. For example, by pushing through an enormous tax rebate that blatantly favored the wealthy, it simultaneously assured that no funds would be available to subsidize programs—such as the democratization of health care, increased unemployment benefits, and protections for pension funds—that might have eased the impact of recession.[19] Instead, at regular intervals, the administration raised the specter of an imminent bankruptcy of Social Security and vigorously campaigned for an alternative. It envisaged a nation of citizen-investors who would be encouraged to convert their accrued benefits into investment accounts. These would be available for speculation in the stock market and would, in effect, lock social security into the ups and downs of Wall Street—in effect an insecurity system and not likely to reduce the anxiety levels that had been the original target of the Social Security Act of 1935.

A similar strategy has been at work regarding health care. After first threatening to reduce Medicare benefits and increase the premiums for recipients, the administration succeeded in passing a reform of Medicare that, while providing some modest benefits, did little to control the obscene prices of drugs. Meanwhile in a concerted strategy businesses and corporations began to insist that workers contribute a higher percentage to monthly premiums for private health plans, and, in some cases, to threaten the withdrawal of business contributions altogether. All of this while wages remained mostly stagnant. In making a political spectacle of rising health care costs with no resolution in sight, the administration would seem to have found it politically more advantageous to leave the issue in doubt and the public uncertain and demoralized.

vi

What can one make of this strange situation? The president assumes an "above politics" pose of a "patriot king" grimly warning the nation that it is locked in a deathly struggle with terrorists. Meanwhile his administration is engrossed in an intensely partisan politics promoting corporate interests and polarizing cultural and religious issues that divert attention. When society is in a state of war, patriotism dictates that divisive economic and cultural issues should be laid aside. In wartime one might reasonably expect that the economy, especially large corporate operations, would be subject to regulation in the interests of sharing the burdens of war. In times of national danger, when the whole society is threatened, the common good appears as obvious and unambiguous. Everyone is expected to make sacrifices, and a kind of rough egalitarianism prevails. But if war is so distant as to seem disconnected from everyday life, if no conscription is introduced, no shortages perceived, if war and the economy appear to be on separate tracks, there is not only no need to rally the citizenry, but it is politically advantageous not to. The common good seems an abstraction, private interests the reality. Equally paradoxical, it is a truism that during wartime the natural expectation is that governmental powers will be expanded. Yet, save for the Patriot Act and the establishment of the hopelessly cumbersome Homeland Security Department, the political rhetoric of the Republicans and of many Democrats continues to repeat the prewar refrain about the need to reduce the size of government, of taxes, and of public spending—in short, all of the themes intended to cater to the citizens' suspicions of their government, all of those themes subversive of a close bond between government and citizenry that one might expect to be encouraged during a "real" war.

Thus a schizoid condition: a war without mobilization, a war where the citizenry is a potential target but not a participant. It is strangely reproduced in domestic political matters. While the war on terrorism induces feelings of helplessness and a natural tendency to look toward the government, to trust it, the domestic message of distrust of government produces alienation from government. The people are not transformed into a manipulable mass shouting "Sieg Heil." Instead they are discouraged, inclined to abdicate a political role, yet patriotically trusting of their "wartime" leaders. The domestic message says that the citizenry should distrust its own elected government, thereby denying themselves the very instrument that democracy is supposed to make available to them. A democracy that is persuaded to distrust itself, that applauds the rhetoric of "get government off your backs," "it's your money being wasted," and "you should decide how to spend it," renounces the means of its own efficacy in favor of a laissez-faire politics, an antiegalitarian politics, where, as in the market, the stronger powers prevail. What is revealed or, rather, confirmed is that the consummated union of corporate power and governmental power heralds the American version of a total system.

What kind of political contests would be characteristic of such a situation and contribute to the regime of Superpower? At the present time most analysts are agreed that some of the major features of contemporary politics and the overall situation are indicative of "deadlock." The nation is said to be almost equally divided in its party loyalties. Accordingly electoral campaigns are primarily attentive to a relatively small number of "undecided voters." At the same time there is a large number of "safe seats" for each party, with the result that parties concentrate more upon primaries than upon the final election and successful candidates tend to become long-term incumbents.

The obvious question is this: what interests would thrive upon a politics of small margins? Clearly, powerful interests that can fund candidates and parties so that when the deadlocked legislatures convene, these interests are positioned to deploy a large contingent of lobbyists to persuade a few legislators from one party to vote with their opponents. This becomes all the more feasible and cost-effective when one party, the Republicans, is openly "pro-business," and a substantial number of Democrats elected to Congress are virtually indistinguishable from Republicans, especially on economic issues. Deadlocked legislatures, prevented from passing legislation opposed by powerful corporate interests, are especially prone to attaching amendments or "earmarks" favoring a particular and usually powerful interest. Conversely, it is especially difficult to muster majorities in favor of broad social programs, such as health care, improved working conditions, and education, when organized corporate interests can easily block those efforts.

A closely divided electorate and a Congress with narrow majorities are also conducive to fanning cultural wars. The point about disputes on such topics as the value of sexual abstinence, the role of religious charities in state-funded activities, the question of gay marriage, and the like, is that they are not framed to be resolved. Their political function is to divide the citizenry while obscuring class differences and diverting the voters' attention from the social and economic concerns of the general populace. Cultural wars might seem an indication of strong political involvements. Actually they are a substitute. The notoriety they receive from the media and from politicians eager to take firm stands on nonsubstantive issues serves to distract attention and contribute to a cant politics of the inconsequential.

When George II declared "war on terrorism," he formalized the politics of the inconsequential. It is common knowledge that, before 9/11, his administration entered office with no serious program for the benefit of the general citizenry. Its "popular" agenda was simple and largely negative: to promote government deregulation, dismantle environmental safeguards, pass tax legislation in favor of the wealthier classes, and reduce social programs. Its positive agenda took advantage of the politics of gridlock and the role of corporate power to promote the economic well-being of corporate sponsors in oil, energy, and pharmaceutical drugs.

Again the inversion is striking: the Nazi Party had a strong antipathy toward big business and, early on, professed a "socialist" tendency that was later reflected in several programs aimed at eliminating unemployment and introducing social services. Indeed, a socialist or, better, a collectivist element figured as well in the Soviet Union and even in Mussolini's Italy. Collectivism might be defined as a conception of society as a compact, solidaristic whole in which the *Volk* or "workers" are exalted—while being reshaped into a manageable mass that loves its solidarity and anonymity. Inverted totalitarianism, in contrast, appears as anticollectivist: it idealizes individualism and adulates celebrities. And yet both constructs of the "outstanding," of those who "stand out," serve to paper over the fact that instead of a sovereign citizen-body there is only a "lonely crowd." The challenge is to give the lonely crowd a sense of belonging, of selfless anonymity, of solidarity with a noble cause. The solution: a mix of patriotism and nationalism, and unthinking loyalty to the troops. That solution is the populist counterpart to the role played by elites in bridging the two constitutions. While corporate power and its ethos are incorporated into the structure of the state,[20] the patriotism, nationalism, and unblinking loyalty of the citizenry connect the constitution for preservation to the constitution for increase. That role becomes all the more important as it becomes clearer that globalizing, multinational capitalism has no political loyalties as such.

It loves offshore bank accounts as much as it loves producing cars in China, where it can pay workers a monthly wage of sixty dollars.[21]

Through the convergence of these developments Americans are being successfully "kneaded" into a citizenry less suited to democratic demands and increasingly more accepting and supportive of the dominant forms of power, not out of Nazi enthusiasm, but from fear and misguided patriotism.

CHAPTER SEVEN

The Dynamics of the Archaic

i

Religiosity distinguishes America from most other
Western societies. Americans are also overwhelmingly
Christian, which distinguishes them from many non-Western
peoples. Their religiosity leads Americans to see the world
in terms of good and evil to a much greater extent
than most other peoples.
—*Samuel Huntington*[1]

We should offer to serve the war effort in any way possible.
God battles with people who oppose him, who fight
against him and his followers.
—*Charles Stanley, pastor and former president of the
Southern Baptist Association*[2]

Not long ago, as Americans were poised to welcome the third millennium, there was much speculation about future discoveries, inventions,
and economic progress, and about the rewards due a society devoted
to science, technology, and capitalism. The anticipation reflected the
kind of national identity to which the society was seemingly dedicated:
to forms of knowledge, their organization, their application, and supporting culture that were worldly, materialistic, ever-changing, and
firmly fixed upon the here and now.

However, in the aftermath of the 2000 presidential campaign and
of the memorializing of 9/11, Americans were confronted with a very
different notion of who they are as a nation. The experience might be
described as another Great Awakening. Some awoke, as it were, to be
told that instead of being identified primarily by their attachment to
science, invention, and the marketplace, they were distinguished as

well by their dedication to spiritual values and to different and higher powers. For others it confirmed what they had suspected. The United States ranks highest among all industrialized nations in the number of citizens who declare that they "believe in God." Thirty-five percent of Americans identify themselves as "born-again Christians." And 75 percent of Americans who attend church regularly are Republicans. While 83 percent of Americans believe in the Virgin Birth of Jesus, only 28 percent admit to a belief in evolution.[3]

These statistics take on added significance in light of the remarkable commingling of politics and religion that has occurred in recent years and gives every indication of increasing in the future. In that mixture it is not religion generally but primarily fundamentalist and evangelical religion whose energetic political activism is helping to shape the course of some public policies (e.g., antiabortion, school vouchers, and welfare programs) and playing a pivotal part in elections. Evangelical Protestants are in the vanguard of these developments, both as foot soldiers for the Republican Party and as influential players in Beltway politics.[4] Contrary to a common assumption—that an "outdated" belief is similar to an old-model refrigerator or auto, that its antique status connotes inefficiency, feebleness, lack of power—the exact opposite is true of religious fundamentalists. Their faith in the Bible as the literal word of God converts zeal into real political energy.

At first glance, that fundamentalists and evangelicals have been embraced by the Republican political establishment seems incongruous with the imperial, corporate, and high-tech strut of Superpower. When contrasted with the outlook of those who looked forward to a new millennium defined by science, technology, and capitalism—and their accompanying conceptions of what counts for truth, how it is to be searched for and subsidized—the beliefs of the biblically inspired millennialists appear as prescientific relics from a distant past, their millennial hopes antithetical to the expectations of those who welcomed the third millennium for its this-worldly promise of high-tech marvels.

In their fundamentalist version, evangelicals believe in the inerrancy of Scripture and the unchanging nature of its truths, particularly those in the book of Revelation. They challenge the hegemony of the natural sciences, preferring the Bible's version of Creation over the findings of biologists, geologists, and astronomers. Unlike the corporate dynamists who may be said to produce and invest in the means of power, the evangelicals invest power itself, sanctify it, and guide its use. "God," Rev. Jerry Falwell declared in 2004, "is pro-war."[5] Yet they, like the dynamists, contribute a future-oriented element to the politics of Superpower. Their energies are fired by their belief in the imminence—how imminent is a matter of intramural dispute—of the Apocalypse or "rapture" of the Last Days when the Lord will unleash death and destruction, the world will go up in flames, the forces of evil will be vanquished and the thousand-year reign of Christ inaugurated.[6] Strangely the apocalypse of the Last Days has a counterpart in the apocalypse of the secular dynamists. In a revelatory moment, while observing the first spectacular display of his handiwork, the father (read: patriarch) of the atomic bomb was moved to cite a religious text: "I am become Death, the destroyer of worlds."[7]

What is most striking about these particular forms of spirituality and piety is the extent to which they are represented in high politics. As Americans were continually reminded, President Bush was a "born-again" believer whose speeches were notable for their biblical allusions; who often struck prophetic poses and assumed the role of divine instrument for combating and overcoming evil. Frequent prayer meetings took place in the White House and the Congress. Even the military was affected; it was only in the wake of special intervention by high-ranking generals and a public protest by a former Jewish cadet that proselytizing activities encouraged at the Air Force Academy were halted.

Many of the main elements in the dynamic of Superpower—corporate capital, Christian evangelism, elitism, American nationalism and exceptionalism—share a triumphalist faith. The distinctive element contributed by religious fundamentalism is a dynamic of hope, nourished on an absolute promise of a climactic, triumphant moment that, despite delays, satanic mischief, and false prophets, will be realized.[8] Strong traces of its influence are evident in the theological imagery adopted by politicians, from Reagan's depiction of the "evil empire" of the Soviet Union to George II's jeremiad: "We will never forget the servants of evil who plotted the attacks [of 9/11], and we will never forget those who rejoiced at our grief.”⁹ Millennial hopes mix with other elements in the totalitarian dynamic to feed an impulse toward limitlessness. Culturally Americans are continuously exposed to exaggerated claims and encouraged by advertising, TV, movies, and popular music to entertain extravagant expectations about their future.

ii

> And if a sparrow cannot fall to the ground without His notice,
> is it probable that an empire can rise without His aid?
> —*From Ben Franklin as reproduced in Vice President Cheney's Christmas card*¹⁰

Evangelicalism is one element in a broader ideological matrix, “archaism,” that includes political and economic variants of fundamentalism. My aim is to show archaism's unexpected affinities with the “dynamism” of science, technology, and corporate capitalism. The archaist, whether political or religious, has a fondness for singling out privileged moments in the past when a transcendent truth was revealed, typically through an inspired leader, a Jesus, a Moses, or a Founding Father. The odd couple of Superpower is an alliance that finds reactionary, backward-looking archaic forces (economic, religious, and political) allied with forward-looking forces of radical change (corporate leaders, technological innovators, scientists) whose efforts contribute to steadily distancing contemporary society from its past. It is as though the archaist believes that by going forward, by allying with dynamic powers, he enables an ever-receding past somehow to bring the revelation closer.

The American zest for change coexists with fervent political and religious convictions that bind the identity of the believers to two “fundamentals,” the texts of the Constitution and the Bible and their status as unchanging and universal truths. Recently an Alabama judge tried to implement that belief by having a huge Ten Commandments monument placed within his courthouse. Although he failed, the significance of the incident went beyond the challenge to the alleged “wall” separating church and state, amounting to an assertion of the supremacy of the "laws of God."

When we say that some belief or object is archaic, we are distinguishing it from a "relic" or artifact from the past that may be preserved but is no longer in common use. An archaic belief is one that flourished in the past and carries identifiable marks of that past, but unlike a relic, it is operative, employed rather than simply preserved. Like a relic, an archaism requires care, preservation, if it is not to decay. Unlike scientific truths, which are cumulative and frequently superseded, archaisms are fixed, impervious to evidence. What is the doctrine of "the framers' original intent" and "constitutional originalism" but a variant of creationism and the denial of historical evolution?

Curiously, the intellectual godfather of many of the neocons, Leo Strauss, was a rigid archaist. His "bibles" were Plato, Aristotle, and (discreetly) Nietzsche. He was deeply hostile toward the social sciences and dismissed virtually all of the major figures in twentieth-century philosophy.[11]

As a system of belief archaism appears to the nonbeliever as anachronistic, as out of synch with the culture seemingly dominated by the dynamists. The latter display or embrace a forward, futurist thrust that celebrates change and trumpets "progress." It is not difficult to grasp the power that the dynamists create: we see the changes they have brought to society, how they have succeeded in converting nature into products, and how their ingenuity has given the military destructive, shock-and-awe capabilities—a revelation of technological prowess.

As we noted previously, the religious archaists, while they look to truths established in the past, have a distinctive forward thrust of their own. Although that dynamic draws its energies from expectations about the Last Days, it has also adapted some of the practices of contemporary business organizations, including their techniques of advertising. The worldly power of the religious archaists depends upon organizing (marketing) a more or less coherent system of beliefs (a religious form of capital), attracting adherents (customers), and making them into converts (consumers) who will behave in accordance with the precepts they have been taught.

As with the history of democracy evangelicalism began as a protest against the domination of congregations by educated elites and as a demand for evangelists who "came from the people."[12] Instead a managerial elite has emerged within a religion once famous for its populism. Thus the evangelicals have followed a path strikingly similar to that of the democratic citizenry. The prominence of these techniques of organization suggests that the recent history of evangelicals—and in this respect they are not unique among religious groups—bears a strong resemblance to the relatively recent displacement of the democratic citizenry: pastoral elites as managers; political elites as pastors. The similarity or interchangeability of secular and evangelical elites was conspicuously confirmed in the so-called Abramoff scandal. It was revealed that one evangelical leader prominent in Republican politics, Ralph Reed, and one Republican politician, Tom DeLay, who boasted of "born-again" credentials, were deeply implicated in a scheme for bilking Indian tribes of several million dollars—and updating Wounded Knee.

The archaist is convinced that his core beliefs are superior to rival beliefs and are true because unchanging. The archaist is also a proselytizer who promises that if unbelievers will adopt the true faith, they, too, can be "born again," transformed. Archaic truths, then, are powerful because they are transforming truths. They save the true believer not only from error but from the consequences of errors that can corrupt existence and, ultimately, decide the fate of one's soul. And, by extension, they can save a nation. Like corporate capital and the marketplace they have an element of ruthlessness, a hardening in the face of death and destruction.

Evangelicals want to change or, in their view, restore the national identity. Along with other religious groups, they have actively pushed to dismantle the so-called wall separating church and state. They want prayer and other religious activities to be a part of public education— the latter arguably the heart of democracy; they want public funds for the charitable activities of religious groups and for the support of religious schools; they want the Bible's account of "creation," or a covert version of it, taught in science courses; and they want public acknowledgment and recognition of the "fact" that, from its beginnings, America was understood by its Founding Patriarchs to be a "Christian nation."

What is being promoted, although not openly acknowledged, is the establishment of a "civil religion."[13] The idea of a civil religion is an old one that predates Christianity. Originally it was based on political rather than religious considerations and fostered by ruling groups. It was assumed that a political society needed cohesion in order to overcome or reduce the centrifugal pulls of class, clan, and the secret "mystery religions" that flourished in antiquity. One solution was to have its citizens embrace, or be indoctrinated into, a common set of beliefs, rituals, and values concerning such matters as the meaning of life and death, the sacred character of society and its governance, and the nature of the higher powers or deities who must be placated and worshiped if the society was to endure, flourish, and triumph over its enemies. One model, that of ancient Israel, was revered during the political and religious struggles of seventeenth-century England and transported to the colonies by the Pilgrim Fathers. It inspired enthusiasm for creating a "holy commonwealth" in the "New World" that God had reserved for the new Israelites. In the pre-Christian system of religion and politics, religion was integrated into the political order and subordinated to it; by contrast the religious archaist is intent on establishing religion as constitutive of the nation's political identity and, potentially, as regulative principles for the whole society. It is a totalizing vision.

iii

Another version of archaism is political and equally fundamentalist. In the narrative of the political archaist the United States was blessed with a once-and-for-all-time, fixed ideal form, an original Constitution of government created by the Founding Fathers in 1787. In that view, the original Constitution is the political counterpart to the Bible, the fundamental text, inerrant, unchanging, to be applied—not "interpreted" by "activist judges." As the political fundamentalists see it, except for the Edenic era of Ronald Reagan, the form of government decreed by the Constitution has been under siege by "the liberal media" and liberal administrations abetted by their minions in Congress and by judges who "legislate" instead of "following the letter" of constitutional scripture. The nation is perceived as a wayward sinner who frequently wanders from the straight and narrow and needs to be sobered, returned to its sacred text, its Word. The vision of an idealized original constitution rarely, if ever, includes the kind of participatory democracy that Tocqueville celebrated. Instead archaism tends to support republicanism rather than democracy, that is, a system in which the responsibility for saving the Many devolves upon a selfless elite, an elect although not necessarily elected.[14]

This fixation upon a timeless and ideal political form and the persistent resurfacing of that notion during controversies over the powers of the national government are all the more remarkable in a society that otherwise enthusiastically embraces change and adores novelty in virtually all of its guises, including ones that mock deeply held convictions, such as the sanctity of human life and traditional conceptions of marriage and sexuality. Americans have a famously voracious appetite for new technological advances, even knowing that they bring radical changes ranging from where we live, how we love, fornicate, procreate, and medicate to how we terminate. During his presidency Bill Clinton informed his countrymen and -women that they could expect to change jobs about eleven times in the course of their lives. Cities and states compete ferociously to attract new industries by offering subsidies and tax abatements despite the almost certain knowledge that success will inevitably destroy established patterns of life and bring new ones with no assurance that the subsidized industry will not yank up stakes before long and accept a more attractive offer elsewhere. Similarly very few Americans live where they were born or raised. Thus a continuous internal migration, a change of place, of vocation, of partners, of cultures and economies that is intensified by immigration from abroad bringing different cultures and political traditions.

Perhaps change can also serve to confirm the appeal of the unchanging; perhaps a hunger for that which is steadfast and true may be a protest against a condition where "Whirl is King." The Question: is the archaic ultimately antithetical to a power-and-profit regime and its technology of continuous innovation; or is the archaists' dedication to the timeless implicitly exploiting the intolerableness of existence under the reigning mania for the new; and is its political support for Super-power a tactic, a way of hurrying society toward the apocalypse?[15]

iv

Surprisingly, archaism resurfaces where we might least expect to see it, in the economic theory of the free market. The proponents of that theory have been prominent in the councils of Republican administrations ever since the Reagan presidency. They have contributed importantly to the general distrust of governmental "intervention" in the economy and hostility to governmental social programs. Their intellectual genealogy can be traced directly to a particular text, Adam Smith's *Wealth of Nations*, which appeared in 1776 at the outbreak of the American Revolution—a sign not to be lightly dismissed as a mere coincidence. It was written to oppose "mercantilist theories" that assigned to the state an active role in regulating and promoting economic activity. Smith offered a sharply opposed vision of the economy as radically decentralized, largely unregulated, consisting of small-scale producers—in short, virtually autonomous (laissez-faire). In place of an explanation (the economy was supervised by the state for the common good), Smith offered a miracle. The decisions of countless individual actors, each acting for his own self-interest, would nonetheless produce the well-being of the society, a state of affairs that the actors had not intended.

How to explain that remarkable result, an outcome unrelated to the actors' intentions? How is it possible to have a "natural harmony" of selfish interests? Smith's answer: an "invisible hand" guided the individual selfish actor "to promote an end which was no part of his intention." "It is his own advantage, indeed, and not that of society which [the individual] has in view. But the study of his own advantage naturally, or rather necessarily leads him to prefer that employment which is most advantageous to society."[16] In spite of its worldly concerns, Smith's economy required a theological sleight of hand—whose but the sure hand of an all-seeing god?—an anticipation of "intelligent design" for a domain that moderns typically consider to be irredeemably secular.

Needless to add, Smith did not anticipate the modern globalizing corporation, although he was an opponent of monopolies. What matters today is that his version of an economy is actively promoted as an ideal at a time when the economy is dominated by economic organizations whose scale and power exceed anything Smith might have imagined. Today when his teaching is invoked to reduce state power and to free entrepreneurial energies, that teaching acquires a mythical quality, another nostalgic yearning, this time for a natural economic order in which intense competition is mere surface to a harmonious order in the interests of all. Meanwhile the actual hand of government distributes corporate subsidies, tax breaks, and the like.

The ideological resources of Superpower represent a curious combination of, on the one hand, the eighteenth-century Enlightenment, with its gospel of rationalism, science, written constitutions, and a "free economy"—what we might call an ideal of the methodical pursuit of power controlled by rational self-interested decision making; and, on the other, the sixteenth- and seventeenth-century religious Reformation, with its emphasis upon scriptural truth (sola scriptura), enthusiastic belief (sola fide, faith alone), evangelizing energy, and millennial hopes about a final showdown between good and evil—what we might call a dynamic of transcendent expectancy.[17] The reluctance to admit that profound changes have taken place in our economic and political institutions points to the curious coexistence of forward-looking and regressive elements in the makeup of "the greatest power in history." The same society that enthuses over economic, technological, and scientific advances, and devours novelty in its popular culture and consumer goods, also includes an extraordinary number of citizens who, when it comes to politics and religion, passionately reject the idea that experiment or novelty is welcome.

Why should that combination be explosive? or, to risk a bad pun, possess an elective affinity—at least among Republicans? Does the fact that Protestant evangelism has historically been well-disposed toward capitalism mean that we are witnessing another confirmation of Max Weber's thesis that Protestantism was a powerful factor in the rise of capitalism? Or could it be the other way round, that instead of Calvinist asceticism's furnishing the driving force behind capitalism's dynamic, the reverse is true: capitalism's dynamic of excess is fueling evangelical dreams of the millennium? According to Max Weber Protestant sects once preached frugality, only to find that this encouraged saving, savings became investments, and, lo and behold! Protestantism had launched capitalism—to vulgarize Weber's thesis. Perhaps in the era of evangelical megachurches and televangelists skilled in eliciting contributions from the faithful, Weber should be revised: capitalism and the rise of religion. As Jerry Falwell, one of the leading fundamentalist preachers, counseled, "the church would be wise to look at business for a prediction of future innovation."[18]

v

Dynamists and archaists share a certain drivenness, the one engaged in an unending quest for markets, new products, new discoveries; the other in quest of personal preparation for a final judgment that lies at the end of historical time. Although the idea of returning to the original Constitution might seem at odds with these drives, its very passivity renders it complicit, easily manipulated, allowing for preemptive wars, torture, and the legitimation of Superpower yet not standing in the way while organized lobbies, responsible only to their sponsors, corrupt the political processes.

The political price exacted when grandiose conceptions of power are in ascendancy is suggested by the remark of an administration official cited earlier. To believe that those in power can make their own reality at will is a sure recipe for losing touch with reality, for ignoring stubborn facts, such as the history and culture of Iraq or the sensibilities of Muslims. The list of misjudgments stretches from North Korea to Iraq, from Social Security and health care reform to Hurricane Katrina, from judicial nominations to the handling of intelligence estimates. These and others are not simply miscalculations but, in the literal sense, acts of willfulness, of overreaching, that are encouraged by assumptions not only about power's potential but about reality's nature. Those assumptions may be exaggerated by the absence of thoughtfulness among the administration's major decision-makers, yet they are not assumptions peculiar to Texans and neocons. The role of fantasy becomes greater when those who had previously been considered responsible for puncturing illusions and discrediting false beliefs have lost their status as truth-tellers.

Roughly a quarter century ago, when fundamentalists of all stripes were relics rather than archaists, the large majority of those who gave much thought to questions of reality would have agreed that the principal methods for discovering, identifying, and predicting reality, whether of the natural or of the social variety, were those employed in the natural sciences and, with less agreement, in some of the social science disciplines. Superpower's uncertain grasp of reality is related to what might be called the dethronement of science. It is not fortuitous that during the imperial administration there have been innumerable instances in which scientific findings have been ignored, or suppressed, or distorted, or denied because they did not support the administration's policies and ambitions.

The Founders' Constitution authorized Congress "to promote the Progress of Science and useful arts" by protecting the copyrights of inventors. Science in the forms we know it could not exist, much less attain its present status, without the resources and organizing skills of government and private enterprise. Conversely, governmental power, and especially military force, would not have reached the magnitudes implied by "superpower" or the "imperial reach" without the weaponry of destruction, intelligence-gathering capabilities, rapid transport, and instant communications that science and technology have made available.

The oddity of American Superpower is that while it readily exploits the power possibilities of science and technology, its ideology depends upon a crucial development, the puncturing of the cultural mystique formerly surrounding science as disinterested "inquiry," leaving in its place a predominantly instrumental, market-oriented understanding.[19] Science is no longer the heroic adventure of loners who challenge orthodoxies but the consequence of a series of investment decisions. Paradoxically, this transformation of science is an essential precondition for the dynamic of the archaic to be asserted.

A half century ago the work of scientists was idealized. Typically science was depicted almost monastically, as pursued within a "community of scientists" that constrained their behavior in accordance with an unwritten code of conduct for protecting scientific objectivity and integrity.[20] Scientists operated outside the marketplace; their autonomy, which was considered to be the necessary condition for scientific honesty, was subsidized by government and universities. Now, however, scientists, have become "incorporated," either as entrepreneurs or as employees in research divisions of corporations and government bureaucracies.[21] The integration of science into the culture and practices of corporate and governmental bureaucracies has destroyed the iconic status it enjoyed for more than three centuries, leaving scientists and their findings more vulnerable to political and corporate manipulation and attacks by religious and economic archaists. Once scientists were universally revered as exemplars of independent truth seeking, of knowledge for its own sake, but in recent years they have been accused of fraud, misrepresenting their findings, and other forms of cheating reflective of a highly competitive, market-oriented culture. More significant, on virtually every major policy issue, from global warming to genetic engineering, apparently reputable scientists can be found appealing to scientific evidence and theories while defending diametrically opposed positions. While some may welcome these revelations for eliminating the last holdout against postmodern subjectivism, there can be little question that they, along with the corporatization of science, further weaken public confidence in the possibility of disinterested policies and public trust in authorities.

Paradoxically, the demystification of science and its incorporation into the power complex have worked to the advantage of religious fundamentalists. Beginning in the nineteenth century and continuing throughout much of the twentieth, science was widely regarded as the most powerful alternative system of beliefs that challenged organized religion for hegemony.[22] Although the echoes of those controversies can occasionally be heard today in the curriculum battles between "creationists" and "Darwinians," what tends to be obscured is the reversal in influence and popularity of the antagonists since the Scopes trial.

Today it is religion, not science, that is in ascendancy, that holds the loyalties of those who "believe."[23] The new vogue of "intelligent design" can be interpreted as a modest theology that hopes to capitalize on the vulnerability of contemporary science.

The demotion of science has had severe public consequences. It means that the ideal of a disinterested arbiter, of a forum where partisan claims might be tested "objectively," is as much a relic of the past as is the ideal of an independent judiciary. In its place we have "virtual reality," imaginary weapons of mass destruction, democracy as a cover for market forces, an ideological rendering of terrorism that transforms its reality into a theological problem admitting of no solution.

vi

> The end of worship amongst men is power. . . .
> But God has no ends.
> —*Thomas Hobbes*[24]

How is it possible for corporate power, worldly, cynical, materialistic, not only to coexist alongside evangelical Christianity but to subsist, to be symbiotic with it? How have Christ and Mammon come to cooperate? Several explanations are plausible. One might emphasize the manipulative genius of Republican Party operatives in attracting the loyalty and contributions of both while keeping each compartmentalized from the other. Or, alternatively, one might argue that, far from being pawns of the party, religionists are as adept as corporate operatives in exploiting the party for their own ends. Or, again, one might point to examples of how corporations—in the belief that piety helps in producing more loyal, honest, hardworking, and nonunion employees—have become increasingly receptive to religious groups who bring their message to the workplace. Or one might conclude that religious fundamentalists, who tend to believe that all are by nature sinners, can take in stride corporate scandals and political corruption as confirmation of mankind's original nature rather than as an outrage. Similarly one might expect fundamentalists to tolerate capitalism's treatment of workers and resistance to welfare programs, to raising the minimum wage, or to guaranteeing pensions and health care as in keeping with the historical decision of fundamentalists to eschew teaching a social gospel out of concern that it might distract people from focusing on salvation. There is a tuneless harmony between, on the one hand, the evangelical belief that this life is destined to pass away and, on the other, industrial practices that threaten to exhaust finite resources while polluting the earth and atmosphere.

While these and other tactical explanations are suggestive, and even true to some extent, they do not do justice to the contradictions between corporate power and evangelical beliefs, to the tension between the materialistic and worldly and the faith-driven, otherworldly. I want to suggest that the alliance between power and faith results because each needs the other, desperately.

To the ancient philosopher who exclaimed, "Whirl is King," all is flux and change, another, Heraclitus, responded, "Listening not to me but to the Logos it is wise to agree that all things are one." If we think of the world as being continuously redefined by contemporary science, technology, corporate capitalism, and its media, it would not be misleading to describe it as a "whirl." Everything seems in flux, from definitions of "family" to specifications of job skills, from the modes of human reproduction to the prospect of space travel, from the near extinction of manners, propriety, and civil discourse to the endless affronts displayed on TV and the cinema screen, from the frequency with which people change jobs to the frequency with which they change partners. When life is defined by "style" and style by the latest mode of provocativeness, then meaninglessness aptly describes much of contemporary life. Or, if that characterization seems overwrought, try "absurd" or "the permanence of a changing contemporaneity."

Whatever the term, the point is the universally uncertain character of contemporary life. The promise of stability, not simply stability itself, but the promise and assurance of certainty, give the archaic its appeal and make it complementary to the politics of fear and antiterrorism. Yet the fact remains that there is no natural affinity, as distinct from tactical advantage, between the relentless drive for change represented by science, technology, and corporate capitalism, on the one hand, and the reverence for changelessness among those defenders of the Logos, the constitutional and religious fundamentalists. The alliance between the dynamists and the fundamentalists is tactical or expedient rather than a matter of fused identities. Corporate entities couldn't care less if all evangelicals and fundamentalists were to suffer a crisis of faith and to disappear tomorrow; and an even greater indifference would be found among scientists and technologists. Among the dynamists there is a greater affinity with constitutional than with religious fundamentalists. Corporate power has utterly transformed the constitutional system of the Founders without acknowledging the transformation. If the fundamentalists wish to believe that the corporate donors who subsidize conservative legal foundations are as fervent as they are about an original Constitution, then corporate types are more than ready to indulge the make-believe. Corporate power is more than eager to tolerate the idiosyncrasies of constitutional fundamentalists; it needs a stable legal framework, and for most of two centuries corporate operatives have successfully cultivated accommodating judges and eager lawyers. As long as the courts are prepared to step in when the federal government tries to flex its regulatory powers, corporations will continue to underwrite the Federalist Society.

One practical consideration that causes the corporationists to play along with religious zealots and political doctrinaires is that archaism helps to neutralize the power of the Many. The religious fundamentalists remind the needy that instead of throwing their energies into gaining the transient goods of this world, they should heed Jesus' teaching and concentrate upon the salvation of their souls and the "pearls beyond price" awaiting them in the Kingdom of God. The constitutional fundamentalists teach the same lesson of quietism but with a different logic. The Constitution, they allege, is one of limited powers, and those powers become especially limited whenever the government "interferes" with property rights in an effort to remedy gross inequities, or threatens the rights of that peculiar species of persons called corporations, a status not mentioned in the "original Constitution."

vii

There is a complementarity among the republican doctrine of elitism, evangelical notions of an elect, Republican Party elitism, and (as we shall see later) neocon elitism. The elect and the elite, the elected and the elect. The combination is as old as the Massachusetts Bay Colony. The Puritans believed in both an elect destined by God for salvation and an elite destined to govern. When modern-day Republicans invoke the imagery of "a city upon a hill," they may think that they are quoting Ronald Reagan, but historically the author was the first governor of the Massachusetts Bay Colony, John Winthrop, who assumed himself to belong to the elect and the elite.

Sadly, the archaists do not temper the dynamists but collude with them. Once upon a time, during the eighteenth and nineteenth centuries, the Great Awakenings helped to further believers' democratic impulses and to urge them into the forefront of the fight to abolish slavery. Once upon a time, too, in the late nineteenth and early twentieth centuries, evangelicals preached a "social gospel" and sided with the poor and the working class. Their fate seems intertwined with that of democracy itself.[25]

CHAPTER EIGHT

The Politics of Superpower: Managed Democracy

i

Tax shelters, many of them illegal, saved big companies at least $14.7 billion in federal income taxes last year, a senior Internal Revenue Service official said. . . . Now all companies are being offered an amnesty in return for confessing their illegal tax avoidance.

The 95 companies that have already confessed their tax avoidance strategies . . . shorted the government an amount equal to a dollar a week for every man, woman and child in America.
—*David Cay Johnson*[1]

Superpower is the union of state and corporation in an age of waning democracy and political illiteracy. This chapter inquires into some of the political changes that are making Superpower and inverted totalitarianism possible and demoting democracy from a formative principle to a largely rhetorical function within an increasingly corrupt political system. The crux of these changes is that corporate power and its culture are no longer external forces that occasionally influence policies and legislation. As these have become integral, so the citizenry has become marginal and democracy more manageable. What follows is an account of these developments.

ii

Superpower has its own "constitution," its own "more perfect union." Unlike the nation's written Constitution, with its emphasis upon checks and balances, limitations upon governmental authority, federalism, and the Bill of Rights, Superpower's unwritten constitution is about powers whose scope and influence derive from available resources, opportunities, and ambitions, rather than legal limits. Its composition is meant for "increase," not constraint.

Superpower's constitution depends upon a symbiotic relation between two elements, one political, the other economic. The first is empire and consists in large measure of military might, of bases scattered throughout the globe, of arms sales, of alliances and treaties with comparatively weak client states. Unlike the Roman Empire, and its extended citizenship, Superpower has only customers and clients, dominated markets instead of incorporated provinces. The second element is the globalizing corporation. It brings to foreign countries economic goods and services as well as the softening power of cultural influences and products.[2] As these elements take hold and develop, the "homeland" is transformed, from a self-governing, predominantly inward-looking political society into a "home base" for international economic and military strategies.

The "dynamic powers" of science, technology, and capital discussed earlier are clearly vital to the imperial reach and the globalizing drive of corporations. They are the basis of the new system of power, replacing the old one and its ideal of a sovereign citizenry. The new constitution conceives politics and governance as a strategy based upon the powers that technology and science (including psychology and the social sciences) have made possible. Exploitation of those powers enables their owners to redefine the citizenry as respondents rather than actors, as objects of manipulation rather than as autonomous.

A distinctive and common feature of organized science, technology, and capital, and of imperial power and the globalizing corporation, is their distance from the experience of ordinary beings. Military and corporate structures are hierarchical, complex, and arcane. Both science and technology employ an esoteric language familiar mainly to the initiates, while military-speak is a language unto itself. Democracy, whose culture extols the common and shared, is alien to all of these practices and their modes of communication.

The politics both of empire and of the globalizing corporation have a special status. In the rhetoric of governmental officials, military spokesmen, corporate executives, and think tank intellectuals imperial and global politics occupy a special plane, that of foreign policy, where, insulated from the pressures and instabilities of domestic politics, problems can be addressed in the language and assumptions common to experts and elites. Throughout American history political leaders, opinion-makers, and academics have maintained that foreign policy should be out-of-bounds politically, not only to safeguard secrets but to insulate decision-makers from the whims of a democratic citizenry and the distractions of populist politics. Prestigious academics have warned that if foreign policy decisions were made sensitive to public opinion, the result would likely be either indecision or constant "shifting" in response to a whimsical populace.[3] A public sage of an earlier era, Walter Lippmann, predicted flatly that if foreign policy were to follow public opinion, the outcome would be "a morbid derangement of the true functions of power" as well as policies "deadly to the very survival of the state and a free society."[4]

In the Bush administration the doctrine of "reason of state" was not only alive and flourishing but extended to domestic politics. Take the incident in which the vice president secretly invited several executives from the energy industry to formulate the government's energy policy while excluding environmental and public-interest representatives. The vice president then refused to disclose the identities of the representatives or the content of their policy proposals. As the elaborate system of wiretapping, secret surveillance, and extreme interrogation techniques suggests, the apparent aim of the administration is to extend the privileged secrecy of foreign policy (*arcanae imperii*) to domestic affairs. This is consistent with its phobia about leaks to the press and its zeal for stamping documents from the distant past as "classified," and thus shaping future interpretations of the past. The totalizing implications in the extension of the doctrine of arcanae imperii to include domestic politics are underscored by the government's surveillance of Internet communications; authorities at first claimed that this eavesdopping was restricted to communications directed abroad, but then later admitted that domestic messages were also being monitored.

The insulated status ascribed to imperial affairs, the secrecy and inhibitions beginning to envelop domestic politics and the operations of globalizing corporations have the net result of excluding the public from a deliberative role in each and all of the major preserves of modern power. The demos is free to enjoy the results of its exclusion, but, as in the political process in general, it has no claim to a significant, let alone a controlling, influence. At the same time, the powers that exclude democracy from their counsels are eagerly exporting it. Thus democracy, like empire and globalization, gains a universal status, but what it universalizes is not the practice of self-governing democracy but American power.

Recently the director of national intelligence, John Negroponte, announced that a new strategy had been adopted by the Bush administration "to bolster the growth of democracy"; henceforth that goal would rank among the three top missions for American intelligence agencies—just below the war against terrorism and weapons proliferation. The director specified that the agencies' "operators" would "forge relationships with new and incipient democracies" in order to help "strengthen the rule of law and ward off threats to representative government."[5] Undercover democracy: one could imagine a day when a grateful democratic movement would express thanks by erecting a monument to the 100,000 spies that the agency claims to employ.[6]

iii

Haven't we already given money to rich people?
Why are we going to do it again?
—*President George W. Bush*

Stick to principle, stick to principle.
—*Karl Rove, responding*

Reagan proved that deficits don't matter. We won the midterm
elections, this is our due.
—*Vice President Cheney. also responding*[7]

State power not only relies upon corporate power for the conversion of scientific advances into technological achievements but depends heavily on corporate personnel for policy advice and managerial skills. Consider this postmodern potpourri. Politicians resign in order to accept lucrative corporate positions; corporate executives take leave (typically with "delayed compensation") to run government departments and set policies;[8] and high-ranking military officers are hired by corporations, become TV commentators, join faculties, and run for presidential nominations. One consequence is that the political has been managerialized. Politics and elections as well as the operation of governmental departments and agencies now are routinely considered a managerial rather than a political skill. Management is not a neutral notion, however. Its roots are in the business culture, its values shaped by the pressures of a competitive economy that persistently push the limits of legality and ethical norms. The arrogance that leads corporate executives to violate the law finds its parallel in the arrogance with which Superpower flouts or disregards international norms.[9]

The consequences are registered in the decline of a public ethic. Disinterestedness has virtually ceased to be celebrated, much less practiced, as a public virtue. Instead it has become a casualty of the process of relentless rationalization and integration. One of the preconditions of disinterestedness, a certain protected isolation, was thought to encourage independence. Ideals such as academic freedom, isolation of the scientist from the marketplace and from politics, the impartial jurist, and the public intellectual (a Walter Lippmann) were valued as especially necessary to the pursuit of truths in matters where interests and passions ran strong in society at large. Another casualty: the ideal of a civil service, disinterestedly devoted to the public good and a noble calling for college graduates. Its place is now occupied either by the "manager" who is equally at home at the Department of Defense, Halliburton, and the Republican National Committee, or by the party apparatchik who is rewarded for loyal service that he is expected to continue to perform, albeit as a public servant. Not coincidentally, generals who later join corporations and corporate executives who take a turn in government have, along with party officials, regularly been charged with corrupt practices.[10]

iv

Corporate power depends on the state in innumerable ways: for contracts, subsidies, protection; for promoting opportunities at home and abroad. Beginning in the last quarter of the twentieth century, the relationship between corporate power and state power began to develop beyond one of reciprocal favors or of a revolving door between corporate headquarters and military headquarters. An important fact of contemporary politics is that, while the scope of government regulatory authority has receded, corporate power has increasingly assumed governmental functions and services, many of which had previously been deemed the special preserve of state power. Corporate expansion extends to military functions, a province once jealously guarded as a state prerogative.[11] To the extent that corporation and state are now indissolubly connected, "privatization" becomes normal and state action in defiance of corporate wishes the aberration.

Privatization supplies a major component of managed democracy. By ceding substantive functions once celebrated as populist victories, it diminishes the political and its democratic content. The strategy followed by privatization's advocates is, first, to discredit welfare functions as "socialism" and then either to sell those functions to a private bidder or to privatize a particular program. A traditional governmental function, such as education, is in process of being redefined, from a promise to make education accessible to all to an investment opportunity for venture capital.[12]

It might seem perverse to warn of the "totalitarian temptation" at a time when the Republican Party—and to a lesser extent, the Democratic—have championed the cause of "smaller government," of trimming the size of the "bloated bureaucracy" and sharply weakening its regulatory powers. To scoff at the warning would be to miss a main object of managed democracy: the expansion of private (i.e., mainly corporate) power and the selective abdication of governmental responsibility for the well-being of the citizenry. These trends are not driven by a desire to reduce control over the populace. Rather they indicate a realization that governance—in the sense of control over the general population and the performance of traditional governmental functions, such as defense, public health measures, assuring the means of communication and transportation, and education—can be accomplished through "private" mechanisms largely divorced from popular accountability and rarely scrutinized for their coerciveness.

The so-called free market is not simply about buyers and sellers, or producers and owners, but about power relationships that are fundamental to the management of democracy. Financial markets are not just about securities but about useful insecurities. These constitute methods of discipline, of reinforcing certain behaviors and discouraging others, of accustoming people to submitting to hierarchies of power, of exploiting the tentative nature of employment—the uncertainty of rewards, pension systems, and health benefits. The union of corporate and state power means that, instead of the illusion of a leaner system of governance, we have the reality of a more extensive, more invasive system than ever before, one removed from democratic influences and hence better able to manage democracy.

v

We support the election process, we support democracy, but that doesn't mean we have to support governments that get elected as a result of democracy.
—*President George W. Bush*[13]

Today references to "corporate culture" are commonplace. Corporate culture might be defined as the norms and practices operative at various levels of the corporate hierarchy that shape or influence the beliefs and behavior of those who work in a particular institutional context. Today corporate culture is not confined to the corporation. Managed democracy depends upon managers, and managers are the product and creators of corporate culture. The question is this: what are the characteristics of the culture that corporate managers bring to government? how are the corporatists likely to approach power and governance, and how does that approach differ from political conceptions?

Over the centuries politicians and political theorists—starting with Plato's *Republic*—have emphasized disinterestedness, not personal advantage, as the fundamental virtue required of those entrusted with state power. In recognition of the temptations of power and self-interest a variety of constraints—legal, religious, customary, and moral—were invoked or appealed to in the hope of limiting rulers or at least inhibiting them from doing harmful or evil acts. At the same time rulers were exhorted to protect and promote the common good of society and the well-being of all of their subjects. With the emergence of democratic ideas during the seventeenth and eighteenth centuries, it fell to the citizen to assume responsibility for taking care of political and social arrangements, not only operating institutions but "cultivating" them, caring for them, improving them, and, ultimately, defending them. Democracy presumed the presence of a "popular culture," not in the contemporary sense of packaged pleasures for a perpetually adolescent consumer, but culture in its original meaning: from the Latin *cultus* = tilling, cultivating, tending. The ideal of a democratic political culture was about cooperating in the care of common arrangements, of practices in which, potentially, all could share in deciding the uses of power while bearing responsibility for their consequences. The assumption was that if decision-making institutions of a community were left untended, all or most might suffer. A medieval aphorism summed up the traditional idea of the political, "that which touches all should be approved by all."

In contrast, the ethos of the twenty-first-century corporation is an antipolitical culture of competition rather than cooperation, of aggrandizement, of besting rivals, and of leaving behind disrupted careers and damaged communities. It is a culture for increase that cannot rest (= "stagnation") but must continuously innovate and expand. It accepts as axiomatic that top executives have to be, first and foremost, competition-oriented and profit-driven: the profitability of the corporate entity is more important than any commonality with the larger society. "The competitor is our friend," according to an Archer Daniels Midland internal memo, "and the customer is our enemy." Enron had "visions and values" cubes on display; its chief financial officer's cube read, "When Enron says it will rip your face off, it will rip your face off."[14]

Perhaps the most striking embodiment of the aggrandizing culture of the corporation is Wal-Mart, the consumer's low-cost paradise and the perfect economic complement to Superpower. In its own way it is an invasive, totalizing power, continuously establishing footholds in local communities, destroying small businesses that are unable to compete, forcing low wages, harsh working conditions, and poor health care on its employees, discouraging unionization.[15] It is inverted totalitarianism in a corporate, imperial mode.

As the scandals about Enron and WorldCom demonstrated, the self-interest of the corporate executive takes precedence over the interests of the institution. During the last decade corporate crimes and abuses involving the highest executive levels have been commonplace: cheating, lying, deceptive practices, extraordinary bonuses despite corporate failure, ruthless conduct, and so forth. Recall that in the Reagan presidency, corporate managers rather than public service–oriented officials dominated the upper levels of government, bringing with them a corporate ethos.[16] Not surprisingly, "conflicts of interest" flourished. Equally unsurprising, the reverse did not occur; no corporate executive stood accused of sacrificing private interest to the common good. The effect of persistent, pervasive corporate misconduct is to promote public distrust of power-holders in general. From Superpower's vantage point public cynicism, far from being deplorable, is one more element contributing to political demoralization and languor.

Although the doctrine of the "preemptive strike" is a controversial topic in discussions of foreign policy, there is less *political* controversy about its economic counterpart. Corporate competition has its preemptive strike in hostile takeovers, poison pills, and the like. These tactics of corporate power politics form a complement to Superpower politics.[17] The corporate ethos is not one that favors conciliation and fairness or worries over collateral damage.

The broad question is whether democracy is possible when the dominant ethos in the economy fosters antipolitical and antidemocratic behavior and values; when the corporate world is both the principal supplier of political leadership and the main source of political corruption; and when small investors occupy a position of powerlessness comparable to that of the average voter. "Shareholder democracy" belongs on the same list of oxymorons as "Superpower democracy."

At stake are the conditions that serve forms of power antithetical to democracy. The citizenry is reduced to an electorate whose potency consists of choosing among congressional candidates who, prior to campaigning, have demonstrated their "seriousness" by successfully soliciting a million dollars or more from wealthy donors. This rite of passage ensures that the candidate is beholden to corporate power before taking office. Not surprisingly, the candidate who raises the most money will likely be the winner. The vote count becomes the expression of the contributor.

"Managed democracy" is the application of managerial skills to the basic democratic political institution of popular elections. An election, as distinguished from the simple act of voting, has been reshaped into a complex production. Like all productive operations, it is ongoing and requires continuous supervision rather than continuing popular participation. Unmanaged elections would epitomize contingency: the managerial nightmare of control freaks. One method of assuring control is to make electioneering continuous, year-round, saturated with party propaganda, punctuated with the wisdom of kept pundits, bringing a result boring rather than energizing, the kind of civic lassitude on which a managed democracy thrives. A large campaign contribution represents the kind of surplus power a dynamic capitalist economy makes available. It begins as the production of an ordinary commodity, say a computer chip, which eventually turns a profit that is then "invested" in a candidate or party or a lobbyist in order to purchase "access" to those who are authorized to make policies or decisions. A law or regulation favorable to the donor mysteriously emerges—an immaculate deception or "earmark" with no apparent "father." No one wants to acknowledge paternity or reveal the consensual act that produced it.[18]

At issue is more than crude bribery. Campaign contributions are a vital tool of political management. They create a pecking order that calibrates, in strictly quantitative and objective terms, whose interests have priority.[19] The amount of corruption that regularly takes place before elections means that corruption is not an anomaly but an essential element in the functioning of managed democracy. The entrenched system of bribery and corruption involves no physical violence, no brown-shirted storm troopers, no coercion of the political opposition. While the tactics are not those of the Nazis, the end result is the inverted equivalent. Opposition has not been liquidated but rendered feckless.

vi

[In a direct democracy] the countenance of the government
may become more democratic; but the soul that animates
it will be more oligarchic. The machine will be enlarged,
but the fewer and often, the more secret will be the
springs by which its motions are directed.
—*James Madison*[20]

Early in the American occupation the Iraqi Governing Council, whose members had been handpicked by the occupiers, proposed a solution to the problem of governance: let the council enlarge itself and then proclaim that body to be the interim legislature. That grab for power seemed too crude for American tastes, and so the deputy secretary of state vetoed it, saying, "I think we need a little bit more transparent and participatory process than that."[21]

That version of democracy has been tested successfully at home, which is why the Bush administration's trumpeting of "regime change" is more ominous than reassuring. It revealed the administration's understanding of democracy, and why control of elections loomed so large for the leaders of the American occupation. The initial attempt by the American authorities to set a June 2004 date for the Iraqi elections may have been an unsubtle maneuver to gain a talking point in the impending American presidential election in the fall, but it was also a tacit admission that the two electoral systems belong to the same project, one that a sympathetic pundit described as "making democracy safe for the world."[22]

While a "managed democracy" might seem a contradiction in terms, the idea of an exportable democracy was not invented on the spur of the moment to justify the invasion of Iraq. The mere existence of Superpower was testimony to democracy's reliability and availability for export—otherwise its leaders would not have felt sufficiently confident to impose it upon Iraq and persuade themselves that the whole Middle East needed only the example of Iraq to incite a regionwide stampede that could be corralled for democracy.

Such confidence was inspired by the ways in which democracy had been shaped at home. Inverted totalitarianism had perfected the arts of molding the support of the citizens without allowing them to rule. Having domesticated democracy at home, the administration knew the specifications in advance; hence a proven product could be exported, along with expert managers boasting honed skills, tested nostrums, and impressive résumés.

For the American conquerors majority rule has certain negative connotations associated with uncertainty of outcome and probable excess. As one important American adviser remarked in warning against introducing direct elections before safeguards were in place, "If you move too fast, the wrong people could get elected."[23] Managing democracy requires a process by which "extreme" views are filtered and control rests with a favored guardian group, the "right people," who have been preselected by the conquerors and rewarded with being the first to gain a foothold in power. From that strategic vantage point, and under the watchful supervision of the conquerors, they are expected to produce the political structures of a democracy in which power is distanced from the people in whose name it is to be exercised.

vii

José Luis Rodríguez Zapatero, leader of the Spanish Socialist Workers' Party . . . campaigned on a pledge to withdraw the 1,300 Spanish troops stationed in Iraq if the United Nations did not assume control of the occupation. . . . The Zapateros of Europe . . . seem bent on validating the crudest caricatures of "old European" cowardly decadence. . . . Paradoxically, Mr. Zapatero can redeem Spanish democracy only if he repudiates the popular mandate he received and announces that there will be no withdrawal from Iraq because of any act of terrorism, Muslim or Basque.
—*Edward N. Luttwak*[24]

That managed democracy should be promoted by an administration steeped in corporate culture reflects a primal concern of globalizing capitalism, indeed, of capital generally: the concern for stable conditions. Typically the principal means of establishing stability include a reliable legal system, effective governance, and an orderly citizenry: in other words, the conditions for assuring that expectations—those accompanying an investment or a contract, for example—will not be upset by destabilizing developments, such as erratic fiscal policies, widespread social unrest, or popular demands for the nationalization of oil.

The attempt to eliminate or radically reduce such contingencies is a tacit admission that a principal source of social instability is capitalism itself. Ever since its inception capitalism has produced not only goods, services, and jobs but also severe social dislocation. The dynamic of capitalism disrupts established practices, beliefs, even whole communities, rendering traditional skills obsolete, and generally emptying "the old ways" or traditions of any practical significance. A vigorous capitalism always carries the potential for producing social unrest that occasionally culminates in demands for anticapitalist, egalitarian policies and governmental intervention.

The vicious circle, whereby capital provokes hostile reactions that threaten the stability it requires, is reproduced in Superpower. With the amalgamation of corporation and state the political ethos of public service is replaced by an aggressive and exploitative ethos. The essential skill that a corporate executive brings to his firm and to a top-level governmental position is the skill of devising and executing strategies of aggrandizement, both within and outside his or her domain. This often requires that one attack rivals, eliminating or weakening them before they can attack you. Preemption.

The symbiosis between corporate and Superpower politics extends beyond the shared value of aggressiveness. Consider the notion of "collateral damage." It has become familiar in the form of the regrettable casualties—typically of civilians, especially women and children—reckoned to be the inescapable "costs" of military actions and the "price" of "winning." Consider "downsizing" as the corporate version. Firms downsize in order to compete more efficiently with rivals. Downsizing means casualties: careers destroyed, lives radically changed, hopes blasted. It is hailed as an essential, inescapable part of the "creative destructiveness" (Schumpeter) of capitalism. Equally important, downsizing is mimicked by a politics that consistently sacrifices the needs of the poorer and often the more vulnerable classes—the counterparts to civilian casualties. Reduction of social benefits, lax enforcement of workplace standards, preserving a scandalously low minimum wage, all these are part of strategies devised to achieve an electoral victory and demonstrate the political superfluousness of the working classes. With the emergence of the phenomenon of "outsourcing," collateral damage is spreading upwards toward the middle and white-collar classes, threatening even those with advanced degrees in computer sciences.

A government responsive to the deepening distress of the Many, to ever-widening class disparities, to impending environmental crises, would need sufficient autonomy to defy corporate wishes. The fact that government rarely challenges corporate power allows capital to define the political terrain to fit its own needs.

In the recognition that it is a structure for organized aggression, corporate capital systematically recruits skilled operatives, individuals who can manage contingency by coordinating operations, seizing fresh opportunities for expanding the resources of the firm, and defending it against the challenges of rivals while its PR experts make certain that the proper spin is attached. The culture is refreshed, systematized, and transmitted by professional schools and increasingly by much of higher education; it is even popularized by television, most recently in *The Apprentice* featuring a real CEO (Donald Trump) who regularly fired some contestants, after first humiliating them, and encouraging each to undercut the others.[25]

Among the main functions of the modern manager are to foresee the unexpected, eliminate or cope effectively with the unforeseen ("risk management," "crisis management"); to exploit or contain change insofar as it affects his or her enterprise; and to seize opportunities and aggressively use them to advance the power advantage of the firm— and of him- or herself.

The executive or manager is, above all, a decision-maker. Accordingly, the effective exercise of managerial skills dictates certain institutional requirements, among them strong and centralized authority, a hierarchical power structure, top-down control, and an aversion to whistle-blowers.

The managerial role has emerged from a context of extreme competitiveness; hence successful managers tend to be known more for ruthlessness than for democratic camaraderie, for intolerance of criticism from associates and subordinates, for demanding huge bonuses—which sometimes prove detrimental to the firm—rather than for the casual indifference to material perquisites supposedly characteristic of traditional elites. Although managerial elites are typically trumpeted for their "objective" skills, their aura of rational decision making sits uncomfortably with the favors, perks, golden handshakes, golden parachutes, and fraudulent, deceptive practices that have been revealed to go far deeper into corporate culture than the pecadilloes of a few. More than one CEO has ruined his firm while "managing" to emerge unscathed and richer for the experience.

viii

Not, one might think, the kinds of qualities desirable in those sworn to "protect and defend" a Constitution of limited powers and checks and balances. That familiar phrase from the oath of office points to the traditional understanding that served to distinguish public from private institutions. Its crucial supposition was that government consisted of nonprofit institutions whose basic responsibility was "to promote the general welfare." The measure of performance was political, not economic; the common good, not the bottom line. That ideal was to be represented in its personnel: they were depicted in democratic terms, as "public servants" whose ranks were open to all who were qualified, and dedicated not to acquisitive pursuits but to defending and improving the lives of citizens.[26] The ideal of public service was meant to embody a mode of conduct and a set of ideals emphasizing the responsibilities accompanying public power and the near absolute contrast between "government service" and business practices.

The ideal of disinterested public service has also figured in the notion of the independence of the judiciary, but now the system of creating an "interested" judiciary has been perfected and without apology. Although political considerations have always been in play in appointments to the Supreme Court, most notably during the administration of FDR, the recent controversies over the judicial nominations of John Roberts and Samuel Alito and in the aborted nomination of White House counsel Harriet Miers marked the moment when disinterestedness was publicly interred. Little effort was made to conceal the "interested" character of the nominations. Rather the partisan loyalty of the nominees became a recommendation—and this before a national television audience. What the "glare of publicity" did not reveal was that the cultivation and production of reliable jurists has become systematized. It is not simply the duck-hunting trips involving the highly partisan vice president and the equally partisan Justice Scalia but rather the systematic effort to identify, encourage, and educate future court appointees through organizations such as the Federalist Society and so-called judicial education programs financed by business interests and held at fancy resorts.[27]

Public servants were supposedly the instruments by which a democracy could be realized. That same ideal of the public servant, chosen solely on the basis of merit, represented the point where the ideals of democracy and of republican elitism converged in a kind of salutary tension: between the values of commonality and equality and the claims of excellence, not of superiority. The idea of a merit system was an offshoot of the classical republican conception of elites. Classical republicanism had conceived elites in purely political terms: disinterested service on behalf of the public good, not the amassing of wealth. The corporate revolution has reshaped the republican ideal in the image of the corporate executive. In the process it has ruptured the alliance between the demos and the elite, between democracy and republicanism.

Instead of a convergence of commonality and excellence, the skills and ethos of aggressive management—its culture of beliefs and practices, its forms of corruption—have been rationalized into a corporate makeover of a politics struggling to be democratic. It signals the defeat and corruption of commonality.[28] Accordingly, recent policies of the Bush administration have deliberately promoted inequalities of wealth, taxation policy, health care, educational opportunities, and life prospects. In the process the egalitarian momentum generated during the thirties and revived during the sixties of the last century has been reversed. As a result democracy has been reduced to a rearguard action, struggling not to advance and improve the lives of the Many but merely to defend the shredded remains of earlier achievements.[29]

One form of inequality that is rarely discussed arises from the inequities and accompanying sacrifices of military service. Since the Vietnam War, and then reaching unprecedented proportions in the wars of George I and George II, the ranks of the armed forces have been filled entirely by volunteers and reservists, that is, by those who need a job, or additional income to survive, or who are trying to earn citizenship by enlisting, or who risk their lives in order to gain the educational opportunities that arguably would be the right of every citizen in a less shameless democracy. In a genuine democracy all citizens (save for obvious exceptions of age, health) would be expected to serve and thereby share sacrifices, which would make foreign adventures a bigger political risk domestically.

It is worth noting that despite the protests of high-ranking military officers that their forces were being strained to the limits by the unexpected armed resistance during the occupation of Iraq, there was an embarrassed silence in Washington and the media when an occasional dissident voice suggested reintroducing a military draft. Superpower warfare is the real, if sardonic, version of class warfare: the less well-off fight wars instigated by the well-off, well-educated, and well-represented.

ix

Democratic legitimation might be defined as the ceremonial and symbolic action whereby citizens invest power with authority. In a truly participatory democracy elections would constitute but one element in a process of popular discussion, consultation, and involvement. Today elections have replaced participation. Elections enact a kind of primal myth in which "the people" designate who is to rule them, that is, who is authorized to wield governmental power. Authority or authorization means not only that some official is enabled to perform a particular action (e.g., has the means to enforce the law) but also that he or she is entitled to assume that citizens will accept the decision and comply. Thus an election, at one and the same time, empowers a Few and causes the Many to submit, to consent to be obedient. Submission entails more than obeying the law. Citizens, regardless of whether or not they voted for the elected candidate, are expected to defer to those who were elected, to give them the benefit of whatever doubts there are about the wisdom of a particular action or law. In the identification of democracy largely with voting, there is the risk that legitimation can become automatic, tantamount to a slippery slope ending in Tocqueville's submissive citizenry.

While the management of elections resembles many of the ways of business management, not least in being competitive, there used to be one important difference. Elections have always been contests in which there were winners and losers. But, in a democratic context, winning acquired an additional element of legitimacy from the presence of party competition. The assumption that the defeated party or parties would continue to exist and compete another day served to bestow legitimacy on both the victorious and the defeated party.

That understanding has been tacitly challenged by the new Republican Party's scheme to establish a permanent majority that will support an agenda aimed at eliminating the social programs essential to democracy.[30]

x

In theory elections should be the nonnegotiable condition of effective demotic power. Its corollary is that elections should be determined fairly. As the infamous Florida recount of 2000 taught, minimal requirements must include a fair count of the votes, with each vote equal to every other, and the maintenance of the conditions that enable citizens to vote free from intimidation or official obstruction. The presidential election of 2000 also taught a bitter lesson that the people have no power over the very process that is supposed to be the prime example of their empowerment. In contrast to organized, well-heeled interests, who have power to spare, ordinary citizens have only the power allowed them by a process they cannot control.

The paradox is that while in the abstract the demos has the authority of electing, it lacks effective power to control or set the terms of actual elections, including the regulation of campaign finance, television ads, and debate formats.[31] Instead we have the phenomenon of highly managed elections controlled by those who use the resources and know-how of economic organizations to manipulate the capture of authority.

To better understand the ideas whose triumph eased the way for managed democracy and eventually for its exportable version, we need to take a brief excursion into the historical controversies behind the strategy of rendering democracy (in the contemporary jargon) "governable" rather than actually controlling. We want to inquire into the ideological antecedents of the peculiar combination of governing elites and a populace that reigns without ruling.

xi

In a culture where names are invented mainly with an eye to their commercial appeal rather than to any historical associations, one revealing exception appears in the names of our major political parties. The Democratic Party—curiously, Republicans think it disparaging to call it the "Democrat" Party—can fairly plausibly claim to be the party comparatively more faithful to the "demos," to poor people, minorities (racial, sexual), trade unionists and workers generally: to persons whose sole form of power lies primarily in their numbers. Throughout much of Western history they were referred to simply as the Many, more recently as "ordinary people" or "folks," an undifferentiated aggregate that stood in sharp contrast to the clever Few who were possessed of distinguishing marks such as pedigree, wealth, and education. The Republican Party tends to attract and reward the wealthy, the better-educated, most business people, especially corporate types: persons whose power derives from their ownership and control over the means of creating and producing the main forms of social power. These forms include the material (cars), the immaterial (the media, popular religion and culture), the financial (banks, investment firms), and the technocratic (managerial, legal, academic)—resources that are readily convertible into forms of political power: organizing electoral campaigns, orchestrating the media chorale, "mounting legal challenges," conducting lobbying, financing and staffing policy tanks, and temporarily lending their talents to governing the nation, though, without conscious irony, only after first placing their wealth in a "blind trust."

Those party labels and the differences they represent are consistent with a long-standing historical opposition between the advocates of democracy and those of republicanism. Managed democracy represents the triumph of the latest version of republicanism.

The distinctions were invented centuries ago, appearing first in ancient Athens. The Greeks formulated it as a contrast between those who supported the idea of having political offices filled by ordinary male citizens (the demos) on the basis of lot and election, and those whose ideal was a leader-oriented democracy of outstanding men, typically aristocrats (*áristoi*), supported by a deferential citizenry. The demos stood for the idea of "the people" in their civic capacity, as a collective actor, not, as later, a passive electorate. The trauma of the Peloponnesian War produced a profound antidemocratic reaction among the Athenian political and intellectual elites. For centuries thereafter and down to the present their ideas colored virtually all descriptions of democracy while inspiring numerous versions of elitism. The demos was categorized as fickle, tumultuous, irrational; envious of the wealthy, the talented, and the well-born. Above all, the "people" became a byword for the tendencies that good governance should hold at bay. After the demise of Athenian democracy elite strategy aimed at discouraging the demos from ever again becoming conscious of its powers.

It was not until the English civil wars of the mid-seventeenth century that the political and intellectual elites' picture of the demos was challenged by modern democratic ideas of equal rights and popular political participation. Although those ideas made their way to the American colonies where they were established as a persisting and powerful presence, English political influences also brought the idea of aristocracy and along with it the notion that "higher" birth, great wealth, and (some) education justified rule of the Few. While the entitlements of nobility failed to take hold in the colonies, the dichotomy between elite and rabble persisted, exacerbated and seemingly confirmed by popular revolutions, first in the colonies and then in France.[32]

When James Madison declaimed, "Had every Athenian citizen been a Socrates, every Athenian assembly would have still been a mob,"[33] he was expressing a political elite's fear of the type of popular pressures for direct democracy that had prevailed in Athens. The fear of assembled numbers was a fear that popular power might "level" all civilized distinctions of wealth and ability. Yet the pressing "weight" of numbers represented the only form of practical power that the Many possessed to challenge its history of exclusions. Despite the obvious fact that the labor of the Many and their military service were essential to the existence of society, throughout Western history—and most other histories—the vast majority of the members of society were excluded from virtually all of the advantages associated with "civilization": literacy and education, safe living conditions, a steady income, adequate diet and shelter, the protection of the law, public office, and political representation. Inevitably, exclusion provoked rage, rioting, demands for equality, and occasional rebellion. The rabble had good reason to be tumultuous.

During the English civil wars of the seventeenth century the excluded found their own voice and a political identity. But little more than a century earlier, republicanism had begun to revive and, in anticipation of the democratic stirrings of the next century, to search for a modus vivendi that would overcome the ancient division between republicanism and democracy, between the Few and the Many.

In early modern times the most famous theorist of republicanism was Niccolò Machiavelli—who happens to be a favorite author among Straussians.[34] In a European world beginning to modernize and to experience the first stirrings of nationalism, Machiavelli concluded that politics could no longer be conducted successfully if it relied on traditional sources of power, remained restricted to hereditary monarchs and nobles, and preserved the dichotomy between elitism and democracy. He proposed a new kind of politics with new players. Effective governance required a combination of skilled elites (the republican principle) and popular support (the democratic principle). Republicanism would depend upon the ability to recruit a select number of idealistic, patriotic young men untempted by the allures of wealth and high privilege but drawn instead toward the idea of power in the service of the common good. They were to be educated in the school of political realism and taught that power was the irreducible means by which a state preserved its existence in a world of predatory rivals. Politics was, first, foremost, and always, about power: how to gain, manage, and increase it. In order to defend the state or advance its interests, rulers must be prepared to flout conventional standards of morality, not for personal gain but for the preservation of the republic.

Machiavelli reasoned that in changing times, when the people, as represented by artisans, merchants, and tradesmen, were beginning to play a part in local political life, a system could not survive for long if it ruled blatantly in the interests of the Few, whether of the nobility or the wealthier classes. Machiavelli argued that the old dogmas about the people as a tumultuous mob were mistaken; they were a far more stable element than the vain and fickle aristocrats. Accordingly, a republic's power should be broad-based, founded on the people, although not in the sense that the citizenry was to share in the actual exercise of power. Rather its function was to support the republic's rulers. Citizens should, for example, serve in the militia and, above all, stand with those who were sworn to defend republican institutions and were skilled in their management. Toward that end the citizens were to be educated, taught that loyalty was owed to their city or state rather than to noble patrons. Among the most important elements in the political education of the citizenry was the promotion of a religion that emphasized sacrifice: inevitably the city or state would be at war and would have to defend itself by expanding its power over other states or cities.

At no point did Machiavelli develop a principled argument in defense of popular participation, much less of democratization of politics. Machiavelli favored the people as a reliable "foundation" for power principally because they did not demand much. The price of their loyalty and support was simple: to be left alone and protected in what modest possessions they had. Accordingly, one principle Machiavelli insisted upon was that his elite respect the property and the wives of citizens.

The people were not only reliable—far more so as soldiers than the usual mercenaries—but malleable, manageable. The pliant qualities that Machiavelli attributed to the "multitude" suggested the possibility of a political science that could show how a culture might be designed to suit political needs, in particular how popular allegiance could be secured by a civil religion. Rulers should institute religious rituals and observances that sanctified the state, cemented the loyalty and obedience of the populace, and rendered them willing to risk their lives if necessary. Religion should be tailored to political requirements and to the limitations of the people. The appropriate model, Machiavelli argued, was not the meek and submissive cult of Christ but a pagan and more dynamic cult. A civic religion should stage bloody spectacles and symbolic violence to stir and toughen the populace. When later the great historian Gibbon remarked of the Roman emperors that they cared less whether a religion was true and more whether it was useful, he spoke the authentic language of Machiavellian republicanism.

Machiavelli believed that the whole question of what kind of institutions a republic should adopt and what sort of social and class basis it should favor depended on a crucial choice: between a republic that aimed at expansion, as in the Roman example of a small republic acquiring an empire by conquest; and, alternatively, a republic shaped primarily to defend itself and content with the status quo, as was the case of the Venetian Republic. The choice also involved whether a republic aimed at "greatness" measured in terms of power or dominion and wealth, or whether it chose a modest life. Machiavelli favored the Roman example, but the interesting aspect of that choice was the crucial role assigned the people, not only in supporting expansionism but in contributing a dynamic. If people feel both free and secure that their "patrimony will not be taken away and that they may aspire to share in rule then riches [will] multiply and abound." Once they are "convinced" that "what they have acquired" will be secure, the competition that ensues brings advantages to individuals and "wonderful progress" to the republic.[35]

Although Machiavelli admired the Roman example, he warned that it was also a model with a briefer life expectancy than that of a contented republic. That difference pointed to the attraction of the Roman example to elites down to the era of the neocons. The Roman way posed greater risks to the safety of the republic, but, at the same time, it brought the possibility of achieving "greatness" and "glory." Thus, while the republic might end in disaster, its "fame" and that of its heroes would survive. That risky path would inevitably bring the leaders up against the cruelest choices: they must not hesitate to commit horrible acts when the survival of the republic was at stake, a likely possibility on the hazardous road to greatness.[36] Elitism thus had a dark side, a fascination with noble death, with death not for low material ends—that was for the multitude and the merchants—but for fame, even immortality.

xii

Machiavelli's teachings made their way to England, filtered first through Elizabethan dramatists, including Shakespeare, and then developed more systematically in the seventeenth century by political theorists, such as James Harrington and Algernon Sidney.[37] During the civil wars of that century republicanism fused with Puritanism to produce an ideology hostile to the claims of kings and aristocrats. The advocates of republicanism proposed a blend of Machiavellian competence with Puritan notions of an "elect" to produce a new variant of elitism, actors as confident of their skills as of their rectitude.

That combination later migrated to the American colonies where it was preserved among New Englanders, beginning with John Winthrop, the first governor of the Massachusetts Bay Colony, continuing with John Adams, and absorbed by aristocratically inclined Southern politicians, such as Jefferson and Madison.[38] A republican elite led the opposition to colonial rule, directed the war against Britain, drafted the Constitution, staffed the new government, and established a party system. During the formative period from colonial times to the Jacksonian era, when fundamental political institutions and practices were being settled, republicanism dominated American politics.

With the possible (and ambivalent) exception of Jefferson, the American republicans were steadfast critics of democracy. When they decided that it was time to draft a new constitution, they treated as axiomatic that a modern political system had to make concessions to democratic sentiments without conceding governance to "the people." Accordingly they composed a masterful translation of republicanism that drew a line indicating what was to be allowed and what excluded from the democratic aspirations aroused by the struggle for independence from Britain. While they recognized the "people" as a political presence, they proceeded to dilute the potential of democratic power by constraints intended to filter out any grand schemes. An elaborate system of checks and balances, separation of powers, an Electoral College to select the president, and, later, judicial review were designed to make it next to impossible for popular majorities to institute policies actually in the interests of the majority. Only the House of Representatives was to be directly elected by eligible (white male) voters; the Senate was to be indirectly elected by the various state legislatures.[39] And it was hoped that the Electoral College would play an active role in the selection of presidents and not merely register popular votes. The framers of the Constitution were the first founders of modern managed democracy.

The republicans assembled at Philadelphia demonstrated their grasp of how, in a popular government, the electoral system could be stacked so as to prevent its being used to promote a populist agenda, and nowhere more clearly than in the provision governing the most crucial power a democracy can have, the power to change its constitution. Article V stipulated that an extraordinary majority was required for constitutional amendments: a two-thirds vote of both houses and ratification by three-fourths of the state legislatures or by three-fourths of special state conventions.[40] That naked empowering of minorities amounted to a subversion of the Constitution's grandly democratic preamble, "We, the People of the United States . . . do ordain and establish this Constitution." Small wonder that, later, when the New Deal attempted to improve the lot of ordinary and poorer citizens, its efforts were attacked by modern republicans as an assault on the Constitution and its protection of property rights.

A major tactic on the way to managed democracy was to encourage what might be called "discouraged democracy." A prime example was the device of requiring extraordinary majorities that became a staple of antitax and -spending forces beginning in the latter part of the twentieth century. Not only did the device increase the power of highly organized minorities, but it served to discourage a majority from using its power to promote social programs intended to meet basic needs and improve the lot of poorer citizens. Voter apathy is importantly a consequence of low expectations that their government will respond to their needs. Why bother? Perhaps because inequalities are not confined to differences of wealth, status, life prospects, and conditions of existence; such inequalities translate into inequalities of power. Arguments about taxation are, at bottom, arguments about the distribution of power.

While low voter turnout might seem a reflection of low civic morale and a dangerous symptom of democratic decline, republicanism would view it in a positive light. A certain amount of nonvoting is especially welcome if it deters the most desperate, those who are likely to be swayed by "populist" demagoguery.[41] When Republicans and conservative Democrats work methodically to reduce or eliminate social programs, the result is tantamount to a deliberate strategy of encouraging political apathy among the poor and needy.

This antipopulist tactic marks a sea change in American politics. Recall that the administrations of Eisenhower and Nixon both followed periods of extensive social reforms that had primarily been the work of Democrats (the New Deal, 1932–40; the Fair Deal, 1945–52; and the Great Society, 1963–68). Yet neither Republican president sought seriously to roll back programs that were widely perceived as beneficial to the country as a whole. That consensus prevailed until the Reagan election of 1980. Thereafter the consensus disintegrated and gave way to a radically different understanding. Rejected was the principle that what legitimized a government as democratic was not solely an electoral majority but the use of governmental power to serve the needs and aspirations of ordinary people. Instead the effort was undertaken—principally, but not solely, by Republican politicians—to hammer home the astounding principle that a democratically chosen government was the enemy of "the people." Reagan promised, accordingly, "to get government off the backs of the people." During the 1990s politicians of both parties educated the populace in antigovernment ideas. Democrats and Republicans alike then raced to see who could propose the most drastic cutbacks in social welfare programs. Government that had prided itself on serving the Many was dismantled in favor of "a leaner government." Predictably this counterrevolution was made easier during the 1980s and 1990s by a spate of ideologically inspired, wildly exaggerated, and racially divisive attacks upon "welfare cheats" and "Cadillac welfare queens."

The successful counterrevolution was doubly significant. Whatever the merits of corporate capitalism, it is not a system whose benefits are equally distributed. It is instead a system that, as a matter of course, produces striking inequalities. The results are evident in the greater concentration and extremes of wealth, a deeper divide between classes, in terms of health care and of educational and cultural opportunities, than at any time in recent history. The wide disparities serve to expose the counterrevolutionary strategy that motivates the champions of managed democracy.

Counterrevolution means, not a return to the past—the powers fostering it are too dynamic—but a closing off of a *demotic direction* and the nudging of society toward a different direction where inequalities will be taken for granted, rationalized, perhaps celebrated. Not the least of the counterrevolutionary conditions promoting cultural, economic, and political inequalities are the ingenious barriers that the Bush administration erected to prevent future administrations from alleviating inequalities. By enacting tax measures that according to virtually every account primarily benefited the wealthiest, and by amassing ever-increasing government deficits to astronomical proportions, that administration has effectively prevented a future democratically oriented administration from enacting social programs for the Many. The aim of the counterrevolutionary strategy is the permanent institutionalization of a counterdemocratic state. Meanwhile military spending is nearly four times greater than the expenditures on social programs; yet neither party would dream of proposing an amendment specifically limiting or controlling military spending—only one prohibiting same-sex marriage.

The antimajoritarian provisions of the Constitution and of various state constitutions are typically touted as a salutary check on the excesses inherent in the practice of majority rule. The "tyranny of the majority" and the specter of "socialism" are the knee-jerk reaction of think tank apparatchiks, business leaders, and Republicans whenever the possibility emerges of government regulation of business practices, or the possibility of real programs for advancing the opportunities of average citizens. Yet the fact is that the most serious incursions into the political and civil liberties, for example, have come not from tyrannical majorities representative of the poor, the needy, or the struggling middle classes but from the representatives of elites, the Justice Department, legislators, judges, police, prosecutors, and media, which, with some honorable exceptions, play sycophant to the powerful.

The crucial problem lies not with rapacious majorities poised to plunder the privileged but with discouraged majorities that have had their hopes raised when social programs to their advantage have actually been enacted, only to see them rolled back or left underfunded.

CHAPTER NINE

Intellectual Elites against Democracy

i

[T]he rule of a tyrant who, after having come to power
by means of force and fraud, or having committed any
number of crimes, listens to the suggestions of reasonable
men, is essentially more legitimate than the rule of
elected magistrates as such.
—*Leo Strauss*[1]

As we saw in the preceding chapter, historically the idea of elite rule conceived democracy as its antithesis and natural enemy. With the emergence of the modern state, postmodern technologies, and post–Cold War complexities elitism's claims, that governance demands a special order of skills lacking in ordinary citizens and should be entrusted to the Few who possess them, would seem irrefutable, especially when democracy is seen as increasingly anachronistic. Today, when the appeal of democracy is being touted by ruling elites and exploited as an instrument of American power, elite contempt is prudently camouflaged, or perhaps sublimated, as managed democracy.

In its belief that the Few should more or less monopolize power, political elitism displays its elective affinity with capitalism. Both believe that the powers of high office, whether in government or business, should be reserved for those who earn them by their personal qualities and exceptional talents—demonstrated under highly competitive conditions—rather than for those who gain power by virtue of popular approval. In the best of worlds, political elites would be entrusted with power and rewarded with prestige; capitalist elites would be rewarded with power and wealth. Because both represent the best, they are, in that view, *entitled* to power and reward.

In theory, the two forms of elitism should be at odds with each other.[2] Political elites are entitled to power, in part, because they possess functional skills but also because they are supposed to be "virtuous," that is, disinterested, principled, and, above all, dedicated to the true interests of the society. Business elites, on the other hand, not only are presumed to be self-interested but work in a context where self-interest is the prevailing motive, even inculcated as principle, and where the common good is more of a side effect or unintended consequence than a guiding principle of decision making. Where "trust" is crucial to the relationship between elites and those they often refer to as "the mass," distrust is operative in the relationship of corporate leaders versus shareholders and the public at large. The tensions between the two versions of elites run far deeper. As recent revelations have shown, corruption is close to being a constant of corporate life. Given the integration of a corporate ethos with that of high-level government offices, one might expect the weakening of disinterestedness and the emergence of a more arrogant and secretive executive branch, one nearly tone-deaf to conflicts of interest. As we shall see, the uneasy alliance between disinterested and self-interested elites shows signs of fraying, suggesting that in the era of the corporate state elitism is merely a cover.

The peculiarity of elitism in the United States is that while the practice of it is securely established in political, corporate, cultural, intellectual, and professional life, and their relationship to democracy much on the minds of elitists, it seems rarely to concern democrats.[3] Although elitism has been a staple topic in the literature of the social sciences for more than a century, and of political theory for more than two thousand years, politically its existence seems unproblematical today even though it challenges directly the democratic principles of equality and shared power. The phenomenon of Superpower makes the issues more urgent, as Superpower is distinctively the creature of elites and the antithesis of democracy.

ii

More members of this year's freshman class at the University of Michigan have parents making at least $200,000 a year than have parents making less than the national median of

about $53,000, according to a survey of Michigan
students. At the most selective private universities . . . ,
more fathers of freshmen are doctors than are hourly
workers, teachers, clergy members, farmers, or members
of the military—combined. An important purpose of
institutions like Harvard is to give everybody a shot at the
American dream.
—*President Lawrence H. Summers, Harvard University*[4]

There are two domains where the contradictory aims of Superpower
elitism and anti-Superpower democracy are most evident and crucially
important for both: education and elections. Neither elections nor democracy is the source of the legitimation to which elites appeal; today,
instead, education is the core legitimating principle of elitism. For its
part, democracy is ultimately dependent on the quality and accessibility
of public education, especially of public universities. Education per se
is not a source of *democratic* legitimacy: it does not serve as a justification for political authority, yet it is essential to the practice of citizenship. The difficult task of public education is to combine civic education with the development of civilized sensibilities and socially useful
types of competence.

Education that is civic and populist is not a formula that accords
with the requirements of American hegemony as elites conceive it.
They envisage public education for Supercitizenship, education for the
masses, as increasingly privatized and specialized rather than civic and
civilizing. Privatization entails a concerted strategy for breaking the monopoly of public education at the primary and secondary levels and
encouraging "private" corporations to establish and operate schools,
including public institutions; financing is provided by public funds that
might otherwise support public schools. Technical education—that is,
the creation of "a skilled workforce"—has been the task assigned to
the two-year "community colleges," the institutions that serve as the
terminal point where formal education ceases for a student body overwhelmingly drawn from lower-income families.[5] Conversely, private
institutions—prep schools, colleges, and universities—are elevated and
assume the function of public institutions, virtually monopolizing the
preparation of ruling elites while receiving substantial public funds and
subsidies. The public is privatized, the private "publicized."

iii

> Former Secretary of State Henry Kissinger talked about the
> Vietnam War and conducting foreign policy in the 21st
> century in a question-and-answer session with 40
> [Princeton] undergraduates. . . .

> With students on couches and chairs around him, Kissinger
> took questions on all topics, telling the students, "Feel free to
> ask any question you want. There are no impolite questions."

> Later he had dinner with a second group of students,
> where he gave a lecture.[6]

How do contemporary elites become elites? What are they taught? Who authorizes them? Or are they recognized rather than authorized—and by what process? are they quietly recruited and initiated like members of Skull and Bones, the secret society of Yale undergraduates, several of whom attained high political positions?

In earlier eras those questions had relatively straightforward answers. One became a member of an elite by heredity. In ancient Greek the word for aristocracy was *aristokratia*, or rule by the best (*áristos*). The assumption was that noble birth went along with "natural" aptitudes for military or political leadership or high religious office. Actual skills were acquired through training and tutoring. Later Jefferson cited the term *áristoi* in extolling the value of a "natural aristocracy" whose members achieved preeminence by ability alone—which assumed a society that welcomed talent regardless of wealth or birth. In the twenty-first-century United States, however, elite status rarely follows a Horatio Alger scenario where an individual of humble origins gains success by dint of hard work and ability, achieving status and fortune while becoming beholden to none.

Elitism might be defined as the political principle which assumes that the existence of unequal abilities is an irrefutable fact. That principle was fundamental to Nazi and Fascist regimes; it is equally fundamental to inverted totalitarianism. The "fact" of unequal abilities is not, however, accidental. Today in the United States there is a circular system whereby elites are produced and the institutions producing them are confirmed as "elite institutions," thereby attracting a fresh supply of promising material that further confirms the institutions' special status. A small number of U.S. institutions select, groom, train, and certify a small number of individuals as exceptionally talented and warranting privilege.[7] "Elite" private preparatory academies, colleges, and universities, including Bible colleges and theological seminaries, perform the function of identifying and producing, not just elites, but authorities.[8] At elite institutions, unlike community colleges and many public and private educational institutions, the humanities and social sciences are featured prominently, whereby those subjects are designated as a badge of superiority distinguishing their students from those at lesser schools emphasizing "work skills." The vocational education of elites is deferred to the highly competitive graduate and professional schools in law, medicine, business, the sciences, social sciences, and humanities, where not only qualified practitioners but "leaders in their field" are produced. Although a few public universities, even an occasional public high school, make the cut, the high costs of elite institutions convert attendance into an investment. The expectation is that there will be a "return" in the form of a prestigious career.

Elitism functions as a self-sustaining enterprise. The key is to produce not only successful alumni but rich ones to feed the virtually insatiable appetite of elite institutions, where fund-raisers are as prolific as scholars and university financial officers are millionaires. While still in school those chosen as future elites are encouraged to "network" with each other for later reference and assistance. Academia is also a privileged setting where the successful return as honored guests and lecturers. There they hobnob with the eager wannabes and provide future "contacts," letters of recommendation, and résumé entries.

Yet while academic institutions are the main manufacturers of elites, there remains the post-postgraduate stage of maintaining and refining them, and utilizing their skills. Bright prospects are passed along to think tanks, institutes, and centers. There they learn the arts of developing "policy proposals" and demolishing the arguments of their enemies. Think tanks are not modeled after Plato's austere Academy; they are not environments where individuals are free to explore a problem, letting the chips fall where they may. Rather the tanks and centers function as ideological auxiliaries mobilized to promote the agendas favored by their sponsors. As an executive at one prominent think tank explained, "We're not here as some kind of Ph.D. committee giving equal time. Our role is to provide conservative public policy makers with arguments to bolster our side."[9] There are also nonpartisan, mercenary "centers" where ex-officials will sell analyses or proposals on a contractual basis. Flanking these are the foundations that support think tanks, supply grants to select recipients, and promote projects to their liking. Foundations subsidize a variety of causes ranging from liberal to reactionary. Liberal foundations give awards to designated geniuses, while the more extreme conservative foundations are aroused by the prospect of investigating the sexual practices of liberal presidents.[10]

The reproduction of elites is an instance of the phenomenon of "rationalization." The existence of elites doesn't just happen; it is systematized, premeditated, refined to a practice assuring that those who are selected as "promising leadership material" will prove to have the right stuff, thus validating the methods of selection and, in the process, perpetuating the system that has made them possible. It is said that at night, when elitists look at themselves in a mirror, they mutter, "The system cannot be all bad . . ."

iv

Elitism is perhaps most pronounced in the areas of politics relating to international relations and foreign policy. This is not surprising because these are precisely the areas where, historically, partisanship has supposedly been taboo—except for bipartisanship. ("Politics stops at the water's edge.") Historically, matters of diplomacy, foreign policy, war, and peace have been singled out as a special province to which both the opposition and the public are admitted only when it becomes politically awkward to bar them or expedient to admit them. Revealingly, foreign policy was once called the domain of "statecraft" and was closely associated with so-called arcanae imperii, state secrets, suggestive of a range of especially sensitive matters involving high risk, great dangers, and swift responses, and demanding superior intelligence, specialized knowledge, lengthy experience, and a relatively free hand. Thus, virtually by definition, foreign affairs were not only "outside" politics but a domain of expertise where notions of democracy seemingly made no sense. Foreign affairs, like military affairs, were about power politics, unpredictable dangers—including threats to the very existence of the nation—complex strategies, and "the" national interest, subjects about which average citizens lacked the experience and competence to judge. The models for the kind of experienced expertise qualified to deal with high matters of state were the "wise men" assembled by President Kennedy during the Cuban Missile Crisis and later by President Johnson for Vietnam strategies.[11] Although the one was a near nuclear disaster (averted because in the end JFK followed his own judgment) and the other a clear disaster (plunged into because LBJ did follow his more hawkish advisers), neither resulted in discrediting the status of elitism or its claims. Two prominent neocons predicted that installing "a decent and democratic government in Baghdad" would be "a manageable task for the U.S."[12] As the second Iraq war proved, failure merely stiffens the resolve of elites and their defenders.

During the first Gulf War George I exulted that "by God, we've kicked the Vietnam syndrome once and for all."[13] The syndrome included not only popular resistance to an adventurous foreign policy and mounting criticism of "the foreign policy elites," but, equally important, widespread experiments in spontaneous "teach-ins" where the pros and cons of foreign policy and military strategies were avidly discussed by ordinary citizens, students, and teachers. One of the reasons why "the sixties" continues to be a favorite punching bag of neocons and neoliberals is that it represented a decade of prolonged popular political education unique in recent American history. The most frequent topics were racism, foreign policy, corporate power, higher education, and threats to ecology—each in one form or another a domain of elitism. Public universities, such as those at Berkeley, Ann Arbor, and Madison, played a leading role in the organization of antiwar activities. That none of those institutions was ruffled by antiwar agitation at the time of the U.S. invasion of Iraq in 2003 testifies to the effective integration of universities into the corporate state.

v

> Elections, open, free and fair, are the essence of democracy, the inescapable sine qua non. Governments produced by elections may be inefficient, corrupt, shortsighted, irresponsible, dominated by special interests, and incapable of adopting policies demanded by the public good. These qualities make such governments undesirable but they do not make them undemocratic.
> —*Samuel P. Huntington*[14]

It is striking that at the very moment in our nation's history when the most vital public questions revolve around foreign policy, the issue of elitism versus democracy should emerge and, equally significant, assume the form of a neoconservative-neoliberal attack upon democratic elections.

Of late, democratic elections in the United States have appeared clouded. They have not been marked, as elections in Weimar Germany were, by the violence of an extreme Communist Left and an extreme racist-nationalist Nazi movement on the right. Nor have they been threatened, as was Italy's weak parliamentary system of the 1920s, by the repetition of a Fascist March on Rome—marches in the United States have been overwhelmingly aimed at defending democratic institutions. Instead, electoral democracy was subverted in the 2000 election by Republican elites assisted by toadying conservative appointees on the Supreme Court; by a code of near silence on the part of the mass media; and by a supine opposition party. The opposition failed to alert the citizenry to the threat posed by the display of managed democracy in Florida and its less publicized equivalents elsewhere in the nation; instead Democrats blamed Ralph Nader. The events heartened the apologists for Superpower who have set about to discredit democratic elections, reducing their status from a first principle to a strategy and, in effect, justifying machinations (*sic*) that engineered a coronation rather than an election.

vi

> Liberal education is the necessary endeavor to found an
> aristocracy within democratic mass society.
> —*Leo Strauss*[15]

Today's elitism reflects one particular development without precedent in American history and, indeed, one that runs counter to much of it. This is the role of academic theories in shaping the management and direction of foreign policy. The academic genealogy of today's elitism consists primarily of two branches, one deriving from the émigré political philosopher Leo Strauss, the other from a native son, Samuel Huntington. Both have furnished recruits to the National Security Council, the Departments of State and Defense, and the ranks of punditry. The Straussians, as befits a highly intellectualized elite, have tended to avoid service in the more prosaic departments of Commerce, Transportation, and Labor.

While Straussians project elitist ideals of heroism and a disdain for the ordinary, Huntington confronts the complexity of a world of large collectivities, of conflicting "civilizations." While Straussians are in principle antidemocratic, Huntington wavers. His early writings are critical and incline toward elitism: democracy "is one public virtue, not the only one."[16] His more recent writings, however, are of uncertain direction, reflective of a candid disillusionment with current elites. Although neither celebrates capitalism, neither ventures a critique nor explores capitalism as a distinct system of power. Both serve an ideological function, contributing to the legitimation of some powers and the delegitimation of others.

Throughout his career Huntington has been a familiar figure in the halls of power of government, corporate-sponsored think tanks, and academia and has never hesitated in exposing his views to a wider public.

Strauss was at the opposite extreme, reclusive, sheltered by his disciples, rarely, if ever, engaged in public debates, never a proponent of specific policies; nonetheless, a passionate teacher of an extremely rarefied "political" philosophy whose disciples have occupied high positions of power and influence in foreign and military affairs.

In his own highly distinctive way Strauss was as much a fundamentalist and archaist as the born-again religionists whose disciples also occupy high positions in government. He believed it his mission not only to recover ancient teachings, especially those of Socrates, Plato, and Aristotle, and to reveal their truths concerning "knowledge of the good life and of the good society,"[17] but also to attract a coterie who were capable of grasping a teaching that was often deliberately esoteric, and who would eventually repeat the process, identifying new disciples and, if possible, putting the teaching into practice. The claims of political philosophy were not confined to knowledge of the morally uplifting; they extended as well to "the nature of political things," especially concerning who should rule, what aims are to be pursued, and what kind of politics is to be shunned.[18]

The singularity of Straussism is not the invention of a doctrine or the creation of a coterie privy to esoteric truths from which the uninitiated are excluded. The Pythagorean brotherhood (sixth century BCE) followed a rule of secrecy about the master's teachings and severely punished those who divulged it to outsiders.[19] One might argue plausibly that secret doctrines are, by definition, incongruous with both the academic world and the public world of democratic politics. Rather what is astonishing is that the Straussian initiates once occupied high political positions even though the secret teaching and the disciples themselves appear incongruous in a governmental setting that is strongly redolent of the corporate world and its values of materialism and self-interest. How is it possible for the adepts of absolute truths hidden in the ancient past to make common cause with powers—such as science, technology, and corporate capitalism—that, if they are anything, are bent toward overcoming past achievements? Is the alliance based on nothing more than expediency in which one side provides access to power and its possibilities while the other supplies ideological cover for what amounts to a drive for economic and political hegemony?

Nowhere is that incongruity more striking than in the leadership of the Defense Department during the first administration of George II. Its secretary, Donald Rumsfeld, was the incarnation of the blending of the corporate and governmental worlds and was renowned for his no-nonsense approach, the last person one would associate with esoterica or love of (abstract) truth, and the first person one might nominate as the embodiment of the crude drive for power per se. He has been an elected representative, a member of the White House staff, and the chief executive of one of the largest pharmaceutical corporations — and he is a former member of the Princeton wrestling team. Notwithstanding, his onetime second-in-command, Assistant Secretary Paul Wolfowitz, was a Straussian who, presumably, would not have been appointed without Rumsfeld's approval. By all accounts, Wolfowitz, along with other initiates, was among the principal architects of the invasion of Iraq. Perhaps it is relevant to note that before leaving Nazi Germany, Strauss enjoyed close intellectual relations with Carl Schmitt, a political and legal philosopher who collaborated with the Nazis and enjoyed official favor; moreover, both before and after he left Germany, he offered no harsh public criticism of either Hitler or Mussolini.[20]

To understand what, at first glance, appeared to be the extremely odd couple of Rumsfeld and Wolfowitz, we must briefly look at the master's teaching, inquiring how its particular form of archaism could contribute to the dynamic of Superpower, to the practice of elitism, and to the subversion of democracy. Like Superpower itself, Straussism is based upon a fantasy about power — in this case, the power to be found in a most unlikely form, philosophy. Unlike most of the fantasts of scientific and technological power, who are rapturous about the material benefits for humankind that such powers can bring, Strauss was a fantast who warned of the harm to the "masses" that the true philosophy would wreak should the Many ever gain even a glimpse of its meaning and implications.

What form does the awesome power of the true philosophy take? The true philosophy knows a great and dangerous truth, that society is founded on and held together by myths, that is, untruths. By nature the masses are credulous; their credulity is necessary to the existence and preservation of society and, not least, of philosophers. So the "Few," "wishing neither to be destroyed nor to bring destruction upon the multitude," must not expose to the Many, or publicly ridicule, the insubstantial basis of mass beliefs.[21] So, while the true philosophy holds that religious teachings are false, its adepts must not openly attack those beliefs or even express contempt. By extension, although Strauss did not commit himself on the subject, the same self-restraint would hold regarding capitalism—but perhaps not for those exceptional "captains of industry" who sought power rather than mere wealth, say, by endowing university chairs or supporting think tanks of the proper persuasion.

For Strauss there is "a" true political teaching found primarily in the philosophies of Plato and Aristotle, with more than a nod now and then to Nietzsche, the apostle of "superman" (*Übermensch*) and a strong believer in the gullibility of the masses. The teaching is about "values," not policies. It is not to be understood or conveyed by ordinary methods of reading, nor is it accessible to the ordinary, even to the skilled reader. The great texts must be deciphered for an esoteric or hidden meaning that can be revealed only by a learned master who has the responsibility of ensuring that true meanings are taught only to those Few of unusual intellect and virtue. The convolutions of the method are such that the master's teachings are also cast in esoteric terms, so that their "real" meaning is comprehensible only to those who have undergone a demanding apprenticeship and instruction in the arts of decipherment. Hence students, implicitly young men, must be carefully selected and nurtured, and are expected to remain loyal to the teacher and each other. The disciples resemble a brotherhood; women rarely figure in the ranks of Straussians. The teaching and teacher must be insulated from the "crowd," from what one prominent Straussian called "native populism and vulgarity."[22]

What is "the" teaching and why the phobia about secrecy? It is not directly about "policies," practical means, or programs, but about principles. The first principle is that power should be in the hands of the virtuous, meaning those dedicated to what is "highest": to absolute truth and "the good," to the supreme value of the intellect, especially as embodied in the philosopher. This worthy is not the pragmatic, or analytic philosopher of the Anglo-American tradition, much less the postmodern philosopher of twentieth-century France; the exemplars are the two preeminent philosophers of ancient Greece and the premature Nazi, Nietzsche.[23] Secrecy is enjoined as a matter of prudence. The philosopher has to be cautious, to conceal his true beliefs from the "many" who have an "unqualified commitment . . . to the opinions on which society rests."[24] (Translated, that means not attacking democracy but using it.)

In order to protect themselves and the "multitude" the philosophical "few" resort to coded language when communicating publicly.[25] Truth and the true philosopher are both dangerous to society, not least because they are subversive of the common beliefs, myths, and prejudices that the vast majority hold: the glue of society.[26] While the teaching is self-described as "lofty," it is far from being fastidious about the uses of power or allergic to a certain ruthless deployment of it as long as it is being wielded by the virtuous, who "know" and value the Good and respect the true hierarchy of values.

There is, as the above account suggests, a marked strain of antimodernism in the ideology: it is hostile toward social science, cool toward the natural sciences, contemptuous of popular culture, and tactful toward capitalism, especially in the form of financial support from right-wing foundations, such as the Olin Foundation.[27]

vii

Straussian ideology outfits its adherents not with specific policies but rather with grandiose ambitions, like "democratizing" the Middle East. The achievement of bringing Straussism to bear upon political actualities belongs unquestionably to Harvey Mansfield, Jr. Mansfield has sought to demonstrate, not so much how, but *why* power and virtue should be combined so that politics can again be a great stage for heroic action and noble deeds. In a dazzling and subtle account Mansfield depicts an ideal political world where the "executive" dominates the political system, not a political system understood in terms of checks and balances or responsibility to the citizenry, but one inspired in almost equal parts by an ideal of monarchy, a patriot king, and a dismissive contempt for democracy.[28] Mansfield's "prince" is not conceived either as an official whose principal responsibility is to execute the laws passed by the legislative power or as "the people's tribune." Far from being "tamed," as the ironical title of Mansfield's book seems to imply, Mansfield's "prince" is instructed to exploit the possibilities of an office that is claimed to be "at least in part outside the law and not explained by the system."[29] Clearly, George II—with his expansive conception of presidential power, as represented by his practice of appending "signing statements" to legislation, proclamations that place his understanding of statutes above that of Congress and his understanding of the proper treatment of prisoners above that of the rule of law—would have no difficulty qualifying as a "prince."

Mansfield's prince governs in the broad sense; he "rules" with a kind of Gaullist *grandeur*, testing the constitutional limits of office, while pursuing a politics of "daring, sacrifice," and "nobility."[30] Above all, ideally the executive stands not for programs but for "virtue." That means, among other things, he is prepared to act in defiance of the popular will. Virtue, or the love of the highest things, is something only the Few can aspire to and the Many never appreciate. A true leader would be justified—not to put too fine a point on it—in concealing his motives and objectives from the public. In Mansfield's polity the citizenry has no substantive share in political power; their lot is to respect the virtue embodied in their governors and, by definition, denied them.

There is a remarkable, although not uncharacteristic, passage where Mansfield refers to a famous incident in the Peloponnesian War between Athens and Sparta and offers it as a telling example of the politics of risk and glory. It reads especially poignantly in the aftermath of the invasion of Iraq. "Not even Alcibiades," Mansfield lamented, "could convince a modern democracy to launch the Sicilian expedition that he persuaded the Athenians to undertake."[31] Mansfield fails to round out the picture: Alcibiades happened to have first betrayed his native Athens and then sided with its deadly enemy, Sparta, only to betray it in turn; upon his return to Athens, his demagogic talents enabled him to regain power and persuade the Athenians to risk a new expedition against Sicily. It resulted in a disastrous defeat, hastening the eventual surrender of Athens and the beginning of its demise.[32] But it was undeniably daring . . .

Mansfield is scathingly contemptuous of the politics dominated by interest groups. "Interests" are viewed primarily as a useful political tool for buying off the demos, distracting them from interfering in what Nietzsche called "grosse Politik," politics on a grand scale. The whole subject of economic policy or of policies of any kind has no place in Mansfield's conception. And, predictably, he is silent about corporate power. Perhaps rightly so: his prince is not that kind of crusader. We need no longer speculate as to what might happen if the "virtuous" wing of the Bush administration, the Alcibiades faction, were to persuade the "corporate wing" to embark on a bold, unprovoked invasion of Iraq that, at this writing, promises neither glory nor profits, only a debacle of unprecedented magnitude and a deceit-filled chapter in the history of the republic. But it was daring . . .

viii

Elitism stands for rightful entitlement to power, and by implication a claim to greater authority than that conferred by the citizenry. The fundamental importance of elections for democracy and, in a more complex sense, of First Amendment rights, is that they are the irreducible means by which consent can be expressed and the conditional basis of authority affirmed. The point of the elaborate grooming of elites discussed earlier is to establish a process of selection that wants to be recognized as an institutionalized alternative to election, as a rite of passage to legitimation. As defined in a previous chapter, legitimation involves the method(s) by which power acquires authority, or the rightful exercise of power. The obvious big step for elitists is to delegitimize its main rivals, the institution of electing leaders and the democratic ideals of which elections are the political expression. The objective is nothing less than to diminish and replace consent as the first principle of legitimation—and to foreshadow the contempt for democratic elections and the subsequent coup of 2000.

Fareed Zakaria, a protégé of Huntington, has obliged with *The Future of Freedom* (2003), a frontal attack on democracy and an attempted apologia for elitism.[33] Zakaria's argument is exactly the opposite of the analysis I have been advancing. Instead of a beleaguered democracy growing ever more powerless, he portrays democracy as all-powerful, total in its influence. At the same time, he contends that while elites actually rule in the United States, they are hesitant to admit it. What is troubling about Zakaria's analysis is not the particular political problems he identifies. Rather it is his account of their causes and his proposed solutions.

According to Zakaria, "For much of the twentieth century, professionals formed a kind of modern aristocracy, secure in its status and concerned with the country's welfare and broader interests. . . . For all of the elitism and privilege that accompanies such a world, American democracy was well served by public-spirited elites."[34] In contrast to my claims about the grooming system and its emphasis upon producing professionals, Zakaria contends that we have become enveloped by a totally democratic society, a reflection of the fact that power has shifted "downward." "[T]he democratic wave is breaking down hierarchies, empowering individuals, and transforming societies well beyond their politics." The term "democratization," as Zakaria employs it, is given an elasticity that allows it to cover virtually any phenomenon he deplores. Thus the "masses" are declared to be "the primary engine of social change." The proof is in the "democratic" character of capitalism whereby "hundreds of millions" have been "enriched."[35] Thanks to money-market funds "suddenly a steelworker . . . could own shares in blue-chip companies."[36] In news that should cheer the homeless, Chase Manhattan Bank is declared guilty of "catering to the great unwashed."[37] Similarly consumerism is the expression of democracy, consumerism conceived not as simple consumption but as the exercise of mass power. Not long ago "patrons of art . . . rarely gave a thought . . . to curry[ing] favor with the public," but now (ostensibly as another expression of democratization) "corporate sponsors support art as part of a business strategy."[38] Democracy is also the beneficiary of the "information revolution." The latter has "made control impossible and dissent easy"—a stunning claim in the light of revelations about government spying on the Internet. Worse, "most anyone can get his hands on anything. Like weapons of mass destruction." The result: we are threatened by "the democratization of violence."[39] (As contrasted with what, aristocratic violence?) At the same time the state has been weakened, its authority "sapped" by "capital markets, private businesses, local governments, [and] nongovernmental organizations." Even more bad news: democracy has been displaced by "a simple-minded populism that makes popularity and openness the key measures of legitimacy."[40]

Zakaria seems not to allow the possibility of a development that appears to have antielitist implications and yet has no causal relation to democratization. Thus he deplores that doctors and lawyers, instead of acting as dignified professionals, have become "hustlers," and presents this is an instance of democratization instead of, say, normal market behavior.[41] One might suggest, however, that recent scandals about the role of doctors in promoting pharmaceutical products are evidence not of an insidious egalitarianism at work but rather of the "opportunities" thrown up by an intensely competitive and dynamic economy that often is at odds with ethical standards in several professions.[42] Zakaria, however, insists the problem is one of "democratization"—his comprehensive term for a porous society where access to every social domain is open to any and all. "Democracy" is its political version. Zakaria defines democracy as "rule of the people" and identifies elections as the essential element of democracy. He never explains or illustrates how the people actually "rule" or even in what sense they form a single coherent entity. For him democracy is concentrated in the single institution of elections. To defend that narrow conception he simply decrees that "the rule of law, a separation of powers, and the protection of basic liberties of speech, assembly, religion, and property" have "nothing intrinsically to do with democracy." In the past "free elections" produced Hitler, and now they might bring "Islamic theocracy or something like it."[43] Throughout the world he sees "illiberal democracies" that violate rights and override constitutional limitations.[44] Dictatorships, such as those of Tito or Suharto, are preferred because they were more "secular" and "tolerant" than some elected regimes. All of this justified because the "people" need "guidance" by authority.[45] He has kind words for Musharraf's coup in Pakistan and for Pinochet, who, we are instructed, "did eventually lead his country to liberal democracy"[46]—and, no doubt, the disappeared reappeared. Zakaria favors "liberalizing autocracies" and "dictatorships [that] opened the economy" and "made the government more and more liberal." His model is the East Asian autocracy, which, he notes, is superior to the American South of the 1950s.[47] In the United States slavery and segregation were "entrenched" by virtue of "the democratic system." Jim Crow was destroyed, Zakaria opines, not by democracy "but despite it." He attributes no significance to the civil rights movement except as part of the sixties' "assault" on "the basic legitimacy of the American system."[48]

Curiously, despite his preoccupation with elites Zakaria maintains an absolute silence about the most ambitious attempts in recent times to proclaim the principle of elitism, to cultivate it systematically, and to put it into practice. Nazi Germany, Fascist Italy, and Stalin's Soviet Union, despite their differences, all shared a basic conviction that their respective societies could achieve their objectives only if led by the exceptional Few, typically represented by the leadership of "the" party.[49] Instead, Zakaria identifies the British colonial system as the ideal regime for preparing a society to become a liberal democracy—American elitists of a non-Straussian stripe tend to be Anglophiles. According to his Kiplingesque view, the British elites imposed "limited constitutional liberalism and capitalism."[50]

As regards the United States Zakaria prefers the early republic when political candidates were chosen by "tightly controlled hierarchies" and legislatures were hierarchical and "closed"—in contrast to today when politicians "do scarcely anything else but listen to the American people."[51] "Special interests now run Washington," and the major responsibility, predictably, is attributed to the attacks on authority launched during the sixties and to the political reforms that followed. Once the floodgates were opened, "minorities," lobbyists, celebrities, and the rich began to dominate.[52] The new elites that now control the political parties are inferior to "the old party elites": the arrivistes consist of Washington professionals, activists, ideologues, pollsters, and fund-raisers. Zakaria's list does not include corporate donors and sponsors.[53]

The main problem, as he sees it, is that those who operate the present system fail to "enact policies for the long run." Instead of "real reform," such as trimming welfare benefits, there is "pandering." His solution is antidemocratic as well as antipolitical: "the economic realm" should be sealed off from politics and "the impartial judge" adopted as our political model.[54] The best examples of that model are institutions protected from political pressures such as the International Monetary Fund (IMF), the World Bank, the World Trade Organization (WTO), and the Federal Reserve Bank.[55] We need to "insulate some decision-makers from the intense pressures of interest groups, lobbies, and political campaigns—that is to say, from the intense pressures of democracy. . . . What we need in politics today is not more democracy but less."[56] As examples of regimes able to enact farsighted policies, Zakaria points to Taiwan, South Korea, Singapore, Chile, Indonesia, "or even China."[57]

Despite his tirade against "democratization" Zakaria acknowledges grudgingly that elites do exist and rule; however, because of the influence of democratization elites don't recognize themselves as such or they hesitate to acknowledge publicly their uniqueness. When Zakaria enters the most damning indictment of the current elites, that they lack true public spirit or the fundamental virtue of disinterestedness, his elites surrender any ethical claim to legitimacy they might have had.

> By declaring war on elitism, we [*sic*] have produced politics by a hidden elite, unaccountable, unresponsive, and often unconcerned with any larger public interest. The decline of America's traditional elites and institutions—not just political but cultural, economic and religious—is at the heart of the transformation of American society.[58]

In the end Zakaria has no solution; he wearily concedes that democracy remains "the last, best hope." That he offers no clues as to how democracy can be expected to cure itself of itself leaves one with the suspicion that either he has misdiagnosed the problem—if it is one—of why there are no "true" elites, or else he is reluctant to pursue his own suspicions. Following his ritualistic indictments of porous democractization he concedes that the corruption of the political process and the abysmal quality of popular culture are, at bottom, due to the influence of money and to those (elites?) who have lots of it. Zakaria's ideal of "constitutional liberalism" is inspired by nineteenth-century liberalism, with its priorities of "individual economic, political, and religious liberty" and its rejection of all forms of "coercion." Far from recognizing the power of capital, Zakaria defends nineteenth-century laissez-faire and argues for freeing economic activity from government regulations—as though by reducing governmental power one reduced the political power of capital. At the same time he fails to recognize that what he chooses to label as "democratization" has in reality been a feature of capitalism since long before modern political democracy and its electoral systems even existed. A French historian of an earlier generation pointed out that what was unique about the early bourgeois capitalist was that in his transactions he was indifferent to a buyer's political affiliation, religious beliefs, or skin color.[59] Historically, however, it did not follow that the bourgeois was similarly indifferent about removing property or racial qualifications for office or for voting, or that he believed that workers had the right to form trade unions, or that black Americans had the same rights as other citizens. Rather he understood that wealth was power and that a society which recognized that equation would allow the wealthy to use their power to further whatever political, social, or cultural goals they favored. They could be public benefactors (Carnegie) or private mischief-makers (robber barons). But to attribute that situation to "democratization" is to invite Anatole France's gibe about the majesty of the law in that it equally allows the rich and the poor to sleep under the bridges at night.

In the end Zakaria can offer no solution to the problem he has identified as democratization operating in collusion with nontraditional elites, presumably including the kind represented by Zakaria himself— immigrant background, graduate of Yale and Harvard, editor at the mass-circulation magazine *Newsweek*.[60] Democratization anyone?[61]

ix

As a leading American institution, Harvard College has
a responsibility to educate its students—who will live and
work in all corners of the globe—as citizens not only of
their home country, but also of the world, with the capacity
not only to understand others, but also to see themselves,
and this country, as others see them.
—*Dean William C. Kirby, Harvard College*[62]

The despair over the condition of elites has recently been expressed in a surprising formulation by Huntington himself. In an essay entitled "Dead Souls: The Denationalization of the American Elite" Huntington in effect signaled that the American experiment of combining democracy with elitism was over—and the causes of the failure lay squarely with the elites. Mansfield had been prepared to suffer democracy because he thought it feckless rather than dangerous, easily distractible through the manipulation of its dreams of avarice. In contrast, Huntington had early on depicted democracy as a threat to the power of the state and as posing the problem of whether an electoral democracy was governable. The ballot enabled the masses to press for policies and social programs that diverted resources which might otherwise be used to strengthen the state.[63]

While the Straussians see the philosopher as their ideal, Huntington, in his earlier writings, had a more robust, less intellectual role model but one that shared the Straussians' disdain for material acquisitiveness. In *The Soldier and the State* (1957) he extolled the professional military officer as the embodiment of the true national ideal, the brave patriot who serves his country by a life of austere self-sacrifice. West Point, not Plato's Academy, could save the United States from its infatuation with democracy and, by implication, its elites from Wall Street.

A half century later Huntington's problem is not that the people have denied elites their rightful place or that they are ungovernable. Rather it is that a transformation of American elites has caused them to turn their backs on their native land. The American establishment, he asserts, has become divorced from the American people.[64] In contrast the people have remained steadfast, loyal, and devoted to the homeland and its values. For Huntington the consequence is a crisis of loyalty produced by the opposing perceptions of "national identity" held by "the more cosmopolitan elites," on the one hand, and the general citizenry, on the other.

> The public, overall, is concerned with physical security but also with . . . sustainability . . . of existing patterns of language, culture, association, religion and national identity. For many elites, these concerns are secondary to participating in the global economy,

supporting international trade and migration, strengthening international institutions, promoting American values abroad, and encouraging minority identities and cultures at home.[65]

"Dead souls," in Huntington's formulation, "refers to not loving one's country."[66] He arranges the soulless under three categories: the "universalists" who believe that the whole world has become American in its values and popular culture; the globalists ("a global superclass"), primarily the leaders of corporate multinationals, who are focused upon "breaking down national boundaries, merging national economies . . . and rapidly eroding the authority and functions of national governments"; and, finally, the "moralistic" types, primarily "intellectuals, academics, and journalists," who decry "patriotism and nationalism as evil forces" and who favor international institutions.[67] This "intelligentsia" is accused of abandoning "their commitment to their nation and their fellow citizens"—and this while "Americans as a whole are becoming more committed to their nation."[68] The supreme stake in this cleavage is "national Identity." The universalists see the world as becoming Americanized; hence the distinctiveness of America disappears. The globalists tend to favor an American imperium by which the United States shapes the world but, in the process, loses its identity.[69] The public, in contrast, is concerned about "military security, social security, the domestic economy and sovereignty."[70]

Huntington is in no doubt as to the crux of American national identity: "America is different and that difference is defined in large part by its religious commitment and Anglo-Protestant culture." "At the heart" of that culture "have been Protestantism" and the "political and social institutions and practices inherited from England, including most notably the English language."[71] Elites, in contrast, tend to be "liberal" and irreligious.[72]

That formulation is intended not as a contribution to dispassionate analysis but as a polemic against the multiple identities favored by multiculturalists and ethnic preservationists; against the demotion of English as the sole language of instruction in the public schools; against the lax enforcement of border controls; and against the ideal of inclusiveness. The really patriotic Americans tend to be native born and white.[73] The fact that immigrants were, in effect, forced to adapt to "Anglo-American culture" is cause for celebration rather than apologetics: "it gave birth to the American Creed."[74]

Huntington's xenophobic and nativist tendencies should be understood as defensive, a circling of the wagons, stemming from his long-standing belief that the hegemonic power of "the West" and of the United States is in decline.[75] An expansionist America is far from Huntington's ideal. If the United States is not the unchallengeable Superpower but a failing hegemon, what grounds does Huntington find to reverse his earlier dim view of the demos and now place his hopes in them rather than in elites? From what quarter does he draw the evidence for his view that the citizenry, long ridiculed by conservative critics, should now represent the last best hope for the survival of the nation? And, crucially, what are the virtues possessed by the demos that recommend it as political saviors?

The peculiarity of Huntington's eulogy of the people is that he supports it by relying exclusively on polling data. "The patriotic public" emerges in response to questions such as "How proud are you to be an American?" Huntington's "public" is thus a construction of the pollsters. He takes pains to point out that the polls also reveal that "significantly fewer blacks than whites think of themselves as patriotic."[76] Hispanics fare only slightly better as patriotic material. Huntington makes no reference to participatory actions or political involvements as characteristics or concerns of his citizenry. The people appear more as a mass with patriotic sentiments, as the stuff of a governable populace, as more ready-made for inverted totalitarianism than for the project of self-government. And while Huntington deplores the tendencies current among the elites, he never disavows the principle of elitism, nor does he encourage rule by the masses. Instead his account of a patriot-nation furnishes a basis for rethinking the ways in which elites can govern, and in this he has shown what he had previously doubted: the masses are governable and democracy manageable.[77] And given his hostility toward corporate and world-conquering elites and his reservations concerning certain foreigners and African Americans, the resulting tendency resembles the elite-mass formula of Nazi Germany, with American Muslims, African Americans, and Hispanics potential pariah groups.

x

A democratic citizenry, finding itself being ruled by awesome powers exercised in its name, might legitimately demand or expect that a ruling elite would at least give lip service to certain virtues, such as self-restraint, disinterestedness, perhaps a touch of humility—qualities arguably urgent in an age of megapower. When power is dependent as never before upon scientists and technologists, one might hope that a ruling elite would strive to emulate some of the scientific virtues by acting rationally, using power prudently, and carefully weighing unwelcome facts that don't fit their cherished assumptions. Instead the governing elite has chosen the path of radical reaction, even primitivism: clinging stubbornly to the claim that Saddam was involved in 9/11, and that he had weapons of mass destruction; displaying a cavalier disregard of legal standards of guilt; admitting no responsibility for the shameless treatment of prisoners of war, even denying that Americans practiced techniques of torture while demanding that the CIA be excused from observing prohibitions; and dismantling or weakening environmental safeguards despite the near unanimous findings of scientists concerning global warming.

What is striking about these actions is that they undermine the principal justification for elitism. Unlike the irrational populace, elites are supposed to be rational actors, not opportunists who constantly "push the envelope" in order to test the limits of power while publicizing the role of faith in their decisions. One would hope that those entrusted with awesome power, especially those whose electoral legitimacy was originally shadowed by doubts, would weigh counterevidence carefully, employ power judiciously, and, above all, consider the consequences of a course of action, especially if it involves grave risks or harm. One might even assume that those who constantly proclaim "the sanctity of human life" and of embryos would extend an equal solicitude to the innocent victims of collateral damage.

Elites are supposed to withstand the gales of popular passions, stand firm for what is right against what the Founding Father Madison described as "the confusion and intemperance of a multitude."[78] And yet the most disastrous wars in American history have been instigated, not by rabid majorities but by elites: the "Southern aristocracy" pro-voked the Civil War; "the best and the brightest" led the country into the quagmire of Vietnam; and Bush's advisory "Vulcans" and the neo-con products of elite universities have made of Iraq a national and international nightmare.

The irrationalism of Superpower is the result of a fearful asymmetry. From one perspective Superpower is inconceivable without the extraordinary intelligence at work in modern science and technology. Among the qualities of that intelligence are exactness, discrimination, sensitivity to counterevidence, skepticism toward faith-based claims, and mindfulness of consequences. From another perspective, however, a willful naïveté is at work. Scientists invent instruments of unprecedented power for those who are motivated, not by intellectual curiosity or the common good, but by power or profit or some combination of the two. Dresden, Hiroshima, Nagasaki were triumphs of scientific knowledge and technological ingenuity, but also of a political irrationality that began with the rationale of "saving" an unknown number of American soldiers' lives and ended by employing against Japanese cities weaponry whose destructive effects were untested, hence uncertain—at least the first time round. A process that began with rationality organized on a human scale—a lab, a university—ended in irrationality, a huge Manhattan Project, devastated cities, the fatally contaminated survivors, the ashes of countless dead, a counterholocaust. The odyssey of Superpower might be described in these terms: from Einstein's abstract equations scrawled on a blackboard to the bunker busters, "shock and awe," unleashed in Iraq against an entire society—notwithstanding President Bush's previous description of an unconventional enemy that had to be hunted down "one terrorist at a time." At this writing, according to one estimate, there have been 100,000 Iraqi civilian casualties since the American invasion.[79]

CHAPTER TEN

Domestic Politics in the Era of Superpower and Empire

i

I think the best part of this job is to set in motion big
changes of history—it's unbelievably exciting to
be in a position to do that.
—*President George W. Bush*[1]

Before attaining power and even afterwards, totalitarian parties all characterized politics as an epical "struggle" or a "war" in which the very fate of society was declared to be at stake. A party was conceived as a "fighting organization" designed for gaining a total monopoly over politics and eventually establishing a one-party state in which opposition parties and contested politics were declared illegal and suppressed. Within the party and its auxiliaries (youth and women's organizations, veterans' groups, business and farm organizations) power was ordered by hierarchical principles of command—and subordination: leadership, loyalty, discipline, and rigid observance of "the party line." Once a totalitarian movement gained control of government, its first objective was to eliminate politics as the expression of divisiveness, hence of weakness, and a barrier to fashioning a "mass." Politics was replaced by homogeneity—with one major exception. Totalitarian regimes were committed to promoting and enforcing select superiorities (e.g., race, party, class, nation) and elevating elitism to a universal principle.

In a one-party state politics is, in effect, "privatized," dissociated from the practices of citizenship and confined within the party, where it takes the form of intramural rivalries for the privileges of power and status. It is a politics that never goes public except to orchestrate unanimity.

Inverted totalitarianism follows a different route. Instead of pursuing unanimity, it encourages divisiveness; instead of rule by a single master race, it promotes predomination—that is, rule by diverse powers which have found it in their interests to combine while retaining their separate identities. The key components are corporate capital, the very rich, small business associations, large media organizations, evangelical Protestant leaders, and the Catholic hierarchy. Models of organization tend to be corporate as well as military. The aim is to control politics by settling the terms of competition in the spirit of Archer Daniels Midland's watchword, "the competitor is our friend, and the customer is our enemy": substitute "the other party" for "competitor" and "active citizen" for "customer" to get the inverted version of totalitarian politics. Opposition is not abolished but neutralized, its politics constrained within limits, allowed a minor concession now and then that keeps its supporters hopeful, and pressed to emulate the victors' strategies. Where totalitarian parties practiced a warlike politics of "struggle," in the inversion politics is at first viewed as a market where a competition rages among rival firms, each striving to develop strategies for beating the others and winning over as large a number of consumers as possible. But then one party perceives that it can significantly ratchet up a mere politics of market competition by attracting adherents as well as consumers. Other than fervor, the key characteristic of the adherent is a combination of acceptance of and superiority to marketplace practices and incentives. The adherent is committed to transcendent values, to Christianity, the sanctity of life, the "traditional family," and premarital abstinence. But he or she is not a critic of capitalism.

ii

Conventionally defined, politics is the struggle waged to gain control of, or influence over, governmental institutions; unconventionally, we might call this "the exploitative view of politics." The aim of its practitioners is to defend or advance the material or ideological interests of those who contribute money and energy, and to claim at the same time that these efforts also serve the interests of the whole society. To gain control of the power of government a party must define its identity, then become an organization, a generator of power/capital capable of formulating a program, mobilizing and directing supporters, and competing against rivals for political power.

A variation shared by both traditional liberals and conservatives might emphasize that, as in the ideal free market, a party system should operate in accordance with "the rules of the game." These stand for elementary principles of fair competition. Parties should be free to organize and compete for power, and the party out of power should be free to compete, to criticize the policies and personnel of the party in power, insist on accountability, propose alternative policies, or draw attention to problems left unaddressed or mishandled.

A democrat might challenge these versions of politics and claim that they have avoided the fundamental question: what kind of citizen or political being would those versions of politics encourage? Would they, for example, connive to stigmatize politics so as to suggest that those who became "involved" would first have to hold their noses, that democratic politics, like all politics, was inherently degrading? or that one should actively participate only for a "higher" cause uncontaminated by material concerns? A related question would be this: if the preceding conceptions of politics were true, in whose interest would it be for such views to be widespread, even encouraged?

If, in contrast, one starts from the notion that democratic politics should contribute to individual development and, at the same time, promote a greater measure of egalitarianism, then a different conception of politics would follow. It would expand the liberal conception by assigning first priority to the role of citizens as participants, demoting their role as voters to a secondary priority. The party's structure and processes would be shaped to encourage the citizen-participant to be involved in the party's decision-making practices and to become acquainted with the ways of power. Party policies and programs would become matters for common discussion and suggestion, not pep rallies for persuading the voter to endorse programs previously decided by the party elite. A democratic party would view politics as the arena of a continuous struggle to alleviate the inequalities of a system whose social, cultural, and economic institutions continuously reproduce them.

The extent to which a politics could be said to be democratic would depend upon how committed parties were to encouraging the citizenry to become an active demos rather than a sometime voter. Yet a democratic politics has suspicions about corporate-inspired party organizations; hence it would allow, even encourage, a large element of the ad hoc, the improvised, the spontaneous. It would not concede to a permanent party organization a monopoly over politics.

The contemporary Republican Party is both antidemocratic and illiberal. It is notable for its contempt for the weaknesses it attributes to its rivals: moral flabbiness, antipreemption, antimilitarism (= "hate America"), welfare laws, poverty programs, respect for treaty obligations, environmental protections (= tree huggers), and French fries. An antidemocratic party tries to prevent the formation of an active, participatory demos—it distrusts popular demonstrations—and is deeply antiegalitarian. An illiberal party, it considers "rules" less as restraints than as annoyances to be circumvented. It exploits the vulnerabilities of a two-party system with the aim of reshaping it into a more or less permanent undemocratic and illiberal system.

The Republican Party is not, as advertised, conservative but radically oligarchical. Programmatically it exists to advance corporate economic and political interests, and to protect and promote inequalities of opportunity and wealth. Pragmatically its elites form alliances with the "elect," evangelicals who, seeing themselves as distinguished by their intimate relation to their savior and privileged by their knowing what their god has in store for mankind, supply an "ideal" element to an otherwise decidedly worldly party. To promote a permanent hegemony, the party adopts the strategies of a movement. It systematically trains future cadres of loyal followers and leaders, enlisting them when they are young (Republican *Jugend*), and carefully tutoring them as it shepherds them through the educational systems from which eventually dependable apparatchiks emerge.[2] The combination of party and movement harbors intimations of inverted totalitarianism, not least because it is driven by forms of extremism, of intolerance, of aggrandizement both materialistic and spiritual.

In keeping with the unpremeditated, even innocent, beginnings of inverted totalitarianism, consider an early effort to reform the organization of American political parties. In 1950 the professional organization of political scientists, the American Political Science Association (APSA), published *Toward a More Responsible Two-Party System*. The report was issued at a time when American and Soviet antagonisms had hardened into the Cold War and the anticommunism crusade had begun to color domestic politics. The APSA document reflected a widespread concern that with the end of the war and the emergence of the United States as a, if not the, leading world power, the party system needed to adapt to a new era of expanded governmental power abroad, while perpetuating the activist state with its New Deal social programs and regulatory agencies. In response the report offered proposals intended to rationalize party politics, render it more manageable and predictable: qualities that were supposed to make it more responsible.

The operative assumption of APSA's manifesto was that American political parties were dysfunctional because disorganized, undisciplined, and lacking ideological consistency. As a result voters were denied a clear choice. A major cause of this condition was said to be the strong pull of local loyalties and interests. The report argued that if the two parties were to become responsible, they would have to create stronger party organizations that would enable them to formulate clearer positions. It reasoned that if the parties were to distinguish themselves more sharply, they could more easily be held accountable. Currently the political parties were "too loose" with "very little national machinery," with the result that sharp and often inconsistent policy differences existed between state and local parties, at one end of the spectrum, and the national party, at the other. To promote "party discipline" and "cohesion," the report recommended that within each party power be centralized in a Party Council. The tasks of the council would be to coordinate policies, clarify issues, vet candidates, and deal with "rebellious and disloyal state organizations" (read: Southern Dixiecrats). The authors also proposed to simplify and centralize party "leadership" in the two houses of Congress.[3]

A major assumption of the report was that "politics" is identical with, or exhausted by, the activities of political parties. And by implication politics was properly the monopoly of the parties and a two-party system was the natural or obvious form. The role of the citizen was pretty much reduced to "choice" between competing candidates.

Without intending to do so, the APSA report foreshadowed the difference between classical and inverted totalitarianism: one sought to eliminate politics, the other to contain politics by introducing structures designed to facilitate managerial control. Unlike the democratic citizen, who, through the experiences of participation, grows into a political being, the voter is akin to a response system engineered by public opinion surveys, pollster strategies, and media advertising that first stimulates voters to vote and afterwards encourages them to relapse into their accustomed apathy. The voter is the flip side to the imperial subject. The model voter-subject and model political milieu were described recently in the *New York Times*. It reported a programmed remark addressed to the president by one of the preselected party faithful at a prearranged and screened event:

> I am 60 years old and I've voted Republican from the very first time I could vote. And I also want to say this is the very first time that I have felt that God was in the White House.[4]

iii

What is democracy doing bearing the stigma of empire? Recall that the United States was born in a revolution against imperial power. Recall as well, however, that the Founders favored a republic over a democracy because the latter could not be accommodated to an "enlarged sphere," to a huge geographical expanse. And recall that the American citizenry has a long history of being complicit in the country's imperial ventures. The imperial impulse is not a tic afflicting only the few. The difference may be that, unlike, say, the Roman and British empires, the American empire is repressed in the national ideology.

Virtually from the beginnings of the nation the making of the American citizen was influenced, even shaped by, the making of an American imperium. The nineteenth-century expansion of the country to the west and southwest was achieved by military victories over various Indian nations and Mexico. It brought new opportunities for enterprise, exploitation, and ownership. It made conquest and violence familiar, part of everyday experience. Foreign observers, such as Tocqueville, were struck by the appearance of a new kind of citizen: mobile, adventurous, highly competitive, and often brutal. At the end of the nineteenth century and in the early decades of the twentieth, Americans wrested Cuba and the Philippines from the Spanish empire: American power was being distanced from the citizen, becoming abstract. During the interwar years of the twentieth century, U.S. Marines were frequently dispatched to put down "rebels" in Latin and Central America — and President Wilson ordered the army to invade Mexico in 1914 — yet during the 1920s the country's foreign policy was inhibited by isolationist sentiments. That changed after World War II. While the American invasions of the Dominican Republic, Grenada, and Panama might be seen as continuations of the Marine expeditions of the twenties, and the Cold War as fought to "contain" Soviet power rather than promote an empire, Vietnam marked a crucial turning point. A fitful, stupid imperial war remarkable not only for the American defeat but for the fact that, unlike earlier imperial ventures, it was vigorously and successfully opposed at home. The reassertion of constitutional limits on executive power and the successful mobilization of a demotic protest movement meant that military defeat was actually a democratic victory — over its own imperial power.

The victory was short-lived. Two decades later the first President Bush declared triumphantly that the importance of the (first) Gulf War was its achievement as a double victory, over Saddam and over "the Viet Nam syndrome." The claim that imperial ambitions had been checked only temporarily by the protests of the sixties was a put-down not only of demotic action but of the efforts of Congress to reclaim its war powers. In the run-up to the first Gulf War the administration encountered virtually no public protests and only small opposition in Congress. In the aftermath of 9/11 the second Bush administration cast aside any inhibitions and began to advance a more expansive notion of American power and to pursue grandiose schemes for the reconstruction of the world. The administration seized on 9/11 to declare "a war on terrorism." The declaration not only transformed that event and the public support it generated into a warrant of legitimation that dispelled the clouded 2000 election, but, casting terrorism in global terms, it also justified the mobilization of imperial power *and* elicited the support/ docility of a fearful citizenry.

Empires are said to be distinguished by whether they occupy foreign lands; whether they rule directly or work through local elites; how much local autonomy is permitted; how the subject populations are treated; and whether imperial rule is meant to be more or less permanent or, instead, a form of tutelage that gradually permits imperial subjects to become mostly or wholly independent. There are differences of opinion about whether the United States actually is an imperial power. Some scholars pronounce it an empire that is bashful about identifying itself as such.[5] Others celebrate the existence of a U.S. empire. "The fact is," opined one commentator, "no country has been as dominant culturally, economically, technologically, and militarily in the history of the world since the late Roman empire."[6] Still others deny that the United States is a genuine empire, primarily because it does not occupy or directly rule foreign territories.[7] Almost without exception these recent discussions avoid evaluating the impact of empire upon domestic politics, much less of its effects upon American democracy.

While all empires aim at the exploitation of the peoples and territories they control, the United States is an empire of a novel kind. Unlike other empires it rarely rules directly or occupies foreign territory for long, although it may retain bases or "lily pads." Its power is "projected" at irregular intervals over other societies rather than institutionalized in them. Its rule tends to be indirect, to take the form of "influence," bribes, or "pressure." Its principal concerns are military and economic (i.e., access to bases, markets, and oil). When policy-makers deem it necessary or expedient, domestic needs are subordinated to the requirements of global strategies and to the economic needs of Superpower's corporate partners.

The U.S. empire is *the* Superpower, unrivaled. The European nations that seized empires during the late nineteenth century and the first half of the twentieth were rival "great powers," but there was no one dominant Superpower. Revealingly, when Vice President Cheney described the current enemy as aspiring "to establish a radical Islamic empire that encompasses a region from Spain, across North Africa, through the Middle East and South Asia, all the way to Indonesia," he was identifying not just an enemy but an imperial rival—though not a superpower.[8]

iv

> [T]he US empire [is] the most magnanimous imperial
> power ever. . . . If this be the workings of empire,
> let us have more of it.
> —*Dinesh D'Souza*[9]

To describe the United States as an imperial Superpower is to say that elements of domination are inescapably present in the power relations between the United States and the rest of the world, and that empire's superior-inferior relationship necessarily means a politics among unequals. The obvious question is this: can imperial power observe a distinction between domestic citizens and imperial subjects? Can it seek to dominate abroad without materially changing power relations at home or without importantly changing the status of the citizenry? Consider the Patriot Act and its inroads on civil liberties; or the continuing campaign of the administration to restrict the power of the courts in matters affecting military "justice"; or the attempts to contain the investigative practices of the media; or the falsehoods arrogantly defended; or the unchecked growth of corporate influence over public policy—all of these suggest that imperial politics represents the conquest of domestic politics and the latter's conversion into a crucial element of inverted totalitarianism. It makes no sense to ask how the democratic citizen could "participate" substantively in imperial politics; hence it is not surprising that the subject of empire is taboo in electoral debates. No major politician or party has so much as publicly remarked on the existence of an American empire. Imperial power is not about restraint, and the consequences of empire are evident in domestic politics: in military expenditures, subsidies to globalizing corporations, mounting deficits, and the decimation of social programs and environmental safeguards.

Whatever else they may be, empires are not about justice. It is thus not surprising that even in matters of procedural justice (e.g., fair trial) the Bush administration should fight strenuously to deny access to American courts for foreign nationals, illegal aliens, and American citizens captured in the empire's war against terrorism; or that the administration sanctions the widespread use of torture, secret tribunals, and unconscionable detention periods before trial. Concurrently, justice has pretty much disappeared from the political vocabulary of domestic politics.[10]

The effects of imperial power are not solely registered abroad, externalized. Under empire the significant actors are not citizens but corporations with the rewards of empire adjusted accordingly. Rewards are reaped more or less according to how strategically placed globalizing players are in the domestic power structure. Halliburton's power begins in Texas, extends to Washington, and then connects with projects (often without competitive bidding) in Afghanistan and Iraq; it returns to the "homeland" enriched and eager to invest its profits in politicians. Politicians, in turn, become responsive to the new sources of pressure, contributions, and lavish favors. The district or constituent back "home" shrinks in significance. The politician's postponed gratifications: the higher rewards of lobbyist or corporate executive.

Since empires are premised upon domination, it is not surprising that an element of imperial ruthlessness infects politics at home. It is commonly observed that today's domestic politics has changed in tactics and ferocity with the avowed aim of establishing a permanent Republican majority, the domestic equivalent of imperial hegemony, heralding a new politics and citizenry.

The emergence of Superpower and its joint imperium of state and corporation have resulted in the institutionalization and normalization of corruption. The doctored accounts, the public misrepresentations, and illegal transactions that have become a commonplace of corporate behavior in recent years have been transmitted to party politics, whose immune system has always been less than robust. There is little to choose between public and corporate morality, to the detriment of both. In bringing democracy to Iraq the United States has also exported our practices of contractual malfeasance, from overbilling to nonperformance to shoddy work to dropped charges despite clear evidence of wrongdoing.

The symbiosis of corporation and governmental institutions and the normalization of corruption are perfectly embodied in the institutionalization of the lobbying industry. In matters of public policy and governmental decision making, lobbying demonstrates how little the actions of the electorate matter. The proliferation of Washington lobbyists, who now number in the thousands, is indicative of a radical change in the meaning of who and what are being represented, and indicative also of the final defeat of majority rule. It is no secret that lobbying is designed to short-circuit the power of numbers, of the ordinary citizenry. In contrast to the citizen-as-occasional-voter, the lobbyist is a full-time "citizen." As the form of politics indicative of where real power lies, lobbying is the perfect complement to empire.

v

In theory the choices presented by parties are supposed to clarify such issues as who is likely to benefit from the policies being advocated; how the burdens will be distributed; and according to what notion of priorities the nation's resources should be assigned. Those concerns do not disappear when they involve empire but become starker. Does current tax policy or social welfare spending provide clues as to who bears empire's burdens, who benefits? will an expanding empire require a military draft or, like other empires, hire mercenaries? Inverted totalitarianism provides the context for reflecting on these questions.

Politically, as well as socially and economically, inverted totalitarianism is best understood as imperialist and hence as a postdemocratic or, better, post–social democratic phenomenon. It is marked by an expansion of the horizons and ambitions of the governing classes and an accompanying increase in the instruments of power, private as well as public, as well as by a decline in demotic power both in its instruments of governance (political democracy) and in its socioeconomic supports (social democracy). This reflects a reversal in the relationship or, rather, the perceived relationship between government and economy. The formulation favored in business circles and among economists stigmatizes government regulation as "political interference" in the economy and emphasizes its dire economic consequences. We need, however, to reverse that account in order to take note of the *political* significance of deregulation, of withdrawing public power and, in effect, renouncing it as an instrument for dealing with the political, social, and human consequences of a market economy.

Deregulation changes the character of domestic politics. In effect, it declares that in a democracy the demos is to be denied the use of state power. It weakens the unaffluent constituencies that have a vital stake in preserving and expanding government social programs. The weaker constituencies are not only hurt economically but depoliticized in the process, discouraged from political participation because government appears unresponsive to their needs. Corporate political power and influence can then take advantage of the capitulation of the demos to strengthen the corporation's own partnership with the state. The results of a weakened social democracy and, conversely, a concentrated political economy are writ large in the shocking character of a tax structure that heavily favors the very rich while damaging most other classes. The favored group can then translate the windfall into political power. They become "a political donor class" that raises millions for the Republican Party and throws a few crumbs and broad hints to the Democrats.[11] To grasp the significance of these developments, we need to see them in the context of inverted totalitarianism.

Inverted totalitarianism is the result of the acceleration of two strategies. One, the politics of reversal, was launched in earnest in the Reagan counterrevolution. It aimed at eviscerating the social programs vital to political democracy, either by dismantling them or, alternatively, assigning them to private entrepreneurs, thereby expanding the dependence of ordinary citizens upon unaccountable "private" powers. The politics of reversal was resumed by the "Gingrich revolution" of the 1990s and accelerated by the second Bush administration. By striking at welfare programs and unemployment benefits, blocking a national health care system, and making threatening gestures toward pension plans and social security, not only did this politics cripple social democracy, but in the process it undermined political democracy, the one political system that depends upon those who work. It might be recalled that the totalitarian regimes of Soviet Russia and Germany each instituted a strong network of social services; inverted totalitarianism seeks to dismantle or significantly reduce them, thereby throwing individuals back on their own resources, reducing their power. How far that power is being reduced can be gauged by the response of businesses to the lack of national health care and guarantees for pension systems. They have cut pensions and health care benefits while lavishing huge bonuses upon departing executives.

Instead of collectivism, inverted totalitarianism thrives on disaggregation, on a citizenry who, ideally, are self-reliant, competitive, certified by standardized testing, but equally fearful of an economy subject to sudden downturns and of terrorists who strike without warning. Classical totalitarianism mobilized its subjects; inverted totalitarianism fragments them. Growing inequalities of power—reflected, for example, in the influence of lobbyists or the concentration of media ownership— render increasingly difficult the mustering of power for a politics that seeks to ameliorate inequalities.[12] Corporate capitalism is creating an imperial workforce of dependent low-wage workers, preferably of large numbers of undocumented, fearful aliens, the new metics, for whom survival, rather than political participation, is uppermost. In the background is the threat of a prison system incarcerating more than two million. Hence the high symbolism of convicted felons who, if released, are likely to be denied the right to vote, that last feeble afterglow of democracy.[13]

The shift, in which Superpower's ascendancy is inverse to the dismantling of social democracy and the weakening of political democracy, reflects the profound transformation of politics effected by the imperium of Superpower. Exit the citizen, enter the corporate actor. Politics comes to replicate the structure and culture of corporate capitalism: it is rationalized, capitalized, managed, elite-dominated, viciously competitive, and technologically dependent.[14] Instead of an expressive politics that encourages the voicing of concerns, grievances, and proposals, we have a controlled politics that tolerates dissent but is unresponsive to protests and proposals from below. In place of the citizen-participant the new politics courts the viewer-consumer. Above all, it is a politics that importantly inverts democracy by being only minimally concerned with domestic policy, preferring to subordinate it to the military and economic issues of terrorism, energy supplies, and globalization.

vi

Despite the efforts made to extend voting rights and lower the voting age to eighteen, national elections typically attract slightly more than half of the eligible electorate while local elections average about 35 percent. While the advocates of democracy view the low turnouts as a warning sign, the technicians of Superpower politics welcome voter apathy, and some Republican operatives have even sought to discourage African American and Hispanic voters: it makes for a more cost-effective and manageable method of purchasing legitimacy.

Numerous reasons have been advanced to explain low turnout: the competing attractions of various forms of entertainment supplied by the mass media; the belief that "my vote doesn't make any difference"; the widespread perception of politics as corrupt; and the like. These explanations reflect a politics that is remote, necessarily abstract, adapted to the needs of Superpower and its distant character. The party politics being fashioned for empire and for inverted totalitarianism is a politics where the parties court voters but do not seek mass membership. Consequently most vote for a party without joining it; a few become party foot soldiers, and fewer still are courted as "contributors" of huge sums of money. A party wants a few zealous cohorts, generous donors, and a mass of occasional, TV-conditioned voters.

Thus in discouraging member participation, the party leads the way from citizen democracy and toward a mass democracy, in search of "followers" who are, first and foremost, patriots who yearn to believe — in America's moral, economic, and political superiority, and in its sanctity; followers who want to feel secure rather than participate, who want the burdens and demands of politics shouldered by leaders who care for "people like me."

According to the liberal theory fashionable among academics, the ideal role of the generality of citizens in a democracy is to "deliberate," that is, discuss rationally and civilly the important political questions of the day. However appealing or remote that ideal may seem, in the reality of the war between imperialism and terrorism the contemporary citizen, far from being invited to a discussion, is, as never before, being manipulated, by "managed care" and by the managers of fear. From one direction the citizen is assailed by fears of terrorism, not knowing when or how terrorists may strike; a fear that the citizen cannot "fight" against has been amplified by fears of natural disasters (tsunamis, hurricanes), of invasions by illegal immigrants and by epidemics (Asian flu, avian flu) for which, according to official spokespersons, only limited supplies of vaccines will be available. The citizen is all but paralyzed by official warnings that an attack of one kind or another may be imminent or certain to happen sometime and somewhere. The implicit message is that the citizen can do nothing except follow the instructions of "authorities." The predictable, and anticipated, response of the citizen is to look to government for protection and to defer to official judgments. Yet the same citizen who is told to follow the instructions of authorities has had it drummed in that "big government" is the enemy who threatens to take away his money and freedom. The citizen is left with no political ally responsive to his economic fears. Unlike classical totalitarianism, which boasted of the unanimity of its citizens, inverted totalitarianism thrives on ambivalence and the uncertainty it breeds.

The ambivalent citizen: where is the power located that can be trusted to protect him and her but not to tax them? And what kind of politics would support that kind of power? The answer: a form of antipolitics that reflects a distaste, bordering on intolerance, for frank discussion of inequalities, class differences, the persisting problems of racism, climate change, or the consequences of imperialism. Antipolitics is expressed as patriotism, antiterrorism, militarism—subjects that brook little or no disagreements, provoking fervor while stifling thought. Ambivalence is temporarily suspended before a patriotic power "above" politics, one represented by the armed forces, symbols of heroism, antimaterialism, sacrifice for others, force purified by a righteous cause. Big government may be the problem; big military is the solution.

That the patriotic citizen unswervingly supports the military and its huge budgets means that conservatives have succeeded in persuading the public that the military is distinct from government. Thus the most substantial element of state power is removed from public debate. Similarly in his/her new status as imperial citizen, the believer remains contemptuous of bureaucracy yet does not hesitate to obey the directives issued by the Department of Homeland Security, the largest and most intrusive governmental department in the history of the nation. Identification with militarism and patriotism, along with the images of American might projected by the media, serves to make the individual citizen feel stronger, thereby compensating for the feelings of weakness visited by the economy upon an overworked, exhausted, and insecure labor force. For its antipolitics inverted totalitarianism requires believers, patriots, and nonunion "guest workers."

Instead of reflecting love of the nation's democratic heritage patriotism has become xenophobic; fixated on might, preemptive war, and hatred of terrorists; suspicious of Muslims and liberals alike; and contemptuous of former allies. The new militarism, glorifying war and sacrifice, and boasting an imperial reach, is being made an integral element of the public piety so conspicuous in American politics. Not surprisingly the Republican Party is its chief curator and beneficiary. It was recently celebrated during the Republican National Convention of 2004. To the sanctifying strains of "The Battle Hymn of the Republic," engagingly sung by a chorale of black youngsters, Vice President Cheney (a notorious draft dodger during the Vietnam War) and Zell Miller (a venomously reactionary Democrat) both lavished such praise upon the armed forces as to stifle any discussion of the mistreatment of Iraqi prisoners, the recent official inquiries about it, and the rationale for the war itself. For the first time in American history that same convention presented the spectacle of about a dozen retired generals and admirals posing on the stage of a party's convention and serving as a claque for the party's candidate; they were followed by General Tommy Franks, former commander of operations in Iraq, who offered a lengthy testimonial to the decisive character of the nominee. Since many of the military men on the stage had also served their country in corporate office, the convention was paying homage to the *cursus honorum* of the

revolving door: enter the military, transfer to the corporate, and graduate a conservative claqueur. The true rivalry among elites is not between Harvard Business School and Yale Law School, but between
them and West Point.

Militarism is not only a distraction from social problems but confirmation that warfare is now a joint undertaking (*sic*) of corporation and
state. Government soldiers fight side by side with enterprising corporate
warriors who, fittingly, are paid thousands of dollars more than GIs.[15]
The United States remains the world's biggest arms dealer. It is no
surprise that ever since the Reagan administration, the Republican
Party, which successfully pinned the label of "big spenders" on the
Democrats, should be the prime mover for making defense appropria-
tions the largest item by far in the annual federal budget. It highlights
a consistent inconsistency: big spending is anti-American when directed to social programs but patriotic if it is funneled to the beneficia-
ries/defenders of the corporate state.

vii

> If class warfare is being waged in America, my class is
> clearly winning. . . . Tax breaks for corporations (and their
> investors, particularly large ones) were a major part of the
> [Bush] administration's 2002 and 2003 initiatives.
> —*Warren Buffett, billionaire investor*[16]

The most dramatic change in party politics has been the transformation
of the Republican Party: from deficit hawks to proponents of the largest
deficit in governmental history; from isolationists to preemptivists; from
a party renowned for its anti-intellectualism to a party that nurtures its
very own intellectual luminaries and think tanks; from a midwestern
party with Grant Wood's American Gothic as its icon to a southern-
southwestern party boasting a cowboy capitalism with the robber baron
as its appropriate icon. All this suggests that inverted totalitarianism has
evolved a politics to support its imperial ambitions.

While the transformed Republican Party reveals what a "party of government" might look like under inverted totalitarianism, the Democrats reveal the fate of opposition politics under inverted totalitarianism. The Democrats' politics might be described as inauthentic opposition in the era of Superpower. Having fended off its reformist elements and disclaimed the label of liberal, it is trapped by new rules of the game which dictate that a party exists to win elections rather than to promote a vision of the good society.[17] Accordingly, the party competes for an apolitical segment of the electorate, "the undecided," and puzzles how best to woo religious zealots. Should Democrats somehow be elected, corporate sponsors make it politically impossible for the new officeholders to alter significantly the direction of society. At best Democrats might repair some of the damage done to environmental safeguards or to Medicare without substantially reversing the drift rightwards. By offering palliatives, a Democratic administration contributes to plausible denial about the true nature of the system. By fostering an illusion among the powerless classes that the party can make their interests a priority, it pacifies and thereby defines the style of an opposition party in an inverted totalitarian system. In the process it demonstrates the superior cost-effectiveness of inverted totalitarianism over the crude classic versions.

This underscores the contribution of the "public ideology" being promoted by elected Republicans and pseudoconservative ideologues. Although ideologies profess consistency and boast of their coherent "worldview," there is typically a suppressed, or downplayed subtext in the message. The suppressed component of the prevailing ideology is the *political* status of corporate power. While the public ideology celebrates economics in the form of "entrepreneurship," "small start-ups," and "free enterprise," it ignores the political significance and power of the corporation. The public ideology of conservatives boasts of their commitment to reducing governmental power; hence the mantras of archaism: returning to "the original Constitution," ending "social engineering," and demanding no taxation—even with representation. In that imaginary "original Constitution" neither Superpower nor empire exists.

viii

> In a general election, the candidate with the most hopeful
> message is going to win it. Most people in the U.S. want
> to be rich, they want to get ahead, and that's why an
> opportunity-oriented message works.
> —*Al From, founder of the Democratic Leadership Council*[18]

What kind of politics is encouraged when the president is strong and Congress weak? A politics set by a decisive leader, a politics of action rather than the deliberative politics that is the forte of the legislative branch.

Ominously, the decline of congressional power and prestige in the United States is one of the most striking recent political developments. Historically, the legislative branch was supposed to be the power closest to the citizenry, the main reason being that lawmaking was held to be the highest, most solemn, and most important of all governmental powers, the symbol of rule by consent of the governed. A law was viewed as a command that all citizens had to obey because the people's representatives had approved it. Legislation made tangible the notion of equality: no one was above the law and everyone was protected by it.

Unlike the classic totalitarian systems that tolerated only the unanimity of pseudolegislatures, our rulers have come to exploit a nearly evenly divided electorate and a consequent near parity of representation of both parties in the Senate and House. Majorities do exist, but either they are narrow or, when they are substantial, they tend to be limited to one chamber. However, the politics of near gridlock, as it works out in Washington, does not mean that all interests are equally and adversely affected by what appears to be a politics of inaction or stalemate. Executive orders can still be issued that roll back environmental gains or withhold funds from programs disliked by the administration, or that insert into trade negotiations items favored by campaign contributors.[19] And regulatory agencies, now stacked against regulation, are not prevented from doing the bidding of the major party and corporate interests. Moreover, even a gridlocked Congress will likely support, even enthusiastically increase, military spending. Similarly, gridlock does not prevent tax breaks for the wealthiest classes from being legislated.

The true significance of near gridlock is not that it paralyzes governmental action but that it prevents majority rule. Sharp and nearly equal divisions, the stuff of gridlock, are in the interest of some powerful groups who would be less influential, more threatened by majority rule.

What is made more difficult by the politics of stalemate is the capture of state power to advance the social interests of the Many. The politics of programmatic social democracy, which had defined politics throughout much of the last century—the politics of populism, Progressivism, the New and Fair Deals, and the Great Society—has all but vanished. Does this suggest that a broad consensus exists, that social conflicts have disappeared even as the society becomes more sharply divided in terms of income and of all the attendant values of education, cultural opportunities, health, and environmental safety? Why are those sharp differences not reflected politically?

Returning to the narrow margin between the major parties in the Congress: if one believes that they correspond to sharp and widespread ideological divisions in the society, one might conclude that social inequalities are in fact being registered, that what is being represented are really deep divisions in society and boiling class conflicts, and that Marx's scenario of class struggle has begun. In reality, the much publicized polarization of the electorate is less a sign of division than of a politics shaped to prevent the expression of substantive differences. Polls that provide the evidence for a sharply divided electorate typically collect responses to questions so broad as to be meaningless. What could follow substantively from questions such as "Do you think the president is doing a good job?" Electoral politics is integrally connected with polling so that elections tend to be contested over narrow differences in emphasis that do not disturb a pseudoconsensus. In the competition for the votes of the center, for the so-called independents or undecided, the deepening social, educational, and economic inequalities remain submerged, unevoked in political rhetoric, immobile.

The resulting despair produces strange contortions of allegiance. Workers find themselves in an era of declining trade union power, yet many respond by opposing unions, voting Republican ("Reagan Democrats"), and hoping to improve their economic prospects by joining the military and going off to defend corporate America.[20]

Traditionally the meaning of the ideal of consensus was that the fundamental institutions and practices of the political system, "the rules of its game," were accepted by all citizens and politicians; that a winning party would not proceed to stack the system against the losers and make it impossible for them to gain controlling power (e.g., gerrymandering); and that some political institutions (e.g., the courts and independent regulatory agencies) should not be systematically and deeply partisan. In recent times, roughly since the Reagan counterrevolution of the 1980s, an ersatz consensus has evolved: from agreement about basic political institutions and practices to one that accepts as permanent the institutions and practices of corporate capitalism and the dismantlement of the welfare state; that equates taxation of the wealthy with "class war"; and that anoints Protestantism as the civil religion of the nation.[21] Traditional consensus stood for agreement upon political fundamentals and, as such, beyond ordinary partisan politics. Ersatz consensus exploits that notion in order to reduce the space for acceptable contestation. Certain matters, such as tax increases, are declared to be "off the table." How influential the phony version can be was illustrated when, during the 2004 elections, the Democratic presidential candidate testified plaintively, "I am not a redistributionist Democrat. Fear not." He identified himself as "an entrepreneurial Democrat."[22]

The nationalistic, patriotic, and "originalist" ideology being hawked by Republicans promotes a myth of national unity, consensus, that obscures real cleavages in order to substitute synthetic ones ("the culture wars," school vouchers, abortion) that leave power relationships unchallenged. Manufactured divisiveness complements the politics of gridlock; both contribute to induce apathy by suggesting that the citizenry's involvement in politics is essentially unneeded, futile. In the one case, of consensus, active involvement is superfluous because there is nothing to contest—who wants to dispute the wisdom of The Founders? In the other, gridlock, it appears that active engagement can accomplish nothing. Meanwhile divisiveness is assigned to the make-believe politics played on talk shows or by pundits. Thus consensus, pseudodivisiveness, and gridlock establish the conditions of electoral politics. In elections the parties set out to mobilize the citizen-as-voter, to define political obligation as fulfilled by the casting of a vote. Afterwards, post-election politics of lobbying, repaying donors, and promoting corporate interests—the real players—takes over. The effect is to demobilize the citizenry, to teach them not to be involved or to ponder matters that are either settled or beyond their efficacy.

One striking example of the suppression of deep differences was the 2004 electoral campaign of John Kerry. There is wide agreement among observers that during the winter and spring presidential primaries the Democratic Party was galvanized by the deep antagonism toward the Iraqi war. Moreover, as a side effect, the growing antiwar sentiments threatened to activate segments of the population that had become resigned to the impotence of the Democratic Party. Yet the party organization and its centrists, abetted by a Dean-hostile media, succeeded in squelching the bid of the antiwar candidates and threw their resources behind Kerry. Kerry's nomination and subsequent meandering campaign furnished no focus for debate over the decision to go to war, the tactics of the administration in misleading the public about the threat posed by Saddam, the need to rethink the terms on which the "war on terrorism" was to be waged, and not least the terms by which "homeland security" had been cast into opposition with civil liberties.[23]

The threat that antiwar sentiments might embolden anticorporate elements to entertain hope of reversing the trends embodied in Superpower, combined with the determination of the Democrats to prevent that from happening, points to the crucial significance of the lack of third party alternatives. The historical role of third parties has been to force the major parties to cherry-pick third party proposals, typically those of a democratic or social democratic tendency. The 2004 presidential election marked the tragicomic playing out of the ineffectualness of third parties: the Democrats employed every dirty trick possible to discourage Ralph Nader from merely gaining a place on the presidential ballot for November 2004. At the same time the Republicans were deploying resources to enable Nader, their severest critic, to secure a place on the ballot. The episode, in its absurdity, shed a sharp light on how the two major parties connive to create as many obstacles as possible—in the form of requirements—for discouraging genuine alternatives to the established parties and their policies. While the Republican Party is ever-vigilant about the care and feeding of its zealots, the Democratic Party is equally concerned to discourage its democrats.

The timidity of a Democratic Party mesmerized by centrist precepts points to the crucial fact that, for the poor, minorities, the working class, anticorporatists, pro-environmentalists, and anti-imperialists, there is no opposition party working actively on their behalf. And this despite the fact that these elements are recognized as the loyal base of the party. By ignoring dissent and by assuming that the dissenters have no alternative, the party serves an important, if ironical, stabilizing function and in effect marginalizes any possible threat to the corporate allies of the Republicans.[24] Unlike the Democrats, however, the Republicans, with their combination of reactionary and innovative elements, are a cohesive, if not a coherent, opposition force.

The character of the Republican Party reflects a profound change: radicalism has shifted its location and meaning. Formerly it was associated with the Left and with the use of political power to lift the standard of living and life prospects of the lower classes, of those who were disadvantaged under current distributive principles. Radicalism is now the property of those who, quaintly, call themselves "conservatives" and are called such by media commentators. In fact, pseudoconservatism is in charge of and owns the radicalizing powers that are dramatically changing, in some cases revolutionizing, the conditions of human life, of economy, politics, foreign policy, education, and the prospects of the planet. It is hard to imagine any power more radical in its determination to undo the social gains of the past century. The transformation of the Republican Party reflects the domestic requirements of an imperial Superpower and is an indicator of the future forms of party politics in this country.

Paradoxically, liberalism and its historical party, the Democrats, are conservative, not by choice but by virtue of the radical character of the Republicans. At the historical moment when the citizenry is strongly antipolitical and responds to immaterial "values," the Democrats, in order to preserve a semblance of a political identity, are forced into a conservatism. Out of desperation rather than conviction, they struggle halfheartedly to preserve the remains of their past achievements of social welfare, public education, government regulation of the economy, racial equality, and the defense of trade unions and civil liberties.

The imbalance between, on the one hand, constitutionally limited state power and, on the other, the relatively unconstrained power of science, technology, and corporate capitalism makes little difference to the Republican Party. It is content with an ancillary role of encouraging capitalism and allowing it to shape the directions of science and technology. By relying on corporate capital to provide major funding for the other two powers, the party can then even adopt a mildly disapproving stance toward public subsidies of some forms of scientific research (e.g., on stem cells) or of some technologies. The Democratic Party mirrors the problem more acutely. As the party with a history of both favoring state regulation of economic activity, especially of large corporations, and being well disposed toward subsidizing science and technological innovations, it would appear to be well positioned to use state authority to redirect the dynamic powers that are driving American imperialism. But in recent decades, as it has become dependent on contributions of corporations and wealthy donors, it has become less willing to mount an electoral challenge that would take on the Republicans at the level of the fundamental political question of whether democracy can cohabit with imperial Superpower.

At best, if state power were to fall into the hands of a reform-minded Democratic administration, that administration would, perforce, expend considerable "capital" (i.e., the patience of its corporate sponsors) playing catch-up. No area of policy better illustrates the "game" of catch-up and how it can assume desperate proportions than that of environmental or ecological issues. Scientific evidence regarding global warming, air pollution, water and food shortages, and dwindling supplies of fossil fuel continues to accumulate; yet, in the face of what appears to be a looming global crisis, the political system, at best, can manage spasmodically to enact regulations in those areas—only to have them weakened or rolled back by a new (i.e., Republican) administration. The frustrations of environmental policy reveal a profound inability of the system to deal with long-range problems requiring consistency of purpose, allocation of public funds, taxes, and a determined commitment to controlling corporate behavior, qualities that a porous policy process lacks. At the same time, the economy, with its highly focused quest for profits, generates new products, new dangers to consumers and the environment, and new tactics for circumventing existing safeguards.

ix

In their beginnings political institutions and their practices typically incorporate a notion of proper scale. Their "sphere" of operations is defined by geography, socioeconomic circumstances, available technologies, and cultural values. Our system was originally conceived as a federal structure that recognized the presence of sovereign states but also envisaged an arrangement flexible enough to absorb the addition of new states. Virtually from the beginning of the republic it was assumed that the nation would expand westward. It was expected that the main national institutions of president, Congress, and courts would be enlarged to accommodate additional representatives in the Senate, the House, and the Electoral College without altering the practices governing those institutions. In other words, while a new scale would come into existence, the old institutions would have to adjust only in a quantitative sense (new states would mean additional senators, representatives, and electoral votes). Thus the operative norms would continue unchanged. It was assumed that the admission of new states to the Union could be orderly and need not disturb issues that the Constitution had either suppressed or postponed, such as slavery, women's suffrage, and the status of native Americans.

The assumption that politics could comfortably accommodate an expanded scale was first put in doubt in the decades preceding the Civil War. The Missouri Compromise of 1820 was an attempt to settle the crucial issue of whether new states entering the Union would be free or slave. It admitted Missouri into the Union as a slave state but prohibited slavery in the rest of the territory acquired under the Louisiana Purchase north of the 36-30 latitudinal line.[25] The Compromise of 1850 allowed inhabitants of the New Mexico and Utah territories, acquired by the Mexican War, to decide the question of whether they wished to enter the Union with or without slavery. In the end these efforts at postponing the issue of slavery failed. The Civil War put in doubt the capability of free politics to keep up with an expanded scale. The proof was in the failure of postwar Reconstruction: despite military occupation democracy and racial equality failed to take hold in the South.

x

Today this failed assumption, that free politics could be reconciled peaceably with an ever-increasing scale, has been demonstrated again by the imperial ambitions of Superpower and its distinctive nonterritorial conception of empire. It used to be said of the late British Empire that it was not the consequence of a premeditated plan but casually established in "a fit of absent-mindedness." There were, of course, "imperialists" who dreamed of empire, and some of them, such as Cecil Rhodes and Winston Churchill, who consciously fought for its realization. But there is a larger truth in the notion of an empire that begins without much forethought or conscious intention at work: empire building is likely to have contributing causes other than, or in addition to, the conscious intentions of imperialists. Those causes could include the actions of non- or even anti-imperialists. Unlike Hitler, Mussolini, and Stalin, who set out consciously to establish one-party dictatorships and to extend their rule beyond their nation's original borders (*Lebensraum, mare nostrum,* world revolution), inverted totalitarianism comes into being, not by design, but by inattention to the consequences of actions or especially of inactions. Or, more precisely, inattention to their cumulative consequences.

The lobbyist who seeks to influence a legislator by campaign contributions or other inducements does not set out to weaken the authority and prestige of representative institutions and thereby contribute to inverted totalitarianism. The legislator who votes in favor of a resolution giving the president virtually unlimited discretion in deciding when to wage war does not intend to weaken the powers of the legislature to the point where it lacks the will to check the president in matters of war, peace making, and foreign policy. The federal regulator who, despite thousands of letters of protest, approves a regulation allowing large media conglomerates to extend further their control over local markets may not intend to eliminate the possibility of outlets that give a voice to dissenting political, economic, and ecological views. The employer who "busts" unions does not seek to weaken the structure of civil society and the power of its associations and nongovernmental organizations to counter the state and corporate capital. The occasional citizen who, muttering about corrupt politicians, retreats into political hibernation and emerges blinkingly to cast a vote does not mean to make himself an easy object of manipulation or to confirm the elite's view of democracy as a useful illusion.

CHAPTER ELEVEN

Inverted Totalitarianism:
Antecedents and Precedents

i

In late November and early December 2004, a million citizens of Kiev and from other parts of Ukraine assembled in the public square of Kiev to protest the results of a national election, claiming that it had been deeply flawed by fraud and that the true winner was the candidate of the opposition party. Foreign observers largely agreed that the election had been marred by widespread irregularities. The protesters demanded a recount and held firm for several days until an agreement was reached that set a date for a new election. This in a society that had no strong tradition of democratic politics.

Following the American presidential election of November 2000, there were numerous claims that proceedings in the crucial state of Florida had been marred by irregularities of various kinds, including fraud, voter intimidation, and racism. The issue was eventually settled by a process that was as flawed and partisan as the election itself. Yet no crowds took to the streets; no one sat down before the Supreme Court in protest; no one mounted a mass march on Washington. This in a society that boasted of being the world's oldest—and presumably the most experienced—democracy.

ii

The crisis, it seems, is that there was no crisis. In its literal meaning a crisis is "a turning point." Adapting the formulation "a turning point but no crisis" to the condition I have designated "inverted totalitarianism," we might ask, why does the existence of that turning point go unrecognized? how are the facts of radical political change concealed when there is no evidence, say, of a coup or revolutionary overthrow? how can we recognize that the country is at the political turning point of inverted totalitarianism?

As a start, we might pause over the notion of "recognition." As commonly used, it implies a prior knowledge of an object: we recognize (i.e., identify) an old schoolmate. But if we bisect the word into "re-cognize," a somewhat different meaning is suggested: to rethink, to reconsider, in our case, to reconceive the possible forms that totalitarianism might assume *and* to question whether the political history of the United States really is the triumph of democracy in America. That double strategy might enable us to avoid the presumption that fascism or totalitarianism necessarily means a distinct break by which a political society is suddenly and radically transformed by a coup or a revolution, as were Lenin's Russia and Franco's Spain.

The second aspect of our strategy calls for collective self-examination: is the United States the model democracy or a highly equivocal one? If we were to list the essentials of a democracy, such as rule by the people, we would find that democracy in that sense is nonexistent—and that may be a substantial part of the crisis that is no crisis. That our system actually is democratic is more of an unquestioned assumption than a matter of public discussion, and so we ignore the extent to which antidemocratic elements have become systemic, integral, not aberrant. The evidence is there: in widening income disparities and class distinctions, polarized educational systems (elite institutions with billion-dollar endowments versus struggling public schools and universities), health care that is denied to millions, national political institutions controlled by wealth and corporate power. While these contrasts are frequently bemoaned, they are rarely considered as cumulative and, rarer still, as evidence of an antidemocratic regime.

To claim that antidemocracy is a regime means expanding the meaning of democracy so that it is not confined to political matters but applies as well to social, cultural, and economic relationships. If it is objected that this stretches the meaning of democracy beyond what it can reasonably bear, my response is this: not to do so implies that democracy can operate despite the inequalities of power and life circumstances embedded in all of those relationships.

An inverted totalitarian regime, precisely because of its inverted character, emerges, not as an abrupt regime change or dramatic rupture but as evolutionary, as evolving out of a continuing and increasingly unequal struggle between an unrealized democracy and an antidemocracy that dare not speak its name. Consequently while we recognize familiar elements of the system—popular elections, free political parties, the three branches of government, a bill of rights—if we re-cognize, invert, we see its actual operations as different from its formal structure. Its elements have antecedents but no precedents, a confluence of tendencies and pragmatic choices made with scant concern for long-term consequences.

For example, the contemporary phenomenon of privatization by which governmental functions, such as public education, military operations, and intelligence gathering, are shared with or assigned to private entrepreneurs represents more than a switch in suppliers. The privatization of public functions is an expression of the revolutionary dynamic of capitalism, of its aggrandizing bent. Capital brings its own culture of competitiveness, hierarchy, self-interest. Each instance of the private inroads into public functions extends the power of capital over society. Services such as public education that had previously been viewed as essential, not only to the literacy of the citizenry but to its empowerment, are now increasingly being ceded to private entrepreneurs. From a democratic perspective the effects of privatization are counterrevolutionary; but from a capitalist viewpoint they are revolutionary. Privatization of education signifies not an abstract transfer of public to private but a takeover of the means to reshape the minds of coming generations, perhaps to blend popular education and media culture so as to better manage democracy.

iii

As the example of privatization suggests, re-cognition enters as we discern connections between phenomena that, when naively noted, seem unrelated. Thus at first glance forms of popular culture such as newspapers, cinema, TV, or radio seem more or less unchanged except in technology. Occasionally we are told of changes that we cannot see, that "ownership is being concentrated in fewer and fewer hands." Even less frequently are we told that ownership brings control of content, how that control is manifested, and what its political bearing might be. TV might present what we recognize as the familiar figure of a uniformed policeman at a political demonstration; but, again, if we have been reading about the new technologies (e.g., databases), tactics of crowd control, surveillance methods, and weapons (stun guns, pepper spray) being used by police, as well as the broader authority available to them by virtue of antiterrorist laws, we may re-cognize the police as a force for controlling popular expression rather than simply as "the arm of the law" dedicated to the protection of life and property.[1]

Antecedents but not precedents: Police repression is far from being novel in American history; it has antecedents. Toward the close of the nineteenth century, not uncommonly, police and National Guardsmen were used to break strikes and to aid employers against unions; and throughout the twentieth century, from Selma to Watts to Berkeley and Chicago, the police have been employed to quell populist political protests; it was National Guardsmen who shot dead antiwar demonstrators at Kent State. Those actions are rarely, if ever, invoked as precedents that justify repression. They are viewed as singular, ad hoc interventions rather than a practice. There are few antecedent examples of repression of the rich, much less precedents.

But does terrorism, that war without end, that perpetual emergency, cause us to re-cognize repression or, instead, to normalize it? When do the police evolve from the obvious but occasional agent of employers into an element within an evolving system of control, intimidation, and repression; or when does the expanded *domestic* role of the military seem a natural response to terrorists—or to a natural disaster such as a hurricane? How does good old American pragmatism, supposedly the least ideological, most practical of public philosophies, become the unwitting agent of a regime with affinities to the most ideological systems?

A possible answer: The normalizing of deviations occurs when the main political institutions, such as legislatures, courts, elected law enforcement officials (e.g., district attorneys), mayors, governors, and presidents are able to exploit a fearful public and promote the powers of an increasingly militarized police but not their accountability. The usual justification is one that draws the citizenry into complicity: the public, according to polls, favors harsh sentences, safer streets, the names of sexual predators publicized and their residences listed, and no coddling of prisoners in those rehabilitation programs favored by liberals at taxpayers' expense. In these examples we see the ingredients whereby antecedents become precedents: an empowered police, an officialdom that sanctions expanded police powers and reduced legal and political safeguards, and public opinion that appears to favor methods which weaken legal safeguards and diminish the institutions whose traditional role is to oversee, check, and alert the public to dangerous tendencies in the system. The remarkable thing about public opinion is that it is self-justifying, never accountable.

Thus the invasive Patriot Act, with its inroads into personal liberties and the reduced power of the courts to check overly zealous officials, is first accepted by the public as a practical response to terrorism, but then it is soon cemented as a permanent element in the system of law enforcement. What may have emerged without premeditation is quickly seized upon and exploited. The response to 9/11 is soon declared to be a "war on terrorism." Then, when that war appears to be flagging, it is redefined as the war against "radical Islamism" or an "Islamic caliphate." It then seems logical to coordinate all the relevant agencies—federal, state, and local, and all armed forces, from police and National Guard to the traditional armed services—and, *voilà!*, we have a system. The Nazis called it *Gleichschaltung* (coordination). We might call it "management" to indicate its place in an opportunity society.

But—returning to TV—we may be led to wonder whether the actual intimidation of populist protests by police and TV's highly selective and unfavorable depiction of them are connected. Invoking history, we may further re-cognize when a significant change occurs. Recall the media's relatively benign portrayal of the civil rights movement and antiwar rallies of the sixties, and recall, too, the media's steady focus on the "police riot" at the 1968 Democratic Convention; then contrast those with its perfunctory coverage of the opposition to the first Gulf War and to the invasion of Iraq (2003). The main continuity between the sixties and the Reagan and George I–II administrations is the close scrutiny of antiwar and antiracist protests by increasingly militarized police forces, a cooperative media, and an ever more intrusive and high-tech national intelligence network.[2]

What is at stake here is the control of public space and the power to depict, to discourage and intimidate, and ultimately to filter what is happening and being expressed at a time when technology makes filtering relatively easy. Consider the attempts on the part of protest groups during the summer of 2004 to enter the public space of streets in the environs of the conventions of the two national parties. As the police herded the protesters into the equivalent of cattle pens, the media presented the groups as bizarre and ignored the serious arguments they were attempting to offer. In effect the media transformed a political action, intended for the civic education of a public, into a spectacle framed for mass entertainment. Earlier, during the election campaigns of 2004, the media enforced the one-and-a-half-party system and a stunted version of an electorate. When they did not caricature, they virtually erased the attempts of third parties to present the electorate with alternative policies and candidates; even Howard Dean, a conventional candidate though an unwelcome one to the party establishment, was pilloried as an extremist and ridiculed as "out of control."[3]

The perfect illustration of a rigidly controlled system at which both parties connive was the so-called presidential debates of 2004. In a fog of vacuous answers to insipid questions the public was treated as props, passive guests rather than citizen-participants. One might reasonably wonder what educational character those debates might have had if, say, Ralph Nader had been allowed to press Bush on issues of corporate power, or Dennis Kucinich had confronted Bush on the likely consequences of his proposals for reforming the Social Security system, or Howard Dean had been present to pursue the issue of a calamitous war and the justification for killing thousands of Iraqis while reducing large parts of their society to rubble.

iv

Police control over demonstrators, combined with the media's censorship of popular protests and of third party activities, produces for inverted totalitarianism what Fascist thugs and censorship accomplished for the classic version.[4] It seems a replay of historical experience that the bias displayed by today's media should be aimed consistently at the shredded remains of liberalism. Recall that an element common to most twentieth-century totalitarianisms, whether Fascist or Stalinist, was hostility toward the Left—in the United States the Left is assumed to consist solely of liberals, occasionally of "the left wing of the Democrat Party," never of democrats. Indeed, a crucial feature of all totalitarian systems is that they were preceded by a pronounced shift in political dynamics from left to right.[5] In the politics of Spain, Italy, and Germany after 1918 and before the Fascist triumphs, liberals, socialists, and communists had been major players, on occasion controlling government and influencing the general political culture.[6] Accordingly, the elimination of the Left became a key objective of Fascist strategies. That strategy was complemented by campaigns to stoke, then reinforce, mass emotions of nationalism and patriotism, and to accuse the Left of being "soft" and "unpatriotic."

In the United States the rise of an extreme and highly ideological Right was driven by an unrelenting assault on liberals, portraying them as both "hating America" and hostile to business, and thus suggesting that the two occupy the same plane, even though a substantial proportion of Americans are reported as being distrustful of corporations.[7] Paradoxically, and unlike classic totalitarians, the Bush administration simultaneously attacked liberalism while professing a determination to establish democracy and free markets abroad. A clue to its real tendencies is that in defending its domestic policies, the Bush administration rarely claimed to be promoting democracy.[8]

That right-wing ideologues, with their staunch defense of elitism and disdain for the demos, should attack liberalism and belatedly discover democracy, smacks of bad faith.[9] Liberal intellectuals, like their conservative counterparts, have traditionally defended a meritocratic elitism—and hence are at one with many conservatives—while democratic theorists have rejected it as incompatible with the principle of equality. Although neocon ideologues manage to muster one cheer for capitalism,[10] most liberals manage at least two, and some leaders of Christian political groups three. Thus liberalism would seem to share important common ground with conservatives, and that, in turn, suggests a certain skepticism about broad distinctions between red and blue politics. Color coding obscures the likelihood that a significant number of liberals hold serious reservations about democracy: what is the color of centrist Democrats?

Thus a muddle: conservative elitists should hate democrats and ally with elitist liberals. Instead they profess to love the former and hate the latter. Is deference to democracy popular among politicos of all shades because its dynamic is spent and its force is mainly rhetorical? If such is the situation, then a rhetorical democracy may hide the contradictory elements that, in the case of conservatives, are joined tactically to produce a dynamic but, in the case of liberals, produce uncertainty.

A short historical detour may shed some light on the changing dynamics of political identities and alliances.

v

d'ynamis (Gr.): power, potentiality.

Historically, the ideology of liberalism came to represent an uneasy combination of elements: elected representative government, limited government, equal rights, property rights, and an economy that, when freed from governmental interference and rid of privilege, nevertheless produced inequalities as striking as any in the traditional regimes.

In early modern Britain capitalism and liberalism had been allies in their revolutionary struggles against the "old regimes" of inherited privilege and power. They represented "forces" of change that promised greater freedom, economic opportunity, and an end to privilege and arbitrary government.[11] In contrast, early modern conservatism had no dynamic, only a reaction in defense of a dying order. In Edmund

Burke's classic version conservatism responded to the French Revolution by preaching quietism, appealing to tradition (represented by the landed gentry and established church), and defending a politics of deference to superiors. Thus conservatism stood as a holding action against radical change from "below," a defense of customary ways and institutions, a skeptical view of marketplace values and types, and an abhorrence of demotic equality.[12]

The liberal apostles of change were the great political economists—Adam Smith, Jeremy Bentham, John Stuart Mill, and David Ricardo. In varying degrees they advocated a politics centered on the middle class and excluding the working class and poor. None were egalitarians—with the possible exception of Bentham. They pitted intellectual elitism against the inherited privileges of an aristocracy, the free market against mercantilist notions of state control of the economy, and they sided with modern science against religious obscurantism. They were only moderately enthusiastic for political participation, favoring, instead, a larger role for disinterested public servants. Except for Adam Smith, whose *Wealth of Nations* appeared in 1776, the English version of liberalism was formulated roughly a quarter century after the American Revolution; hence it was not their liberalism that initially took hold in America.[13] When the American colonists protested the taxes and import duties that the mother country had imposed, their arguments were primarily based on political principles concerning representation, not on economic theories. Moreover, in the years after the revolution, many among the emerging political elites believed that the most pressing need was to establish a strong government and especially one that would play a major role in overseeing economic affairs and promoting economic growth—the opposite of the teachings of many nineteenth-century English liberals. That viewpoint was embodied in the American Constitution, in provisions for political institutions and individual rights and for checking majoritarian democracy. In assigning to Congress broad legislative powers to regulate commerce, the framers aimed at preventing the states from interfering in business transactions or with the flow of commerce. Other clauses provided for a central government with authority to promote as well as protect the new nation's economy. In other words, a strong element of neomercantilism was perpetuated.

When Alexander Hamilton became secretary of the treasury in the Washington administration, neomercantilism became policy, thus establishing precedent for a long tradition of government favors and subsidies to business.

The neomercantilist concordat between liberalism and capital, which continued throughout most of the nineteenth century, was an expression of the dynamic comprising the centralized state emerging from the Civil War, an expanding economy, and ideologies of nationalism and competitive individualism ("social Darwinism"). It began shaping the habits, outlook, and material circumstances of the population, extending the reach of the state, and encouraging the corporate revolution of the last half of the nineteenth century. As Karl Marx, no less, repeatedly emphasized, capitalism is by nature a revolutionary force. When, toward the end of the century, that dynamic was opposed by a different dynamic—the challenge of populist forces demanding that the state intervene to regulate railroad rates, promote paper money, and prohibit monopolies—the alliance between state and corporation, while strained, held against the threat of neomercantilism in the service of populism. When antitrust legislation was introduced, it was inconsistently enforced. The great Progressive reformers of the early twentieth century, while sharply critical of corporate concentration and growing political influence, were not anticapitalist.

America's entry into the First World War was an intimation of what was to come: a Democratic, reformist administration that redirected its energies into making a world safe for democracy. Following victory the party went into decline, along with reformism.

The first sustained parting of the ways between liberals and capitalism came with the New Deal, when liberalism displayed a degree of independence that, if not anticapitalist, appeared highly critical.[14] Serious governmental regulation of the economy and legislation favorable to trade unions and social democracy were introduced, suggesting that liberalism was about to redefine its alliance with capital. What made that moment possible was the Great Depression and the consequent weakened condition of capitalism, plus the heightened political consciousness of workers, small farmers and businessmen, teachers, artists of all kinds. Throughout the Western world at the time there were wide-ranging discussions of alternatives, especially of governmental planning as the means of reorganizing economic life to serve the needs and aspirations of the vast majority of citizens. From today's vantage point it is difficult to recognize a time when politicians, public intellectuals, even some businessmen were convinced that capitalism was in mortal danger and in need of serious reform, possibly by some type of "collectivism."

The aftermath of World War II should have witnessed the high tide of liberalism; instead it was as though liberalism became frozen in time, its dynamic spent. It might promise more New Deal–type social legislation, but not more regulation of the economy. One of the last important pieces of New Deal–type legislation was the GI Bill of Rights with its educational subsidies for veterans; significantly, no regulation of capital was involved. Ideologically, it seemed as though there was nothing more to reform—very few party leaders were concerned about civil rights, much less racial equality.[15] After the years of wartime controls over the economy accompanied by rationing and shortages, the public seemed to have little desire for the expansion of government but a huge appetite for the material comforts denied during wartime. The substantial governmental apparatus assembled during the war was adapted to the new mode of Cold War and containment and produced near disastrous hot wars in Korea and Vietnam. Neoliberalism emerged as the New Deal's residuary legatee and found its icon in JFK. Its proponents were willing to sacrifice some elements of social democracy in order to promote a "strong state" for opposing Soviet communism abroad.[16] Many liberals shared with conservatives a distaste for the participatory politics of the sixties. About civil rights neoliberals tended to be either indifferent or lukewarm, as witness the JFK and Carter presidencies, or rhetorically friendly only after the fact (Clinton). In short, liberalism had lost the robust dynamic that had enabled it to intervene to control the "excesses" of capital and to respond, at least minimally, to the new challenge of broadening political along with social democracy. The contrary tugs of liberalism—toward a defense of the "free world" against communist aggression, and toward social and racial equality at home—were played out in the Johnson administration. It floundered helplessly in an unwinnable "hot" war abroad, while at home its reformist energies were pretty much exhausted by efforts to secure equal voting rights. The climactic moment symbolic of its exhaustion was Lyndon Johnson's decision to withdraw from the race for his party's presidential nomination in 1968. By its own actions and inactions, not through any conservative strategies, liberalism had failed in Korea and Vietnam, and proved unable to come to terms with the participatory energy of the sixties.

vi

Meanwhile American business underwent its own revolution. During the 1950s and 1960s publicists announced that American capitalism was in the throes of "the managerial revolution."[17] A new cult figure emerged: the executive trained and certified in the dynamics and intricacies of organizing, administering, and exploiting power. Thanks to the role of business and law schools, a new component of a ruling class, educated in the ways of power and of innovation in its uses, was introduced, not only in businesses but throughout society, in university administration, philanthropic foundations, cultural institutions (museums, symphonies), and the communications industry. The managerial revolution made possible the modernization of the Republican Party.

Managerialism, by definition, was not only elitist in principle but, in an age dominated by large-scale forms of "organization," a claim to rule. That claim was distinctive, for it concerned ruling in a context of intense competition, high risk, and big stakes. Accountability figured mainly as profitability. In that sense organizational power, with its emphasis upon expansion, dynamic leadership, and risk taking, contrasted with constitutional authority, with its emphasis upon restraint, settled ways, checks and balances. The differences between organization and constitution would loom large when the corporate manager, the risk-taker, succeeded the governmental bureaucrat, and when the president trained at the Harvard Business School succeeded the Rhodes Scholar president.

The managerial character of capital assumes particular significance in light of the fact that no distinct, self-conscious conservative ideology existed in the United States before the mid-twentieth century. The major exception was the Civil War era's Southern apologists for slavery. Modern conservatism was a post–World War II invention. And when capitalism and conservatism merged in the latter part of the twentieth century, conservative intellectuals, while occasionally paying homage to "absolute values," rejected the conservative temptation to look backwards and instead joined their cause to the dynamic of an expanding, globalizing capitalism and its managers.

Conservative intellectuals date the beginnings of "the modern Republican Party" from the presidential campaign of Barry Goldwater in 1964. That happens to have been when conservative intellectuals first played an influential political role. By the time that the party returned to power in 1980, it had become increasingly radicalized and its reactionary elements converted into a political dynamic symbolized by managerialists such as Cheney and Rumsfeld. The revelatory moment came when the neocons joined with the managerialists to proclaim the "New American Century" and lay plans for the expansion of American power.

A case might be made, however, that the origins of the party's transformation and the source of its dynamic are earlier than either the Goldwater campaign or the Reagan presidency or the managerial revolution. They can be traced to the Cold War with the Soviet Union that began in the late 1940s and early 1950s. The distinctive element in that transformation was the party's success in blending foreign threats and domestic suspicions to lay the basis of a totalizing dynamic. America, scarcely finished with a global war in 1945, had to be mobilized again, aroused to confront the "challenge" of a new and peculiarly insidious enemy. Thus began the first efforts at constructing an enemy who, while not mythical, was given mythical proportions.

Republicans and their supporters claimed that Soviet communism had launched a "conspiracy," a "plot" for "world domination" whose operations were secret and hidden, dependent upon spies and traitors. That allegation led to a crucial decision, to reflect the "crusade against Communism" inwards, into domestic politics. That move led to a campaign to expose Communist Party members and sympathizers. Its beginnings were in the McCarthy "crusade" (as its supporters called it) to ferret out "disloyal" citizens and "Communist sympathizers."

In effect the party first invented, then launched a culture war. What was striking about many of those accused as "subversives" or "un-American" was the large number of academics, writers, actors, and Hollywood directors and executives. Thus the targets were the makers of popular and "highbrow" culture. The ideology for that counterdynamic was quickly formulated by a new breed of highbrow conservative intellectuals. Decades before neoconservatism became a buzzword, there were true intellectual revolutionaries bent on overthrowing and replacing the liberal establishment that, in their view, had dominated the nation from the 1930s to the 1960s. Their assault gained more standing when, as the liberal intelligentsia hesitated, conservative intellectuals united in discrediting the populist and democratic politics of the sixties. The new ideology can be fairly described as totalizing and unapologetic for its absolutism. Its targets were not confined to Democratic politicians but included a wide range of matters: education, morality, religion, and popular culture. The great evil was "relativism," the favorite remedy "discipline." They charged that liberal relativism, permissiveness (= moral laxity), affirmative action, and secularism were softening the national will, mocking ideals of loyalty and patriotism, and in the process undermining national unity in the global struggle with Soviet communism.

To describe Republicanism as a dynamic party is to say that the party succeeded in organizing and focusing powers that challenge limits, be they limits regarding church and state, presidential powers, environmental protections, the distinctions between public and private, the protections for civil liberties, the observance of treaties, or respect for local markets. The party united otherwise disparate powers, producing the momentum for change as well as dictating its direction. And that direction has been self-consciously antiliberal and not infrequently reactionary. While packaging democracy for export, at home it hacked away at the social supports for democracy.

Doubtless there are several factors underlying the party's success, but there is one in particular that may explain the party's distinctive combination of forward-looking (science, technology, venture capital) and retrogressive elements (fundamentalists, creationists, originalists, moral absolutists, and classroom disciplinarians). An age of rapid, relentless, and uncertain changes leaves many, perhaps most, people yearning for stability, for relationships, beliefs, and institutions that abide. The retrogressive elements seek reassurance that there are religious, moral, and political verities, unchanging truths. Thus the party is able to have it both ways, encouraging and subsidizing the powers that undermine the status quo while publicizing prayer in the Oval Office and making abstinence in the third world a condition of foreign aid.

vii

At present the national government is embarked upon a war in which our leaders first deceived the public about the threat to the nation and then followed a course of action that consistently evaded and violated constitutional limitations. Nonetheless its actions and official justifications are in certain important respects compatible with some of the broad aims of some of the Founders of our constitution. The point is not whether the Founders had a totalitarian vision, but rather what forms of power they were bent on encouraging and what forms they were determined to check. What did they hope for and what did they fear?

The main hope of the framers of the Constitution was to establish a strong central government, not one hobbled at every turn by an intrusive citizenry or challenged by the several "sovereign" states. They professed to be choosing a republic, but it is closer to the truth to say that they were focused upon establishing a system of national power to replace what they considered the hopelessly ineffectual system of decentralized powers under the Articles of Confederation.

The new system, with its emphasis upon a strong executive, an indirectly elected Senate composed (it was hoped) of the educated and wealthy, and an appointed Supreme Court also represented the fears of the Founders. Theirs was a counterrevolution against not only the system of politics that had led the revolution against Britain but against the democratic tendencies and populist outbreaks that had persisted from the end of the seventeenth century and throughout the eighteenth.

Why should one oppose democracy, that is, a government that advanced the interests of the vast majority, of the less powerful? During the eighteenth century there were many attempts at answering that awkward question. The people, it was said, were not competent to rule (i.e., they were uneducated and/or inexperienced); hence they would be unable to govern according to their (true) interests. Or allegedly the people were subject to wild mood swings. Or it was claimed that, at best, democracy was possible in a society of small scale; an extended society made it impracticable for the people to assemble—as though democracy depended upon assembling the entire nation. In the course of its arguments for the ratification of the Constitution, *The Federalist* made much of a contrast between "reason" and "passion," the one associated with the Few, the latter with the Many. Passions were attributed to uncontrolled self-interest: they were "immediate," "private," "selfish," "strong," "irregular." Because "the people" symbolized the threat of irrational politics, the task of elites was to hold popular forces at bay by establishing and defending a "reasonable" politics.[18] According to *The Federalist* the main purpose of the Constitution was to control "interests," explicitly the interests of a majority. Interests were depicted as selfish, irrational, and potentially destructive.

In fact in the early years of the republic ordinary people had concrete interests, such as small businesses (a tanner, a butcher), manufacturing, trade, and agriculture. Interests, although not the same ones, were what most Americans had in common; the system of exchange (the butcher bought from the farmer) was an important bond in a relatively large country without an extensive system of communication. Ordinary Americans welcomed democracy as the only political system that encouraged them to use power to promote and defend their interests. As early as the 1760s groups of New York artisans declared: "Every Man who honestly supports a Family by useful Employment is honourable enough for any office in the State, that his abilities are equal to. And in the great essential Interests of a Nation, which are so plain that every one may understand them,—as every individual is interested, all have an equal Right to declare their Interests, and to have them regarded."[19] In short, democracy and the interests of individuals were complementary.

For *The Federalist* interests were legitimate so long as they satisfied two conditions: they were nonideological and not organized politically into a national majority.[20] For *The Federalist*, and for Hamilton in particular, the consolidation of national power and its extension required the promotion of certain interests, such as banking, finance, and commerce. These were "national interests," even a "common interest" of which "the state" would be "guardian."[21] In other words, some interests were expansive, the constituents of national power, while the interests of the butcher were parochial and unrelated to state power. That understanding continues today.

The history of the revolution that most Americans are taught emphasizes the role of selfless generals, patrician leaders—in short, an elite.[22] However, thanks to the efforts of some historians, we now are able to learn about the extraordinary political activities of working-class members, small farmers, women, slaves, and Indians during the period from roughly 1690 throughout most of the following century. It took several forms: street protests and demonstrations, attacks on official residences, petitions, mass meetings, pamphlets, and newspaper articles. Virtually without exception the motive animating these actions was to protect or advance interests that the existing system ignored or exploited unfairly. And, since most lacked the economic resources necessary to qualify for the suffrage, protest was also directed against the exclusion of the lower classes from the political decision-making institutions. Democracy, in this early meaning, stood for a politics of redress, for common action to alleviate the sharp inequalities of wealth and power that enabled the more affluent and educated to monopolize governance.[23] It was, of necessity, a fugitive democracy, given to moments of frustration, rage, and violence that inspired the dominant classes to describe the people as "tumultuous." That "turbulence" was, in effect, the demotic form of political dynamics. It drew its strength from sheer numbers, but also from the indispensable role of artisans, laborers, small farmers and merchants not only in the economy but as common soldiers and sailors in the military. Except for periods of unemployment, those who protested, marched, organized, or propagandized had neither leisure time nor the resources to sustain their own dynamic.

The American political system was not born a democracy, but born with a bias against democracy. It was constructed by those who were either skeptical about democracy or hostile to it. Democratic advance proved to be slow, uphill, forever incomplete. The republic existed for three-quarters of a century before formal slavery was ended; another hundred years before black Americans were assured of their voting rights. Only in the twentieth century were women guaranteed the vote and trade unions the right to bargain collectively. In none of these instances has victory been complete: women still lack full equality, racism persists, and the destruction of the remnants of trade unions remains a goal of corporate strategies. Far from being innate, democracy in America has gone against the grain, against the very forms by which the political and economic power of the country has been and continues to be ordered.

viii

The contortions that the Founders underwent in order to contain demotic power produced a lasting fault line: on the one side a national establishment and preserve for an elite politics concerned with the grand issues of war, defense, diplomacy, regulation of commerce, national credit, and public finance, and whose operations were to be "regular," "efficient and well administered";[24] on the other a collection of decentralized societies whose politics and culture displayed—as virtually every foreign observer attested—democratic and egalitarian tendencies, rowdiness ("irregular"),[25] local loyalties, a parochial suspicion toward a remote power claiming sovereignty over local life, and a destabilizing politics often "turbulent" and "tumultuous."[26] Thus two countertendencies housed within the same framework: national power could not, even with the best of intentions, be wielded democratically; local powers could not easily submit except by suspending democratic instincts and suspicions and surrendering to the seductive passions of nationalism and patriotism.

The result was a two-tiered system that, at the national level, might be called one of "dissociated democracy." There the people reigned but did not rule. At the state and local level, alongside "great families" whose wealth and status enabled them to play a considerable role in politics, were elements of a widespread and robust democracy, often inspired, sometimes crude, and where the bias of numbers occasionally prevailed.

The framers of the Constitution understood clearly that majority rule was the first principle of democratic government and the essential means of expressing a popular will. It was the method by which "the people" asserted itself politically and acquired self-consciousness. But the Founders, almost without exception, believed that democratic majority rule posed the gravest threat to a republican system. It stood for collective irrationality or, as Madison put it, the "wishes of an unjust and interested majority."[27]

The dilemma of many of the Founders was that, while they feared "the people," they recognized that the political culture of the largely self-governing communities that preceded the Constitution made it unrealistic to attempt a political system without the consent of the power they distrusted most, the people. So they fashioned a variety of devices intended to "filter" expressions of a popular will, hoping to rationalize the irrational. They limited direct popular elections to one branch, the House of Representatives, and designed an elaborate system of separation of powers and checks and balances to make it as difficult as possible for a majority to control simultaneously all branches of the government. The president and Senate were to be indirectly elected; the federal judges were to be nominated by the president and confirmed by the Senate, while personnel of the executive branch were to be appointed by the president and some required approval of the Senate. Neither the original Constitution nor the Bill of Rights contained any provision guaranteeing the right to vote for national offices.

The "great experiment" was aimed not at inventing self-government or individual freedom—these were already the prized achievements of the several states—but at managing democracy. As Hamilton wrote, "When occasions present themselves in which the interests of the people are at variance with their inclinations, it is the duty of the persons whom they have appointed to be the guardians of their interests, to withstand the temporary delusion, in order to give them time and opportunity for more cool and sedate reflection."[28] Thus the people, like wayward minors, needed "guardians"—not executors of their will but interpreters of their true interests. Accordingly, the great purpose of the system of indirectly elected politicians and officials was to legitimate a guardian class, an elite with sufficient leisure to devote itself to governing and schooled in what Hamilton called the "science of politics."[29]

ix

> We no longer have the luxury of having a threat to plan for.
> What we plan for is that we're a superpower. We are the
> major player on the world stage with responsibilities around
> the world, with interests around the world.
> —*Colin Powell (1991)*[30]

While the Founders invested their principal hopes for checking the formation of demotic power by erecting complex constitutional barriers, they also discovered that the large geographical expanse of the nation naturally encompassed a variety of differences of interest and belief, and thereby automatically rendered the organization of a democratic majority difficult. "Extend the sphere," Madison wrote, "and you take in a greater variety of parties and interests; you make it less probable that a majority of the whole will have a common motive to invade the rights of other citizens; or if such a common motive exists, it will be more difficult for all who feel it to discover their own strength, and to act in unison with each other."[31]

We might call this a vision of the saving weakness of a "disaggregated majority." Later it recurs in different guises. A disaggregated majority is a majority prevented from developing its own coherence. Its majoritarian character is fabricated externally, by its opponents, whose aim is to produce a majority at once manipulable (i.e., electoral), self-justifying ("moral majority"), and for the most part "silent." Richard Nixon was being true to that original conception of the majority when he appealed to "the forgotten American, the non-shouters, the non-demonstrators."[32]

The disaggregated majority is fabricated to endorse a candidate or a party for reasons that typically pay only lip service to the basic needs of most citizens (health, education, nontoxic environment, living wage), even less to the disparities in political power between ordinary citizens and well-financed interests. Its speciousness is the political counterpart to products that promise beauty, health, relief of pain, and an end to erectile dysfunction.

Following the 2004 elections the political and media establishment discovered or invented the notion that the salient issue had been "values"—not an endless and increasingly bloody war, nor a faltering economy, burgeoning deficits, and widening class differences.

What was the value of "values"? To obscure more fundamental issues and to divide society along ideological lines rather than class conflicts: the religiously obedient Catholic worker, the evangelical African American, the church- and family-oriented Hispanic, the struggling white family with a son in the military because he aspired to go to college: all vote for the party trumpeting values that impose virtually no cost on its affluent and corporate beneficiaries and their heirs.[33]

There have been other techniques of dispersing popular power without repressing it. During the early years of the republic, it is startling how common were imperialist aspirations, especially among the political notables. One might plausibly presume that in that period political leaders would have had enough daunting challenges to occupy them in firming up a union of fractious states. Yet Hamilton was eager to annex Canada to the new Union, while President Jefferson justified the Louisiana Purchase by claiming that the huge expanse of southern and western land would "enlarg[e] the empire of liberty ... and provide new sources of renovation."[34] Although later commentators would hail the notion of an "empire of liberty," the more revealing phrase was Jefferson's "new sources of renovation." Jefferson had also famously, if recklessly, remarked that it would be healthy for a society to be shaken up by revolution every twenty years. What could prompt the vision that a nation hardly two decades old needed "renovation"—that is, renewal?

Were these expressions of democratic exuberance or of fears that a democratic self-consciousness, bound to a place, might consolidate a majority, and thus become settled into institutions of its own devising?

In an effort to forestall that possibility, the imperial idea was broadened to associate the geographical extension of national power with new economic opportunity.[35] Expansion would mean substituting economic opportunity and independence for political involvements, and trading competitiveness for equality. For a brief moment expansion seemed to encourage democracy. So long as geographical expansion was not aided by centralizing technologies, or incorporated into the framework of a national market, or subjected to a national administration, it could provide space for local forms of democratic self-government to emerge.

For later generations, for whom the notion of empire was becoming associated with European subjugation of conquered peoples, "frontier," rather than empire, became the preferred name for expansionism. The change becomes comprehensible once it is realized that "frontier" signified not a distinct boundary or limit but the expression of a dynamic seeking an outlet for potential power frustrated by the lack of available land or opportunity. It then remained to claim that democracy was peculiarly the product of the frontier experience. For the historian Frederick Jackson Turner (1861–1932), the frontier, the conquest of new space, had been the crucible of democracy.[36] The Western frontier experience, he declared, had been a main force in developing democratic virtues of independence, freedom, and individualism. It had supplied "what has been distinctive and valuable in America's contributions to the history of the human spirit." Although often mentioned in Turner's account, Indians never appear as autonomous actors. "Our Indian policy," he smoothly explained, "has been a series of experimentations on successive frontiers."[37] His main concern was with the crisis created by the vanishing of the frontier. For Turner the democracy in crisis was not participatory democracy in any collective sense. His crisis was the opposite, the disappearance of individualism. "The free lands are gone, the continent is crossed, and all this push and energy is turning into channels of agitation." Discontent would lead to demands for government intervention; the nation would be "thrown back upon itself" and would face the dangers posed by the differences previously absorbed in "the task of filling up the vacant spaces of the continent." A "new Americanism" was emerging, and "it might mean a drastic assertion of national government and imperial expansion under a popular hero."[38]

Turner's pessimism was premature. The idea that democracy depended upon the nation's being forever on the go was revived after World War II. In the early 1960s, as part of his promise "to get America moving again," President John Kennedy announced a "New Frontier," the "race for space." Over the next decades Americans "probed" outer space, circled the globe with satellites, contained communism, and expanded their nation's power to forestall "domino effects." Before long venture capitalists entered, offering "space tourists" reserved seats on future spaceships. Outer space was soon overshadowed by the discovery of "cyberspace," the domain where Turner's frontier thesis took on new meaning as its champions proclaimed that democracy had been reinvented. A band of young pioneers, personified in Bill Gates, explored and exploited a hitherto unknown world where physical power was irrelevant. The new frontiersmen were enterprising in the extreme, hypercompetitive, ruthless in their methods ("take no prisoners"), and able to accumulate staggering amounts of wealth in a relatively brief time. Above all they invented forms of technology that appeared to have the potential for endless innovation: Turner's utopia, a frontier land that, like the universe, appeared to have no borders. Predictably, the introduction of the Internet was hailed as the perfect expression of democracy: that everyone could enter the Web and voice whatever happened to be on his or her mind = democracy.

The achievement represents the removal of the barriers that make Superpower's empire possible: the conquest of space and the compression of time. Endless space: the fulfillment of Madison's strategy for dispersing the demos. Compressed time, instantaneous communication, rapid response: the tyranny of efficiency and the subversion of democracy's requirement that time be defined by the requirements for deliberation, discussion, reconciliation of opposing viewpoints, all of which suddenly seem "time-consuming."

Superpower's mission of spreading democracy throughout the world would seem to fit into the tradition of American expansionism, the resumption of the Wilsonian crusade to "make the world safe for democracy." But the unstated assumption behind that genealogy is that democracy has first to be made safe for the world. Managed democracy is that achievement—and it has precedents and antecedents.

x

The task of elitism in the so-called age of democracy was not to resist democracy but to accept it nominally and then to set about persuading majorities to act politically against their own material interests and potential power.

The solution had been sketched in the seemingly opposed but actually complementary strategies represented by the political ideas of Madison and Hamilton in *The Federalist*. Stated simply, Madison was so intent upon preventing rule by the demos that his system of institutional and geographical complexity seemed destined to end in deadlock. Amidst the welter of contending interests, Madison noted, "justice ought to hold the balance." But, he continued, when politics and governance reduce to interests, "impartiality" is not to be found. Further, "Enlightened statesmen will not always be at the helm." Despair not: the geographical expanse, ideological differences, and socioeconomic complexity of the new system would splinter the demos—"the society . . . broken into so many parts, interests and classes of citizens"—and thereby prevent it *permanently* from gaining the unity of purpose necessary to concert its numerical power and dominate all branches of government.[39]

Madison had, in effect, produced the theory of how—at the national level—to render majoritarianism forever disaggregated and incoherent. The new system might produce majorities, but the elements composing them would be so disparate as to make concerted action unlikely. The downside was that in his determination to enfeeble majorities, Madison appeared to be championing a government tied into knots and hence destined to repeat the colonial experience of impotent and ineffectual rule, the curse of the Articles of Confederation.

The solution to a system that seemed to be designed for deadlock was to craft an institution that had, like monarchy, a certain remoteness, an element of popular legitimacy and yet sufficient independent power that it could furnish genuine governance, possess the requisite "energy" to give direction to the nation. The institution was the executive, or president; its theoretician, Alexander Hamilton. Unlike the divided legislature, with its numerous and diverse representatives, the executive would possess "unity" or "power in a single hand."[40] (The doctrinal inspiration for George Bush's "unified executive.") The fact that the chief executive was elected indirectly, and by an Electoral College that was intended to be a deliberative body, meant that he would have a significant degree of independence, not only from the legislative branch but from the citizenry as well. It was not until the twenty-first century that the Hamiltonian version of the presidency was fully realized.[41]

That the current president has come to embody and reflect the expansive notions of power associated with empire and Superpower does not mean that he was the first. Harry Truman stated that the world could be saved only if "the whole world [were to] adopt the American system." Truman added, "For the American system" could survive only by "becoming a world system."[42] Earlier presidents had justified extraordinary power because the nation was at war. Thus Lincoln, in defending his decision to suspend habeas corpus, cited the ongoing Civil War. Later presidents, such as Wilson and FDR, have also applied expansive notions of executive authority during wartime. In those earlier instances the clear assumption was that once the emergency was over, the powers would cease to be exercised. There was no strategy for normalizing emergency power by pronouncing a new and sweeping doctrine of presidential authority and making it a part of the everyday exercise of executive power. Further, there was no attempt to use a wartime emergency as a pretext for permanently reducing the constitutional authority of the other two branches of government.

Under the present administration the president has claimed the authority to conduct secret wiretaps without the judicial approval required by law; to order the "secret rendition" and detention of enemy combatants; to violate treaties despite the fact that the Constitution declares that treaties passed by Congress are "the supreme law of the land." These and other sweeping claims have been defended as exercises of authority belonging to the president as "commander in chief" and as "chief executive." Clearly, these broad assertions are related to the nebulous character of the "war on terrorism" and to the thoughtless action of Congress when it agreed, unconditionally, that combating terrorism constituted a "war."

Perhaps the most remarkable of all the efforts to expand executive authority at the expense of the constitutional balance of powers is the practice of "signing statements." When presidents sign a congressional bill into law, it has sometimes been the practice of a president to attach a statement in which he may indicate his understanding of the intention of the bill. President Bush, however, has taken that practice and converted it into a sweeping claim that he can ignore provisions of a bill with which he disagrees. On this basis he has claimed the authority to ignore congressional attempts to regulate the military, affirmative action provisions, requirements that he report to Congress about immigration service problems, whistle-blower protections, and safeguards against political interference in federally funded research. He has asserted that he does not have to obey congressional laws forbidding U.S. troops to engage in combat in Colombia; or laws requiring him to inform Congress when he diverts money to start secret operations; or laws prohibiting the military from using intelligence unlawfully collected. Frequently he has deceived Congress by first promoting compromises on legislation and then reneging in his signing statement.[43] In the light of these expansive claims to presidential authority to override congressional power and thereby radically alter the system of checks and balances, the successful strategy of packing the Supreme Court with "reliable" justices completes the picture of a dramatically changed political system. Prior to their nominations to the Court, John Roberts and Samuel Alito helped to formulate the rationale for these expansive doctrines while serving the president.[44]

Although the sum of these actions might seem prima facie grounds for impeachment of the president, they are entirely consistent with the imperial presidency of a superpower.

xi

If we have to use force, it is because we are America.
We are the indispensable nation. We stand tall.
We see further into the future.
—*Madeleine Albright, secretary of state (1998)*[45]

The global pursuits of Superpower have a paradoxical effect. They cause the "homeland" to appear shrunken in comparison with its global status, Lilliputian compared to the Gulliver of Superpower. The usage "homeland" itself is revealing of a certain sense of diminution, of reduction to a beleaguered refuge. "Superpower," "empire," and "globalization" all presuppose and depend upon inequalities of power while maintaining the illusion that somehow those inequalities are not retrojected into the homeland, that the refinement of methods of controlling "crowds" or the denial of due process to American citizens is, at worst, an aberration rather than a prerequisite of Superpower and a contribution to inverted totalitarianism.[46] In fact empire and Superpower undermine and implicitly oppose two presumably fundamental principles of American political ideology: that the Constitution provides the standard for a government of limited powers, and that American governance and politics are democratic.

Despite the incongruity and inherent tensions between unlimited global hegemony and constitutionally limited domestic power, between arbitrary power projected abroad (unilateralism, preemptive war) and democratic power responsible to the citizenry at home, the implications of Superpower, imperial power, and globalizing capital for democracy and constitutionalism have not been publicly confronted, least of all during the 2004 presidential campaign. On the contrary, the defenders and practitioners of these extraordinary forms of power profess to be employing Superpower to force the values of American democracy and the institutions of the free market upon the world. For their part American citizens are expected to support the project of imposing democracy while remaining in denial of their own complicity in ravaging foreign populations and economies. Americans have conveniently forgotten their own disastrous experiment in imposing democracy at the point of a bayonet when, after the Civil War, the victorious North tried to "reconstruct" the South.

Innocents at home, Terminators abroad . . .

CHAPTER TWELVE

Demotic Moments

i

We of the United States, you know, are constitutionally
and conscientiously democrats.
—*Thomas Jefferson*[1]

America, the world's first land of opportunity to
become a democrat . . .
—SSW

Morning/Mourning in America
—SSW

. . . a mourning over the failure of a project that
nonetheless cannot be relinquished.
—*Jürgen Habermas*[2]

Any prospect of revitalizing democracy in America should not assume
that we can start afresh. It is not morning in America. The first step
should be to reflect on the changes of the past half century that have
distorted the cultural supports of democracy and eroded its political
practices while preparing the way for a politics and political culture
favorable to inverted totalitarianism.

Inverted totalitarianism marks a political moment when corporate
power finally sheds its identification as a purely economic phenomenon, confined primarily to a domestic domain of "private enterprise,"
and evolves into a globalizing copartnership with the state: a double
transmutation, of corporation and state. The former becomes more political, the latter more market oriented. This new political amalgam
works at rationalizing domestic politics so that it serves the needs of

238

both corporate and state interests while defending and projecting those same interests into an increasingly volatile and competitive global environment.

Antidemocracy, executive predominance, and elite rule are basic elements of inverted totalitarianism. Antidemocracy does not take the form of overt attacks upon the idea of government by the people. Instead, politically it means encouraging what I have earlier dubbed "civic demobilization," conditioning an electorate to being aroused for a brief spell, controlling its attention span, and then encouraging distraction or apathy. The intense pace of work and the extended working day, combined with job insecurity, is a formula for political demobilization, for privatizing the citizenry. It works indirectly. Citizens are encouraged to distrust their government and politicians; to concentrate upon their own interests; to begrudge their taxes; and to exchange active involvement for symbolic gratifications of patriotism, collective self-righteousness, and military prowess. Above all, depoliticization is promoted through society's being enveloped in an atmosphere of collective fear and of individual powerlessness: fear of terrorists, loss of jobs, the uncertainties of pension plans, soaring health costs, and rising educational expenses. Unlike the Nazis, who made life uncertain for the wealthy and privileged while providing social programs for the working class and poor, inverted totalitarianism exploits the poor, reducing or weakening health programs and social services, regimenting mass education for an insecure workforce threatened by the importation of low-wage workers.[3] Employment in a high-tech, volatile, and globalized economy is normally as precarious as during an old-fashioned depression. The result is that citizenship, or what remains of it, is practiced amidst a continuing state of worry. Hobbes had it right: when citizens are insecure and at the same time driven by competitive aspirations, they yearn for political stability rather than civic engagement, protection rather than political involvement.

That the issues of empire, its consequences for civic values and the practice of liberty, participation, and equality, were never raised during the 2004 elections attests that empire's tacit precondition—of an uncurious and apolitical citizenry—is being consolidated.[4] Empire prefers a passive but patriotic subject. While much has been made of the deep divisions allegedly at work in the electorate, the fact remains that the 2004 election attracted a modest turnout of roughly 60 percent of eligible voters. This suggests that inverted totalitarianism does not want or need active citizens, only periodic ones, a citizenry on call.

One shouldn't expect empire to promote liberty, participation, or equality other than as versions of economic opportunity. The object of its managed democracy is not to persuade the citizens but, depending on the objective, to neutralize or incite them. Managed democracy is not the creature of a tyrannical majority—as the Founders feared. On the contrary. Managed democracy thrives not on active suppression but on an electorate so evenly divided as to prevent the formation of a strong majority will. While an evenly divided electorate stymies the formation of effective majorities, it enhances the power of corporate lobbies, that is, of determined, single-minded, lavishly financed minority wills that operate independently of electoral results. Near deadlock diminishes the legislature's ability to exercise vigorous oversight of the executive and opens the way for an unprecedented assertion of executive power, especially if a legislature is riddled with corruption.

ii

Yet there are grounds for believing that while the American empire may persist, American hegemony is weakening. The debacle of Iraq, the mounting American casualties, pictures of soldiers without limbs, Iraqi casualties so numerous that the American military is loath to report them, the destruction of that society's entire economy, educational system, and culture have by this time begun to shame the American conscience. The huge cost of the war, the escalating share of the national budget claimed by defense spending, the spiraling national deficit, mounting foreign debts, looming oil shortages, a fitful economy, and a shredded social net suggest that the nation can no longer afford to subsidize grandiose imperial ambitions, that retrenchment of American power is necessary. From midsummer of 2005 to the spring of 2007, public opinion surveys consistently indicated that a majority of Americans were losing confidence in the president and beginning to doubt the merits and public rationale for the invasion of Iraq. That finding is of a piece with a spate of articles, books, independently produced movies, and occasional TV shows critical of "the mess in Iraq," and with the public criticism by retired generals of the administration's handling of the war.[5] Even some conservative supporters began to question the administration's loose spending habits and appetite for foreign adventures.

The twilight of empire will not necessarily spell the demise of inverted totalitarianism. The fact of terrorism, combined with the imaginary it has assumed in the national consciousness, will provide justification enough for retaining the security apparatus, subsidizing the defense industry, and nurturing "the fear factor," while accustoming the citizen to a legal regime that sanctions extraconstitutional powers, including the torture of prisoners and domestic spying. Nor is it likely that the Republican Party will abandon its goal of attaining a permanent majority, much less renounce the alliances it has cultivated with corporations, religious groups, conservative intellectuals, and powerful lobbies.

iii

Granted that the invasion of Iraq was politically immoral, duplicitous, and stupid, the blame game is at bottom an unwitting acknowledgment of the shallowness of the political culture of American democracy and of the persistence of antidemocratic tendencies. For the public disenchantment with the Iraq war unintentionally reveals how deeply leadership-dependent the democracy has become.[6] Fault is attributed exclusively to the White House, never to the citizenry for its unthinking support of the venture. If, by luck, the war had been won as quickly as the administration assumed—or purported to assume—it would be, would "democracy" have even blinked? Not only did the citizens endorse the president's war by reelecting him; in 2000 that same citizenry had watched supinely as the Bush team defied the electorate and achieved a political coup. Strong democracy's Weimar?

Much as one is justified in blaming Bush and his coterie, one also needs to figure in the culpability, complicity, and apathy of the citizenry. And that brings us back to the question of how shallow or deeply entrenched in U.S. politics, economy, and society is the democratic ideal of shared power, civic involvement, and egalitarianism. Does "democracy" truly describe our politics and political system, or is it a cynical gesture used to camouflage a deeply manipulative politics?

iv

Not only does the people have no precise consciousness of
its own historical identity, it is not even conscious of the
historical identity or the exact limits of its adversary.
—*Antonio Gramsci*[7]

Throughout most of Western history democracy, far from being the establishment, was virtually unknown. With the exception of ancient Athens, where democracy generally prevailed from, roughly, 450 to 322 BCE, no example of a democratic regime appeared during the subsequent two thousand years. Even in the Constitution of our Founders democracy was only one element and by no means the most valued. Only in the twentieth century were there political regimes that were democratic, when judged by formal criteria such as a universal franchise for all adult citizens, legal rights to which all citizens were equally entitled, a free press and political parties, and comprehensive public educational systems.

Broadly postulated, the struggle for democracy went through three distinct moments widely separated in time. The earliest sustained attempt at inventing a demos occurred in ancient Athens. There a popular challenge was mounted against prevailing notions that the political domain was the exclusive prerogative of the "well-born" and wealthy. Athenian democracy initiated a more inclusive politics open to all adult male citizens regardless of wealth or noble lineage. From that conception there emerged the idea of a demos, a politically engaged and empowered citizenry, one that voted, deliberated, and occupied all branches of public offices.[8] The emergence of a demos also provoked pejorative characterizations: the rabble, the vulgar, the unruly.

"Democracy" (*demokratia = demos + kratia*, or power) stood for rule or power of the people, the political supremacy of an entirely new presence, and also for a certain defiance in an Athens continually beset by class conflicts: on one side nobility, wealth, and education; on the other small farmers, artisans, and merchants.[9] It was also closely associated with equality (*isonomia*) and expressed through such practices as election of officials by lot, the accountability of officials, popular jury courts, and the powers of the popular assembly (*Ekklesia*). Citizens were paid for attendance at the assembly and for participation in jury service. There were no property qualifications for voting or officeholding.

Athenian democracy was said to place a high value on freedom (*eleutheria*). While some critics, such as Plato, satirized it as encouraging the lowliest citizens to take on airs beyond their "place," more generous commentators, such as Aristotle, interpreted democratic freedom as meaning "to rule and be ruled in turn."[10] The precondition was that the Athenian demos should give itself democracy, not have it bestowed by a great lawgiver or benevolent conqueror or Founding Father.[11]

Athenian democracy had serious shortcomings. Women were excluded from politics, and, despite a large population of foreigners in Athens, it was extremely difficult for them to acquire citizenship. Hence the citizen body consisted of a relatively small percentage of the Athenian population; some scholars have estimated it at 14 percent. Further, a large slave population, vital to the economy, had no political voice. Most important, the flourishing of the Athenian economy became strongly intertwined with the transformation of a city-state into an imperial power with an appetite for expansion. The imperial thrust was novel for having its power base in the dynamic of a demotic democracy, bursting with self-confidence and enthusiastic for conquest. "They were," according to one of their opponents, "born into the world to take no rest themselves and to give none to others."[12] Athenians proved to be harsh conquerors, demanding tribute to support their empire and even tolerating the slaughter of a rebellious population that had surrendered.[13]

Inevitably Athens overreached and was challenged by an alliance headed by Sparta. The Peloponnesian Wars (430–404) led to the collapse of the Athenian Empire. It was preceded by several military reverses, climaxed by a disastrous expedition against Syracuse, an adventure stoked by the demagoguery of political rivals, each seeking to outbid the other by firing up mass enthusiasm.[14] Although its democracy survived attempted coups by disgruntled aristocrats and oligarchs, its imperial reign was over. After 324 BCE Athens was incorporated into the Macedonian Empire.

v

What had gone wrong? Broadly, the problem lay in the transformation of political identity from a city defined by circumscribed power to an identity unconfined and imperial. Its preimperial identity was best expressed when, to protect themselves against invaders, Athenians built a wall around their city. We might interpret the wall as defining a political space and symbolizing the scope and limitations of demotic rule. The enclosed space was commensurate with the everyday commonsense capability of a demos for exercising power while preserving democratic egalitarianism. City politics, because of its immediacy, represented a set of practices that a citizenry could comprehend. Rather than pursuing power on a scale without predefined limits, with its paradox of being necessarily abstract while practiced as ruthless *Realpolitik*, the city had once cultivated a politics where it was possible to be both democratic and rational.[15]

One of the striking effects of imperialism upon Athenian democracy was a hardening and increasing ruthlessness of the citizens. They themselves became practitioners of *Realpolitik*. Athenians never pretended to justify their domination over conquered peoples by claiming to bestow the benefits and values of democracy. "As the world goes," an Athenian envoy instructs the representative of a city that refused to submit, "the strong do what they can and the weak suffer what they must."[16] The assumption was that within the city's walls democracy could be preserved undistorted by empire; meanwhile its power was being expanded outwards where, clear-eyed and unconstrained by democratic inhibitions, it could practice domination.

A twofold moral might be drawn from the experience of Athens: that it is self-subverting for democracy to subordinate its egalitarian convictions to the pursuit of expansive politics with its corollaries of conquest and domination and the power relationships they introduce. Few care to argue that, in political terms, democracy at home is advanced or improved by conquest abroad.[17] As Athens showed and the United States of the twenty-first century confirmed, imperialism undercuts democracy by furthering inequalities among its citizens. Resources that might be used to improve health care, education, and environmental protection are instead directed to defense spending, which, by far, consumes the largest percentage of the nation's annual budget. Moreover, the sheer size and complexity of imperial power and the expanded role of the military make it difficult to impose fiscal discipline and accountability. Corruption becomes endemic, not only abroad but at home. The most dangerous type of corruption for a democracy is measured not in monetary terms alone but in the kind of ruthless power relations it fosters in domestic politics. As many observers have noted, politics has become a blood sport with partisanship and ideological fidelity as the hallmarks. A partisan judiciary is openly declared to be a major priority of a political party; the efforts to consolidate executive power and to relegate Congress to a supporting role are to some important degree the retrojection inwards of the imperial thrust.

Second, if Athens was the first historical instance of a confrontation between democracy and elitism, that experience suggests that there is no simple recipe for resolving the tensions between them. Political elites were a persistent, if uneasy and contested, feature of Athenian democracy and a significant factor in both its expansion and its demise.[18] In the eyes of contemporary observers, such as Thucydides, as well as later historians, the advancement of Athenian hegemony depended upon a public-spirited, able elite at the helm and a demos willing to accept leadership. Conversely, the downfall of Athens was attributed to the wiles and vainglory of leaders who managed to whip up popular support for ill-conceived adventures. As the war dragged on and frustration grew, domestic politics became more embittered and fractious: members of the elite competed to outbid each other by proposing ever wilder schemes of conquest. In two attempts (411–410 and 404–403) elites, abetted by the Spartans, succeeded in temporarily abolishing democracy and installing rule by the Few.

vi

According to its elitist critics, a democracy is an incomplete political system because its theory contains no justification or provision for recruiting or attracting great leaders, men who are exceptional and distinguished from the demos by their grasp of what is required for a society to be well-governed and flourishing.

Elitism is typically not a claim about a practical division of labor where the question is how we get from here to there, with the demos deciding where "there" is and the elites supplying the expert know-how. In part the problem centers on whether elite positions of power and decision making are open or tracked, that is, whether or not there are privileged paths to membership. In part the problem also concerns the level of political sophistication of those who are not in the elite but, as citizens, are called upon to judge the performance of elites. The danger lies in the circularity that circumscribes the division of labor whereby elites control the means (e.g., elite preparatory schools and universities, the popular media) and mostly determine the criteria by which they are to be judged.

There is an additional problem, one underscored by the fatal overreaching of Athens, both on the part of the demos and on that of its elite. To overreach involves not only stretching resources beyond their limits or underestimating the pitfalls likely to be encountered but entertaining delusions of grandeur that, typically, are fueled by a conviction about elite entitlements. Overreaching is about crossing the line separating rationality from irrationality. Thucydides vividly portrayed how the gullibility of the demos and its susceptibility to flattery, as well as the inability of its leaders to control either the mass emotions that they had aroused or their own ambitions, produced disastrous misjudgments: overestimations of the Athenian capabilities and underestimations of its foes.[19] Thucydides uses these episodes to contrast political rationality with demagogic leadership swept along by an out-of-control demos. He depicts Pericles, who led the city during the earlier and successful phases of the war, as the model of political rationality and a virtuoso at restraining the dynamics of the demos:

> For as long as he was head of the state during the peace [i.e., an interval during hostilities], he pursued a moderate and conservative policy; and in his time Athens' greatness was at its height. When the war broke out, here also he seems to have rightly gauged the power of his country. . . . He told them to wait quietly, to pay attention to their marine [i.e., navy], to attempt no new conquests, and to expose the city to no hazards during the war, and doing this, promised them a favorable result.[20]

Then, after the death of Pericles, the citizens, did "the very contrary," according to Thucydides. They "allowed private ambitions and private interests" to prevail. Where Pericles had "led the multitude instead of being led by them," the new leaders catered to the "whims of the multitude," each outbidding the other in vying for popular approval. The result was "a host of blunders" culminating in a disastrous defeat in Sicily.[21]

We might restate Thucydides: By its nature imperial conquest imposes a heavy, perhaps unbearable demand upon human rationality, not just upon virtue. There are too many unknowns, contingencies, unpredictable consequences as well as a vast scale on which things can go wrong. The kind of power that democracy brings to conquest has been formed in a local context and according to well-understood norms and traditions. In order to cope with the imperial contingencies of foreign war and occupation, democracy will alter its character, not only by assuming new behaviors abroad (e.g., ruthlessness, indifference to suffering, disregard of local norms, the inequalities in ruling a subject population) but also by operating on revised, power-expansive assumptions at home. It will, more often than not, try to manipulate the public rather than engage its members in deliberation. It will demand greater powers and broader discretion in their use ("state secrets"), a tighter control over society's resources, more summary methods of justice, and less patience for legalities, opposition, and clamors for socioeconomic reforms. It is unlikely that the restraints of rationality can be expected to come from the demos, for its emotional state will have been deliberately inflamed by its leaders, and, more important, the magnitudes of empire and (what amounted to) global war will exceed the demotic ability to comprehend situations, strategies, and likely outcomes alien to their experience. The practical judgments of ordinary life, which under normal circumstances might supply a "reality check" to power, are beyond their depth, suggesting that democracy cannot simultaneously pursue *Realpolitik* and practice demotic politics. For their part the leaders, rather than being able to focus on various choices and their likely consequences, are trapped by the popular moods they had fostered and are tempted to respond by ever more grandiose proposals. The upshot is that there is no reality check for the demos on the elite or for the elite on the demos; neither can control the recklessness of the other but can only encourage it.

vii

Over the next two millennia democracy did not exist in Europe.[22] The politically entrenched classes and interests succeeded in keeping the middle and lower classes out of politics. Although a few wealthy bourgeois might occasionally gain entry into the charmed circle, this moment might be described as one in which the particulars excluded the generality of the population from politics. They succeeded in establishing forms of power that functioned as principles of exclusion. The Few were declared to be "distinguished," set off from the Many by special family genealogies, large fortunes, or privileged access to the sacred. They were, so the logic ran, entitled to rule. The Few thus represented the elements constitutive of a political realm that was as much defined by who was "out" as by who was "in." Power was often sanctified— kings were anointed; popes by virtue of apostolic succession were invested with a "holy office"; and aristocracy was declared an essential element in the hierarchical order of "higher" and "lower" decreed by the Creator. Accordingly, authority was claimed to be wide or general in its scope but particular or restricted in its source. This presaged a continuing tension between power and authority: power was dependent upon organizing cooperation, enlisting the generality of human and material resources in society, while authority claimed to derive from sources said to be rare or special—from Holy Scripture, from God, or from a great Lawgiver, a Moses or Founding Fathers.

viii

The succeeding moment, which may be said to have lasted until the mid-seventeenth century, occurred when the Many came to understand that if they were to regain entry into politics, they had to relearn how to be a political "people," a demos. During this same period the charmed circle of the governing Few was being challenged and reconstituted as a distinctively modernizing and secularizing elite. This was the phenomenon of "civic republicanism." It appealed in the main to those with special skills that were largely independent of birth or ecclesiastical rank: bankers, scientists and engineers, skilled administrators, military leaders, and political advisers boasting of the strategizing talents immortalized by Machiavelli. At the beginning whatever these new auxilliaries of power may have lacked in authority, they more than compensated with their command of new forms of knowledge and skill focused upon material power rather than ecclesiastical authority or dynastic claims.

A modern version of the demos, of necessity, followed a route different from republicanism. It had to arm itself as a threat rather than as a Machiavellian protégé with a résumé. A demos represented power consciousness on the part of the Many. For that power to crystallize, the ordinary people have to change themselves, somehow finding ways and means to go beyond their immersion in the daily struggle to exist. The demos becomes aware of their potential power: raw numbers, physical strength, and individually scant resources in desperate need of aggregation. Demotic politics means a change from being objects of power to becoming agents. Because a demos has no allotted place within the system, it is compelled to challenge the exclusionary politics of the Few and demand as a matter of right entrance into the political realm and participation in its political deliberations.

By definition "the people" was an inclusive notion. Accordingly early democrats appealed to general principles of inclusiveness (e.g., the "natural rights of all mankind"), to what was common (e.g. equally human) rather than to what distinguished one person or class from others. Eventually, but not universally, the Many succeeded in becoming political citizens and thereby an accepted element in political life, although by no means the predominant one. We may call this the struggle by which an inchoate people or "multitude" attempts to convert itself into a demos, into a politically self-conscious actor confronting societies in which wealth and inequality were being reinforced in terms different from those employed by the sacred and privileged hierarchies of the past.

In early modern western Europe and America of the seventeenth century the principal institutional form by which social forces gained expression was through representation in legislatures. Representation was pretty much restricted to the nobility, the higher clergy, and substantial landholders. This meant that when the "lower" or excluded orders tried to gain entry into politics, they could not assume, as the Athenian demos had, that they would take over the legal and political institutions in their entirety and proceed to democratize them. Accordingly, the ambitions of the early modern demos had to be limited to gaining a foothold, which meant representation in a particular branch of the legislature rather than control of a whole system. The sense in which they could constitute anything other than an incomplete demos would be determined by how much of itself the new demos would or could commit and how determined the opposition would be.

ix

An early attempt to give expression to a modern demos with access to political life occurred in the so-called Putney debates during the English civil wars of the 1640s. In contrast to the constitution-writing convention of 1787 in Philadelphia where there would be many delegates representative of the modern elites but none from the demos,[23] at Putney the lower classes and the poor were present and democratic arguments were advanced. Those debates also saw the appearance of a new and self-conscious presence defending the *political* hegemony of nascent capitalists.[24]

The events at Putney have been preserved in a verbatim account of actual debates when the demand for political membership was put forward. The debates reveal a moment when, by their own actions, people were struggling to become "the people," to create themselves as political actors. The exchanges were triggered when the spokesmen for the rank and file of the revolutionary army, representing the views of the Leveller movement, proposed that the army demand the nation's adoption of a written constitution ("An Agreement of the People") ensuring that ordinary men would be guaranteed the right to vote. That would have meant the abolition of the prevailing property qualifications then governing elections and parliamentary representation. Most of the officers, including Cromwell, the army's leader, opposed the demands; in the person of Henry Ireton, Cromwell's son-in-law, they would have an articulate spokesman.

The crucial importance of the debates was to expose the tensions between political democracy and economic power, between demotic claims on behalf of political equality and an elite defending the principle that political inequality was the natural, even logical reflection of economic inequality: between a claim that economic status should not determine political inclusion and a claim that economic status should dictate political status. Underlying these tensions was a further disagreement as to whether the nation was to be tended in the spirit of commonality, equality, and shared power, or governed by those who represented newly emerging interests—mercantile, professional, smaller landowners—intent on challenging the older dominant groups of aristocracy, established church, and wealthy landowners.

The Leveller position was put forward in a famous speech by Colonel Thomas Rainsborough:

> I think that the poorest he that is in England hath a life to live as the greatest he; and therefore . . . I think it's clear that every man that is to live under a government ought first by his own consent

to put himself under that government; and I do think that the poorest man in England is not at all bound in a strict sense to that government that he hath not had a voice to put himself under. . . . [E]very man born in England cannot, ought not, neither by the law of God nor the law of nature, to be exempted from the choice of those who are to make laws and for him to live under, and for him (for aught I know) to lose his life under.[25]

Ireton responded by rejecting the view that natural right supplied a ground for "disposing of the affairs of the kingdom, and in determining or choosing those that shall determine what laws we shall be ruled by here." Only persons with "a permanent fixed interest in the kingdom," he argued, were qualified to serve as electors and as representatives. The reason: "those who shall choose the law makers shall be men freed from dependence upon others."[26] Ireton then went on to identify those who represented the permanent interest of the society as "the persons in whom all land lies, and those in corporations in whom all trading lies. This is the most fundamental constitution of this kingdom, and which if you do not allow, you allow none at all."[27] The Levellers' appeal to natural right, he warned, put all property at risk: any man might "take hold of anything that a[nother] man calls his own."[28] If "you admit [as electors] any man that hath a breath and being" along with those itinerants who are "here today and gone tomorrow,"[29] if those who had no property were allowed to vote, then there could be no guarantee that they would not "vote against all property."[30] Ireton also added a reassuring note that those who had no property would nonetheless have an "interest" under rule by the propertied, for they would be protected and enjoy the freedom "of trading to get money and to get estates by" and would eventually join the ranks of the propertied.[31]

x

In Ireton's argument wealth signified independence, autonomous actors. Dependence, in contrast, meant being compelled by need and circumstance to submit to the superior power of another. When power is organized in the form of an economy based upon private capital and the division of labor, then ipso facto the lives of most persons will be directed by others. Dependence is thus institutionalized as inequalities of reward and, consequently, of power. A future task of intellectual elites is also set: to provide the ideology (e.g., meritocracy, freedom) by which inequality would be acceptable and consistent with principles of democracy and equality, thereby countering Rainsborough's argument that elections without a property qualification empower those who represent numbers but little or no economic or intellectual power.

Thus two forms of power were being pitted against each other. One claimed that superior economic power should translate directly into political power; the other that political life involved transactions among equals, a formula which required that social status, economic power, and religious loyalties be suspended temporarily so that citizens might deliberate as equals—a formula that realists would dismiss as magical while egalitarians would see it as magic realism, as a moment of possibility when the powerless are empowered and experience independence.

In the centuries that followed, the economy of capitalism became increasingly powerful, both as a system of production and as a system of inequalities. While, unquestionably, the new economy would raise the "standard of living" of the "masses," it would also succeed in translating concentrated economic power into political power. Rather than a purely economic system supplying "goods and services," capital acquired political attributes. Faced with that reality, the magic realists, in desperation, would introduce their trump card, the threat of revolution. This meant arousing the dependents, organizing their numbers, and confronting the realists with their worst nightmare—instability, uncertainty, and, worst of all, the subordination of economic to demotic power—compounded by a wholly novel development, a new species of leader who, instead of hoping to join the governing elite, opted to remain with "the people."

Such a description might perhaps seem applicable to revolutionary France of the 1790s; however, that attempt at creating a modern demos with a revolutionary leadership was directed against the Old Regime of monarchy, aristocracy, and church, against forms of power that were already being undermined by modern science, skepticism, and rationalism.[32] For the third moment of democracy, the attempt to resurrect the idea of a demos, we might look to eighteenth-century America, not to the contest over the ratification of the federal Constitution of 1789, nor directly to the revolution of 1776, but to the political consciousness that emerged among the colonists early in the eighteenth century and intensified in the agitation of the 1760s against British taxation and trade policies. An American political system would have its origins in protesting imperial policies only to succumb later to the temptations of empire.

Our present-day hagiography celebrates Founding Fathers but almost entirely overlooks the emergence of an American version of a demos in the decades before and during the revolution.[33] In the years preceding the war for independence new political actors appeared: artisans, workers, small farmers, shopkeepers, seamen, women, African slaves, and native Indians. Typically they were reacting to a particular grievance: a tax, an ordinance, mistreatment of one of their own, a dispute over land titles—even more broadly, the institution of slavery. Under the imperial system there were no official institutions in which the lower and working classes, women, and slaves participated or were represented. The typical colony was ruled by a royal governor appointed by and responsible to the British government; colonial assemblies were largely composed of wealthy landowners and well-to-do merchants, while voting requirements invariably excluded those without considerable property or wealth.

If a demos were to form, it would have to act from outside and against the system. Consequently demotic action tended to be "informal," improvised, and spontaneous—what can be called "fugitive democracy." There were demonstrations, protest meetings, petitions, tarring and feathering of royal officials, burning of effigies, destruction of official residences, and storming jails to free one of their own. Because of property qualifications and financial requirements, few could vote or run for office; hence leadership was frequently provided by middle-class sympathizers who contributed organizational skills so that slates of candidates could be presented or committees of correspondence formed to coordinate common action with their counterparts in other colonies.

xi

Demotic action is typically triggered by felt grievances—not, initially, by a yearning for political participation. Because of the exhausting demands of making a "living," surviving under harsh circumstances, dedication to a political life is hardly a conceivable vocation. While governing is a full-time, continuous activity, demotic politics is inevitably episodic, born of necessity, improvisational rather than institutionalized. It is "fugitive," an expression of those who lack leisure time and whose work skills in modern times would become increasingly foreign to the kinds of experience and prerequisites deemed essential to governing and, conversely, more hospitable to those with experience in command or possessed of technical qualifications.

A would-be demos is drawn to democracy not because ordinary people expect to rule, but because, in theory, democracy legitimates the expression of widely felt and usually deep-seated grievances, the possibility that those who have only numbers can use them to offset the power of wealth, formal education, and managerial experience.

Foreign observers were impressed by the intensity of political interest among ordinary Americans. During the years from roughly the 1760s to the Constitutional Convention of 1787 an American demos began to establish a foothold and to find institutional expression, if not full realization. State constitutions were amended by provisions that broadened the suffrage, abolished property qualifications for office, and in one case instituted women's suffrage. There were also efforts to ease debtor laws, even to abolish slavery.

Those "attacks" on property and the concomitant threat of demotic rule were crucial considerations prompting several outstanding politicians (Madison, Hamilton, John Adams) to organize a quiet counterrevolution aimed at institutionalizing a counterforce to challenge the prevailing decentralized system of thirteen sovereign states in which some state legislatures were controlled by "popular" forces. A new system of national power was proposed, at once centered yet with authority coextensive with the boundaries of the nation, and designed to discourage demotic power both by reducing the authority of the states, several of which had enacted legislation favorable to the lower classes, and by minimizing the role of the demos in national institutions. Only the House of Representatives would be more or less directly elected.[34] The theory was this: the less the demotic presence, the more likely that the populace would defer to men of talent, judgment, and political experience—a governing class composed largely of lawyers, financiers, and plantation owners who would serve the common good although not necessarily all classes to the same extent. Thus was reborn the idea of a republican elite. The aim, which Madison, Hamilton, Adams and several other members of the emerging political class bluntly stated, was to ensure that the new regime, while abstractly based upon "the people," would be directed by the representatives of wealth, status (slave-owners), and achievement rather than of democratic majorities.

Republican theory emerged as the counterforce to demotic power, thus perpetuating a dualism that had first appeared in ancient Athens. As noted earlier, republicanism promoted the notion of a governing class, an idealized aristocracy, virtuous, able, and public spirited. When the theory was transported from Britain to America, it had to accommodate to bourgeois values of wealth and competence and to acknowledge in some degree the presence of democratic ideas and practices.[35] In America republicanism had to find a place for democracy, eventually even endow it with sovereignty—if only in the abstract—while contriving obstacles to popular power that simultaneously advantaged the Few (e.g., a property qualification for voting) and defined governing in ways that corresponded to the abilities of a new class of merchants, bankers, lawyers, and manufacturers.

Thomas Jefferson, more than any other early national hero, anticipated the form that the republican-demotic dualism would take in the "first new nation" and the possible terms of reconciliation. Jefferson defined a republican system as "action by the citizen in person, in affairs within their reach and competence."[36] That formula pointed to the split nature of the new system. Although claiming that the people were "constitutionally and conscientiously democrats," Jefferson proceeded to circumscribe "action by the citizens." Thus while citizens were "competent to judge of the facts of ordinary life," as when serving as jurors, they were "unqualified for the management of affairs requiring intelligence above the common level." In these higher matters their powers should be delegated to more intelligent representatives whom, if necessary, the citizens could remove by elections.[37]

Jefferson's assumption of an unproblematical transition from "democracy" to representative government, from situations (jury trial) where the competence of citizens is deemed adequate to the task, to the ongoing, continuing "management of affairs" where their "intelligence" is "unqualified," testified to a conception of democracy's limited role even among its sympathizers. The tacit conviction was that when it came down to the actual work of governing, an elite ("intelligence above the common level") was a prerequisite.

While governance might be connected to democracy by elections, the act of voting for representatives and a president would seem more demanding than jury service. Not surprisingly that conclusion was drawn by the Founding Fathers, who proceeded to configure and "refine" elections so as to control their demotic potential and thus take the first step toward managing democracy. The Constitution of the Founders compressed the political role of the citizen into an act of "choosing" and designed it to minimize the direct expression of a popular will. As noted earlier, the citizen would not directly elect the president. Instead the citizen chose electors who would cast votes after deliberating in the Electoral College where, presumably, they were not necessarily bound by the wishes of voters. Similarly the citizen was not invited to vote for a senatorial candidate; senators would be selected by the legislatures of the states. As for the courts, the citizen had no part in the process: justices were initially nominated by a president chosen by the Electoral College and then confirmed by senators selected by state legislatures.

While later efforts at expanding the suffrage may have contributed to improving the lot of some groups previously excluded, such as women, elections mainly posed a challenge to the arts of management. Those arts soon became an integral, even a decisive element in the electoral process. Thus, early on, while the people were declared "sovereign," they were precluded from governing. That distinction, between passive sovereignty and active governance, would be contested, defined, and redefined over nearly three centuries as Jacksonian democrats, abolitionists, suffragettes, Populists, and Progressives fought to promote and defend demotic power while the political elites—many of whose representatives early on would defect and transfer their loyalties to the Southern pro-slavery cause—worked to professionalize politics and to make governance a technical art.

xii

In past centuries, with their economies of scarcity, the struggle for democracy was often described as a war between "the haves and the have nots." The element of truth in that formula throws into sharp relief the crucial changes in the stakes. In times past democracy struggled against the "old regimes." Today in the United States the status of democracy and the role of its adherents are the opposite of what they have been in the past. Put simply, the early democrats fought for what they did not have. Today the challenge for democrats is to recover lost ground, to "popularize" political institutions and practices that have become severed from popular control. It involves renewing the meaning and substance of "representative democracy" by affirming the primacy of Congress, curbing the growth of presidential power, disentangling the stranglehold of lobbyists, democratizing the party system by eliminating the barriers to third parties, and enforcing an austere system of campaign finance.

Reforming these institutions is not the same as democratizing them: to only a limited extent can the citizenry itself and by itself inject democracy into a political system permeated by corporate power. It can provide the initial impetus but not the sustained will. Or, stated differently, democracy has, first, to find itself, become a self-conscious demos; and, then, it has to reconceive its relationship with its ancient nemesis, elitism.

CHAPTER THIRTEEN

Democracy's Prospects:
Looking Backwards

i

Generally when I ride it is the one time when I feel
alone, even though I know people are behind me. I ask people
a lot of times not to be in my line of vision because all I can
see straight ahead is, you know, space.
—*President George W. Bush*[1]

At the critical moment when a volatile economy and widening class
disparities require a government responsive to popular needs, government has become increasingly unresponsive; and, conversely, when an
aggressive state stands most in need of being restrained, democracy
proved an ineffectual check. A public fearful of terrorist attacks and
bewildered by a war based on deceit is unable to function as the rational
conscience of the American state, capable of checking the impulse to
adventurism and the systematic evasion of constitutional constraints. A
politics of dumbed-down public discourse and low voter turnout combines with a dynamic economy of stubborn inequalities to produce the
paradox of a powerful state and a failing democracy.

But is it only democracy that is failing? Every day brings fresh evidence that American power is being challenged throughout the world,
that its imperial sway is weakening, that its global economic hegemony
is a thing of the past, and that it has been sucked into an unwinnable
and interminable "war against terrorism." Is failing empire the opportunity for a democratic revival, or does that failure leave intact the tendencies toward inverted totalitarianism?

A democracy failing in what ways? What was democracy supposed
to bring into the world that was not there before? A short answer might

be this: democracy is about the conditions that make it possible for ordinary people to better their lives by becoming political beings and by making power responsive to their hopes and needs. What is at stake in democratic politics is whether ordinary men and women can recognize that their concerns are best protected and cultivated under a regime whose actions are governed by principles of commonality, equality, and fairness, a regime in which taking part in politics becomes a way of staking out and sharing in a common life and its forms of self-fulfillment. Democracy is not about bowling together but about managing together those powers that immediately and significantly affect the lives and circumstances of others and one's self. Exercising power can be humbling when the consequences are palpable rather than statistical—and rather different from wielding power at a distance, at, say, an "undisclosed bunker somewhere in northern Virginia."

What is at stake today is the choice between the two forms of politics, Superpower and democracy. The contrasting nature of those two forms was best revealed by the invasion of Iraq. Beyond those stark and familiar facts about the war—the poor planning that preceded it, the hapless attempts to administer the country following the fall of Saddam, the sacrifice of American lives to a shameful cause, and the incalculable harm done to the country and its inhabitants—there was the political loss of nerve among Democrats, the press, and the punditry, a failure so profound as to call into question the health of the political system as a whole. That failure extended to all but a minority of the citizenry; the vast majority waved an occasional flag and then, when possible, heeded the advice of their leader to "fly, consume, spend."

While there are many lessons to be learned from the war's debacle, there is one that is crucial to any future which democracy, especially participatory democracy, may have. It concerns the primary importance of truth telling and the destructive effects of lying.

ii

If democracy is about participating in self-government, its first requirement is a supportive culture, a complex of beliefs, values, and practices that nurture equality, cooperation, and freedom. A rarely discussed but crucial need of a self-governing society is that the members and those they elect to office tell the truth. Although lying has figured in all forms of government, it acquires a special salience in a democracy, where the object of deception is the "sovereign people." Under nondemocratic forms of government, where the people are politically excluded as a matter of principle, lying is typically done by the sovereign or its agents, usually in order to mislead those presumed to be enemies or rivals of the sovereign. In modern dictatorships lying to the public was a matter of systematic policy and assigned to a special ministry (*sic*) of propaganda. Statecraft as an especially bad joke . . .

Self-government is, literally, deformed by lying; it cannot function when those in office assume as a matter of course that, when necessary or advantageous, they can mislead the citizenry. This is especially true when democracy has been reduced to a form of representative government. Such government is, by its nature, distanced from the citizen. And instead of a representative's politics representing the citizen, the reverse is true: Beltway politics is re-presented to the citizen. The less viable and flourishing democracy at "home," the less democratic representative democracy and the more prevalent a "re-presented" politics, a politics lacking directness, authenticity. And never more so than in the age of spin doctors, public relations experts, and pollsters.

In the face of declining political involvement by ordinary citizens, democracy becomes dangerously empty and not only receptive to antipolitical appeals to blind patriotism, fear, and demagoguery but comfortable with a political culture where lying, misrepresentation, and deception have become normal practice.

It is only mildly hyperbolic to characterize lying as a crime against reality. Lying goes to the heart of the never-ending questions, what is the world really like? what is in fact happening? Accepting something as true is not the same as agreeing that it is. To witness the role of lying and its consequences, we need look no further than to Iraq and to the death and destruction made possible by misrepresentations. Lying and its variants of deception and misrepresentation are no more simple aberrations than the unprovoked war itself. Lying and irrational decisions are connected, as are lying and unreasoning popular support for the decision-makers.

In a preliminary way lying can be defined as the deliberate misrepresentation of actuality and the substitution of a constructed "reality." The problem today is that lying is not an isolated phenomenon but characteristic of a culture where exaggeration and inflated claims are commonplace occurrences. For more than a century the public has been shaped by a relentless culture of advertising and its exaggerations, false claims, and fantasies—all aimed at influencing and directing behavior in the premeditated ways chosen by the advertiser. The techniques developed for the marketplace have been adapted by political consultants and their media experts. The result has been the pollution of the ecology of politics by the inauthentic politics of misrepresentative government, claiming to be what it is not, compassionate and conservative, god-fearing and moral.

While the principle of popular participation in decision making is fundamental to democracy—and we shall return to it—thoughtful participation is dependent upon certain commonplaces: first, the availability of knowledge in the form of reliable factual information and, second, a political culture that values and supports the honest effort to reach judgments aimed at promoting as far as possible the best interests of the whole society. There is a third principle, intellectual integrity. One aspect of it is the responsibility of those who, as teachers, publicists, researchers, and scientists, practice truth telling as their vocation. It is not a vocation to which many pundits, talk show hosts, for-sale journalists, and think tank residents are committed.[2] The public vocation of truth telling cannot be consistently practiced without public and private respect for, and defense of, intellectual integrity.

Totalitarian regimes viewed intellectual integrity as subversive and imposed ideological or political orthodoxy upon all intellectual pursuits and professions. Under the Bush administration there have been repeated instances of governmental or corporate attempts to distort or suppress unwelcome expert reports and scientific findings. As President Bush testified, "One of the hardest parts of my job is to connect Iraq with the war on terror."[3] A common thread connects false claims about WMDs with denials of global warming. The one insists that there was evidence; the other denies that there is evidence. Both are denials of actuality; both are irrational decisions of huge consequence; and both are aided by the lack of intellectual and public integrity among our scandal-ridden corporate and governmental leadership.[4]

iii

> I know what the president thinks. I know what I think.
> And we're not looking for an exit strategy [from Iraq].
> We are looking for victory.
> —*Vice President Dick Cheney*[5]

Lying is more than deception; the liar wants the unreal to be accepted as actuality, so he sets about to establish as true what is not actually the case, not really real. A lie by a public authority is meant to be accepted by the public as an "official" truth concerning the "real world." At bottom, lying is the expression of a will to power. My power is increased if you accept "a picture of the world which is a product of my will."[6] Of course the skilled liar should not be taken in by his own lies; that would be self-deception. Yet the skilled liar might also become a habitual liar, the success of one lie encouraging another with the result that a leader is tempted to try to make untruth into a reality—as with, for example, the vice president's feverish efforts to press the CIA to dredge up evidence of WMDs where there was little or none.

It is a virtual cliché that in unusual circumstances, and especially in extraordinary ones, it may be necessary for leaders to lie to or mislead or conceal facts from the public when lying serves the broad interests of the nation. Throughout Western history questions of when to lie, what form a lie should take, and whether it is or was justified usually presumed that lying was a dispensation allowed only to elites who, theoretically, are more politically knowledgeable and experienced than ordinary citizens.[7]

It seems, however, paradoxical to say that democracy should deliberately deceive itself. Supposing, nonetheless, that elites, instead of simply enjoying access to greater or more reliable information, claimed for themselves a special order of rationality that allowed them access to a higher, extra-ordinary Reality and enabled them to see deeper, beyond the actuality experienced by the average citizen. Would that result in a conception in which lying was not a minor deviation but a reconstitution of "reality"? If, for example, the initial reason for invading Iraq (WMDs) was exposed as a lie but the ruling elites then claimed that a higher purpose was to promote democracy in the Middle East, would that justification amount to a claim that elites possessed the substantively superior form of reasoning required by those who contend with problems whose complexity and possible consequences far exceed the experience of the ordinary citizen?

iv

Perhaps the most influential justification for political lying as a higher form of reason, and for lying as the prerogative of a special type of political elites with access to a higher reality unknown to ordinary mortals, was set down by Plato more than two thousand years ago. His justification for lying has contemporary echoes in the systematic lying of the Bush administration, and those echoes have an intellectual genealogy. Plato was awarded canonical status by Leo Strauss, while Straussians and the neocons, who played a decisive role in deceiving the public about the reasons for attacking Iraq, have similarly canonized Strauss. From canon to cannon-fodder . . .

Rulers, according to Plato, "will have to give subjects a considerable dose of imposition and deception for their good."[8] Plato's ideal political system is founded upon sharply defined and enforced political inequalities designed to ensure that a specially educated class of philosophers would monopolize political decision making and the practice of lying. Thus the crucial distinction, one that is cultivated and enforced, is between those whose exceptional mental endowments and subsequent training enable them to glimpse true reality and those who are judged to lack ability and therefore denied "higher" education.

The ideology that sanctions these inequalities is the so-called noble lie.[9] The inhabitants are to be told that although they are all descended

from a common "mother," they are assigned, according to a hierarchical principle, to one of three classes: the ruling, or golden, class of
philosopher-guardians, where true knowledge and the ability to rule
exclusively reside; the military, or silver, class; and the farmer-artisan,
or bronze, class.[10] Political power and authority are reserved to the specially educated golden class, and they alone are allowed the prerogative
of lying. Plato's justification of elite rule is set out in his famous Allegory
of the Cave.[11] It contrasts the unreality of the images by which the
Many live and the true reality that only the Few can approximate.

Imagine men living in a cave set deep in the ground. From child-
hood they have been kept immobile by chains; because they can see
only what is directly before them, they assume it is reality. Behind them
is a fire with a track built along it. Imagine also some persons carrying
artificial objects of wood or stone, some resembling human figures or
animals, whose shadow images appear on the wall. The "prisoners"
cannot see themselves or other prisoners; they see only the shadows cast
by the fire on the wall facing them. "Such prisoners would recognize as
reality nothing but the shadows of those artificial objects."

Plato continues: Suppose, however, one of the cave-dwellers is spirited outside the cave and thrust into bright sunlight. Dazzled at first,
he believes the "real" world is illusion but, after becoming accustomed
to the light, realizes that now he sees the world in the light of true
reality—that is, he has knowledge, and what he had formerly believed
to be reality was illusion. The vast majority of mankind remain imprisoned in the cave and incapable of grasping the true nature of things.
Their best hope is to accept the power of those versed in the true philosophy. Plato darkly concludes: by nature the masses prefer an illusory
reality, and so they may turn on the philosopher, making him a martyr
to the truth. Thus the masses fear the truth, and their instinct is to cling
to the unreal.[12]

But what is real? For Plato it was not the world of tangible objects,
of everyday experience, things we touch, sense, and experience: these
are too ephemeral or subjective to be true or real. Or perhaps too accessible, for they constitute the everyday world shared by those who are
looked down upon as common. The truly real is immaterial idea, intan-
gible, unchanging, and belongs to a different and higher order of being.

Knowledge of it gives privileged access to the meaning of the world and the nature of the Good. The Few alone are capable of grasping reality but only after they have undergone a rigorous intellectual discipline presided over by the true philosophers. Since the Many are incapable of knowing reality, the Few make no effort to elevate the level of common political understanding. Instead the Few divulge what is politically expedient and in a vulgarized (i.e., untrue) form, such as a myth, which the masses can comprehend.

Democracy was, of course, anathema to Plato, not least because it stands for the regime where those who rule tend to be guided by experience of the tangibles of everyday existence, by "common" sense.[13]

Although there are no contests for political power in Plato's scheme, in another sense his republic is all about politics, the politics of who defines and controls access to "reality," and what the role of truth and lying is in that politics. Plato assumed that the small scale of his imagined state would make it easier for his elite to control the extent to which, and in what form, the Many would benefit from a reality they could never understand, much less truly know.

To press the point: supposing the elite found themselves in a democracy instead of Plato's Republic. Further, supposing they had been sufficiently influenced by modernity to be somewhat skeptical of the existence of "Reality," might they not go down to the cave and seek control of the images cast on the screen, especially if they could ally with those who were in the business of manufacturing images and determining their content?

v

A politics that aims at commonality places a high premium on trust among the participants or between representatives and the people they represent. Trust, in turn, requires not only that the participants and representatives convey the considered views of the citizenry, but that they accurately represent the actualities of the political world to the citizenry. Trust is the precondition of an authentic politics. An authentic politics is not univocal; there will always be contested views about actuality, and how it is to be understood and acted upon. But it makes a great deal of difference if the parties concerned can assume that each has made a good-faith effort to speak truthfully.

Although it would be naive to suggest that democracy eliminates lying, arguably its politics tends to encourage authenticity. A smaller political context is more congenial to nurturing democratic values, such as popular participation, public discussion, and accountability through close scrutiny of officeholders. A smaller scale brings with it modest stakes and a consequent scaling down of power, of expectations, and of ambitions. Precisely because public discussion, debate, and deliberation are fundamental to democracy, deliberate misrepresentation is more easily exposed.

Democratic deliberations deepen the political experience of citizens, but they are time-consuming: time is needed for the expression of diverse viewpoints, extended questioning, and considered judgments. When the pace of life is slower, there is "plenty of time" and a greater possibility of considered judgments and the likelihood of durability, of more lasting decisions, of a public memory.

vi

Attuned to slower rhythms once dictated by long distances and slow communications, democracy now struggles against a context where scale is defined and dominated by Superpower, globalizing capital, and empire; by aggrandizing forms of power that are equipped with the means of annihilating the barriers created by distance. And because distance serves to consume time, those powers have succeeded in annihilating conventional time as well, a precious resource of democracy. Decisions, like weapons, are rapid-fire, with the crucial result that while there may be a transcript, there is less likely to be a memory.

Another result, whose political implications will be explored later, is that the nature, indeed the very notion, of actuality—what the public world is really like, what its inhabitants are really experiencing, and what the effects are of response-time measured in instants—becomes virtual at worst, abstract at best. These unprecedented powers and the scales they can command appear as especially favorable to elitism, to the quick-witted and manipulative, but uncongenial to democratic values and deliberative practices.

These new tempos make for strange bedfellows. Thus modern technology and communications represent the means of "hurrying time" in the sense that less time is required to achieve a desired end—for instance, a Wall Street speculator can communicate instantly with a Shanghai banker. But the believer in a Last Days eschatology is also in a hurry, convinced that the world is hurtling toward a Last Judgment. Oddly, neither the speculator nor the apocalypse-lover is much given to reflection: he hasn't the time to waste or "tarry" if he is to attain his end in time.

The powers that subvert reality—especially everyday reality, the tangibleness vital to democratic deliberations—can also be the nemesis corrupting the judgment of power-holders ("we make our own reality," as the Bushman boasted). Unreality is related to the dominant tendency toward abstraction and the belief that statistical measures can be a shorthand for reality rather than an obfuscation. For example, today there is general agreement that inequality is on the increase in our society.[14] In today's media-speak growing inequality is frequently described by being *measured* in economic terms, as differences in income or as what percentage of the population owns what percentage of the national wealth. While these measures reveal sharp economic differences between the wealthy and the poor, as well as a decline in the percentage of national income going to the middle and lower-middle classes, there is a crucial sense in which the abstract terms (e.g., "below the poverty line") are the expression of a mentality that "doesn't get it." Its "methodology" is unable to convey the "feel" of the grinding impact of poverty on the daily lives of "the millions who lack health insurance."

Put starkly, the crucial political issue of our times concerns the incompatibility between the culture of everyday reality to which political democracy should be attuned and the culture of virtual reality on which corporate capitalism thrives. Despite claims that the opportunity to be stakeholders, or to form start-ups, to revel in consumer choices, or just to get rich demonstrates the democratic possibilities of capitalism, there is no political affinity, only a disjunction between democracy and a system that assumes inequality among investors and reproduces inequality as a matter of course, depends upon individual self-interest as an incentive, practices a politics of misrepresentation, and hence is inconsistent with such democratic values as sharing, caring, and preserving.

The fate of democracy is to have entered the modern world at the same moment as capitalism, roughly during the seventeenth century. As a consequence the course of each became intertwined with the other. This meant, among other things, that the attempts to establish a democratic culture were an uphill struggle. At first democracy and capital were occasional political allies pitted against the stratified order of monarchy, aristocracy, and established church. Then, as each became more politically self-conscious, more aware of divergent concerns, each began to define an identity and pursue strategies that reflected the reality of opposed interests, contrasting conceptions of power, and disagreement as to what degree of equality or inequality each could tolerate without compromising their respective systems.

The persisting conflict between democratic egalitarianism and an economic system that has rapidly evolved into another inegalitarian regime is a reminder that capitalism is not solely a matter of production, exchange, and reward. It is a regime in which culture, politics, and economy tend toward a seamless whole, a totality. Like the regimes it had displaced, the corporate regime manifests inequalities in every aspect of social life and defends them as essential. And like the old regimes, the structure of corporate organization follows the hierarchical principle of gradations of authority, prerogative, and reward. It is undemocratic in its structure and modus operandi and antidemocratic in its persistent efforts to destroy or weaken unions, discourage minimum wage legislation, resist environmental protections, and dominate the creation and dissemination of culture (media, foundations, education).

vii

The tendencies toward inverted totalitarianism do not stem solely from the "Right," and that is one reason why a reversal presents a formidable challenge. Twentieth-century liberalism, or neoliberalism as it was later called, was instrumental in promoting a strong, controlling state, a conception essential to Superpower; it gave limited, even lukewarm allegiance to democracy, except as a demand for equal rights. To be sure, among liberals in the first half of the twentieth century one of the main justifications had been that only a strong, centralized government could effectively control corporate monopolies, punish corporate misbehavior, and promote social welfare. Significantly, that progressive thrust virtually disappeared once the United States prepared for World War II, but not before liberal reformers had discovered that social programs and, later, the war effort were deeply dependent upon a new type of elite of skilled managers.[15] These tendencies continued after 1945. The Cold War and the Marshall Plan for Western European reconstruction both required the expansion of state power and managerial expertise. However, from the end of the Truman administration in 1953 to the end of the Clinton administration in 2001, and with the exception of LBJ's presidency, liberal administrations were unable to sustain much enthusiasm for using state power to promote new social programs or even for promoting civil rights.[16] In place of President Kennedy's stern rebuke, "Ask not what your country can do for you—ask what you can do for your country," the new mantra would be " liberal on social issues" (gay rights and women's equality) but "fiscally conservative," except for defense spending. By the end of the century the Democratic president, who had failed to enact health care reform but did succeed in promoting a tough welfare reform, could boast that his administration had achieved the conservative goal of a budget surplus. Shortly thereafter, deficit spending, which had been a prominent element in financing New Deal social programs, was adapted to a Republican strategy for promoting tax relief for the rich while discouraging social spending.

Significantly, the liberal administration that embarked upon the disastrous unprovoked war in Vietnam and would engage in extensive government lying, as *The Pentagon Papers* would reveal, was also unabashed in advertising its elitism, especially during the Kennedy years, when the country was reassured that "the best and the brightest" and the "wise men" were in power.[17] In the footsteps of Alcibiades, this persuasive elite brought us the Bay of Pigs fiasco, the Gulf of Tonkin lie.

The Reagan era marked the beginning of a new conception of the presidency, one that reinforced the twentieth-century tendency toward presidential domination of the political system. It was symbolic that Reagan attained the presidency by defeating the one president who had promised the American people that he would never lie to them. In 1985 Reagan's administration proceeded to violate the law by covertly supplying weapons to Iran and, in further violation, diverted some of the profits derived from the arms sale to the Nicaraguan "contras," despite a congressional restriction on such assistance. Then the administration proceeded to lie about the transactions.[18] Reagan would come to symbolize the emergence of a political culture in which lying was merely one component in a larger pattern wherein untruthfulness, make-believe, and actuality were seamlessly woven.

The Reagan formula featured a president with little comprehension of, indeed little interest in, most of the major issues of the day but with an actor's skill in assuming a symbolic role, that of quasi-monarch. That same formula also aimed at replacing the idea of an engaged and informed citizenry with that of an audience which, fearful of nuclear war and Soviet aggression, welcomed a leader who could be trusted to protect and reassure them of their virtue by retelling familiar myths about national greatness, piety, and generosity. It was demagoguery adapted to the cinematic age: he played the leader while "we the people" relapsed into a predemotic state.

Ronald Reagan converted a life of inauthenticity into a political art form by which the artist internalizes the inauthentic but expresses it as authenticity, the artful as artless. He had begun his career as a sports broadcaster who, without viewing the actual baseball game, "re-created" it for an invisible radio audience, embroidering the bare facts with colorful and imagined detail. Next followed a career of "real" acting. Reagan came not only to identify himself with his various roles but also to imbibe and reuse bits of wisdom from assorted movie scripts. Then came his stint as paid apologist ("host") for General Electric, extolling the virtues of capitalism, technological progress, the free market, and a notion of government whose principal—almost sole—responsibility was national defense.[19] All that was required of the audience was to suspend disbelief.

Inauthenticity need not imply deceit or insincerity. Rather it could simply mean imagining and believing in the imagined—which is what actors do. Reagan believed in all of the dynamics we have previously associated with inverted totalitarianism: unqualified admiration for the marvels of technology, free market corporate capitalism, and even a deep eschatological belief in the coming of Armageddon.[20] What was the image of Reagan standing triumphantly beside the ruins of the Berlin Wall but that of a latter-day Joshua tearing down the walls of Jericho before entering the promised land?

The roles Reagan played in his earlier career were an apprenticeship for his original contribution to American government, the creation of a "performance president" who fashioned illusion (a tough leader who had learned to throw a crisp salute) from inauthenticity (almost persuading himself that he had been present when inmates were freed from concentration camps).[21] With little or no interest in policy and the details of governance he took on the task of evoking nostalgia, overlaying the present with an idealized past, warmer, believing, guileless, "a shining city on the hill" that provided an illusion of national continuity while obscuring the radical changes at work.[22] The other element characterizing his administration was a presidential entourage that included hard-nosed, ideological zealots and operatives from the corporate world and the public opinion industry. These agents were intent on expanding the powers of the president, reducing governmental oversight of the economy, overriding environmental safeguards,[23] and dismantling welfare programs; simultaneously they expended vast sums in order to build up a military sufficiently intimidating to stare down an "evil empire," causing it to collapse, exhausted, unable to compete, its power spent from being outspent.[24]

The Bush II administration, with its peculiar amalgam of futurism and originalism, would press inauthenticity to extremes. It brought grandiose notions of expanding American power, of creating a new imperium, and, while professing reverence for an original Constitution, systematically undermined constitutional protections for individual rights and constitutional limitations on presidential power. Above all, endless lies and misrepresentations: about Abu Ghraib, Guantánamo, the number of Iraqi civilian deaths, global warming, ad infinitum.

The culmination of inauthentic politics was The Great Hoax concocted by the Bush team. While rhetorically exploiting democracy in support of imperial ambitions abroad, it undermined at home the process by which the democratic ballot bestows legitimacy. In both the 2000 and 2004 presidential elections Bush's minions employed tactics that revealed a chain of corruption extending from local officials to the highest court, all with the intention of thwarting the popular will.[25] The long-run consequences may prove more significant than the clouded elections: a popular distrust of the significance of elections themselves.

In sum, Republicanism has given the nation, not an alternate but a genuine alternative: an inegalitarian social democracy and a bogus political democracy.

viii

A situation of Republican hegemony based on a generally conservative electorate and a consequent inability of Democrats to muster a coherent, effective majority requires a radical rethinking of democratic possibilities, a different perspective from the one that motivated earlier democratic movements. As we saw in the discussion of the three democratic moments, democratic energies had aimed at innovation, at replacing the "old order" by introducing political innovations that could claim little or no precedent. As the cliché had it, the democratic forces "broke with the past." That vision of democracy was perfectly represented in the idea of a "New Deal" and reflected in the title of a volume by one of its eminent historians, *The Crisis of the Old Order*.[26] That thinking is preserved by today's liberals when they refer to themselves as "progressive," with that term's connotation of moving past the present toward a better future.

If, instead of associating democracy with progress toward something new, something more in synch with the ever-advancing tempos of our times, we were to list some obvious preliminary actions that redemocratization would require, then a different temporal perspective is suggested. Examples of "obvious measures": rolling back the empire; rolling back the practices of managed democracy; returning to the idea and practices of international cooperation rather than the dogmas of globalization and preemptive strikes; restoring and strengthening environmental protections; reinvigorating populist politics; undoing the damage to our system of individual rights; restoring the institutions of an independent judiciary, separation of powers, and checks and balances; reinstating the integrity of the independent regulatory agencies and of scientific advisory processes; reviving a representative system responsive to popular needs for health care, education, guaranteed pensions, and an honorable minimum wage; restoring government regulatory authority over the economy; and rolling back the distortions of a tax code that toadies to the wealthy and corporate power.

I have labored unfashionable verbs—"roll back," "revive," and "restore"—in order to suggest the need for a reversal of temporal perspectives so that we might remember or relearn the reasons for believing that the nation could combine restraints on governmental power with social democratic programs. Democracy cannot coexist, much less flourish, under either the antisocial-democratic legacy of the Reagan era or the unconstrained president of the Bush era. The enemies of democracy are the radicals of our day, the futurists bent on substantially narrowing the social and constitutional democracy of the recent past, and committed, in Vice President Cheney's phrase, to "an aggressive posture in terms of our national security strategy."[27] Small "d" democrats need to rediscover and rethink rather than mindlessly embrace "the latest" and thereby become trapped in the regime's futurist dynamic. This does not mean adopting a democratic version of originalism, or fetishizing some revelatory moment or iconic forebears. It does mean relearning some hard-earned lessons.

Our reversal of perspective involves recognizing that in contrast to earlier centuries, when democracy represented a challenge to the status quo, today it has become adapted to the status quo, which lends a certain sheen of legitimacy to a system of complicitous democracy. What complicates the problem and makes it unique is that today's status quo is dynamic. It is not about clinging to what is but about changing continuously in ways that undermine the conditions for a viable democratic politics. The amount of "leisure time," for example, has lessened, which means that time potentially available for politics has also diminished. And since the latter has become scarcer, political media wizards have found it easier to focus their resources upon simplifying politics. A politics dominated by slogans and sound bites is tailored to the voters' limited time and attention span. In combination they discourage public rationality. That situation captures precisely the neat conjunction of political irrationality induced among large segments of the citizenry and the systematic exploitation of popular irrationality by elites.

A society fixated on the future and caught in the frenzy of rapid change has difficulty knowing how to think about the consequences of loss, especially of things once widely shared. Many forms of change are inevitably destructive, displacing or replacing existing ways of life and belief. Obsolescence becomes the norm. Notions that were once common coin—"social justice," "objectivity," or "the common good"— now seem anachronisms, as do the commitments they implied. Unburdened by collective conscience, one feels no complicity in the killing fields of Iraq or in the actions and policies that have allowed the president—whom the Constitution entrusts with responsibility for enforcement of the laws—to proceed as though he had received a mandate to relax constitutional limitations. Rapid change not only blunts the collective conscience but dims the collective memory. So many "pasts" have flashed by and vanished that the temporal category itself seems obsolete. No collective memory means no collective guilt: surely My Lai is the name of a rock star.

Rapid change is not a neutral force, a natural phenomenon that exists independently of human will, or of considerations of power, comparative advantage, and ideological biases. It is a "reality" constructed from decisions arrived at within a certain framework—itself not accidental. We might call it "the political economy of change." That framework involves a wide range of factors: players with unequal resources, available capital, investment opportunities and decisions, market conditions, scientific discoveries, technological innovations, cultural dispositions, and the relative strength of contending political forces. Political corruption and lobbying are the principal expedients for conveying the concerns of the most powerful actors in the political economy of change.[28]

Democracy is not a player in that political economy; it is not even regarded as relevant except as a pawn.[29] The political environment is so hostile to the norms that govern ordinary life, so destructive of commonality, that for many citizens it requires an act of uncommon courage to become engaged. The viciousness of "attack politics" and the degradation of civil dialogue further encourage citizens to distance themselves, declaring a plague on both houses, and abandoning politics to the organized zealots. A turned-off citizenry makes for a more efficiently managed and rationalized politics.

Clearly, recovering democracy presents a task that runs counter to the political dynamics of our times.

ix

"Originalism" is the doctrine that exhorts politicians to be guided by the wisdom of the Founding Fathers, the Constitution of 1789, and the Bible.[30]

"Going back" for democracy differs from originalism. It is not the quest for a privileged moment when a transcendent truth was revealed. Rather it is the attempt to remind ourselves what democracy is about by becoming acquainted with forms of democratic experience, their possibilities and limitations—not with imitating. In the historical "moments" discussed in the previous chapter democratization was associated with a conscious effort to throw off the past and to challenge the present with a vision of a future for which there was no precedent. We saw how a newly self-conscious demos, thitherto excluded from politics, succeeded in forcing entry and gaining recognition. In the process it heralded something new: a more accessible politics, freer, more equal, attuned to popular needs and grievances and to the needs of the everyday lives of those whose personal powers were exhausted by the demands of survival. The possibility of a demotic politics meant that over time submissive subjects might evolve into active citizens, into a different kind of being. Demotic politics also meant a conversion of politics from a preserve of the privileged and powerful into a public domain.

The paucity of actual democracies historically suggests that democratic political institutions are established only after a series of struggles against the "natural" tendency for political power to be monopolized by the Few, by those who possess the skills, resources, and focused time that enable them to impose their will on a society the vast majority of whose members are overburdened and distracted by the demands of day-to-day survival. Leisure signifies time that is at one's own discretion. More than two thousand years ago Aristotle noted that leisure was a necessary condition in the politics of a good society.[31] Or, as an early twentieth-century populist rephrased it, "Raise less corn and more hell."

That contrast between the leisured and the leisureless was literally written into the Constitution. In 1787 many of the delegates to the Constitutional Convention "had time" for politics because they owned slaves whose labor freed their masters for political activity. No working man or ordinary farmer or shopkeeper helped to write the Constitution.

The "fugitive democracy" referred to earlier can be seen as the form of political expression of the leisureless. That politics of protest appeared in prerevolutionary America, where the politically excluded irrupted periodically and took to the streets or relied upon improvised organizations to denounce political decisions in which their interests and views were unrepresented. There was no single mass, no one demos, only episodic actions. Throughout the nineteenth and twentieth centuries a fragmented demos, frustrated by the political system devised by the Founders, retained the practice of fugitive democracy and irruptive politics. Jacksonian democrats succeeded in electing their man and gaining a foothold in the system of federal offices; abolitionist forces agitated for the elimination of slavery; women pressed for the right to participate in political life; trade unions were established to protect workers against employers who were often backed by governmental power; grassroots populists mounted a flurry of protests attacking the power of railroad owners and pressuring legislators to control railroad rates; early twentieth-century Progressives campaigned successfully for government regulation of the economic power of large monopolies; in the 1950s and 1960s African Americans took to the streets and eventually succeeded in ending racial segregation, vigilante justice, and political exclusion; and throughout the 1960s spontaneous movements

arose to protest the Vietnam War, racism, sexism, environmental degradation, and corporate power, not least for the latter's influence over
higher education.[32]

x

Does a demos have a future in the age of globalization, instant communication networks, and fluid borders? Is the notion of "a" demos as a
single, compact body with a "will" and an identity that persists over
time at all possible or even a coherent notion in the age of the political
bloggers? Is there time for a more authentic politics, more reflective of
the pluralistic character of reality?

Those fugitive moments when the demos acted, challenging the
structure of power, even influencing it, were typically the initiatives of
a fraction, not of a collective whole. Such holistic notions as "We, the
People" are the remains of a day when the "people" implied the vast
majority of persons and the reality of a common pariah status: they
were all excluded from politics. As the barriers to participation were
gradually lowered and citizenship opened to all adults, what stood exposed, however, was not a compact body of citizens but the reality of a
society fragmented—first, by economic interests, occupations, and social classes, each of which could be almost endlessly subdivided; and,
second, by cultural identities that resisted absorption. There were small
manufacturers and big ones; manufacturers who produced for a local
market and those who relied on exports; and so on for virtually every
industry. Comparable divisions existed among workers and farmers.
Later cultural fault lines were articulated and organized for political
purposes: race, ethnicity, gender, sexual preference, and religious allegiance. One result was that notions and aspirations reflective of the
simpler divisions of an earlier age—common good, general interest, the
good of the whole—appeared as problematical as the ideal of demotic
solidarity and as elusive as the values of commonality.

The numerous divisions and conflicting interests of contemporary
society that make it difficult to muster a coherent majority appear a
striking confirmation of the prescience of James Madison's argument

in the tenth *Federalist*. Madison's essay is worth recalling, not only because conservative writers and politicians treat it as constitutional gospel, and not only because Plato's antidemocratic argument resurfaces in it, but also because it reveals the conception of a constitution designed to frustrate the politics of commonality.

Bearing in mind Plato's insistence that political power had to be kept out of the reaches of those most closely in contact with the grubby realities of everyday existence and most prone to irrationality, Madison claimed that a basic reason for the weakness of the central government under the Articles of Confederation, and a major argument for a new constitution, was the domination of politics by "interests" and "factions." These he defined as either "a majority or minority" united by a "common impulse of passion, or of interest, adverse to the rights of other citizens, or to the permanent and aggregate interests of the community."[33] Madison's defense of the proposed constitution was not a call for the extirpation of factions or for their regulation. Rather he argued that factions and interests were the inevitable consequence of a free society. The challenge was to devise a system that would make it difficult politically for a majority of interests to coalesce or, failing that, to control all branches of government.

But if, for the sake of argument, we claim that Madison's "factions" are potentially the stuff by which diverse "fugitives" form a momentary but authentic, rather than a tyrannical, majority, then the true target of his attempt to thwart majority rule was not the threat of a numerical majority but that of a heterogeneous movement aimed at redressing real political and economic inequalities. Accordingly, Madison traced the immediate origins of different interests of society to the "different and unequal" abilities in "acquiring property." From these differences in abilities there emerged diverse forms of property and "different degrees" of accumulation. These differences and inequalities shaped the views of their owners "concerning religion" and "government" and led to "different interests and parties" and "mutual animosities." "But the most common and durable source of factions has been the various and unequal distribution of property." The eradication of these differences, Madison argued, would be impossible without destroying liberty; hence "the first object of Government" should be "the protection of different and unequal faculties of acquiring property."[34] Thus he posed inequality as both reality *and* ideal against the authenticity of equality.

Madison's portrayal of democracy's politics as brimming with "passions," "animosities," ideological and religious "zeal" and as essentially irrational was meant as a warning about the dangers of popular rule and as a preliminary to showing that the proposed new constitutional system would simultaneously establish safeguards against it while protecting economic inequalities.[35] But if we ask what kind of politics is being established and what kind is being discouraged, the conclusion might well be that Madison, who is usually regarded as the "father of the Constitution," was bent on creating an artificial politics, the residue left after the authentic politics of popular grievance had been hamstrung by checks and balances. The greatest source of danger to a free government, he argued, was a majority faction's gaining control of governmental power; that was most likely to occur when the society was governed by a "democracy," a system based upon majority rule. Since the revolution of 1776 had depended upon popular participation and as a result aroused democratic hopes, political expediency dictated that democratic impulses be controlled rather than suppressed. In short, how to manage democracy, or how to exploit division and thereby dilute commonality?

The solution required identifying the conditions for an antimajoritarian republic, for nullifying the single most important power element of democracy, not sheer numbers but differences that might discover their commonality. The solution required an expanded society where the geography of huge distances combined with "a greater number of citizens" and "a greater variety of parties and interests" would render it "less probable" that "an unjust and interested majority" or a single "religious sect" or "a rage for paper money, for an abolition of debts, for an equal division of property, or for any other improper or wicked project . . . [could] pervade the whole body of the Union."[36] The political mobilization of "rage" or popular irrationality in pursuit of "improper or wicked project[s]" was thus what the new system was designed to prevent. What Madison described as "rage" would probably have been described by the *enragé* as protesting the actualities of economic hardship and political exclusion. The obvious instrument that, potentially, could express popular grievances was the legislature, the institution that stood closer to the people and was hence the more dangerous.

If, as Madison claimed, the legislature "is every where extending the sphere of its activity, and drawing all power into its impetuous vortex,"[37] how could the legislature as well as other governmental bodies be prevented from committing acts of demotic willfulness? Madison's answer was to superimpose capitalism's principle of market behavior upon the political system, the principle that operated in "private as well as public affairs." Arrange the constitution to imitate an economy so that the various offices "may be a check on the other; that the private interest of every individual may be a centinel over the public rights."[38]

Thus Madison's plan blocked popular irrationality and its misguided view of self-interest, and played off against each other the self-interest of the various government officials; the problem remained that the rationality essential to governing and policy making appeared to have been replaced by, or at least subordinated to, self-interest. Accepting explicitly that all men were driven to act by and for self-interest meant rejecting the ideal of disinterestedness associated with Plato's guardian class. The latter lusted after knowledge, not political power, and, indeed, had to be dragged into fulfilling their public duties, and then only for a limited period.

Madison appeared to argue that the proposed constitution would not depend upon a disinterested elite. Instead its elaborate checks and balances and the separation of powers would provide a systemic restraint, a mechanistic kind of reason, "a machine that would go of itself."[39] "You must first enable the government to controul the governed; and in the next place, oblige it to controul itself."[40]

Hamilton went beyond Madison's negativism and sketched the outlines of an elite that would supply the skills needed for an active state. Writing in *Federalist* No. 35, he indicated from what quarters a guardian class characterized by a certain higher kind of reason could be recruited: "land-holders, merchants, and men of the learned professions," whose very "situations" required them to acquire "extensive inquiry and information," even "a thorough knowledge of the principles of political economy." Hamilton concluded: "The man who understands those principles best will be least likely to resort to oppressive expedients, or to sacrifice any particular class of citizens to the procure-ment of revenue."[41] In the fifteenth *Federalist* Hamilton had introduced a specifically political element to the formulation when he referred to "knowledge of national circumstances and reasons of state which is essential to a right judgment."[42] Thus elite reason was represented by those with a drive for acquisition, accumulation, and exploitation lead-ing to wealth and power, the modern reality principles for a political society conceived as a political economy.

These qualities and classes were incorporated into Hamilton's design for a powerful executive who was clearly intended to dominate a system designed to control populist politics and to promote economic develop-ment. That role was to be facilitated by the relative isolation of the president from the citizenry. As a single official the president would provide the "energy" and direction that a numerous and divided Con-gress could not. If Madisonian checks and balances and the system's political economy of conflicting interests were designed to prevent con-certed action by a demos, the Hamiltonian executive was conceived for action. "Decision, activity, secrecy, and dispatch will generally charac-terise the proceedings of one man," he explained, but not of a legisla-ture. Moreover, the fact that the president was not directly elected by the citizenry afforded him independence. He would not have to bend "to every sudden breese [*sic*] of passion, or to every transient impulse which the people may receive from the arts of men" who "flatter their prejudices to betray their interests." When the people misunderstood their own true interests, it was "the duty" of their "guardians to with-stand the temporary delusion."[43]

Thus in the new system the irrationality of the "multitude" was to be checked by the Madisonian devices that would, at the same time, allow sufficient leeway for rational governance by the new "guardians": an elite of planters and successful business and professional men who could be relied upon to withstand the gusts of demotic irrationality while developing and expanding the new system of power. Elite reason possessed the quality of being able to deal with power on an extended or national scale, and to devise the means of achieving expansive ends.

There was a further, darker side to the exploitative rationality of the republican elite, an "Alcibiades factor." This was the driving force of the quest for public recognition and distinction—in short, for the sort of fame associated with the exercise of great power over the lives of those who had little or no power. It was suggested in a comment by Hamilton when he defended the constitutional principle of no term limits on any of the branches of government. He imagines the frustrations of those who would be compelled to relinquish power and office.

An ambitious man . . . when he found himself seated on the summit of his country's honors, when he looked forward to the time at which he must descend from the exalted eminence forever; and reflected that no exertion of merit on his part could save him from the unwelcome reverse: Such a man, in such a situation would be much more violently tempted to embrace a favorable conjuncture for attempting the prolongation of his power, at every personal hazard, than if he had the probability of answering the same end by doing his duty.

Such men, Hamilton warned, might end by haunting the republic, "wandering among the people like discontented ghosts."[44] Denied power, elite rationality threatens to turn into irrationality with a vengeance.

xi

In order to suggest what is at stake in the gathering tendencies toward inverted totalitarianism, I want to recall a development that occurred broadly in sixteenth-century England and which historians refer to as the "enclosure movement." By custom some land was designated "commons" or "open fields" to indicate that it was not owned by particular individuals but could be tilled or otherwise used by the local populace. However, wealthy men and nobles proceeded to erect hedges around parts of the common and, in effect, to appropriate it and exclude the general, and typically poorer, population.[45] What had been common was now privatized.

Recall that for centuries politics, too, had been "enclosed," and that the demotic "moments" represented attempts to open it up, to make it, as it were, public land, devoted to common purposes. In recent decades, however, there has been a steady and relentless effort to reverse "common" gains, to privatize public functions, notably education, welfare programs, administration of prisons, military operations, postal services, even space travel. In addition to the strong push toward privatizing Social Security, there are persistent efforts to privatize public lands or exploit their resources. Most instances of privatization reverse achievements that had originally been gained in the face of determined opposition from the very forces now operating or administering them. The privatization of public services and functions manifests the steady evolution of corporate power into a political form, into an integral, even dominant partner with the state. It marks the transformation of American politics and its political culture, from a system in which democratic practices and values were, if not defining, at least major contributory elements, to one where the remaining democratic elements of the state and its populist programs are being systematically dismantled.

It is all too evident that political campaigns, elections, legislation, and even judgeships have become so dependent on private funds, especially from wealthy and corporate donors, that our politics, too, is being enclosed and the citizenry largely excluded. The tragedy is that social programs, government regulation of corporate excesses, environmental safeguards, and public education were commonalities won by dint of prolonged struggles against powerful resistance; the gains encouraged hope that democratic goals, reflecting the actualities of everyday life, were achievable.

In the United States the late twentieth-century elites shaped a politics and culture by which the stunting of popular rationality became an art form devised to solve the problem created by the admission of the demos into political life and the comparatively high levels of popular participation in electoral politics around the turn of the last century. The aim was a new kind of electorate, a hybrid creation, part cinematic and part consumer. Like a movie or TV audience, it would be credulous, nurtured on the unreality of images on the screen, the impossible feats and situations depicted, or the promise of personal transformation by a new product. In this the elites were abetted by the long-standing American tradition of dramatic evangelism and its fostering of collective fervor and popular fantasies of the miraculous. It was no leap of faith from the camp meetings of the nineteenth century and the Billy Sundays of the twentieth to the politically savvy televangelist of the twenty-first century megachurch.

In a world where the incredible has become banal, public rationality is overmatched. In 2006, two years after the lie of Saddam's WMDs had been exposed, the percentage of Americans who continued to believe that there were such weapons in Iraq increased from 35 to 50, and a near majority believed in links between Saddam and al Qaeda, lack of evidence notwithstanding.

The credulousness that displaces public rationality tends to relax elite rationality so that elites are tempted by grandiose objectives and unscrupulous means. The mayhem depicted on screens certainly worked not to deter but to invite official forbearance, even approval, for torture, that is, for ignoring normal practice. The temptation of "shock and awe," of actually employing weapons of mass destruction, seems not to deter elites or to violate the sensibilities of citizens conditioned to the violence in most action movies; contemporary Baghdad seems just another cinematic episode in a long-run series.[46] The sense of proportion needed by those with immense powers at their disposal is sadly lacking, as when a secretary of state, Madeleine Albright, demanded of then Chief of Staff General Powell: with all of those troops and arms at your disposal, why not use them?

How can elite calculation promote demotic irrationality that then feeds elite miscalculation? How are elites able to manipulate the demos, shape it into an irrational electorate, and then capitalize on it? The answer to both questions is this: by turning Madison's theory of interests on its head and constructing artificial majorities. Instead of discouraging "factions" from forming a majority, elites *temporarily* assemble or rally diverse interests without integrating them. Instead of seeking ways to block the coalescence of diverse interests, they employ the strategy of "targeting" them with a "message." That message, without necessarily promising to bestow the specific benefits the group might want, appeals to some broad "value"—for instance, a blue-collar "Reagan Democrat" might be attracted by appeals to patriotism that are, at the same time, silent about promoting labor's right to organize.

Thus elites apply a certain type of instrumental or tactical rationality in devising means, including lies (Swift boat ads), to achieve a given end (electoral support). In the course of doing so, they nourish a public discourse of irrationality. Appeals to patriotism or religious faith are invoked because their status lends them the aura of the unarguable. The consequences of blinkered support are not limited to the more specific objectives that patriotism or religious fervor enables the leaders to pursue, but recoil on the decision-makers. When whipped up, as in the calculations after 9/11, patriotism and millenarianism can tempt leaders to undertake adventures that they might otherwise abandon for lack of popular enthusiasm. Thus what begins as rational calculation about voting behavior eventuates in both an irrational citizenry and the compilation by "the best and the brightest" of an alarming record of irrational decisions, a Vietnam, a Lebanon (1982), or an Iraq.[47]

A paradox: in matters of foreign and military policy the demos is said to lack the knowledge, experience, and analytic ability to make rational judgments, yet when they have their attention directed upon national and international problems or crises, they are encouraged to respond viscerally to appeals to patriotism, nationalism, and political evangelism. These forms of collective self-righteousness serve as blinders to the consequences, some horrendous and grossly immoral, of its support. The demos becomes at once complicit and irrational.

xii

In the summer of 2007, as the military and political situation of Iraq steadily worsened, popular support of President Bush sank to its lowest levels. Unlike the classical totalitarian regimes of Hitler and Mussolini—which were toppled by military defeat and, most crucially, vanished shortly thereafter, leaving few traces—inverted totalitarianism will likely survive military defeat and public scorn of its leader. The system is not dependent upon his particular persona. That the system will survive his retirement, would survive even if the Democrats were to become the majority party in control of both the presidency and Congress, something that has not occurred since the Carter administration. Consequently, the fixation upon Bush obscures the real problem. The political role of corporate power, the corruption of the political and representative processes by the lobbying industry, the expansion of executive power at the expense of constitutional limitations, and the degradation of political dialogue promoted by the media *are* the basics of the system, not excrescences upon it. The system would remain in place even if the Democratic Party attained a majority; and should that circumstance arise, the system will set tight limits to unwelcome changes, as is foreshadowed in the timidity of current Democratic proposals for reform. In the last analysis the much-lauded stability and conservatism of the American system owe nothing to lofty ideals, and everything to the irrefutable fact that it is shot through with corruption and awash in contributions primarily from wealthy and corporate donors. When a minimum of a million dollars is required of House candidates and elected judges, and when patriotism is for the draft-free to extol and for the ordinary citizen to serve, in such times it is a simple act of bad faith to claim that politics-as-we-now-know-it can miraculously cure the evils which are essential to its very existence.

xiii

The best hope for a democratic revival is to make use of the experience represented by the demos and by fugitive democracy, thereby identifying promising sites for a democratic revival. An essential preliminary is to distinguish popular from elite-managed democracy.

How are the two distinguished by the characteristic political disposition of each governing their approaches to the world of human and other natural beings, and to the natural world? We might put it as the difference between a commonality and an economic polity, between managing a society and its ecology in terms of the common good and subordinating the political system to economic criteria—for example, being driven by the possible effects of a political decision on the sensibilities of "financial markets."

The institution that provides a model for the economic polity is, appropriately, the free market. It has as its motor principle individual self-interest and its variant, the national interest. Accordingly, no one excepting the deluded, and no nation excepting one led by starry-eyed idealists, is assumed to act disinterestedly to promote the interests of others. In contrast, democracy's idea is based on a culture that encourages members to join in common endeavors, not as a flagellating form of self-denial but as the means of taking care of a specific and concrete part of the world and of its life-forms. At stake are not only the natural environment but institutional and especially democratic institutions that, too, need tending.[48] It is not solely a question of what kind of physical environment we leave to those who follow, but of what will be the condition of the political institutions and the Constitution that later generations inherit.

Commonality stands for the idea that the care and fate of the polity are of common concern; that we are all involved because we are all implicated in the actions and decisions which are justified in our name. What makes political power "political" is that it is made possible by the contributions and sacrifices of many. The perfect example of the difference between the politics of democratic commonality and corporate politics is represented by the contrast between the present Social Security system and the proposed alternative of a system based on private investment accounts. Under the current system one generation contributes to the support of another, so that the program becomes a shared endeavor resulting in a common good. Under the proposed replacement each would be on his or her own; commonality would be lost and inequality promoted. That contrast, between self-interest and commonality of concerns, involves contrasting mentalities, each with its own form of rationality; one is exploitative, the other protective.

To examine both the fugitive character of the modern demos and its form of rationality, consider how a citizenry materialized in response to the Hurricane Katrina disaster. That response was a political act on behalf of commonality. While the administration's vaunted "Homeland Security" agencies and highly disciplined White House floundered, there was a spontaneous outpouring of aid, financial and material, from ordinary citizens, civic and religious groups, and local governments from all parts of the nation. It was as though the

United States could express democracy only by bypassing a national government preoccupied with distant fantasies of being democracy's agent to the world.[49] In other words, the effectiveness of demotic action can go beyond the local when it can empathize. The fact that New Orleans and parts of Mississippi were in dire need of the necessities of life—food, shelter, clothing, medical assistance, and the like—was something that ordinary Americans elsewhere could spontaneously understand.

The survival and flourishing of democracy depends, in the first instance, upon the "people"'s changing themselves, sloughing off their political passivity and, instead, acquiring some of the characteristics of a demos. That means creating themselves, coming-into-being by virtue of their own actions. While it cannot be emphasized too strongly that democracy requires supporting conditions—social, economic, and educational—the democratization of politics remains merely formal without the democratization of the self. Democratization is not about being "left alone," but about becoming a self that sees the values of common involvements and endeavors and finds in them a source of self-fulfillment. Transformation is not a rarity but happens all the time. Generic high school students can, before long, become principled lawyers, doctors, nurses, teachers, even MBAs who learn to behave, think, and speak according to ethical and demanding mores.

To become a democrat is to change one's self, to learn how to act collectively, as a demos. It requires that the individual go "public" and thereby help to constitute a "public" and an "open" politics, in principle accessible for all to take part in it, and visible so that all might see or learn about the deliberations and decision making occurring in public agencies and institutions.[50]

Demotic rationality is rooted in a provincialism where commonality is experienced as everyday reality and "civic spirit" is unapologetic. In that setting schools, businesses, law enforcement, the environment, the conduct of public officials, taxation all have an immediacy. That immediacy serves to chasten the actions of those entrusted with power, whether as council members, teachers, business-owners, police, or environmentalists. Inhibition does not preclude fierce controversies, strong grievances, prejudices, animosities, or nasty tactics, but usually they do not result in the victors' pursuing Rove-like fantasies of a "permanent" grip on power. And this because most decisions, rather than being abstract, visibly affect daily life, and hence their consequences can be evaluated by ordinary reasoning tempered by past experience.

Demotic political interventions are, at the national level, necessarily episodic or fugitive. Among other considerations, this means dependence on the political elite and its modes of engaging political matters. What is at stake is a fundamental difference between, on one hand, reason in the service of commonality and, on the other, elite rationality or reason in the service of the economic polity. It is revealing that the Bush administration's negative view of social programs and environmental regulations is that these fall outside the paradigm of profit; or that its favorite form of public spending is for the military, for sheer power; or that it should promote privatization of public functions that transforms a public service into a form of profit making.[51] Elite irrationalism is encouraged by the ethos and ethic shared by political and corporate elites. Their mentality is expansionist, opportunistic, and, above all, exploitative; it exhausts resources—natural, human, public. It is not just the earth's atmosphere that is being destroyed or human beings who are "burned out" at fifty. Public institutions are being savaged. A legislature, a court, a system of law, a civil service are the equivalent of a public ecology and, like the natural world, an inheritance to be cared for and passed on. They can easily be "used up" by, for example, corruption, partisanship in the wrong places, denigration of public servants, dismissal of scientific evidence and the reports of whistle-blowers, systematic lying to the public, and the stretching of legal authority to the point where it sanctions torture.

xiv

The demos will never dominate politically. In an age where identities are potentially plural and changing, a unified demos is no longer possible, or even desirable: instead of *a* demos, democratic citizenries. Democratic political consciousness, while it may emerge anywhere at any time, is most likely to be nurtured in local, small-scale settings, where both the negative consequences of political powerlessness and the positive possibilities of political involvement seem most evident. Further, a vital local democracy can help to bridge the inevitable distance between representative government and its constituencies. There is a genuinely valuable contribution which democracy can make to national politics, but it is dependent upon a politics that is rooted locally, experienced daily, and practiced regularly, not just mobilized spasmodically.

Democratic experience begins at the local level, but a democratic citizenry should not accept city limits as its political horizon. A principal reason is that the modern citizenry has needs which exceed local resources (e.g., enforcement of environmental standards) and can be addressed only by means of state power.

While the project of reinvigorating democracy may strike the reader as utopian, it requires an accompanying, even more utopian project: to encourage and nurture a counterelite of democratic public servants. The ideal is not of neutral, "above politics" technocrats who would service any master. Ideally a public servant of democracy would combine knowledge and skill with a commitment to promoting and defending democratic values, lessening the inequities in our society, and protecting the environment. For decades that ideal has been the target of corporate-inspired attacks on "government bureaucrats" aimed at preventing a revival of effective regulation of corporate power and of social democracy.

A democratic counterelite would not consist solely of government workers. In fact such a corps already exists among the numerous nongovernmental organizations (NGOs) devoted to environmental conservation, famine relief, human rights, AIDS prevention, and other likeminded endeavors. A crucial element in these efforts is that solutions are typically aimed at the local level and at encouraging the local populations to take responsibility for their own well-being.

As I have argued earlier, the local character of democracy can provide a crucial reality check on the conduct of national politics and governance, perhaps even inhibit the elite's temptation to foreign adventures. But that will require serious changes in the quality of public discussion, which, in turn, would depend upon the reclamation of public ownership of the airwaves and encouragement of noncommercial broadcasting. This contemporary version of the old struggle between "enclosure" and the "commons," between exploitation and commonality, pretty much sums up the stakes: not what new powers we can bring into the world, but what hard-won practices we can prevent from disappearing.

Notes

PREFACE

1. There are numerous instances, such as in the practice of torture or of elevating political or ideological considerations to limit or override scientific findings (e.g., in the areas of birth control, stem cell research, and environmental pollution), wherein the Bush administration approximates totalitarian practice. Throughout this volume I try to avoid the mistake of claiming that in a particular matter inverted totalitarianism "substitutes" one of its policies for a particular policy of the Nazis—for example, racism. That would be to presuppose that inverted totalitarianism and classical totalitarianism have the same structures. My point is that they do not. For a discussion of these problems, see Anson Rabinbach, "Moments of Totalitarianism," *History and Theory* 45, no. 1 (2006): 72–100.

2. Consider the Internet. It is touted as a revolutionary development for promoting popular political participation and providing for "democratic input." But, as recent disclosures demonstrate, it also allows for expanded governmental surveillance of the opinions and actions (e.g., financial transactions) of citizens.

PREVIEW

1. Cited in Richard J. Evans, *The Third Reich in Power, 1933–1939* (New York: Penguin, 2005), 183.

2. *National Security Strategy of the United States,,* sec. 1, pp. 3–4. Hereafter NSS. I have used the text from nytimes.com of Sept. 20, 2002. This document was drawn up by the National Security Council for transmission to Congress as "a declaration of the Administration's policy" and released in September 2002.

3. Quoted in Ron Suskind, "Without a Doubt," *New York Times Magazine*, October 17, 2004.

CHAPTER ONE
MYTH IN THE MAKING

1. *New York Times*, September 12, 2003, A-19.

2. Michael Mandelbaum, *The Ideas That Conquered the World* (New York: Public Affairs, 2002), 2.

3. According to the 9/11 commission's report, the White House was originally on the list but was later omitted for reasons that are not clear.

4. According to one survey 74 percent of the TV coverage of 9/11 was "all" or "mostly pro-U.S.," while 7 percent dissented "all" or "mostly." Cited in Corey Robin, *Fear: The History of a Political Idea* (New York: Oxford University Press, 2004), 143.

5. After Giuliani completed his term, he became an entrepreneur whose business advised governments and corporations on the arts of leadership under conditions of extreme stress. In 2007 he announced his presidential candidacy and indicated that his actions in the aftermath of 9/11 would be his major qualification.

6. A notable fact about the contemporary political climate and its widespread fear is that when some striking event occurs, such as the power failure of August 14, 2003, when several of the northeastern states and parts of Canada were blacked out, the first response of authorities was to reassure the public that it was not the result of a terrorist attack. Yet a few weeks later, and a few weeks before the anniversary of 9/11, officials of the Port Authority of New York and New Jersey (the body that had administered the World Trade Center) released new audiotapes of the voices of victims trapped in the Twin Towers, thus ensuring that the events would remain fresh in the public memory.

7. *New York Times*, September 10, 2003, A-11.

8. The phrase "holy politics" was used by an English divine, Richard Baxter, during the seventeenth-century civil wars.

9. Subsequently the families of the victims were awarded sums equivalent to their expected earnings had they survived. Even death has a salary scale. Meanwhile, the police and firefighters whose heroism was praised to the skies at the time were later unable to gain the wage increase they had bargained for prior to 9/11.

10. At the memorial service commemorating the second anniversary of those killed at the Pentagon, the director of the FBI read this from Ephesians 6:12–18: "We do not wrestle against flesh and blood, but against the rulers, against the authorities, against the cosmic powers over the present

darkness, against the spiritual forces of evil in the heavenly places." Quoted in *New York Times*, September 12, 2003, A-19.

11. A classic example is the *New York Times*'s "public editor," the self-described "readers' representative." He characterizes himself as "a registered Democrat but notably to the right of my fellow Democrats on Manhattan's Upper West Side." He declares he can be located between the "left" of the *Times*'s editorial page and the "right" of William Safire's "right." "But," he declares audaciously, "on some issues I veer from the noncommittal middle" to become "an absolutist on free trade and free speech and a supporter of gay rights and abortion rights." He thinks it "unbecoming" for the rich to "whine about high taxes" and "inconsistent for advocates of human rights to oppose all American military action." He prefers "exterminating rats" to reading a book by "either Bill O'Reilly or Michael Moore."

12. *New York Times*, December 28, 1993, A-4.

13. Quoted in David Sanger, "U.S. Goal Seems Clear and the Team Complete," *New York Times*, February 13, 2002, A-14.

14. President George W. Bush, September 14, 2001, in the National Cathedral, cited in *NSS*, 5.

15. *Myth and Society in Ancient Greece*, trans. Janet Lloyd (Atlantic Highlands, N.J.: Humanities Press, [1974], 1980), 196.

16. Blaise Pascal, *Pensées*, trans. William Finlayson Trotter (London: Dent, 1948), no. 233, p. 67.

17. I have followed the text as printed in the *New York Times*, January 24, 2007, A-16.

18. Max Weber, "Science as a Vocation," in *From Max Weber: Essays in Sociology*, trans. and ed. H. H. Gerth and C. Wright Mills (New York: Oxford University Press, 1946), 139, 148, 155.

CHAPTER TWO

TOTALITARIANISM'S INVERSION: BEGINNINGS OF THE
IMAGINARY OF A PERMANENT GLOBAL WAR

1. Quoted in John Lewis Gaddis, *The Cold War: A New History* (New York: Penguin, 2005), 46. Kennan was speaking at the Naval War College.

2. Edward S. Corwin, *Total War and the Constitution* (New York: Knopf, 1947), 4. A respected contemporary of Corwin's, Bernard Brodie, wrote, "To a community alerted to national danger the F.B.I. or its counter-

part becomes the first line of defense, and the encroachment on civil liberties which would necessarily follow would far exceed in magnitude and pervasiveness anything which democracies have thus far tolerated in peacetime." *The Atomic Bomb and American Security*, 9, cited by Corwin, 9.

3. *The Oxford Universal Dictionary*, rev. and ed. C. T. Onions, 3rd ed. (Oxford: Clarendon Press, 1955).

4. Quoted in Andrew J. Bacevich, *The New American Militarism: How Americans Are Seduced by War* (New York: Oxford University Press, 2005), 45.

5. Thomas Hobbes, *Leviathan*, ed. Michael Oakeshott (Oxford: Blackwell, n.d.), 64, 112, 113.

6. The Doolittle study group on foreign intelligence, reporting to President Eisenhower, advised that the nature of the enemy set the standard for American intelligence: "We are facing an implacable enemy whose avowed objective is world domination by whatever means and at whatever cost. . . . There are no rules in such a game. Hitherto acceptable norms of human conduct do not apply. We must develop effective espionage and counterespionage services and must learn to subvert, sabotage and destroy our enemies by more clever, more sophisticated and more effective means than those used against us." Quoted in Stephen J. Whitfield, *The Culture of the Cold War*, 2nd ed. (Baltimore: Johns Hopkins University Press, 1996), 34.

7. Michael Ignatieff, as quoted in Bacevich, *The New American Militarism*, 25.

8. In what follows I am not suggesting that the New Dealers and FDR entertained totalitarian designs. They did not; it is, however, a well-tested homily that power claims may be established and exercised by those who have no dark designs, but those same claims may be exploited by successors whose purposes are unbenevolent.

9. Quoted in Arthur M. Schlesinger, Jr., *The Age of Roosevelt: The Coming of the New Deal* (Boston: Houghton Mifflin, 1959), 1. *The Age of Roosevelt* consisted of three volumes; in citing them, I shall refer to the subtitles, e.g., *The Coming of the New Deal*.

10. Cited in Schlesinger, *The Coming of the New Deal*, 95, 13, 3.

11. At the time there were writers and journalists who strongly sympathized with Mussolini (e.g., George Bernard Shaw) or the USSR (Walter Duranty, John Reed).

12. See Schlesinger, *The Coming of the New Deal*, 92.

13. See ibid., 184.

14. For examples of the hostile anticapitalist rhetoric, see ibid., 92–93, 115, 120–21.

15. The three movements are discussed—for the most part critically—in Arthur M. Schlesinger, Jr., *The Age of Roosevelt: The Politics of Upheaval* (Boston: Houghton Mifflin, 1960), 43 ff., 242 ff., 327 ff. (Long); 16 ff., 556 ff., 627–30 (Coughlin); and 33–41, 550–60, 626–27 (Townsend). For a perceptive account of Long and Coughlin, see the splendid study by Alan Brinkley, *Voices of Protest: Huey Long, Father Coughlin and the Great Depression* (New York: Random House, 1982). For a broader discussion of populism prior to as well as beyond the 1930s, see Michael Kazin, *The Populist Persuasion: An American History* (New York: Basic Books, 1995); for the earlier movement, see Lawrence Goodwyn, *Democratic Promise: The Populist Moment in America* (New York: Oxford University Press, 1976).

16. Long's record is discussed in Brinkley, *Voices of Protest*, 24–35.

17. Brinkley unfavorably contrasts the Populist movement of the late nineteenth century with Long's Share the Wealth and Coughlin's Social Justice. Ibid., 160–67. He argues persuasively that the Populists succeeded in genuinely involving the rank and file, while Long and Coughlin did not.

18. James MacGregor Burns has drawn attention to FDR's speech of January 1944 that called for "a second Bill of Rights" which would emphasize education, jobs, health care, and housing. *Roosevelt: The Soldier of Freedom* (New York: Harcourt Brace Jovanovich, 1970), 424. This speech came to my attention in the essay by Taylor Branch, "Justice for Warriors," *New York Review of Books*, April 12, 2007, 40–43, at 42.

19. Quoted by Bacevich, *The New American Militarism*, 14. As his source Bacevich cites Ronald Radosh, *Prophets on the Right: Profiles of Conservative Critics of American Globalism* (New York: Simon and Schuster, 1975), 128.

20. Quoted by Bacevich, *The New American Militarism*, 12. Oddly, Reagan was quoting the eighteenth-century radical Tom Paine.

21. The depiction of Japanese soldiers and kamikaze fliers excepted.

22. Shortly after the end of World War I the so-called Palmer Raids (Palmer was the U.S. attorney general) resulted in the violation of virtually every procedural safeguard including deportation of aliens without trial.

23. It is often forgotten that the United States actively intervened in the Bolshevik Revolution, siding with its opponents, the so-called White Russians.

24. Michael J. Hogan makes the point that conservatives succeeded in decoupling "the national security state" from "the economic and social policies of the New Deal." *A Cross of Iron: Harry S. Truman and the Origins of the National Security State, 1945–1954* (Cambridge: Cambridge University Press, 1998), 364–65.

25. Ibid., 365.

26. Senator Hubert Humphrey, who became the Democratic presidential nominee in 1968, was the primary sponsor of the Communist Control Act of 1954, which declared the American communists to present "a clear and present danger" and deprived the party of "all rights, privileges, and immunities attendant upon legal bodies."

27. Arthur M. Schlesinger, Jr., *The Vital Center: The Politics of Freedom*, 2nd ed. (Boston: Houghton Mifflin, 1962), xxii–iii, xxiv. The first edition was published in 1949. Although the first edition was published before the McCarthy phenomenon, the second edition made no mention of it. Schlesinger also followed the line of NSC-68: the United States is in "a permanent crisis" with "no assurance that any solution is possible" to "the tensions between ourselves and Russia." *The Vital Center*, 9, 10. There is an interesting contrast between the critical view of the business community expressed in the first edition and the more comfortable views in the foreword to the second edition. See 33–34, 153. For Schlesinger's critical view of workers and unions, especially for the communist influences, see 46–47, 120, 187–88. Schlesinger's embrace of Niebuhrian pessimism leads to a remarkable passage where war becomes the savior of American democracy because it heals divisions. "It is perhaps fortunate for the continuity of the American development that the Civil War came along to heal the social wounds opened up in the age of Jackson; that one world war closed the rifts created by the New Freedom and another those of the New Deal" (173).

28. According to Bernard Baruch, one of the unofficial sages consulted by American officials since World War I, "Our aim should be to organize the nation so that every factory and farm, every man, every dollar, every bit of material can be put to use where it will strengthen our defenses." Quoted in Hogan, *A Cross of Iron*, 342.

29. This is the viewpoint of Gaddis, *The Cold War*, especially 222–24, 264.

30. The quotations are from the National Security Council (1950), and the officials cited include Dean Acheson, Robert Lovett, and Paul Nitze. I have taken the quotations from Hogan, *A Cross of Iron*, 300.

31. Ibid., 12. NSC-68 is reproduced and discussed from various perspectives in *American Cold War Strategy: Interpreting NSC 68*, ed. Ernest R. May (Boston: Bedford/St. Martins, 1993).

32. "The potential within us of bearing witness to the values by which we live holds promise for a dynamic manifestation to the rest of the world of the vitality of our system. The essential tolerance of our world outlook, our generous and constructive impulses, and the absence of covetousness in our international relations are assets of potentially enormous influence." *NSC-68: United States Objectives and Programs for National Security*, in *Naval War College Review* 27 (May–June 1975): 51–108; VI-A, p. 2.

33. Ibid., Analysis, I, II, p. 3.

34. Ibid., III-A, pp. 4–5.

35. Ibid., V-A, p. 9.

36. Ibid., IV-B, p. 6.

37. Ibid., VI-A, p. 3.

38. Ibid., VIII, p. 14.

39. Ibid., VIII, p. 13.

40. Ibid., III-B, p. 6; C, p. 7. The strategy of encouraging peoples in the satellite nations to revolt was tested in the ill-fated Hungarian revolt in 1956 when, despite the desperate pleas from Hungarian resistance fighters, the United States did nothing.

41. NSC-68, VI, pp. 7, 10, 11.

42. Ibid., VI-B, p. 10.

43. Ibid., VIII, pp. 13, 14.

44. Ibid., VI-A, pp. 2–3.

45. Ibid., VIII, p. 13.

46. See John P. Diggins, *Up from Communism: Conservative Odysseys in American Intellectual History* (New York: Harper & Row, 1975), 3–4, 441–44.

47. NSC-68, VII-A, p. 9.

48. Ibid., Conclusions and Recommendations, p. 1.

49. Ibid., IV-B, p. 6; C, p. 7.

50. Quoted in Hogan, *A Cross of Iron*, 330.

51. Quoted in Whitfield, *The Culture of the Cold War*, 8.

52. Quoted in ibid., 7. According to the minutes of the March 1953 meeting of the National Security Council, "the President and Secretary Dulles were in complete agreement that somehow or other the tabu which surrounds the use of atomic weapons would have to be destroyed." Quoted in ibid., 8.

53. Richard M. Freeland, *The Truman Doctrine and the Origins of McCarthyism: Foreign Policy, Domestic Politics, and Internal Security, 1946–1948* (New York: Knopf, 1975), 196, 243, 272, 298.

54. Gaddis, *The Cold War*, 80.

55. See Hogan, *A Cross of Iron*, 469–70, 473; also the spirited contemporary polemic, *The Cold War and the University: Toward an Intellectual History of the Postwar Years*, by Noam Chomsky et al.(New York: The New Press, 1997).

56. I have relied on the excellent account in Hogan, *A Cross of Iron*, 119–57. See also Freeland, *The Truman Doctrine*, 281–85.

57. See the numerous references and discussion in Hogan, *A Cross of Iron* (see references in his index under "garrison state").

58. The fact that the Nazi regime was proudly racist evoked little self-examination by Americans of their own support and toleration of racism. Throughout the war segregation was enforced in the American armed forces.

59. On the government's recruitment of intellectuals, see Frances Stonor Saunders, *The Cultural Cold War: The CIA and the World of Arts and Letters* (New York: The New Press, 2000).

60. Cited in Whitfield, *The Culture of the Cold War*, 44.

61. See Hogan's account in *A Cross of Iron* (426–44) of the "Freedom Train" and the role of corporate sponsors; and also of the tragicomic episode in Mosinee, Wisconsin, where the town produced a mock communist takeover of the town.

62. Quoted in Whitfield, *The Culture of the Cold War*, 34. The study group was chaired by General James Doolittle, who had led the first bombing raid on Tokyo during World War II.

63. Ibid., 92–97. See also the brilliant study by Michael Rogin, *McCarthy and the Intellectuals: The Radical Specter* (Cambridge: MIT Press, 1967). For the impact on the State Department, see Dean Acheson, *Present at the Creation: My Years at the State Department* (New York: Norton, 1969), 362–65. For a readable account emphasizing the effects of McCarthyism upon the media, see Haynes Johnson, *The Age of Anxiety: McCarthyism to Terrorism* (Orlando: Harcourt, 2005).

64. Gaddis, *The Cold War*, 192.

65. NSC-68, Conclusions, p. 4.

66. Gaddis, *The Cold War*, 79.

67. On the messianic element, see Hogan, *A Cross of Iron*, 298, 384; and on the defense economy, see ibid., 472–73.

68. See the discussion in James P. Young, *Reconsidering American Liberalism: The Troubled Odyssey of the Liberal Idea* (Boulder, Colo.: Westview Press, 1996), 60 ff., 166 ff., 276 ff. Also Christopher Lasch's splendid *The True and Only Heaven: Progress and Its Critics* (New York: Norton, 1991), especially 455 ff.

69. "The effective operation of a democratic political system requires some measure of apathy and non-involvement on the part of some individuals and groups." Samuel P. Huntington, "The Democratic Distemper," in *The American Commonwealth: 1976* (New York: Basic Books, 1976), 37.

70. Elitism was not solely an academic construction. Here is Dean Acheson describing NSC-68 as "a formidable document [that] presents more than a clinic in political science's latest, most fashionable, and most boring study, 'the decision-making process,' for it carries us beyond decisions to what should be their fruits, action. If it is helpful to think of societies as entities, it is equally so to consider their direction centers as groups of cells, thinking cells, action cells, emotion cells, and so on. The society operates best, improves its chances of survival most, in which the thinking cells work out a fairly long-range course of conduct before the others take over—provided it also has a little bit better than average luck. We [i.e., the authors of NSC-68] had an excellent group of thought cells. . . . In the State Department we used to discuss how much time that mythical 'average American citizen' put in each day listening, reading, and arguing about the world outside his own country. Assuming a man or a woman with a fair education, a family, and a job in or out of the house, it seemed to us that ten minutes a day would be a high average. . . . [Our] points to be understandable had to be clear. If we made our points clearer than truth, we did not differ from most other educators and could hardly do otherwise." Acheson, *Present at the Creation*, 374–75.

CHAPTER THREE
TOTALITARIANISM'S INVERSION, DEMOCRACY'S PERVERSION

1. *New York Times*, June 9, 1991. See Stefan Halper and Jonathan Clarke, *America Alone: The Neo-Conservatives and the Global Order* (Cambridge: Cambridge University Press, 2004), 30. Jean Edward Smith, *George Bush's War* (New York: Henry Holt, 1992), 68.

2. "2nd Presidential Debate . . . ," *New York Times*, October 12, 2000, A-20.

3. Hans Mommsen, "Cumulative Radicalisation and Progressive Self-Destruction as Structural Determinants of the Nazi Dictatorship," in *Stalinism and Nazism: Dictatorship in Comparison*, ed. Ian Kershaw and Moshe Levin (Cambridge: Cambridge University Press, 1997), 75.

4. "The Bush Doctrine," *Weekly Standard*, June 4, 2001. Cited in Bacevich, *The New American Militarism*, 83.

5. Richard J. Evans, *The Coming of the Third Reich* (New York: Penguin, 2004), 72 describes how after World War I, German politics and culture were saturated with talk of violence.

6. The remark is attributed to Grover Norquist, founder of Americans for Tax Reform.

7. On the military and the Nazis, see Michael Mann, *Fascists* (Cambridge: Cambridge University Press, 2004), 63, 65, 68–69, 104.

8. On evangelical capitalism, see Malcolm Gladwell, "The Cellular Church," *New Yorker*, September 12, 2005, 60–67.

9. In connection with the rationalization of the universities, note the persistent efforts of think tank critics and right-wing operatives (e.g., David Horowitz) to demand an end to tenure for professors and to "liberal domination" of faculties.

10. See Bacevich, *The New American Militarism*, chap. 3.

11. The German scholar Götz Aly (*Hitler's Beneficiaries: Plunder, Racial War, and the Nazi State* [New York: Metropolitan, 2007]) has argued that the economic lot of ordinary Germans during the Nazi years was better than scholars have allowed, and helped to secure popular allegiance more firmly while making resistance less likely. But see the critical review by Richard J. Evans, a leading contemporary historian of Nazism,"Parasites of Plunder?" in *The Nation*, January 8/15, 2007, 23–28.

12. Robert Dahl, "Business and Politics: A Critical Appraisal of Political Science," in Robert Dahl et al., *Social Science Research on Business: Product and Potential* (Columbia University Press: New York, 1959), 53.

13. Josh Meyer, "Unprecedented Domestic Surveillance since 9/11," reprinted from the *Los Angeles Times* in the *Santa Rosa Press Democrat*, September 9, 2006, A-1.

14. Robert O. Paxton, as quoted by Alexander Stille, "The Latest Obscenity Has Seven Letters: F-a-s-c-i-s-m," *New York Times*, September 13,. 2003, A-19. See also Robert O. Paxton, *The Anatomy of Fascism* (New York: Knopf, 2004), 42 ff., 78 ff.

15. Both Mussolini and Hitler employed violence during the run-up to the elections. See Evans, *The Coming of the Third Reich*, 266 ff.,

285; Mann, *Fascists*, 98–99, 104, 116; Paxton, *The Anatomy of Fascism*, chaps. 4, 5.

16. Mussolini launched his "March on Rome" in 1922; by 1924 Fascists were firmly in control. See Ernst Nolte, *Three Faces of Fascism*, trans. Leila Vennewitz (New York: Holt, 1966), 217 ff.; Hitler's first sustained, although unsuccessful, attempt at an electoral victory was in September 1930. With the cabinet's decree of February 1933 and the Enabling Act of 1933, the Nazis were able to proceed as they wished. See Paxton, *The Anatomy of Fascism*, chaps. 4–5, and Evans, *The Coming of the Third Reich*, 259 ff., 332, 351.

17. "The Decline of America's Armed Forces," in *Present Dangers: Crisis and Opportunity in American Foreign and Defense Policy*, ed. Robert Kagan and William Kristol (San Francisco, 2000), as cited by Bacevich, *The New American Militarism*, 86.

18. The *New York Times* reported that the then head of CNN "made a public show of meeting with Republican leaders in Washington to discuss CNN's perceived liberal bias." According to the *Times* CNN subsequently became more conservative. April 16, 2003, B-9.

19. See Marie Gottschalk, *The Prison and the Gallows: The Politics of Mass Incarceration in America* (Cambridge: Cambridge University Press, 2006), 2, 15, 19. See also Timothy V. Kaufman-Osborn, *From Noose to Needle: Capital Punishment and the Late Liberal State* (Ann Arbor: University of Michigan Press, 2002), 166–68, 173–74.

20. During the Katrina disaster the federal government suspended minimum wage requirements for some businesses under contract for the cleanup operations.

21. In keeping with the spirit of inverted totalitarianism the program was later shown, but on a more obscure TV channel.

22. See the *Oxford English Dictionary*, under "patient."

23. One definition of "popularize" in the *OED* is "to render democratic."

24. *NSS*, sec. 1, p. 3.

25. See *The Corporation: A Theological Inquiry*, ed. Michael Novak and John W. Cooper (Washington: American Enterprise Institute, 1981). Also my chapter, "The Age of Organization and the Sublimation of Politics," in *Politics and Vision*, expanded ed. (Princeton: Princeton University Press, 2004), 315 ff. There are good discussions of the modern corporation and of managerialism in Alfred D. Chandler, Jr., *The Visible Hand: The Managerial Revolution in American Business* (Cambridge: Harvard University Press, 1977); Alfred D. Chandler, Jr., and Herman Daems, eds., *Manage-*

rial Hierarchies: Comparative Perspectives on the Rise of the Modern Indus-trial Enterprise (Cambridge: Harvard University Press, 1980); and Rakesh Khurana, *Searching for a Corporate Savior: The Irrational Quest for Charis-matic CEOs* (Princeton: Princeton University Press, 2002). For a critical view, see Edward S. Herman, *Corporate Control, Corporate Power* (Cam-bridge: Cambridge University Press, 1981).

26. Michael Ignatieff, "Barbarians at the Gate?" *New York Review of Books*, February 28, 2002, 4.

27. See Jeffrey Toobin, *Too Close to Call: The Thirty-Six-Day Battle to Decide the 2000 Election* (New York: Randon House, 2001).

28. The remarks were by Joshua B. Bolten, the president's budget direc-tor and former chief domestic policy adviser. "Bush 'Compassion' Agenda: An '04 Liability?" *New York Times*, August 26, 2003, A-14.

29. There were, of course, the unsavory incidents of repression and gen-uine damage during the McCarthy era, especially by the House Un-Ameri-can Activities Committee, and the later, far less effective attempt by Presi-dent Nixon at compiling an "enemies list" of academics and intellectuals. See the fine work by David M. Oshinsky, *A Conspiracy So Immense: The World of Joe McCarthy* (Oxford: Oxford University Press, 2005).

CHAPTER FOUR
THE NEW WORLD OF TERROR

1. Cited in Karl Dietrich Bracher, *The German Dictatorship: The Ori-gins, Structure, and Effects of National Socialism*, trans. Jean Steinberg (New York: Praeger, 1970), 318n29.

2. Cited in Lewis L. Gould, *Grand Old Party: A History of the Republi-cans* (New York: Random House, 2003), 350.

3. *New York Times*. April 4, 2003, B-2.

4. Recall that the celebration was relatively short-lived when glitches were discovered that prevented computer systems from registering the change in millennial dating. Financial reporting, security systems, and the military were temporarily disrupted.

5. The antiballistic missile program (ABM or Star Wars) championed by the Reagan administration was an admission of American vulnerability.

6. NSS, Introduction, p. 2.

7. "Campaign 2000: Promoting the National Interest," *Foreign Affairs*, January/February, 2000, 53.

8. Cited by Roger Cohen, "A Global War: Many Fronts, Little Unity," *New York Times*, September 5, 2004, sec. 4, p. 1.

9. NSS, Introduction, p. 1.

10. Speech of January 22, 2004, in *New York Times*, January 23, 2004, A-19, A-23.

11. At the second anniversary of 9/11 the ceremonies of remembrance featured children who read the names of the victims and supplied the music.

12. Ignatieff, "Barbarians at the Gate?" 4.

13. *New York Times*, September 11, 2003, A-1.

14. NSS, Introduction, p. 1.

15. Ibid., sec. 3, p. 5.

16. See the interesting analysis in Robin, *Fear*. Fear has long been exploited in American politics. The Oklahoma bombing triggered fearful responses that were quickly exploited. In 1995 a Conference of the States, which was being organized by the usual groups concerned with problems of state governance, quickly became the stuff of conspiracy theories alleging that the aim of the conference was to establish a totalitarian "One World Government." A campaign was launched that eventually led to the cancellation of the conference as one state legislature after another withdrew. In 1994 fifteen states adopted resolutions asserting their sovereignty and insisting upon a narrow view of federal power. See Dirk Johnson, "Conspiracy Theories Impact Reverberates in Legislatures," *New York Times*, July 6, 1995, A-1.

17. To be sure, "empire" had been ascribed to the United States as long ago as the Spanish-American War of 1898, and "superpower" first began to be used in 1950 to describe the USSR and the United States as the "world's only superpowers."

18. Prior to the invasion of Iraq the main, perhaps the sole, official institutions protesting were the city councils in several regions of the nation. Over one hundred of them passed resolutions opposing the action.

19. *Leviathan*, chap. 31, p. 237.

20. Ibid., chap. 42, p. 356.

21. William and Lawrence Kaplan, *The War over Iraq* (2003), 121, as cited in Bacevich, *The New American Militarism*, 92.

22. Hobbes meant his state of nature and war of each against all not merely as imaginary constructs but as descriptions of what life is like whenever there is no "common power" to "awe" men into behaving peaceably. Such a condition, Hobbes argued, existed in the international relations among sovereign states and in a society in the midst of a revolution.

23. *De Cive*, ed. Howard Warrender (Oxford: Clarendon Press, 1983), chap. 10, sec. 9.

24. See "On the Office of the Sovereign Representative," *Leviathan*, chap. 30, p. 219 ff.

25. Hobbes on violent death: *Leviathan*, chap. 13, pp. 81–83.

26. In converting the citizen into a subject, Hobbes was reacting against the more democratic conceptions of the citizen circulating during the English civil wars of the 1640s.

27. *Leviathan*, chap. 28, p. 209; chap. 17, p. 112.

28. *New York Times*, January 23, 2004, A-19, 23.

29. For a further discussion see my *Tocqueville between Two Worlds:. The Making of a Political and Theoretical Life* (Princeton: Princeton University Press, 2001).

30. *Democracy in America*, trans. Harvey C. Mansfield and Delba Winthrop (Chicago: University of Chicago Press, 2000), 663.

31. *Leviathan*, 64.

CHAPTER FIVE

THE UTOPIAN THEORY OF SUPERPOWER:

THE OFFICIAL VERSION

1. *New York Times*, April 15, 2003, B-3.

2. *New York Times*, March 7, 2003.

3. Not long after it had been issued, the administration withdrew it without offering an explanation or disavowal.

4. NSS, sec. 3, p. 5.

5. *The Philosophy of Right*, trans. T. M. Knox (Oxford: Clarendon Press, 1945), p. 210, par. 325.

6. NSS, sec. 9, p. 24.

7. Ibid., sec. 1, p. 3.

8. Ibid., Introduction, p. 1.

9. Ibid., p. 2.

10. Ibid.

11. Ibid., p. 3.

12. Ibid., sec. 6, p. 13.

13. Ibid., sec. 9, p. 24

14. Ibid., sec. 9, p. 23. This claim is accompanied by recognition of the need for "effective international cooperation . . . backed by American readiness to play our part." The current controversy over reconstruction of Iraq suggests that the formula has been reversed: effective American action backed—it is hoped—by international willingness to accept a subordinate part.

15. Later some foreign businesses from France and Germany were selected to compete for contracts. Clearly this was intended as bait to weaken the opposition of those governments to the invasion.

16. See, in particular, Jeremy Scahill, *Blackwater: The Rise of the World's Most Powerful Mercenary Army* (New York: Nation Books, 2007).

17. NSS, sec. 9, pp. 22–24. Compare Chalmers Johnson, *The Sorrows of Empire: Militarism, Secrecy, and the End of the Republic* (New York: Henry Holt, 2004), 159–60.

18. NSS, sec. 8, p. 18.

19. Ibid., Introduction, p. 2; sec. 3, p. 6; sec. 5, pp. 11, 12; sec. 9, p. 24.

20. Ibid., sec. 9, p. 23.

21. In the light of the Bush administration's record, the NSS's promise to "protect the environment and workers" hardly needs comment.

22. NSS, sec. 9, pp. 23, 24.

23. Note that following the Katrina hurricane disaster of September 2005 when the administration was accused of having responded tardily and ineptly, it dispatched federal troops and began a public relations campaign to amend the Posse Comitatus Act of 1878 that restricted the employment of federal troops to "the purpose of executing the laws, except in such cases and under such circumstances as such employment of said force may be expressly authorized by the Constitution or by act of Congress."

24. It is true that when trying to quell civil insurrections or civil wars, constitutional governments have appealed to reason of state in claiming extraordinary powers, but the justification was that a war existed.

25. NSS, Introduction, p. 1.

26. Ibid., sec. 9, p. 24.

27. James Fenimore Cooper, *The Deerslayer* (New York: New American Library, 1963), 78.

28. See the fine study by Michael J. Graetz and Ian Shapiro, *Death by a Thousand Cuts: The Fight over Taxing Inherited Wealth* (Princeton: Princeton University Press, 2005).

CHAPTER SIX
THE DYNAMICS OF TRANSFORMATION

1. Leo Strauss, *Natural Right and History* (Chicago: University of Chicago Press, 1953), 160.

2. *Edward S. Corwin's "The Constitution and What It Means Today"*, rev. Harold W. Chase and Craig R. Ducat (Princeton: Princeton University Press, 1978), 106.

3. See Niccolò Machiavelli, *Discourses on Livy*, trans. Harvey C. Mansfield and Nathan Tarcov (Chicago: University of Chicago Press, 1996), bk. 2, chaps. 4, 19; *The Political Works of James Harrington*, ed. J.G.A. Pocock (Cambridge: Cambridge University Press, 1977), 320–25.

4. The Greek and Roman political theorists, such as Plato, Aristotle, Polybius, and Cicero, were aware of the existence of contemporary empires, yet they ignored them in their classification of types of political regimes.

5. *New York Times*, April 19, 2003, A-3.

6. For an engrossing account see Toobin, *Too Close to Call*.

7. According to Toobin, ibid., 193–94, President Clinton wanted Gore to urge street demonstrations, but the latter chose not to.

8. Ironically, while the Republicans constantly attack the Democrats for their close association with Hollywood celebrities, it is the Republican presidents who emulate the action-heroes of the movies.

9. *New York Times*, June 9, 1991.

10. The resolution required that the president consult with Congress "in every possible instance" before committing forces; further, Congress, by a concurrent resolution, could direct the president to remove forces already engaged abroad if there had been no declaration of war by Congress or authorizing statute. I have borrowed from the account given in *Edward S. Corwin's "The Constitution and What It Means Today"*, 108–10.

11. On the Nazi assault on democracy and constitutionalism see Bracher, *The German Dictatorship*, chaps. 3–5; Paxton, *The Anatomy of Fascism*, chaps. 4–5; Evans, *The Coming of the Third Reich*, chaps. 4–5.

12. See Corwin, *Total War and the Constitution*.

13. Ibid., 8.

14. At this writing American generals and civilian officials have stated that the occupation of Iraq may require that the United States remain in control for up to five years. The continuing Iraqi resistance and daily Amer-

ican casualties suggest that the second Gulf War, if only of a guerrilla type, will be a prolonged one.

15. During the preemptive war against Iraq, television and newspaper photographers were prohibited from taking pictures of the caskets of American soldiers at funeral ceremonies on military bases.

16. A consulting business (Frank N. Magid Associates) that advised the major news media about commercial prospects provided a survey for its clients showing that war protests registered last of all topics tested among 6,400 viewers nationwide. See Frank Rich, "Happy Talk News Covers a War," *New York Times*, July 18, 2004.

17. Secret tribunals outside the legal structure were an important fixture of Nazi rule. See Bracher, *The German Dictatorship*, 210, 213, 263, 351, 352, 359, 364, 418.

18. One should not forget that Nazi success in these elections was facilitated by violence against rival parties, especially against the Communists and Social Democrats. See ibid., 178 ff.

19. Jonathan Weisman, "Study: Bush Tax Cuts Add to Middle-Class Burden," *Washington Post*, as reprinted in the *Santa Rosa Press Democrat*, August 13, 2004, A-7. See also David Cay Johnson, *Perfectly Legal: The Covert Campaign to Rig Our Tax System to Benefit the Super Rich—and Cheat Everybody Else* (New York: Portfolio, 2004).

20. One notorious example was the secret meetings between Vice President Cheney and representatives of various energy corporations. Every effort to force the divulgence of the identity of the participants was rebuffed on the grounds of "executive privilege." Court decisions upheld the Cheney position.

21. See "GM Thrives in China with Small Thrifty Van," *New York Times*, August 9, 2005, A-1.

CHAPTER SEVEN
THE DYNAMICS OF THE ARCHAIC

1. Samuel Huntington, "Dead Souls: The Denationalization of the American Elite," *The National Interest*, November, 2002, 16.

2. Cited in Charles Marsh, "Wayward Christian Soldiers," *New York Times*, January 20, 2006, A-19.

3. Cited by Nicholas D. Kristof, "Believe It, or Not," *New York Times*, August 15, 2003, A-29. Kristof also notes that among non-Christians in the United States 47 percent also believe in the Virgin Birth.

4. Certainly not all, or even the vast majority, of evangelicals and fundamentalists are seriously involved in politics. Many scrupulously avoid political engagement and many are involved in social programs that benefit the poor. It is a matter of dispute as to whether their charitable activities are ever separated from proselytizing.

5. The quotation is the title of a book by Falwell. Cited by Marsh, "Wayward Christian Soldiers," A-19.

6. For a study of the salvational and millenarian elements in Nazi ideology and their influence in the Weimar period, see David Redles, *Hitler's Millennial Reich: Apocalyptic Belief and the Search for Salvation* (New York: New York University Press, 2005).

7. The line is from the Bhagavad Gita, which Oppenheimer had read in the original Sanskrit.

8. For details on the historical formation of fundamentalist notions of "inerrancy" and "the Last Days" in the United States, see George M. Marsden, *Fundamentalism and American Culture: The Shaping of Twentieth-Century Evangelicalism, 1870–1925* (New York: Oxford University Press, 1980), 49–52, 54, 56–57, 107–8.

9. *New York Times*, September 11, 2003, A-1. It is worth recalling that fundamentalism in the United States is also distinguished by its lack of interest in social programs. This attitude dates back to the first part of the twentieth century, when the forerunners of the current fundamentalists broke away in protest over attempts to develop a "social gospel" attuned to the problems of industrialism. In contrast, evangelical leaders are strong defenders of capitalism. One of the notable Washington collaborations is that between evangelicals and the radically antigovernment (and politically well connected) Norquist Americans for Tax Reform organization. See Marsden, *Fundamentalism and American Culture*, 90 ff.

10. Cited by Nicholas D. Kristof, "The God Gulf," *New York Times*, January 7, 2004, A-25.

11. The exceptions were Heidegger and Husserl. See Leo Strauss, *Studies in Platonic Political Philosophy* (Chicago: University of Chicago Press, 1983). See the essay "Philosophy as Rigorous Science and Political Philosophy."

12. See Nathan O. Hatch, *The Democratization of American Christianity* (New Haven: Yale University Press, 1989), especially chaps. 2 and 7.

13. See my essay, "America's Civil Religion," *democracy* 2, no. 2 (April 1982); 7–17. For historical background, see Charles Norris Cochrane, *Christianity and Classical Culture* (New York: Oxford University Press, 1944), chaps. 8–9.

14. For the background to the idea of republicanism, see J.G.A. Pocock's classic *The Machiavellian Moment: Florentine Political Thought and the Atlantic Republican Tradition* (Princeton: Princeton University Press, 1975) and the fine studies by Joyce Appleby, *Liberalism and Republicanism in the Historical Imagination* (Cambridge: Harvard University Press, 1992) and *Capitalism and a New Social Order: The Republican Vision of the 1790s* (New York: New York University Press, 1984). See also Bernard Bailyn, *Ideological Origins of the American Revolution* (Cambridge: Harvard University Press, 1967), and Gordon Wood, *The Creation of the American Republic, 1776–1787* (Chapel Hill: University of North Carolina Press, 1969), especially chaps. 2, 3. and 11.

15. Still suggestive is Harold Rosenberg's *The Tradition of the New*, 2nd ed. (Boston: Da Capo, 2001).

16. Adam Smith, *An Inquiry into the Nature and Causes of the Wealth of Nations*, ed. W. B. Todd (Oxford: Clarendon Press, 1976), 1:454, 456.

17. I do not want to be understood as assuming that in the distant or recent past the United States was in possession of a more or less ideal system and that it has suddenly been hijacked by right-wing fanatics. Our system has always been a work in progress and a contested terrain. We need only recall that "democracy" was not in favor among many of our Founding Fathers; that the original Constitution explicitly accepted slavery and did not include a bill of rights.

18. Cited in Fareed Zakaria, *The Future of Freedom* (New York: Norton, 2003), 210–11.

19. The classic statement of this view is Max Weber's "Science as a Vocation," in *From Max Weber*, 129–56.

20. See Thomas S. Kuhn, *The Structure of Scientific Revolutions* (Chicago: University of Chicago Press, 1962), chap. 2; J. Bronowski, *Science and Human Values* (New York: Harper, 1956), especially 65 ff.

21. See Sheldon Krimsky, *Science in the Private Interest* (San Francisco: Rowman & Littlefield, 2003).

22. In the nineteenth century there were several proposals for substituting science for religion as the basis of society, the most notable being that of Auguste Comte.

23. It is relevant in this connection that the iconic place of Leo Strauss in the formative thinking of the neocons means the adulation of a thinker notoriously hostile to modern science. Strauss's antiscience teaching is strongly evident in Alan Bloom's *The Closing of the Modern Mind* (New York: Simon and Schuster, 1987): Bloom's aim is exactly what the title says, but the book, while ostensibly an attack on "modern" culture for being "closed," is actually a strategy for recommending the teachings of a closed mind, i.e., Strauss's.

24. Hobbes, *Leviathan*, 237.

25. For the contribution to democracy of evangelicals and Pentecostals generally, see Hatch, *The Democratization of American Christianity*, 206–9.

CHAPTER EIGHT
THE POLITICS OF SUPERPOWER: MANAGED DEMOCRACY

1. "I.R.S. Offers Amnesty to Companies That Admit Tax Indiscretions," *New York Times*, December 26, 2001, C-1.

2. See the thoughtful and engaging study by Victoria de Grazia, *Irresistible Empire: America's Advance through 20th-Century Europe* (Cambridge: Harvard University Press, 2005).

3. Hans J. Morgenthau, *Politics among Nations* (New York: Knopf, 1973), 135, 146–48.

4. Walter Lippmann, *Essays in the Public Philosophy* (Boston: Little, Brown, 1955), 15, 20, 26–27.

5. "Spy Agencies Told to Bolster 'The Growth of Democracy,'" *New York Times*, October 27, 2005, A-10.

6. One of the historical ironies of the current crusade for democracy is that during the 1940s and 1950s American officials, and especially Republican politicians, made a ritual of protesting the presence of agents and spies of communist Russia who were "interfering in the internal affairs" of our country. Today the American government subsidizes the efforts of NGOs to change the internal politics of former Soviet republics.

7. These comments are reported by then Secretary of the Treasury Paul O'Neill. They occurred in November 2002 at a meeting to discuss a second round of tax cuts. See Ron Suskind, *The Price of Loyalty: George W. Bush, the White House, and the Education of Paul O. Neill* (New York: Simon and Schuster, 2004), 291.

8. An example: a high-ranking lobbyist of the National Association of Manufacturers, one of the most powerful business organizations, was nominated by President Bush to head the Consumer Product Safety Commission. He was given a payment of $150,000 by the NAM after they learned of his nomination. The CPSC enforces consumer laws that cover many of the NAM's members. Stephen Laboton, "Bush Pick Gets Extra Payment from Old Job," *New York Times*, May 16, 2007, A-1. A week later, in response to public protests and Democratic criticisms, the nomination was withdrawn.

9. See Kurt Eichenwald, "Even If Heads Roll, Mistrust Will Live On," *New York Times*, October 6, 2002, sec. 3, p. 1, for an account of a series of crimes committed by business executives.

10. See "Military Brass and Military Contractors' Gold Mine," *New York Times*, June 29, 2004, C-1.

11. See P. W. Singer, *Corporate Warriors* (Ithaca: Cornell University Press, 2003).

12. Job training was the motivating concern in President Bush's support for increasing government contributions to two-year community colleges.

13. Cited in Elizabeth Bumiller, "Bush Rejects Idea of Boycotting Meeting in Russia," *New York Times*, March 30, 2006, A-10.

14. Cited by Floyd Norris, "Business Ethics and Other Oxymorons,"*New York Times*, April 20 2003, sec. 7, p. 16.

15. See the important article, originally published in the *Los Angeles Times*, by Abigail Goodman and Nancy Cleeland, "Wal-Mart: Empire Built on Bargains." I have used the reprint in the *Santa Rosa Press Democrat*, December 7, 2003, A-1.

16. See the example of Richard Perle, who combined corporate and government employment simultaneously (Scahill, *Blackwater*, 306–7) and the "deft" travels of Edward C. Aldridge, Jr., between the Pentagon and private aircraft corporations. Leslie Wayne, "Pentagon Brass and Military Contractors' Gold," *New York Times*, June 29, 2004, C-1.

17. The *New York Times* (November 27, 2003, A-1) reported that after the American pharmaceutical industry had succeeded in blocking efforts to control the prices of prescription drugs in the United States, it turned its attention abroad. In trade talks with the Australian government U.S. officials were pressing for the weakening of price controls over prescription drugs. In the Medicare Reform Act of 2003 the administration succeeded in prohibiting the government from negotiating lower drug prices.

18. The Democratic majority elected to Congress in 2006 passed a law requiring that the sponsors of earmarks be identified.

19. In preparation for the presidential election of 2004 the Bush campaign established a hierarchy of contributors. Those who succeeded in raising $100,000 in $2,000 individual contributions qualified as "Pioneers," while those who raised $200,000 qualified as "Rangers." The "bundling" of $2,000 contributions was a way of defeating the purpose of the law while observing the letter. It was also a means by which superiors exercised power over those who were called upon to contribute but received little recognition.

20. *The Federalist*, ed. Jacob E. Cooke (Middletown: Wesleyan University Press, 1961), No. 58, p. 396.

21. *New York Times*, November 23, 2004, A-1. Paul Wolfowitz, then assistant secretary of defense during the second Gulf War and reputed neoconservative, offered a revealing contrast between election possibilities. In Serbia, he noted, "communism collapsed with demonstrations on the street, which invested the population with a pride in embracing democracy." In contrast "Iraq has this advantage that we are there, with the coalition [forces], and with an enormous commitment to get it right." *New York Times*, May 22, 2003, A-16. Thus there is an "advantage" to having democracy imposed by foreign troops rather than being chosen by the "population."

22. Another nice example: in February 2004 the Bush administration decided to give in to pressure by Democrats and agreed to establish an independent inquiry into the "intelligence failures" regarding Saddam Hussein's "weapons of mass destruction. A day later, having been whitewashed by the Hutton Report absolving it of any attempt to "sex up" intelligence reports to justify its participation in the Iraqi invasion, the Blair government in Britain announced that it, too, would set up a bipartisan commission to inquire into possible intelligence lapses. But the cat was let out of the bag when the Liberal Democratic Party refused to participate on the commission because the investigation would focus exclusively on intelligence failures and would not inquire into the government's uses of that intelligence. Both Blair and Bush thus followed the same strategy of ensuring that the focus of investigations be centered upon the CIA, etc., not on the White House. Both the planned independent commission and the commission investigating possible intelligence failures before 9/11 are under specific injunctions *not* to deliver their reports until after the November presidential election.

23. Noah Feldman, cited by Dilip Hiro, "One Iraqi, One Vote," *New York Times*, January 27, 2004, op-ed page.

24. Edward N. Luttwak, "Rewarding Terror in Spain," *New York Times*, March 16, 2004, op-ed page.

25. Trump was replaced by Martha Stewart, fresh from serving a jail term for perjury.

26. The landmarks are the Civil Service Reform Act of 1887 and the Hatch Act of 1934.

27. See Dorothy Samuels, "Golf Anyone? The Movable Feast Called 'Judicial Education,'" *New York Times*, April 24, 2004, A-24. Between 1992 and 1998 more than a quarter of the federal judiciary, some 230 federal judges, accepted free vacations, thanks to a loophole in the law.

28. See Paul Krugman, "Victors and Spoils," *New York Times*, November 19, 2002, A-31.

29. It is striking that recent public opinion polls repeatedly confirm that the citizenry's strongest desire is for improvements in health care and education, yet the response from their government is to devise programs, such as the 2004 Medicare reform, that benefit health care corporations rather than the public. Similarly the public has been emphatic in wanting the Social Security system to be preserved, yet the Bush administration responds by proposing privatization, while milking the Social Security Trust Fund in order to meet the deficits created by the administration's tax cuts and escalating military expenditures.

30. For details, see the study by Jacob S. Hacker and Paul Pierson, *Off Center: The Republican Revolution and the Erosion of American Democracy* (New Haven: Yale University Press, 2005).

31. Midway through the 2004 Democratic presidential primary elections the *New York Times* suggested that all of the candidates except the two front-runners should abandon the race. This would have meant that the viewpoints represented by the left wing of the party would lack a public forum, and that the electorate would be denied the opportunity to hear views other than those of the party establishment. It was only after the center-right candidate of the *Times*, Senator Lieberman, withdrew for lack of support that the paper issued its call for the Left to commit hari-kari.

32. For an illuminating discussion of the various political roles played by ordinary people, slaves, and Indians in the years leading up to and including the revolution of 1776, see Gary Nash, *The Unknown American Revolution: The Unruly Birth of Democracy and the Struggle to Create America* (New York: Viking, 2005).

33. *The Federalist*, No. 55, p. 374.

34. See Leo Strauss, *Thoughts on Machiavelli* (Glencoe, Ill.: Free Press, 1958), and Harvey C. Mansfield, Jr., *Taming the Prince: The Ambivalence of Modern Executive Power* (New York: Free Press, 1989).

35. *The Discourses of Niccolò Machiavelli*, trans. Leslie J. Walker, 2 vols. (New Haven: Yale University Press, 1950), vol. 2, II.2.10 (pp. 359–60).

36. "For when on the decision to be taken wholly depends the safety of one's country, no attention should be paid either to justice or injustice, to kindness or cruelty, or to its being praiseworthy or ignominious. On the contrary, every other consideration being set aside, that alternative should be wholeheartedly adopted which will save the life and preserve the freedom of one's country." Machiavelli, *Discourses*, III.41.2 (pp. 572–73).

37. Jonathan Israel has pointed to a significant divergence in the republican traditions as they developed in seventeenth-century England and the Dutch republic. While republican theorists in both countries drew upon Machiavelli, the English writers tended to contrast republicanism and democracy, while their Dutch counterparts looked more favorably upon democracy and tried to incorporate elements into their theories. See Jonathan Israel, "The Intellectual Origins of Modern Democratic Republicanism, 1660–1720," *European Journal of Political Theory* 3, no. 1 (2004): 7–36.

38. On the republican tradition, see Pocock, *The Machiavellian Moment*. There are several excellent essays in the collection *Machiavelli and Republicanism*, ed. Gisela Bock, Quentin Skinner, and Maurizio Viroli (Cambridge: Cambridge University Press, 1990). There is an extended, forceful criticism of Pocock in Appleby, *Liberalism and Republicanism in the Historical Imagination*.

39. It is usually forgotten that the weakening of popular majorities was built into the structure of Congress. The different terms (two and six years, respectively) for representatives and senators were intended to establish the Senate as a smaller, aristocratic body that would attract more reliable, respectable men, who would serve to place a brake on the popular passions that the House was expected to reflect. Further, while the House's members would face a turnover every two years, which would reduce the effectiveness of the body itself, the terms of senators would be staggered so that that body would enjoy greater stability and continuity.

40. It has been remarked that "[a] proposed amendment can be added to the Constitution by 38 states containing considerably less than half of the population of the country, or can be defeated by 13 states containing

less than one-twentieth of the population of the country." *Edward S. Corwin's "The Constitution and What It Means Today"*, 271.

41. See Seymour Martin Lipset, *Political Man: The Social Bases of Politics* (New York: Doubleday, 1963), 102–3, 227 ff.

CHAPTER NINE

INTELLECTUAL ELITES AGAINST DEMOCRACY

1. Leo Strauss, *On Tyranny* (Ithaca: Cornell University Press, 1968), 76–77.

2. Bloom's *The Closing of the American Mind*, an important text among Straussians, simply ignores the power of capitalists.

3. Perhaps the most recent critical discussion was that of C. Wright Mills, *The Power Elite* (New York: Oxford University Press, 1957). As a sign of the times consider the changing character of the American Academy of Arts and Sciences, an honorary society that, until recently, recognized distinguished contributors to the traditional academic disciplines and the arts. Now it includes a section for "Business, Corporate and Philanthropic Leadership (Private Sector)."

4. "As Wealthy Fill Top Colleges . . . ," *New York Times*, April 22, 2004, A-1.

5. In California tuition at the state universities has been raised in an effort to reduce enrollments at the major institutions; students are then shunted to the community colleges and told that at the end of two years they may apply to the four-year universities. Most university teachers are of the opinion that community college graduates enter the four-year institutions at a distinct disadvantage. It is worth noting that during the 2004 elections both major candidates made a point of campaigning at community colleges and stressing their role in job training.

6. "Kissinger Reflects on Vietnam War and Foreign Policy," *Princeton Weekly Bulletin*, March 1, 2004, 3.

7. See the discussion of "enrollment management," which is now practiced at many institutions, both public and private. It attempts to systematize the recruitment and retention of students. According to one experienced student of the subject, "the emergence of enrollment management is simply one small indicator of the ascendancy of capitalism and the extent to which the market metaphor has taken hold throughout the United States and the rest of the world." Donald R. Hossler, "How Enrollment Manage-

ment Has Transformed—or Ruined—Higher Education," *Chronicle of Higher Education*, April 30, 2004, B-3–5.

8. "Enrollment management" extends to watching out for the progress of a student during his or her studies, through graduation and beyond. It has also influenced curricula and faculty recruitment. See Hossler, "How Enrollment Management Has Transformed—or Ruined—Higher Education," B-3–5.

9. Burton Pines, director of research at the Heritage Foundation. Cited by Greg Easterbrook, "Ideas Move Nations," *Atlantic Monthly*, January 1986.

10. Foundations are dependent on their tax-exempt status, which encourages a certain wariness because of past incidents in which the Internal Revenue Service used its powers of withholding exemptions when foundations crossed the political administration in power. It might be noted that there is little doubt of the major role that private foundations played in funding and engineering the impeachment of President Clinton.

11. See Walter Isaacson and Evan Thomas, *Wise Men: Six Friends and the World They Made* (New York: Simon and Schuster, 1997), for a hagiographic depiction, and, for a more critical appraisal, David Halberstam, *The Best and the Brightest*, 20th ed. (New York: Modern Library, 2001).

12. Lawrence Kaplan and William Kristol (*The War over Iraq: Saddam's Tyranny and America's Mission*), cited by Halper and Clarke, *America Alone*, 219.

13. Cited in George C. Herring, "America and Vietnam: The Unending War," *Foreign Affairs*, Winter 1991/92.

14. *The Third Wave*, cited (but no page given) in Zakaria, *The Future of Freedom*, 18.

15. Leo Strauss, *Liberalism Ancient and Modern* (New York: Basic Books, 1968), 5. By "liberal" education Strauss did not mean the liberalism associated, say, with philosophers such as Dewey, Rawls, or Dworkin. Instead, "liberal" is identified with "virtuous" and is closer to conservatism as Strauss defines it. See vii–viii.

16. *The Third Wave*, cited in Zakaria, *The Future of Freedom*, 18–19.

17. Leo Strauss, *What Is Political Philosophy? and Other Studies* (Glencoe, Ill.: Free Press, 1959), 10.

18. Ibid., 12.

19. See G. S. Kirk and J. E. Raven, eds., *The Presocratic Philosophers* (London: Cambridge University Press, 1957), 220 ff.

20. For Strauss and Schmitt, see Heinrich Meier, *Leo Strauss and the Theologico-Political Problem*, trans. Marcus Brainard (Cambridge: Cambridge University Press, 2006), 77–87 (first published in Germany in 1988); for a critique of Meier, see Jan-Werner Müller, *A Dangerous Mind: Carl Schmitt in Post-war European Thought* (New Haven: Yale University Press, 2004), 202–5. On Strauss and Mussolini, see Nicholas Xenos, "Leo Strauss and the Rhetoric of the War on Terror," *Logos* 3, no. 2 (Spring 2004): 4. For a thoughtful defense of Strauss as a moderate, see Steven B. Smith, *Reading Leo Strauss: Politics, Philosophy, Judaism* (Chicago: University of Chicago Press, 2006). Smith attempts to dissociate Strauss from the Bush adventure in Iraq by presenting Strauss as a moderate. See 199 ff. For a sophisticated appraisal, see Anne Norton, *Leo Strauss and the Politics of American Empire* (New Haven: Yale University Press, 2004).

21. Shadia Drury, *The Political Ideas of Leo Strauss* (New York: St. Martin's, 1988), 7. This is a very useful analysis and account of its subject.

22. Bloom, *The Closing of the American Mind*, 324.

23. On Nietzsche see my *Politics and Vision*, chap. 13.

24. Cited in Drury, *The Political Ideas of Leo Strauss*, 11.

25. Ibid., 7.

26. "Philosophy or science, the highest activity of man, is the attempt to replace opinion about 'all things' by knowledge of 'all things'; but opinion is the element of society; philosophy or science is therefore the attempt to dissolve the element in which society breathes, and thus it endangers society." Strauss, *What Is Political Philosophy?*, 221.

27. These attitudes are displayed, if rather vulgarly, in Bloom's *The Closing of the American Mind*. For some critical remarks on that work, see my essay, "Elitism and the Rage against Postmodernity," in *The Presence of the Past* (Baltimore: Johns Hopkins University Press, 1989), 47–65.

28. "Executive power . . . has a natural basis in monarchy." *Taming the Prince*, 295. One of Mansfield's earlier books was a highly suggestive study of Viscount Bolingbroke, who was the author of *The Idea of a Patriot King* (1738).

29. *Taming the Prince*, 297. See my review, "Executive Liberation," and Mansfield's spirited rejoinder, "Executive Power and the Passion for Virtue," in *Studies in American Political Development* 6 (Spring 1992): 211–16.

30. *Taming the Prince*, 271.

31. Ibid., 294.

32. Thucydides, *History of the Peloponnesian War*, trans. Richard Crawley (New York: Random House, Modern Library, 1951), VI.15–18, 48, 53, 61, 74, 89–92; VIII.6, 12, 17; VIII.45, 46–54, 56, 81–82, 86–89. In Strauss's view, Alcibiades was first "compelled" by the Athenian demos to be a traitor, and was then a tyrant who promoted the Sicilian expedition from self-interest. See Leo Strauss, *The City and Man* (Chicago: Rand McNally, 1964), 192–93, 196–99. See the fine study by Josiah Ober, *Mass and Elite in Democratic Athens: Rhetoric, Ideology, and the Power of the People* (Princeton: Princeton University Press, 1989).

33. The book comes with the highest recommendations not only from Huntington but also from Henry Kissinger and Arthur Schlesinger, Jr. See the book jacket.

34. Zakaria, *The Future of Freedom*, 220–21.

35. Ibid., 14, 15.

36. Ibid., 203.

37. Ibid., 200.

38. Ibid., 219.

39. Ibid., 15, 16. Zakaria neglects to point out that al Qaeda is financed by elite money from the Saudi royal family.

40. Ibid., 162.

41. Ibid., 23.

42. See Gardiner Harris and Janet Roberts, "After Sanctions, Doctors Get Drug Company Pay," *New York Times*, June 3, 2007, 1.

43. Zakaria, *The Future of Freedom*, 17, 18. Zakaria makes no mention of the role that conservative elites, including a military, led by an aristocratic, antidemocratic class (the Junkers)—which Huntington should have loved—played in conniving to elect Hitler and, more important, manipulating the Reichstag (parliament) to give him extraordinary powers. Also the "free" election of 1933 was marked by considerable violence. See Bracher, *The German Dictatorship*, 178 ff. and Evans, *The Coming of the Third Reich*, 266 ff.

44. Zakaria, *The Future of Freedom*, 17.

45. Ibid., 220.

46. Ibid., 95, 100–101.

47. Ibid., 56.

48. Ibid., 21, 169. Except for the Civil Rights Act of 1964, all progress on emancipation, Zakaria claims, was due to the "executive" and the courts. The "executive," one might have thought, was popularly elected.

49. See Walter Struve, *Elites against Democracy: Leadership Ideals in Bourgeois Political Thought in Germany, 1890–1933* (Princeton: Princeton University Press), chap. 13; Bracher, *The German Dictatorship*, 96; Paxton, *The Anatomy of Fascism*, 138 ff.

50. Zakaria, *The Future of Freedom*, 57. Curiously, despite his praise of the tutelage provided by British colonialism, Zakaria has harsh things to say about postcolonial India (105–6). And he does cite Kipling in support of the view that elites have power but have not accepted "responsibility" (235).

51. Ibid., 165–66, 167–68.

52. Ibid., 169–73, 181.

53. Ibid., 183–84.

54. Ibid., 20.

55. Ibid., 242.

56. Ibid., 242–43, 246.

57. Ibid., 251.

58. Ibid., 198.

59. Bernard Groethuysen, *Origines de l'esprit bourgeois en France* (Paris: Gallimard, 1927).

60. Zakaria gratefully explains in a footnote that "*Newsweek*, where I work, is one of the few mass-circulation publications that still covers the news seriously and in depth." The explanation: "It is able to do so because *Newsweek* is owned by the Graham family, which also owns the *Washington Post.*" *The Future of Freedom*, 232. It should be noted that Zakaria has criticized elites for the Iraq war. See his article "The Price of Arrogance," *Newsweek*, May 17, 2004, 39.

61. According to Bob Woodward's *State of Denial*, in November 2001 a dozen policy-makers, Middle East experts, and members of research organizations met in a meeting called by Paul Wolfowitz, then deputy secretary of defense. The purpose was to produce a report for the president proposing a strategy for dealing with Afghanistan and the Middle East after 9/11. Present at the meeting were Zakaria and other columnists. Those who attended had to sign a confidentiality agreement promising not to discuss what happened. Zakaria denied being told that a report would be issued. Lawrence Kaplan claimed that the attendees all knew that a report would result, and all signed on. The report, according to Kaplan, was "a forceful summary of the best pro-war arguments at the time." Zakaria insisted that his "column [in *Newsweek*] is an analytical column." Adding that he is in the practice of giving advice to policy-makers and elected officials, he

declared, "If a senator calls me up and asks me what should we do in Iraq, I'm happy to talk to him." See "Secret Iraq Meeting Included Journalists," *New York Times*, October 9, 2006, C-6.

62. Quoted in Sarah Rimer, "Committee Urges Harvard to Expand the Reach of the Undergraduate Curriculum, *New York Times*, April 27, 2004, A-17.

63. See Huntington's contribution to Michel J. Crozier, Samuel P. Huntington, and Joji Watanuki, *The Crisis of Democracy: Report on the Governability of Democracies to the Trilateral Commission* (New York: New York University Press, 1975), 59–118.

64. Huntington, "Dead Souls," 8.

65. Ibid., 1.

66. Ibid.

67. Ibid., 2–3. The title refers to Sir Walter Scott's famous poem that begins, "Breathes there a man with soul so dead / Who never to himself hath said: / This is my own, my native Land?"

68. Huntington, "Dead Souls," 5, 7.

69. Ibid., 12–13.

70. Ibid., 9.

71. Ibid., 14.

72. Ibid., 9.

73. Ibid., 8.

74. Ibid., 14, 15.

75. *The Clash of Civilizations and the Remaking of World Order* (New York: Simon and Schuster, 1996), 90, 306–7, 310. At that writing Huntington feared an intercivilizational war, most likely from Muslims or the Chinese (311–14). It should also be noted that in *The Clash*, 306–7, he declares that in the looming apocalypse the United States should stick to "the Western family" because if that family should go under, it would also mean the "end" of the United States as we know it.

76. Huntington, "Dead Souls," 8.

77. For his doubts, see his essay in the Trilateral Commission Report, *The Crisis of Democracy*, 63–64, 74 ff., 102 ff.

78. *The Federalist*, No. 55, p. 374.

79. According to BBC radio (October 29, 2004) the figure was arrived at by a study conducted by the prestigious British medical journal *Lancet*. The chief investigator estimated that the figure might be as high as 200,000.

CHAPTER TEN
DOMESTIC POLITICS IN THE ERA OF SUPERPOWER AND EMPIRE

1. Cited by Philip Gourevitch, "Bushspeak," *New Yorker*, September 13, 2004, 41–42.

2. As shown by the case of a former Young Republican loyalist, Jack Abramoff, ideological fervency is no prophylactic against corruption, in this case fleecing Indian tribes, even as it keeps faith with the long tradition of special treatment, including racist insults, of Native Americans. It is also instructive to note how the last three candidates proposed for Supreme Court appointments by the Bush administration—Miers, Roberts, Alito— had served long apprenticeships in Republican Party organizations and in Republican administrations. In a recent but not unrelated development, right-wing groups have mounted a campaign in several states to make it possible to indict judges whose opinions run counter to the ideology of the groups.

3. *Toward a More Responsible Two-Party System: A Report of the Committee on Political Parties, American Political Science Review* 44, no. 3, pt. 2, Supplement (1950): 1–9. Details concerning the composition of the Party Councils can be found at 43.

4. "On the Road, Bush Fields Softballs from the Faithful," *New York Times*, August 16, 2004, A-11.

5. Niall Ferguson, *Colossus: The Rise and Fall of the American Empire* (New York: Penguin, 2004), vii ff., and "America, Unconscious Colossus," *Daedalus*, Spring 2005, 18–33. Mann, *Incoherent Empire*, 13, sees the United States as "a disturbed, misshapen monster stumbling clumsily across the world."

6. Charles Krauthamer as quoted by Mann, *Incoherent Empire*, 10.

7. Anthony Pagden, "Empire, Liberalism and the Quest for Perpetual Peace," in *Daedalus*, Spring 2005, 46–57, at 52.

8. "Cheney Sees 'Shameless' Revision on War," *New York Times*, November 22, 2005, A-1.

9. Cited in Mann, *Incoherent Empire*, 11.

10. The major exception is the continuing controversy over procedural rights. This contrasts with the lively academic discourse on justice during the last three decades of the twentieth century, thanks primarily to the focus provided by the magistral work of John Rawls.

11. See Johnston, *Perfectly Legal*.

12. The long-term objective of the tax reformers is to establish a flat tax. The originators of the idea of a flat tax candidly wrote that the tax "would be a tremendous boon to the economic elite. . . . It is an obvious mathematical law that lower taxes on the successful will have to be made up by higher taxes on average people." Cited by John Cassidy, "Tax Code," *New Yorker*, September 6, 2004, 75.

13. In attempting to erase felons from the voter rolls, the state of Florida managed to erase legal voters as well.

14. In much of previous American history spontaneous movements have played an important role in invigorating politics. Such were the Grange movement, the Populists, and, recently, the Green party. It could be argued that spontaneity also drove the campaign of Howard Dean. The successful effort to crush him, undertaken by both the media and his opponents, illustrates the rigidity of the current party system and what it feels threatened by.

15. For details and examples, see Singer, *Corporate Warriors*, especially 73 ff.; Scahill, *Blackwater*, 321 ff., is especially interesting for the policing role assumed by private security forces in the aftermath of Hurricane Katrina. Scahill, chap. 1, is also revealing of the religious element in the Blackwater hierarchy.

16. *Santa Rosa Press Democrat*, March 7, 2004, A-3.

17. A remarkable variation on winning was described recently in the *New York Times*. There a former congressman and now consultant suggested that it might be better for the party if it were not to win the 2006 midterm elections. This would force the Republicans to "struggle" through the remainder of President Bush's term and better position the Democrats for 2008. See Adam Nagourney, "Hey Democrats, Why Win?" May 14, 2006, sec. 4, p. 1. Yet another symptom of the party's failure to oppose was the large number of its candidates in the 2006 midterm elections whose views were strikingly similar to those of conservative Republicans. See Shaila Dewan and Anne Kornblut, "In Key House Races, Democrats Run to the Right," *New York Times*, October 30, 2006, A-1.

18. Quoted in David M. Halbfinger, "Shedding Populist Tone, Kerry Starts Move to Middle," *New York Times*, May 8, 2004, A-14.

19. For a discussion of the strategies of welfare opponents, especially as they relate to bureaucracy, see Jacob S. Hacker, "Privatizing Risk without Privatizing the Welfare State: The Hidden Politics of Social Policy Retrenchment in the United States," *American Political Science Review* 98,

no. 2 (May 2004): 243–60. Another tactic favored by lobbyists is to have their proposals inserted in appropriation bills at a stage where the items cannot be removed except through the defeat of the entire bill.

20. Thomas Frank's *What's the Matter with Kansas? How Conservatives Won the Heart of America* (New York: Metropolitan Books, (2004) is devoted to the question of why the less powerful and poorer classes vote against their own interests.

21. A majority of Americans are said to favor having a religious president.

22. Cited in Halbfinger, "Shedding Populist Tone, Kerry Starts Move to Middle," A-14.

23. Only in the last month before the election did Kerry attempt a clarification of his views on these matters, and even then the differences seemed more rhetorical than substantive.

24. The takeover of the Democratic Party by the "center" is an eerie echo of the fate of the Centre Party (largely Catholic) in the Weimar Republic. Amidst the increasingly polarized politics of the 1920s and early 1930s, the party could not make up its mind whether to support the Right (Nazis and extreme conservatives) or the Left (Social Democrats and Communists). It ended up supporting the Right and was abolished soon after the Nazis took power.

25. The Missouri Compromise also stipulated that Kansas and Nebraska would be organized as free territories.

CHAPTER ELEVEN
INVERTED TOTALITARIANISM: ANTECEDENTS AND PRECEDENTS

1. In March 2006, in response to a lawsuit, New York city police commanders made public reports on their arrest tactics during political demonstrations of 2002. These included "pro-active arrests," covert surveillance, seizure of demonstrators who were "obviously potential rioters," and the deployment of undercover officers to infiltrate political gatherings. It was proposed that a tactic of "utiliz[ing] undercover officers to distribute misinformation within the crowds" be resumed, although it had been disavowed thirty years earlier by the city and federal governments. For a further description of police tactics, see Jim Dwyer, "Police Files Say Arrest Tactics Calmed Protest," *New York Times*, March 17, 2006, A-1.

2. During the traditional New Year's Eve celebration in New York City to usher in 2005, police armed with machine guns patrolled the crowds.

3. The twofold threat presented by Dean was, first, his forthright insistence that the war in Iraq was a gigantic blunder and that the United States needed to withdraw as soon as feasible; and, second, the threat of a popular mobilization, especially of the young. The Democratic Party wanted voters, not militants.

4. On the role of paramilitary forces in preparing the way to power in Italy, see Mann, *Fascists*, 68–69.

5. Ibid., 37 ff.

6. See Carl Schorske, *Fin-de-Siècle Vienna: Politics and Culture* (New York: Knopf, 1980), 116 ff.

7. The *New York Times* reported that in a Roper poll in the summer of 2005, 72 percent of the respondents believed that wrongdoing was widespread in industry; that only 2 percent described CEOs of large corporations as very trustworthy. In a Harris poll of November 2005, 90 percent of the respondents said that big companies had too much influence in Washington. The *Times*'s photo accompanying the report pictured an executive shackled helplessly to a target dotted with knives that had apparently missed. "Take Your Best Shot," December 9, 2005, C-1.

8. See the curious piece in the *New York Times*, "An Unexpected Odd Couple: Free Markets and Freedom," June 14, 2007, A-4, where a few American intellectuals are said to have become doubtful that capitalism and democracy "need each other to survive." Those interviewed were perplexed primarily by China, which is becoming more capitalistic but hardly more democratic; some also seemed to believe that while democracy depends upon capitalism, the reverse is not true. Marx would have agreed. One appeared to suggest that democracy and capitalism were incompatible.

9. Neoconservatives, according to one neoconservative, accept that they live in "a democratic age." They "recognize" the "fundamental justice of democratic equality" (which the author left undefined). Democracy's "shortcomings" are its "low aspirations and dehumanizing tendencies." He concludes: "Only neoconservatism among contemporary conservative modes of thought has made its peace with democracy. That fact might also be considered a serious weakness, but would be a subject for another day." Adam Wolfson, "Conservatives and Neoconservatives," in *The Neocon Reader*, ed. Irwin Stelzer (New York: Grove Press, 2004), 223, 231.

10. Here the essay "The Neoconservative Persuasion" by Irving Kristol, regarded by many as the intellectual godfather of neoconservatism, is indicative. While he supports "economic growth" as the means to "promote the spread of affluence among all classes" so that "a property-owning and tax-paying population will, in time, become less vulnerable to egalitarian illusions and demagogic appeals," he rejects the notion that conservatives should favor a weak "State." In Stelzer, *The Neocon Reader*, 35. In the same volume he begins his essay "A Conservative Welfare State" by writing, "I shall pay no attention to the economics of the welfare state." He goes on: "What conservatives ought to seek, first of all, is a welfare state consistent with the basic moral principles of our civilization and the basic political principles of our nation. . . . [W]e should figure out what we want before we calculate what we can afford, not the reverse, which is the normal conservative predisposition" (145).

11. See John Brewer, *The Sinews of Power: War, Money, and the English State, 1688–1783* (New York: Knopf, 1988). Brewer writes, "The late seventeenth and eighteenth centuries saw an astonishing transformation in British government, one which put muscle on the bones of the British body politic, increasing its endurance, strength and reach. Britain was able to shoulder an ever-more ponderous burden of military commitments thanks to a radical increase in taxation, the development of public deficit finance (a national debt) on an unprecedented scale, and the growth of a sizable administration devoted to organizing the fiscal and military activities of the state" (xvii).

12. Burkean conservatism resurfaced in the late 1950s and early 1960s in writers such as Russell Kirk and William Buckley. They are now somewhat scornfully labeled "paleoconservatives" by some neocons.

13. The infatuation of American academics with Bentham and J. S. Mill was mostly a twentieth-century phenomenon.

14. Schlesinger, *The Coming of the New Deal*, chaps. 2–5.

15. A major exception was the directive of President Truman ending segregation in the armed forces.

16. See Eric Nordlinger, *On the Democratic State* (Cambridge: Harvard University Press, 1982), for a defense of the neoliberal state.

17. Among the influential studies are James Burnham, *The Managerial Revolution* (New York: John Day, 1941); Peter Drucker, *The Practice of Management* (London: Heinemann, 1956); and Chandler and Daems, *Managerial Hierarchies*; and, more critically, Herman, *Corporate Control, Corporate Power*. The great forerunner of these studies was Thorstein

Veblen. See his *The Theory of Business Enterprise* (New York: Mentor, 1904, 1932) and *The Engineers and the Price System* (New York: Harcourt, 1921), 1963.

18. On the opposition between reason and passion, see *The Federalist*, No. 49, p. 343; No. 50, p. 346; No. 58, p. 396. On passion and interest, see No. 10, p. 61; on passion as strong, irregular, and selfish, see No. 6, p. 29; No. 20, p. 128; No. 41, pp. 264, 275; No. 42, p. 283; No. 63, pp. 423, 425.

19. Quoted in Gordon S. Wood, *The Radicalism of the American Revolution* (New York: Knopf, 1991), 246. I am much indebted to Wood's discussion of interests.

20. In *The Federalist*, No. 35, pp. 219–21 Hamilton dismissed as "visionary" the claim that "actual representation of all classes of the people by persons of each class" could be achieved. He argued that "merchants" were "the natural patron and friend" of "mechanics and manufacturers" and "have acquired endowments" lacking in the other classes.

21. Ibid., No. 23, pp. 150–51; No. 46, p. 318.

22. Note also the recent spate of celebratory biographies of Washington, Hamilton, and Adams; at the same time Jefferson's standing as a leader and democratic spokesman has fallen sharply.

23. See the important work by Nash, *The Unknown American Revolution*.

24. Madison, *The Federalist*, No. 58, p. 397; John Jay, No. 4, p. 22.

25. See Madison's usage, "the people stimulated by some irregular passion." Ibid., No. 63, p. 425; and Hamilton, "Are not popular assemblies frequently subject to to the impulses of rage, resentment, jealousy, avarice, and of other irregular and violent propensities?" No. 6, p. 32.

26. See the stimulating account in Charles Wiebe, *Self-Rule: A Cultural History of American Democracy* (Chicago: University of Chicago Press, 1995), especially pts. 1 and 2; and my *Tocqueville*, chaps. 12 and 19.

27. James Madison, *The Federalist*, No. 10, p. 64.

28. Ibid., No. 71, p. 482.

29. Ibid., No. 9, p. 51; No. 31, p. 95.

30. Cited by James Mann, *Rise of the Vulcans: The History of Bush's War Cabinet* (New York: Viking, 2004), 203.

31. *The Federalist*, No. 10, p. 64.

32. Cited in Gould, *Grand Old Party*, 379.

33. See the lively study by Frank, *What's the Matter with Kansas?* It is rarely pointed out that the racial categories of pollsters serve to reinforce racism and its stereotypes.

34. Cited in Merrill D. Peterson, *Thomas Jefferson and the New Nation: A Biography* (New York: Oxford University Press, 1970), 773.

35. There is a helpful discussion of Hamilton's ideas on empire, as well as of the various emphases given to the term by earlier and contemporary writers, in Gerald Stourzh, *Alexander Hamilton and the Idea of Republican Government* (Stanford: Stanford University Press, 1970), especially 189 ff.

36. There is a judicious assessment of Turner in Richard Hofstadter, *The Progressive Historians: Turner, Beard, Parrington* (New York: Knopf, 1969), 47 ff.

37. *The Frontier in American History* (New York: Holt, 1920, 1947), 10. Turner was suspicious of certain immigrant groups: "But even in the dull brains of great masses of these unfortunates from southern and eastern Europe the idea of America as the land of freedom and opportunity to rise, the land of pioneer democratic ideals, has found lodgment, and if it is given time and is not turned into revolutionary lines it will fructify" (278).

38. Ibid., preface, ii; 219–21.

39. *The Federalist*, No. 51, p. 351.

40. Ibid., No. 70, p. 472.

41. More accurately, Hamilton's vision of the executive was more expansively developed at the Constitutional Convention at Philadelphia. There he argued for an executive who would serve for life and similarly for one branch of the legislature. See Max Farrand, ed., *The Records of the the Federal Convention*, 3 vols. (New Haven: Yale University Press, 1911), 1:289, 292.

42. Cited in Ferguson, *Colossus*, 80.

43. Charlie Savage, "Bush Asserts Power to Ignore Laws," *Santa Rosa Press Democrat*, May 1, 2006, A-1.

44. Justice Alito, who served under Attorney General Meese during the Reagan administration, helped devise a strategy for circumventing congressional intentions.

45. Quoted by Emmanuel Todd, *Après l'empire: essai sur la décomposition du système américain* (Paris: Gallimard, 2002), 22.

46. In Hegel's famous allegory of the interaction between master and slave the master is degraded by the practices of mastery while the slave is elevated by inventing ways of resistance. See Hegel's *Phenomenology of Spirit*, trans. A. V. Miller (Oxford: Clarendon Press, 1977), 111–19.

CHAPTER TWELVE
DEMOTIC MOMENTS

1. To P. S. Dupont de Nemours, April 24, 1816, in *Writings* (New York: Library of America, 1984), 1385.

2. "Popular Sovereignty as Procedure," in *Deliberative Democracy: Essays on Reason and Politics*, ed. James Bohman and William Rehig (Cambridge: MIT Press, 1997), 43. Italics in original.

3. See the proposals for congressional action in "Budget to Hurt Poor People . . . ," *New York Times*, January 30, 2006, A-14.

4. One of the striking features of the recent spate of literature celebrating the American empire is the near universal silence of its authors about the internal or domestic consequences of empire. See Ferguson's *Colossus* and Walter Russell Mead's *Power, Terror, Peace, and War* (New York: Knopf, 2004).

5. At the beginning of Bush's second term a series of personnel changes signaled a pause in imperial ambitions. The imperial face was remodeled as democracy's worldwide advocate, the grumpy Rumsfeld traded in for the stylish Rice. Wolfowitz was transferred from the Defense Department to the World Bank; Bolton, the assistant secretary of state for arms control with an appetite for bullying, was given a recess appointment as ambassador to the UN; and other hawks have left government in order to be with their families.

6. During the 2004 presidential campaign it was obvious that the Democrats and their supporters were united almost exclusively by their dislike of Bush. The same tendency to focus primarily on the leader was also evident in the immediate aftermath of the Hurricane Katrina disaster.

7. Antonio Gramsci, *Selections from the Prison Notebooks*, ed. and trans. Quintin Hoare and Geoffrey Nowell Smith (New York: International Publishers, 1971), 273.

8. My discussion of Athenian democracy is much indebted to R. K. Sinclair, *Democracy and Participation in Athens* (Cambridge: Cambridge University Press, 1988).

9. On this topic, see Moses I. Finley, *Democracy Ancient and Modern* (New Brunswick, N.J.: Rutgers University Press, 1973); G.E.M. de Ste. Croix, *The Class Struggle in the Ancient Greek World* (Ithaca: Cornell University Press, 1981).

10. Aristotle, *Politics* 1291b30–38, 1310a28–36, 1317a40–b7.

11. Solon and Cleisthenes were described by some ancient writers as precursors of democracy.

12. Thucydides, *The Peloponnesian War*, I.70, p. 40.

13. The most notorious example of mass slaughter was the Mytilene revolt. See ibid., bk. III.

14. See J. K. Davies, *Democracy and Classical Greece* (Stanford: Stanford University Press, 1983), 139, for examples of these rivalries.

15. Finley, *Democracy Ancient and Modern*, 48–50, argued that empire made Athenian democracy possible by supplying revenues that could pay for the political attendance of poorer Athenians, by providing land overseas for settlements and investment opportunities for the wealthy.

16. Thucydides, *The Peloponnesian War*, V.89, p. 331.

17. Finley argued that both the average Athenian and the wealthy classes derived economic advantages from the empire. See Moses I. Finley, "The Fifth-Century Athenian Empire: A Balance-Sheet" in *Imperialism in the Ancient World*, ed. P.D.A. Garnsey and C. R. Whittaker (Cambridge: Cambridge University Press, 1978).

18. See the fine study of the relationships between elites and demos in Ober, *Mass and Elite in Democratic Athens*, and the earlier treatment concentrating on the "demagogues": W. Robert Connor, *The New Politicians of Fifth-Century Athens* (Princeton: Princeton University Press, 1971).

19. See Thucydides, *The Peloponnesian War*, III.36–48; IV.28–29, 108; VI.8–19, 89.

20. Ibid., II.65, p. 120.

21. Ibid., II.65, pp. 120–21.

22. The closest were the Italian city-states of the late Middle Ages and Renaissance, some of which were republican in character but often dominated by the aristocracy. It is significant that they were cities. See Lauro Martines, *Power and Imagination: City-States in Renaissance Italy* (New York: Random House, 1980), 131–40.

23. See Farrand, *The Records of the Federal Convention of 1787*, 1:26, 48, 49, 51, 58, 123, 132, 146. There were some rare exceptions, e.g., the speeches of James Wilson in Farrand.

24. For background, see Christopher Hill, *The World Turned Upside Down: Radical Ideas during the English Revolution* (Harmondsworth: Penguin, 1975); Perez Zagorin, *A History of Political Thought in the English Revolution* (London: Routledge & Paul, 1954), chaps. 2–3; and the fine collection of essays in Margaret C. Jacob and James R. Jacob, *The*

Origins of Anglo-American Radicalism (Atlantic Highlands, N.J.: Humanities Press, 1991).

25. I have relied on the passages reproduced in G. E. Aylmer, ed., *The Levellers in the English Revolution* (Ithaca: Cornell University Press, 1975), 100, 102. See the important essay by Mark A. Kishlansky, "Consensus Politics and the Structure of Debate at Putney," in Jacob and Jacob, *The Origins of Anglo-American Radicalism*, 89–103.

26. Aylmer, *The Levellers*, 121.

27. Ibid., 100, 101.

28. Ibid., 113.

29. Ibid., 107.

30. Ibid., 107.

31. Ibid., 114.

32. See Arno J. Mayer, *The Furies: Violence and Terror in the French and Russian Revolutions* (Princeton: Princeton University Press, 2000).

33. I am indebted to the following: Nash, *The Unknown American Revolution* and his earlier work, *The Urban Crucible: Social Change, Political Consciousness, and the Origins of the American Revolution* (Cambridge: Harvard University Press, 1979). Also Pauline Maier, *From Resistance to Revolution* (New York: Vintage, 1974), and the essays in Jacob and Jacob, *The Origins of Anglo-American Radicalism*, 185>th>ff.

34. According to Article I, sec. 2, the House was to be chosen by "the people," but the people were promptly defined as "electors" whose "qualifications" were those of "the most numerous branch of the State Legislature." Thus in states where suffrage qualifications were based on wealth or property, this could mean that most of "the people" would have no voice in the selection of their representatives.

35. See Gary Nash, "Artisans and Politics in Eighteenth-Century Philadelphia," in Jacob and Jacob, *The Origins of Anglo-American Radicalism*, 258–78.

36. To Dupont de Nemours, April 24, 1816, in *Writings*, 1387.

37. Ibid., 1385.

CHAPTER THIRTEEN

DEMOCRACY'S PROSPECTS: LOOKING BACKWARDS

1. Cited in Elizabeth Bumiller, "Not 'the Decider,' but Stirring Anxiety," *New York Times*, April 24, 2006, A-17.

2. See Michael Barbaro and Stephanie Strom, "Conservatives Help Wal-Mart, and Vice Versa," *New York Times*, September 8, 2006, C-1, which describes how the major conservative think tanks were paid handsome sums by Wal-Mart and responded by supplying articles praising Wal-Mart at a time when it was facing growing criticism of its low wage and benefit practices. See also Mark A. Smith, *American Business and Political Power: Public Opinion, Election, and Democracy* (Chicago: University of Chicago Press, 2000), who emphasizes the role of think tanks in influencing public opinion and furthering the political power of business.

3. Cited in Maureen Dowd, "The Unslammed Phone," *New York Times*, September 9, 2006, A-27.

4. See Frank Rich, *The Greatest Story Ever Sold: The Decline and Fall of Truth from 9/11 to Katrina* (New York: Penguin, 2006).

5. Cited in Michael Abramowitz and Thomas E. Ricks, "Strategy: Pressures Mount on Bush Policy," *Santa Rosa Press Democrat*, October 20, 2006, A-1, 15. Reprinted from the *Washington Post*.

6. Bernard Williams, *Truth and Truthfulness: An Essay in Genealogy* (Princeton: Princeton University Press, 2002), 118. This book is the best available discussion of the subject.

7. In his biography, *President Reagan: The Role of a Lifetime* (New York: Public Affairs, 2000), 315–31, Lou Cannon describes the anguish suffered by Reagan when he was finally persuaded to confess to the American public that he had lied about the sale of arms to Iran in order to aid the Nicaraguan "contras."

8. *Republic*, trans. Francis M. Cornford (Oxford: Oxford University Press, 1945), 158 (V.459c–d).

9. For discussions of lying in Plato's works, see Julia Annas, *An Introduction to Plato's Republic* (Oxford: Clarendon Press, 1985), 106–8, 166–67; John R. Wallach, *The Platonic Political Art: A Study of Critical Reason and Democracy* (University Park: Pennsylvania State University Press, 2001), 273–74. For a defense of Plato's tactic, see C.D.C. Reeve, *Philosopher-Kings: The Argument of Plato's Republic* (Princeton: Princeton University Press, 1988), 50 ff.

10. *Republic*, 105 ff. (III.414 ff.)

11. José Sarramago has written a remarkable novel on the theme, *The Cave*, 2nd ed. (New York: Vintage, 2003).

12. *Republic*, 227 ff.(VII.514a ff.).

13. Plato portrays his rulers as begrudging the time spent on politics and as looking forward to the day when they can retire and pursue philosophy.

They are strictly limited in the years spent in office. A crucial difference between Plato and the neocons is that his polity is forbidden to expand or embark on foreign conquests. Further, in Plato's antidemocracy there is no provision for interaction between the elite and the populace; hence while there is no provision for holding rulers accountable to the ruled, by the same token there is no likelihood of the Alcibiades dynamic of a demagogic elite exploiting mass emotion or of a mass inciting leaders to foreign adventures.

14. The *New York Times* headlined a front-page story with the innocuous title "Real Wages Fail to Match a Rise in Productivity," but in the continuation of the story on the inside pages a sharper heading was used: "Workers' Share of the Economy Hits Record Low, as Corporate Profits Skyrocket." August 28, 2006, A-1, A-13.

15. Some of the important works are the following: Adolf A. Berle and Gardiner C. Means, *The Modern Corporation and Private Property* (New York: Macmillan, 1932); President's Report on Administrative Management (1937); Hoover Commission Reports (1946 ff.); Elton Mayo, *The Human Problems of an Industrial Civilization* (New York: Macmillan, 1933); Chandler, *The Visible Hand*; Burnham, *The Managerial Revolution*; Drucker, *The Practice of Management*.

16. The administration of Lyndon Johnson was the last instance of a Democratic administration that struggled to combine the welfare state with a crushing defense budget.

17. See Halberstam, *The Best and the Brightest*; Isaacson and Thomas, *Wise Men*.

18. See Cannon, *President Reagan*, 521 ff.

19. For details, see the excellent biography by Cannon, *President Reagan*, 66–67; Gary Wills, *Reagan's America* (Garden City, N.Y.: Doubleday, 1985).

20. On Reagan's belief in Armageddon, see Cannon, *President Reagan*, 247 ff. It might seem astonishing that a political figure as ill-prepared as Reagan and who presided over more than his fair share of fiascos should become a cult figure with an impressive hagiography. The *Times* carried a revealing account of a summer camp for young conservatives funded by the usual conservative foundations. The young people attending went on a pilgrimage to the shrine of the Reagan ranch and were eager to voice unqualified adoration for Reagan. Jason deParle, "Passing Down the Legacy of Conservatism," *New York Times*, July 31, 2006, A-13.

21. For Reagan and concentration camps, see Cannon, *President Reagan*, 428 ff.

22. This is not to say that Reagan had no influence over policies. He was a major influence in modifying the Cold War fundamentalism regarding the Soviet Union by initiating groundbreaking discussions with Gorbachev. He was also instrumental in various schemes for missile defense and arms reduction. For details, see ibid., 671 ff., and especially Frances Fitzgerald, *Way Out There in the Blue: Reagan, Star Wars and the End of the Cold War* (New York: Simon and Schuster, 2000).

23. It was the Reagan administration's James Watt whose record as secretary of the interior was the equivalent of the classic horror movie for environmentalists.

24. One should not be misled into believing that the Reagan White House was streamlined, all marching to the same drummer. On the internal battles, petty jealousies, and conflicting ambitions within the administration, see Cannon, *President Reagan*, 495 ff., 564–69, 611–24.

25. Part of this story is the subservience of the Supreme Court in *Bush v. Gore*, where the Court halted the Florida recount and then solemnly declared that its majority opinion was not to be taken as a precedent. Vice President Cheney's hunting companion, Justice Scalia, when asked about the opinion, tartly responded, "Come on, get over it." Cited in Adam Cohen, "Has Bush v. Gore Become the Case That Must Not Be Named?" *New York Times*, August 15, 2006, A-22. Another part of the story is the "judicial education" programs financed by wealthy individuals and business interests. See Samuels, "Golf Anyone?" A-24.

26. Arthur M. Schlesinger, Jr., *The Crisis of the Old Order, 1919–1933* (Boston: Houghton Mifflin, 1957).

27. Quoted in Adam Nagourney, "Democrats Back Lamont in Show of Unity," *New York Times*, August 10, 2006, A-1.

28. James Glanz, "Series of Woes Mark Iraq Project Hailed as Model," *New York Times*, July 28, 2006, A-1.

29. In Vice President Cheney's notorious closed meeting with the most powerful energy corporations, a major environmental group, the National Resources Defense Council, was denied admission.

30. An interesting addition to the idea of originalism among conservatives is the elevation of certain conservative books as canonical and their authors as founding fathers of conservative theory.

31. Aristotle, *Politics*, VII.ix, 1329a.

32. On higher education and campus protest, see Sheldon S. Wolin and John H. Schaar, *The Berkeley Rebellion and Beyond* (New York: New York Review of Books, 1970).

33. *The Federalist,,* 57.

34. Ibid., 58, 59.

35. For a spirited use of Madison's tenth *Federalist* as a critique of the excesses of the Bush administration, see Stephen L. Elkin, "Republicans and the End of Republican Government," *The Good Society* 14, no. 3 (2005): 1 ff. Elkin makes no reference to corporate power and proposes "a moderate measure of economic equality" as a part of a reformed republicanism, "a well-ordered version of which requires a large and secure middle-class, one that can keep in check the desire to expand the political control that wealth already gives the richest of the 'haves', and that can restrain the desire of the 'have-nots' to use the power of government in any fashion that will alleviate their misery" (5).

36. *The Federalist*, No. 10, 63, 64–65.

37. Ibid., No. 48, p. 333.

38. Ibid., No. 51, p. 349.

39. Madison posed the question of what would preserve the balance between the branches of government; his answer: "by so contriving the interior structure of the government, as that its several constituent parts may, by their mutual relations, be the means of keeping each other in their proper places." *The Federalist*, No. 51, pp. 347–48. See Michael Kammen, *A Machine That Would Go of Itself: The Constitution in American Culture* (New York: Random House, 1987).

40. *The Federalist*, No. 51, p. 349.

41. Ibid., No. 35, pp. 220, 221.

42. Ibid., No. 15, p. 97.

43. Ibid., No. 70, pp. 471–72; No. 71, p. 482. See also the discussion in Wood, *The Creation of the American Republic, 1776–1787*, 508.

44. *The Federalist*, No. 72, p. 489.

45. A classic account is that by R. H. Tawney, *The Agrarian Problem in the Sixteenth Century* (New York: Harper, 1967). The work was originally published in 1912.

46. General Tommy Franks, the commander of Central Command at the beginning of the Iraq war, had a special fondness for movies. See Michael R. Gordon and General Bernard E. Trainor, *Cobra II: The Inside Story of the Invasion and Occupation of Iraq* (New York: Knopf, 2006), 25, 115, 164.

47. On presidential decision making during the Lebanon crisis, see Cannon, *President Reagan*, 521 ff.; on military decisions for the Iraq war, see Gordon and Trainor, *Cobra II*. See also Bruce Kuklick, *Blind Oracles: Intellectuals and War from Kennan to Kissinger* (Princeton: Princeton University Press, 2006).

48. See my essay "Tending and Intending a Constitution: Bicentennial Misgivings" in *The Presence of the Past*, 82–99.

49. The secretary of homeland security testified recently that the agency's inept response to Katrina was due in large part to its preoccupation with security.

50. A prime counterexample was Vice President Cheney's refusal to make public the meetings he held in his office with representatives from the great energy corporations while denying representation to environmental groups and despite the fact the discussions concerned policies.

51. Recently the Bureau of Internal Revenue privatized the collection of small debts, even though it would have been more cost-effective for the bureau to have hired its own agents to perform that function. David Cay Johnston, "I.R.S. Enlists Outside Help . . . Despite the Higher Costs," *New York Times*, August 20, 2006, A-12.

Index

abolitionism, 257–58, 277
abortion debate, 62, 115
Abramoff, Jack, 119, 323n2
academia. *See* educational institutions
Acheson, Dean, 301n70
Adams, John, 154, 255–56
advertising, 12–13, 118. *See also* media
affirmative action, 224, 236
Afghanistan, 193
African Americans, 57–58, 101, 181, 197, 228, 277
Albright, Madeleine, 236
Alcibiades, 172–73, 282–83
Aldridge, Edward C., Jr., 313n16
Alien and Sedition laws of 1798, 78
Alito, Samuel, 146, 236, 323n2
American colonies, 150–51, 254, 255
American Political Science Association (APSA), *Toward a More Responsible Two-Party System*, 188–89
American Revolution, 154, 155, 219, 227
Anti-Ballistic Missile Treaty, 89
antidemocracy, xx–xxi, 150, 212–13, 239, 241
The Apprentice (television series), 144
archaism, 117–21, 122–23, 124, 125–26, 169, 201
Archer Daniels Midland, 138, 185
aristocracy, 97, 151, 162, 174, 183, 219, 248, 251, 253, 256, 269. *See also* elites/elitism; Few, the
Aristotle, 118, 168, 170, 171, 243, 277
Articles of Confederation, 225, 234, 279
Athens, 95, 150, 151, 172–73, 242–48, 250, 256. *See also* Greece, ancient

Bay of Pigs, 270
Bechtel, 88
Bentham, Jeremy, 219
Bible, 4, 115, 117, 119, 123
Bill of Rights, 229
Blair, Tony, 314n22
Bloom, Alan, 317n2, 319n27
Brewer, John, 327n11
Buckley, William, 38, 327n12
Buffett, Warren, 200
Burke, Edmund, 218–19
Bush, George H. W., 41, 147, 165, 190, 216, 314n19
Bush, George W., 104, 112; circle of, 63; and corporations, 94; and democracy, 43; election of, 64; and election of 2000, 94, 101; executive authority of, 235–36; and free society, 11; and Hitler, xvii, 42–43, 44; and inverted totalitarianism, 44; and Iraq War, 11, 16; lack of support for, 240–41, 286–87; and Mansfield, 172; and media, 1–2; and military, 147; and myth, 103; and preemptive war, 48–49; quoted, 10, 80, 82, 134, 137, 184, 259; and reason of state, 133; and religion, 116–17; and Schiavo case, 45; and September 11, 2001, attacks, 5, 65; signing statements of, 172, 236; and social democracy, 274; State of the Union address of January 2007, 11–12; and terrorism, 70–71, 72, 74; and unified executive branch, 235; and *USS Abraham Lincoln*, 1, 2, 3, 44; and war on terrorism, 190–92
Bush (George W.) administration: attack on liberalism by, 217; and

339

Mandelbaum, Michael, 4
Manifest Destiny, 61–62
Mansfield, Harvey, Jr., 171–73, 179
Many, the, 147, 158; and archaism,
121; and Constitution, 226; and cor-
porations, 144; and Democratic
Party, 149; and elections, 148; and
George W. Bush administration,
157; and Mansfield, 172; and Plato,
265, 266; and political futility, 65; in
postclassical Europe, 248, 249, 250;
power of, 151; and religion, 129;
Strauss on, 169, 170, 171. *See also*
demos; majority; masses; people, the
Marshall, George, 37
Marshall Plan, 270
Marx, Karl, 51
masses, 53, 54, 169, 170, 174, 181.
See also Many, the; people, the
McCarthy, Joseph, 37, 38, 223–24,
304n29
McCarthyism, 37, 38
media: and archaism, 118; and Cold
War, 36; concentrated ownership of,
58, 196, 210, 214; credibility of, xx;
criticism by, 77; and defendants'
rights, 78; and degradation of political dialogue, 287; depiction of protests by, 215–16; and election of
2000, 101; and election of 2004,
216; and empire, 192; George W.
Bush's use of, 1–2; and instability,
128; and inverted totalitarianism,
44, 47, 185; and Iraq War, 216; and
loss of liberties, 158; and manipulation of electorate, 284; and myth, 2,
12–13; opinion management by, 7–
8; and populism, 23; and Reagan,
120; and religion, 12–13, 117; and
revival of democracy, 292; and Roosevelt, 22; and September 11, 2001,
attacks, 5, 6; and terrorism, 70, 71–
72; and third party alternatives, 216;
and Vietnam War, 107; and World
War II, 106

Medicare, 109, 201. *See also* social
programs
mercantilism, 122, 219
Mexican War, 209
Mexico, 105, 190
Meyer, Josh, 51–52
Middle East, 49, 93, 142, 171
Miers, Harriet, 146, 323n2
military: and Cold War, 39; and corporate economy, 34; and corporations,
45, 135, 136, 199–200; and democracy, 147; detention centers run by,
57; domestic role of, 214; and dynamists, 118; and empire, 191, 192,
245; and executive branch, 70; and
foreign policy, 90; and George W.
Bush administration, 157, 290; and
George W. Bush's signing statements, 236; and government, 199;
and inequality, 147; and inverted totalitarianism, 45, 47, 61; and Iraq
War, 93; and McCarthy, 37; and
*The National Security Strategy of
the United States,* 83, 88; privatization of, 213, 284; and Reagan, 272;
and religion, 116; and Republican
Party, 199, 200; and science, 125;
and September 11, 2001, attacks, 5;
and Superpower, 60, 62, 132, 147;
support for, 112, 198–200; and terrorism, 73; universal training for,
34–35, 39; and World War II, 106
Mill, John Stuart, 219
Miller, Zell, 199
Missouri Compromise of 1820, 208
Mommsen, Hans, 41
monarchy, xxi, 53, 96, 171, 234, 248,
253. *See also* sovereign
Mubarak, Hosni, 47
Musharraf, Pervez, 175
Muslims, 124, 181, 199
Mussolini, Benito, xvii, 21, 22, 44, 51,
53, 84–85, 112, 169
Mutual Assured Destruction, 33
myth: and Cold War, 223; cosmic, 10–
11; definition of, 10; democratic, 52;